Who's Who
in
Wagner's
Life & Work

Who's Who in Wagner's Life & Work

Phillip Hodson

Weidenfeld and Nicolson
London

For Anne and Alexander
With thanks to Maggie

Filmset by Deltatype, Ellesmere Port
Printed in Great Britain by
Butler & Tanner Ltd.,
Frome and London

'A work like the *Ring* is, with respect to its beginning, growth and completion, the only one of its kind in the world and perhaps the mightiest work of art of the last millenium.'

Gerhard Hauptmann

The Wagner Family Tree

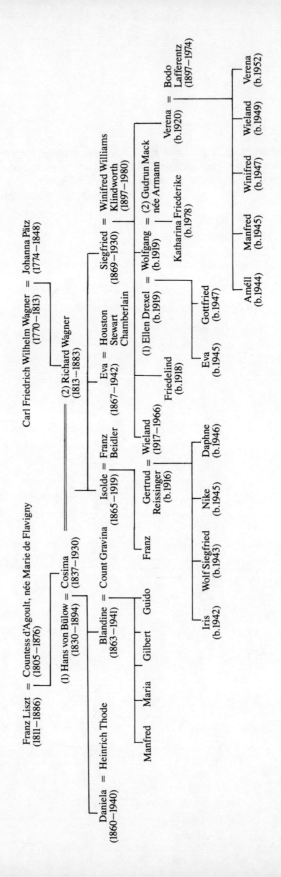

Contents

Acknowledgements

To George and Louise Browning for bibliographical research; Erika O'Byrne and Eva Wilson for assistance with translations; the staff of the British Library, the Library of Times Newspapers Ltd, Swiss Cottage Music Library and the Library of the Royal College of Music, London; the administrative staff of the Bayreuth Festspielhaus and the trustees of the Richard Wagner Foundation in Bayreuth; and most of all to Maggie Gee and Anne Hooper.

I am indebted – as are all Wagnerians – to Andrew Porter's glittering translation of the *Ring* into English (London, 1976) and must also acknowledge my great obligation to a miscellany of Wagnerian translators. I have been helped at many turns by Raymond Furness's excellent study, *Wagner and Literature* (London, 1982); by Robert Hartford's fascinating book *Bayreuth, The Early Years* (London, 1980) and Martin Gregor-Dellin and Dietrin Mack's superb edition of the *Diaries of Cosima Wagner, 1869–1883* (two volumes, London, 1976–7). The chronology of Wagner's life has been partly based on the work of Otto Strobel and Robert Hartford, to whom my thanks.

Introduction

The purpose of this book is to provide, in the new age of televised Wagner, an A-Z of Wagner's life and work for the most general audience. Wagner himself wished to acquire a mass following and a hundred years after his death is beginning to get one. But prejudice still bars the path, some of it from critics reluctant to see their hero fall into the hands of mere fans, some from philistines, some from politicians.

To scrape away some of this prejudice means that Wagner, now more than ever, needs a little explanation. He needs protecting from professional Wagnerites who refuse to share him with the wider world. He needs introducing to musical people who draw the line at Wagner *because* they've never heard him, *because* they know he's a German bore, *because* they understand neither the language of the operas nor the intentions of the composer, and *because* they simply feel intimidated by all the critical fuss. He needs to recover from the dishonest attentions of Hitler and the Nazis. Some Europeans still believe Hitler and Wagner were close friends, despite the fact that the former was born in 1889 and the latter died in 1883. And Wagner needs an even bigger apology in Israel, where the music is unofficially banned and riots break out whenever the ban is challenged.

Wagner still needs to be rescued from charges of heaviness because a number of singers and conductors once mangled his scores. Above all, he needs elucidation because we can derive so much pleasure at so many levels from Wagner once wc know what's intended. Put simply, Wagner is gibberish if you cannot follow the details of plot and musical purpose. While most opera is largely tuneful, Wagner invented a new art-form in which the words constitute a play it is vital to follow. When you realize that the play is a very modern one – a psychodrama, no less – and that some of the drama is occasionally expressed in the music and not in the words, you can see that ignorance of the plot puts the audience at an uncomprehending disadvantage.

Wagner created great modern art explicitly in keeping with the age of psychological self-discovery. It is amazing to find a first-rate musician, a sometimes second-rate human being and often third-rate philosopher providing answers from beyond the grave to many of the questions bothering people today about matters of life and love.

His greatest musical dramas unquestionably transcend their bourgeois origins as well as his own early anarchism: neither Marxists nor liberals can absolutely claim Wagner for their own – nor reject him with justice. Fascists may feast on his racial theories, but will only find bitter fare in the operas, where love is always exalted over power. With the right introduction, his musical art may speak sensuously, erotically and humanistically to all.

I hope this book will persuade you of the truth of this. It's meant to serve as a soft-spoken butler – pointing out who's who and what's what in the privileged and sometimes aloof world of the Wagnerites – but it's written out of personal pleasure in Wagner's music, the only starting point.

I have also saved space by writing entries on only the more significant names in Wagner's life. Readers wishing to gather information on the minor figures should consult the notes at the end of *Diaries of Cosima Wagner, 1869–1883* and also the lives of Wagner by Ernest Newman (*The Life of Richard Wagner*, 4 vols, London, 1933–47) and Curt von Westernhagen (*Richard Wagner: Sein Werk, sein Wesen, seine Welt*, Zurich, 1956).

Asterisks are used to refer the reader to other entries in the *Who's Who*.

Wagner's Operas

The abbreviations in brackets are used at the beginning of entries to place a character or theme. Dates of composition are from early drafts of the music to completion of the full score.

Die Hochzeit (Ht), a fragment	1832–3
Die Feen (F)	1833–4
Das Liebesverbot (Lt)	1835–6
Rienzi (Ri)	1838–40
Der Fliegende Holländer (H)	1841
Tannhäuser (T)	1843–7
Lohengrin (L)	1846–7
Das Rheingold (R)	1853–4
Die Walküre (W)	1854–6
Siegfried (S)	1856–69†
Tristan und Isolde (T I)	1857–9
Die Meistersinger von Nürnberg (M)	1862–7
Götterdämmerung (G)	1869–74
Parsifal (P)	1877–82

Wagner's non-operatic music, and his minor prose writings, are listed collectively at the end of the book.

† The last few pages were scored in 1871.

Chronology

Leipzig
1813
RW born on 22 May, probably the son of Carl Friedrich Wilhelm Wagner* and his wife, Johanna*. Carl Friedrich dies on 23 November.

Dresden
1814
RW's mother marries Ludwig Geyer, RW is henceforward known as 'Richard Geyer' (until 1827).

Eisleben
1821
Geyer dies. His brother at Eisleben undertakes RW's education.

Dresden
1822
RW returns to Dresden and begins studies at the Kreuzschule.
1823
RW enthusiastically studies Greek verse; he is less enthusiastic about Greek grammar.
1824
RW begins piano studies at the age of eleven, but shows a keen interest in opera as well. Becomes fascinated by the work of Weber*, an acquaintance of his mother's.
1825
RW shows poetic ability, winning a prize at school.
1826
The rest of the family move to Prague. RW stays in Dresden, and imagines he is a second Shakespeare. Begins a large-scale Shakespearean tragedy (Leubald)*.

Leipzig
1827
RW and family remove to Leipzig.
1828
RW goes to the St Nicholas School, finishes his tragedy and, after hearing Beethoven's* symphonies, decides to compose music for it.

1829
RW studies violin and musical theory. He is overwhelmed by the singing of Schröder-Devrient* as Leonore in Fidelio. The conductor Dorn* takes an interest in RW at the newly-completed Leipzig Theatre.
1830
Revolution in Paris. Wagner thrilled. Echoes of this revolution in Leipzig and RW takes part. RW arranges Beethoven's Ninth Symphony for piano. Dorn conducts RW's overture in B flat major; not a success.
1831
Weinlig* teaches RW more musical theory, including counterpoint and harmony. RW is an able music student. RW composes an overture in D minor and enters university. He is now eighteen.
1832
Wagner composes his only symphony, in C major, and some shorter pieces. His symphony is played in Prague.
RW begins his projected opera Die Hochzeit. Rosalie, his sister, suggests it is too bizarre, and he destroys the work.

Würzburg
1833
RW is appointed chorus master at Würzburg. Works on his second opera, Die Feen.

Magdeburg
1834
RW completes Die Feen, but it is not produced at Leipzig, contrary to his expectations. At Lauchstädt RW joins a theatre company that travels to Magdeburg. One of the actresses is Minna Planer, later his first wife. RW commences Das Liebesverbot. RW develops erysipelas (a serious and painful subcutaneous skin disease difficult to treat before modern antibiotics).
1835
RW's Columbus Overture given a performance at Magdeburg.
1836
Première of Das Liebesverbot at Magdeburg, but it fails after only two evenings.

On 24 November RW marries Minna, although they have little to live on. RW writes libretto for a new opera, based on Heinrich Koenig's novel, *Die Hohe Braut*, which he offers to the French dramatist Scribe*, but then abandons.

Konigsberg/Dresden/Riga
1837
RW starts to write another opera (*Die quickliche Bärenfamilie*), which he fails to finish. Minna runs away with another man, shortly after Wagner is appointed conductor at Konigsberg, and after the first performance of his 'Rule Britannia' Overture. RW goes to his sister, Ottilie Wagner*, in Dresden, Conceives the idea for *Rienzi*. He is then appointed conductor at Riga, re-woos Minna and gets heavily into debt.
1838
RW works on *Rienzi*.

Norway/London/Paris/Meudon
1839
RW escapes his creditors by taking a boat to Paris, experiencing a near-shipwreck off Norway and proceeding via London. RW gets idea for *Der Fliegende Holländer* from this experience. Meets Meyerbeer at Boulogne. The visit to Paris is a disaster. More debt. Inspired by Beethoven's Ninth Symphony, decides to compose a Faust Overture.
1840
Privation and still more debt. RW takes any hack and writing work he can get. Fails in efforts to have *Das Liebesverbot* produced. Completes *Rienzi*.
1841
RW still not well provided for. Writes text for *Der Fliegende Holländer* for 500 francs. At Meudon with Minna, RW extends the piece to three acts, finishing the score. *Rienzi* is accepted for production at Dresden.

Dresden
1842
RW sketches *Die Bergwerke zu Falun*, but this project is soon abandoned. The Wagners now go to Dresden, since that is where their living lies. *Der Fliegende Holländer* is accepted at Berlin. RW sketches out *Tannhäuser*. *Rienzi* is performed at Dresden on 20 October: a success at last.
1843
RW succeeds Weber* as conductor – a solid paying job.
Der Fliegende Holländer given at Dresden on 2 January. Wagner writes choral works.
1844
RW writes musical elegy for Weber.
1845
Tannhäuser finished; performed at Dresden on 19 October. RW sketches texts of *Lohengrin* and *Die Meistersinger*.
1846
Wagner meets von Bulow*, conducts Beethoven's Ninth Symphony and makes composition sketch of *Lohengrin*.
1847
Work on *Lohengrin* continues. *Rienzi* given in Berlin. RW discontinues composing operatic work until autumn 1853.
1848
RW writes the text of *Siegfried's Death*. Becomes friends with Liszt*. Grows increasingly radical and joins radical group.

Weimar/Paris/Zurich
1849
Joins revolution in Dresden. It fails and RW has to flee as a wanted criminal, first to Liszt at Weimar. He decides to endure his exile in Zurich, where Minna joins him. Decides art requires social evolution, which he now explains in *The Art Work of the Future*.

Paris/Zurich
1850
RW very discontented and unsettled. He falls in love with Jessie Laussot* and proposes to elope with her. Jessie breaks off the relationship and RW returns to Minna and Zurich. First performance of *Lohengrin* in Weimar on 28 August. Writes *Judaism in Music* under a pseudonym; it is published in September.

1851
RW gets subsidy from Julie Ritter. Writes *Opera and Drama*. Completes the text for the *Young Siegfried** and decides to write a Nibelung cycle in four parts.

1852
Writes texts for *Die Walküre* and then *Das Rheingold*; reworks other parts of the *Ring* as *Siegfried* and *Gotterdämmerung*.

1853
RW meets the young Cosima Liszt on a visit to Paris. RW is forty and she is sixteen. Having befriended Mathilde Wesendonck*, writes a piano sonata for her. Begins composing the music of *Das Rheingold* at the beginning of November.

1854
Das Rheingold is completed and *Die Walküre* is begun. Wagner friendly with Mathilde Wesendonck while Minna is visiting in Germany. RW gets inspiration for *Tristan und Isolde*.

London/Zurich

1855
RW goes to London to conduct a series of concerts for the Philharmonic Society. He meets Queen Victoria and Prince Albert. The British Press are hostile towards him. RW encounters Berlioz*, who is also in London conducting an orchestra. RW returns to Zurich.

1856
Home in Zurich, RW completes *Die Walküre*. He makes a sketch for *Die Sieger** ('The Conquerors'), but then abandons the project. Begins work on *Siegfried* and makes musical sketches for *Tristan und Isolde*.

1857
RW begins work on outline for *Parsifal*. He starts living at 'Das Asyl'* on the estate of the complaisant Otto Wesendonck, with Mathilde living next door. RW completes the text of *Tristan und Isolde* and begins to compose the music. He writes *Wesendonck Lieder* for Mathilde.

Paris/Zurich/Venice

1858
RW goes to Paris for a visit. After his return, Minna gets wind of his affair with Mathilde and there is an ugly scene between the two women. RW flees to Venice and works on *Tristan und Isolde*.

Lucerne/Paris

1859
RW completes *Tristan und Isolde* at Lucerne, then joins Minna in Paris.

1860
Wagner has a successful Paris concert. He revises *Tannhäuser* for performance at the Opéra, but refuses to include a ballet. He is granted a partial amnesty, allowing him to return to Germany, apart from Saxony.

Paris/Vienna/Venice

1861
After an immense expenditure of time and money, *Tannhäuser* is performed in Paris but destroyed by the claque of the Jockey Club; it has to be withdrawn. RW listens to *Lohengrin* for the first time in Vienna. RW visits the Wesendoncks in Venice, then works on *Die Meistersinger*.

Biebrich-am-Rhein/Leipzig/Vienna

1862
Finishes text of *Die Meistersinger*; begins work on score at Biebrich-am-Rhein. His amnesty extended to Saxony. Concert of RW's music in Leipzig. He has affairs with Mathilde Maier* and Friederike Meyer.

On Tour: St Petersburg/Moscow

1863
RW's debts threaten to crush him, so he embarks on a concert tour. Debts become worse than ever.

Stuttgart/Munich

1864
Leaving Vienna, to escape his creditors, RW moves via Mariafeld (near Zurich) to Stuttgart, where he is rescued by a miracle in the shape of King Ludwig II of Bavaria*, who invites RW to be his permanent guest. Debts are paid off. Von Bülow, appointed conductor of the Munich court

opera, plans with the King to produce Wagner's works in Munich. R W writes *Huldigungsmarsch* for the King. New scheme for a special theatre to built in Munich. Endless plans, but court intrigues against Wagner begin to stir. R W starts to score Act I I of *Siegfried*.

Munich/Geneva
1865
Tristan und Isolde given in Munich on 10 June. R W begins his autobiography, *My Life*. The scandal of R W's relations with Cosima ends Wagner's immunity from court intrigue, and the King is forced to ask him to withdraw from Bavaria, but continues to support him financially. Wagner moves to a villa near Geneva.

Lucerne
1866
Minna dies at Dresden; R W not unhappy with the news. Cosima and R W publicly set up home at Triebschen*, by the Lake of Geneva. Hans Richter becomes R W's assistant. Cosima becomes amanuensis for *My Life*.
1867
Die Meistersinger finished. Preparations for production of *Lohengrin* in Munich go ahead.

Lucerne/Leipzig/Lucerne
1868
Die Meistersinger produced on 21 June. Nietzsche, then aged twenty-four, visits Triebschen.
1869
R W composes Act III of Siegfried, apart from last few pages. On 6 June his only son, Siegfried, is born. Judith Gautier* and her husband visit Triebschen. Contrary to R W's wishes, *Das Rheingold* is performed at Munich on 22 September. R W reprints *Judaism in Music* under his own name. He starts work on *Götterdämmerung*.
1870
Cosima divorced from von Bülow and married to R W. R W has first plans for Festival Theatre at Bayreuth*. Composes

Siegfried Idyll for Cosima's birthday; performed on 25 December at Triebschen.

Lucerne/Bayreuth/Berlin/Leipzig/Lucerne
1871
Last few pages of *Siegfried* scored. The *Kaisermarsch* written to celebrate Prussia's victory over France. R W makes trips to Germany to prepare the way for his Festival Building at Bayreuth. Wagner Society* founded.

Bayreuth
1872
The Wagners leave Lucerne for Bayreuth. Foundation stone of theatre laid on R W's birthday. *Götterdämmerung* finished in draft. Wagners tour Germany to engage singers for the *Ring*.
1873
Wagners mount concert tour to raise money for Bayreuth. First act of *Götterdämmerung* completed.
1874
Ludwig saves Bayreuth with subsidy. Wagners' new house 'Wahnfried'* finished in Bayreuth; they move in. *Götterdämmerung* finished.

Vienna/Budapest/Berlin/Bayreuth
1875
R W gives fund-raising concerts in Europe. In the summer, rehearsals begin in Bayreuth for the *Ring*. Vienna stages the 'Paris' version (1861, with R W's Corrections) of *Tannhäuser*.

Bayreuth/Italy
1876
Festival finally saved by R W earning more money. He composes American Centennial March. Felix Mottl* joins staff at Bayreuth. *The Ring of the Nibelungs* is given in three complete cycles at Bayreuth; makes a large loss, but is a success with the public who see it. Wagner bitterly disappointed artistically as well as financially. R W and family go to Italy to recuperate.

London/Bad Ems
1877
Wagner in love with Judith Gautier. He elaborates sketches for *Parsifal*, and begins to compose music. RW gives more concerts, this time in London, to help defray the Bayreuth loss. He has start of heart trouble; goes for cure at Bad Ems.

Bayreuth
1878
RW's periodical, the *Bayreuther Blätter*, begins to appear. Coronary disease and rheumatism afflict RW. Complete *Ring* given at Leipzig.
1879
Parsifal finished in short score. RW develops erisypelas again.

Italy/Venice/Munich/Bayreuth
1880
RW goes to Italy for further cure. Meets Humperdinck* who is engaged as assistant at Bayreuth. Visits Venice and Munich.

Bayreuth/Berlin/Palermo
1881
First two acts of *Parsifal* completed. RW has a heart attack during a performance of the Berlin *Ring*. Leaves to winter in Sicily.

Palermo/Bayreuth/Venice
1882
Parsifal finished at Palermo on 13 January. First performed at Bayreuth on 26 July, sixteen performances given. RW conducts last act of last performance. RW and family go to Venice; RW's health worsens and he suffers severe heart attack. He conducts his symphony in C (1833) at the Teatro la Fenice.

Venice
1883
On 13 February RW has final heart attack and dies. On 18 February he is buried at 'Wahnfried', Bayreuth.

'Actors and Singers'

Wagner's late (1872) essay which drew attention to the importance of mime. Shakespeare's plays, he claimed, alone among the supreme developments of theatre, were mimed poetic improvisations. To excel Shakespeare would require the addition of music. The opera-maker of the future should first attempt to write Shakespearean verse, allowing the actor to perform realistically, and then set his text to music like Beethoven's, if he could. A tall order, but the resulting music-drama would take the mind by storm.

Ada (F)

A spellbound fairy queen, compelled to suffer for the love she feels for Arindal*, a mortal. Her punishments for offending against caste rules are legion. For instance, she may not marry her lover for eight years nor in that period tell him her name. And on the final day of this trial period she must afflict him with trial by torment to try to force him to curse both her and her undisclosed identity.

In the opera, this involves subjecting Arindal to the profound hallucination that his friend Morald* has been slain, his country conquered by hostile forces and his two illegitimate children cast into a fiery chasm by none other than his beloved Ada. Provoked beyond endurance, Arindal curses Ada despite her warnings that this would cause them all disaster.

As if it were possible, more punishment is heaped on Ada's hapless head. She is not allowed to assume mortal form after all or get married in an earthly church; instead, she must remain immortal, after first serving a hundred years' penance frozen in the shape of a stone statue.

A bewitched and cursed existence does not allow a character much room for free will or for the expression of individual personality – even less when they have been turned to stone. Accordingly, Ada is merely a vehicle for the force of compul-

sive magic – nevertheless, she foreshadows the more sophisticated, semi-divine personality of Brünnhilde*, who is faced with more poignant and telling choices and dilemmas.

Adorno, Theodor Weisengrund (1903–69)

German Marxist sociologist and philosopher. His polymath writings include important studies of modern music (*Philosophy of Modern Music*, 1949) and Wagner (*In Search of Wagner*, 1952). Adorno claims that Wagner not only 'made music for the unmusical' he also used 'magnificence to sell us death'. Adorno therefore stresses the ritual, non-musical content of the operas, the 'inherent ideology', eagerly noting that 'in Wagner there is hardly any humane collectivity'. Wagner himself is variously described as an 'anti-semitic terrorist' and 'casuistical'. But Adorno's criticism penetrates to much deeper levels than that of Marx* or Lukács because Adorno possessed profound musical knowledge. He therefore notices those extensive passages in Wagner where the writing is slovenly or the remorseless chromaticism seems over-bland. To a good Marxist the reason seems clear: 'Wagnerian method is a sort of mental flight, the jettisoning of everything unequivocal, the negation of everything with an individual stamp'. Wagner is seen as a reactionary composer as well as a 'semi-feudal' librettist.

Agoult, Marie Catherine Sophie de Flavigny Countess d' (1805–67)

Cosima Wagner's* mother by a love affair with Franz Liszt*. Under the pen-name 'Daniel Stern', Marie d'Agoult wrote novels and political and historical essays. Her fiction included *Nélida* (1846) and the drama *Jeanne d'Arc* (1857).

Alberich (R, S, G)

The Nibelung dwarf who in the first scene of *Rheingold* renounces love for power. Throughout the *Ring* he is the evil genius whom Wotan* fights and fears. Alberich represents the dark side of the human personality: a creature dwelling under the ground, conjuring up visions of chaos and tyranny. He has been used to symbolize a number of different 'target' groups. The Nazis conceived him to be Jewish; Marxist producers see him as a crypto-Nazi. Alberich may also be seen as a purely egotistical force of primeval lust: a being freed from the restraints of the conscious mind and, by means of his curse on love, from those limits imposed by man's desire for affection. All the same, in Wagner's allegory, Alberich is unsuccessful in his desire to dominate the conscious world. In the last resort, a purgative mental breakdown ensues (*Götterdämmerung*), offering more than a hint of optimism that by eliminating both Alberich and Wotan from the system, man may subordinate his lust for power and wealth to his desire for love and wisdom. The world of the *Ring* is disinclined to tolerate Alberich's autocracy. Opposition forces of legality, heroism, fearlessness and altruism in the persons of Wotan, Siegmund,* Siegfried* and Brünnhilde* eventually combine to eliminate the forces of tyranny from the drama, although we hear no news of his death.

IN *Rheingold*

In the opening drama of the *Ring* we see Alberich in the bass-baritone role of a naive fornicator attempting to make love to the Rhinemaidens. They cruelly taunt him with his physical deficiencies but this scorn turns to fear when he proves himself man enough to steal their Rhine gold. To do so, he must pronounce a comprehensive curse upon love. Since his only experience of love would appear to be a rather rudimentary form of rapid intercourse, we may be forgiven for thinking Alberich is proposing to renounce a great deal less

than a mature Siegfried or a Tristan* would give up in comparable circumstances. Scene 3 shows us Alberich in his true element as the slave-driver of a hellish goldmine. His Nibelung people work day and night to satisfy his insane cravings for the precious metal; he even inflicts corporal punishment on his own brother, Mime,* for attempting to disobey his instructions. His drive and energy are apparent for all to see. So, too, is his increased self-confidence. However, Wotan and Loge* still find him to be a gullible simpleton. In order to trap and bind him, they simply ask Alberich to put on his magic Tarnhelm* and turn himself into a toad and he does so. It is then an easy matter for Wotan to stretch forth a foot and halt him – merely a pantomime.

Alberich only reveals his ultimate strength after the Rhinegold and the magic Ring* which he has fashioned from it have been extorted from his grasp. Now, as a free agent again, he passes the most terrible curse upon the Ring, which will remain in force throughout four operas until the skein of destiny, winding the gold back into the glittering waters of the Rhine, drowns Alberich's curse, together with his own son Hagen*. See 'Curse on Love'.

IN *Die Walküre*

Wotan brings us up to date with news of Alberich, who does not appear himself. According to the lord of the Gods, whose information is supplied by Erda,* 'the dwarf has forced a woman; his gold bought her embrace and she will bear Alberich's son; the seed of spite stirs in her womb. . . .' However, the dwarf is still plotting to overthrow Wotan and, if Erda is to be believed, he will succeed in this aim if the Ring comes back into his possession.

IN *Siegfried*

Alberich is waiting beside Fafner's* cave, ever on duty to advance his cause, hoping to repossess the magic Ring. He has an argumentative meeting with Wotan, who is disguised as the 'Wanderer'; although Wotan hopes Siegfried will win the Ring, he assures Alberich that he has done nothing to help him (which is not true). Alberich is delighted to be told that the only other party interested in the Ring is his crafty brother, Mime. Fafner declines to hand the Ring into Alberich's safe-keeping, and so the Nibelung resumes his patient vigil after Wotan's departure. It is with intense delight that Alberich watches Siegfried kill the dragon soon afterwards; but it is with the bitterest sense of disappointment that he also sees Siegfried take the magic Ring and Tarnhelm for himself. A lesser spirit than Alberich might have given up at this point in despair, but the Nibelung is prepared to wait: 'in the end, the Ring will return to its Master!' At least he can have one good laugh when his brother Mime, the crafty blacksmith, is also killed by Siegfried.

IN *Götterdämmerung*
Alberich appears to his son, Hagen, in a dream in order to galvanize him into destroying Siegfried. He explains that Siegfried is 'safe' from the curse of the *Ring* (so far), and that therefore Hagen must eliminate him by a spontaneous act of his own, seizing the Ring from Siegfried's innocent hand. It is not made clear by Wagner whether Alberich is now alive or dead. He appears, in the stage directions, crouching before Hagen, which seems to suggest that he is alive. Either way, his implacable Nibelung spirit lives on in Hagen's breast.

Alvary, Maximillian (1856–98)
An outstanding German tenor. From the mid-1890s, he devoted himself to the music of Richard Wagner. He was America's first Siegfried*; in 1891 he gave Tristan*, and Tannhäuser* at Bayreuth and the following year he performed Siegfried in the London *Ring* under the direction of Mahler*. His other roles included Lohengrin*, Loge* and Siegmund*. In 1894 he was injured in a fall on stage (from which he never fully recovered) while rehearsing *Siegfried*.

Ambassadors, The (Ri)
A chorus which registers the international acceptance, albeit on a temporary basis, of the election of Rienzi as Tribune of Rome. The embassies come from Lombardy, Naples, Bavaria and Bohemia.

Amfortas (P)
Son of Titurel* and Leader of the Grail knights.* His name means 'amor fortis' ('love is strong') and therein lies his downfall. Throughout the opera, until Parsifal* purges his pain on Good Friday in Act III, Amfortas, a baritone, is suffering from a physical and spiritual lovesickness. He it was who, on entering his inheritance as Grail* leader, decided to destroy Klingsor's* offensive pleasure palace, which is situated so close to the sanctuary of Montsalvat.* Possibly he realized that Klingsor, purveyor of sexual temptation, represented his greatest personal insecurity. Unable to resist the amorous snares of the bewitchingly lovely Kundry,* Amfortas sins before he can kill Klingsor and therefore loses his virtue and half his power. The sacred spear* of Longinus* is taken into Klingsor's blasphemous grasp and turned against Amfortas, who is wounded with a wound that only the spear itself can heal. Yet who can retake the spear from Klingsor? Certainly no ordinary man can seize it again by force. This is made clear by the Grail, which prophesies that only the arrival of a 'pure fool, made compassionate by suffering' will herald the end of Amfortas' pain. This pain is extreme, since whenever the Grail is unshielded to allow the knights to renew their store of energy, it has the opposite effect on their leader, who sickens in ever-greater pain. For a while Amfortas can take pity on his brethren

3

and preside over the Grail ceremony as usual. He can also appreciate the suffering of Kundry in her vagabond guise (or does he still yearn for her without knowing why?), and he is grateful for all the help of Gawain* and the others in searching for some balm to ease his pain. But the Grail ceremony is progressively neglected until the Brotherhood is virtually destroyed. Amfortas himself begs for death on the swords of his remaining knights: 'Slay the sinner and his torment!' Of course he intends this as an act of sacrifice on their behalf – 'Then shall the Grail glow again for you!' – but he effectively requests them to commit murder, which must count as a further sin. Not the least of Amfortas' sorrows is that he has to let his own father die in order to survive himself. Titurel is eventually deprived of the life-giving Grail ceremonies because Amfortas can no longer endure the pain from his own wound.

Has all this woe of Amfortas been in vain? No, because, through his Christ-like suffering, Parsifal is able to bless Amfortas, remove his pain and grant atonement. Only by appreciating the full extent of Amfortas' agony has Parsifal learned the meaning of pity and achieved human sympathy for all sinners. This makes a certain amount of Christian sense, but the less pleasing side effect is the renewed suggestion that sexuality is the Creator's black joke. He gave love to men in order that they should refrain from expressing it. To the modern temperament it might be more congenial to think of Amfortas' sin as disobedience rather than loss of chastity.

Anders, Peter (1908–54)

A German tenor famous as Walter von Stolzing* which he sang under Beecham in 1951.

Angelo (Lt)

A noble hanger-on in *Das Liebesverbot*.

Annunzio, Gabriele d' (1863–1938)

Italian poet, novelist, playwright and man of action who once made himself ruler of the small territory of Fiume (1919–21) and who was much influenced by Wagner. His best play is agreed to be *La Figlia di Iorio* (1904) and his best poetry can be found in *Alcione* (also 1904).

He produced perhaps the most thrilling evocation of the *Tristan* music in all literature with his novel *Triumph of Death* (1894) in which two fiercely passionate lovers flee to a lonely retreat, to devote themselves to love. They take with them the score of *Tristan und Isolde**; the memory of an overwhelming performance of the opera at Bayreuth never leaves them. Unable to accept life on the terms available, the lovers finally fling themselves over a cliff to destruction.

d'Annunzio completed his homage to the Bayreuth genius in *The Flame of Life* (1900). At one point, in a superb vision, the composer even appears to the hero of the novel as a god.

Anti-semitism

Wagner was a pernicious anti-semite in his general social, political and above all musical views. At the same time he was good friends with a number of individual Jews. The conductor, Hermann Levi, was specially selected to conduct the 1882 première of *Parsifal* at Bayreuth*, even explaining to his parents in a letter home that Wagner was only anti-semitic 'for the noblest artistic reasons'. The theatre director, Angelo Neumann,* and the pianist, Joseph Rubinstein*, were both close friends of Wagner, and were by no means the first Jews to be ardent Wagnerites. Ever since Wagner achieved fame, leading Jews have been his devotees, beginning with Theodor Herzel himself, the founder of modern Zionism.

It cannot be denied that Wagner was in some respects a thoroughly degenerate personality. The early reverses he suffered in Paris disturbed him for life. He felt that the Jewish composers Meyer-beer* and Halévy* had deliberately plotted to prevent him earning fame and fortune and he never forgave them. This is why he wrote an infamous self-redressing pamphlet called *Judaism in Music** in 1850. In it, he accuses the entire Jewish race of being incapable of achieving the higher levels of culture, thus ignoring the evidence of his own senses and all historical fact. Apologists suggest that he merely repeated the views of his friend Count Arthur de Gobineau,* the racial theorist. This is false. Gobineau actually held the Jews in considerable esteem. Wagner adapted Gobineau's theory of races to elevate his own contribution to music by denigrating his Jewish competitors. Wagner married dubious European racial theory to traditional Bavarian petty anti-semitism. The consequence was serious for music and the world. Mendelssohn's music, for example, failed to get its just deserts from the German public. And the Jews paid practically the highest price in history for what later theorists, such as Wagner's son-in-law Houston Stewart Chamberlain,* and Hitler* himself, managed to do with Wagner's intellectual legacy. After all, Hitler was more inspired by the life and teachings of Wagner and Bayreuth than practically anything else. Wagner's operas are explicitly anti-Nazi. But for the period after 1850, Wagner's personal ideology had more in common with the spirit of *Mein Kampf* than many Wagnerians would care to admit.

Antonio (Lt)

A noble hanger-on in *Das Liebesverbot*.

Apel, Theodor (1811–67)

A friend from Wagner's youth, Apel was the son of a playwright and poet, August Apel, on whose play *Freischütz* Weber's* opera was based. He and Wagner shared a riotous holiday together in 1834, appropriately enough in Bohemia, and Wagner later wrote Apel an important series of letters.

Apples, golden: *see* Freia, goddess of Spring

Apprentices, First, Second, and chorus (M)

A choral gang employed by Wagner to represent the idea of anarchic urban youth in mediaeval Nuremberg. They spend much of their time teasing David,* Hans Sachs'* apprentice, and starting minor fist-fights.

Arindal (F)

A bewitched, Siegfried-like figure who is the mortal and earthly King of Tramond. His misfortune is to go out deer-hunting one day together with his ranger Gernot* and run into a party of fairies. A sweet-voiced doe leads them inexorably towards a stream and before they know it they are trapped in an enchanted castle. A fairy queen (Ada*) is soon telling Arindal that she 'loves him as he loves her' but for eight years he must not ask her name. Arindal and Gernot are duly trapped in fairyland for those eight years and Arindal's bewitching consort bears him two children. When the period is up, he asks her what she is called. The spell breaks, the castle vanishes and the two mortals are back on the rocks they had left all those years before. They hasten home to defend Tramond, which is being ravaged by the wicked King Murold after the death of Arindal's father, the previous king. But on his return home, Arindal, a plaything of the fates, is deceived into cursing Ada and thus loses her, apparently, forever. He goes mad and sings a King Lear-inspired ballad of desperation and disorder. However, all comes right in the end when the magician Groma* tells him he may regain his beloved Ada and defy the fates if he is armed with the right weapons (a shield, a sword and a lyre).

5

Since Arindal, like Ada, is a vehicle for the forces of enchantment, his outstanding virtue is his capacity to love even unto madness and death – at one point he welcomes a 'warrior's death' if he should never see Ada again. Arindal's tenor role is gruelling for the singer – long, high and florid.

Art and Revolution
Aesthetic pamphlet written by Wagner in exile in 1850 after the failure of the 1848–9 revolutions in Europe. It was a defiant attempt to rekindle the flame of reform and start a cultural revolution. He took the Greeks as his model. According to his account, their art had not been created for profit and their artistic geniuses were never at the mercy of speculating patrons. Instead, their work was a solemn celebration of the community. Each individual art worked in harmony with the others to that end. In fact, the arts of music and drama and poetry and dance were festally combined into a 'whole artwork'. This perfectly reflected the spiritual aspirations of the common people, which is art's true purpose. Such art must be deemed intrinsically good. In a market society art of this type was impossible. Therefore, a thoroughgoing social revolution was necessary before artistic progress could be made.

The paradox underlying this argument – that the long-term future of civilization depends on the destruction of civilization, at least in the short term – troubled Wagner increasingly as he grew older. But he never fully renounced the idea of 'community art' (witness Bayreuth*) or the concept of the 'whole artwork' which might regenerate, if not overthrow, existing society.

Art-work of the Future, The
The second of Wagner's aesthetic pamphlets written in 1850 (the first was Art and Revolution*), following the failure of the European revolutions of 1848–9.

Elaborating his previous argument, Wagner stressed the importance of creating a new 'community' or 'folk' art from a merger of all the arts. This mélange would produce a total identity between art and society. All members of the community would feel a similar 'need' to refresh themselves with such art. No art could do this singly. Music, for example, was solid sound, although it produced ideas; poetry was 'only ideas', lacking any other tangible reality; painting and sculpture were prisoners of form, lacking dynamism. Thus each art could only obtain proper fulfilment through a union of all the arts. Music and poetry would lend each other substance; drama would mobilize painting; painting would bring the force of 'nature' on to the stage.

This was an interesting theory and Wagner's operas are innovative largely because he thought at length about this question. It proved, however, impossible to merge the arts even in Wagnerian opera, where the music predominates. His ideal remains unfulfilled to this day. See 'Gesamtkunstwerk'.

Ash-tree
Hunding's* hut in Die Walküre is built around an ash-tree in which a gleaming sword lies buried up to the hilt. This tree is reminiscent of the 'World Tree of Life' (see 'Yggrdasil') on which, according to the legend, Wotan* hung for nine days and nights in an attempt to acquire wisdom.

'Asyl, Das'
'Das Asyl' ('The Sanctuary') was the name of a small, exquisite house which Wagner rented at a low figure from Otto Wesendonck* from the spring of 1857. It was situated on the left bank of Lake Zürich and was decorated and furnished to Wagner's precise instructions.

'Das Asyl' was an asylum both for art

and love. It was offered to Wagner at the suggestion of Wesendonck's infatuated wife, Mathilde Wesendonck* (the inspiration for Isolde* and Sieglinde*) and soon after Wagner took up residence she moved into a mansion next door. Otto Wesendonck had to tolerate the situation to protect his children. As Wagner smugly records, 'for their sake [Otto] accepted his renunciatory position'. But 'Das Asyl' did yield, besides a fractured marriage, a great deal of sound Wagnerian hard work in the form of *Tristan*, the *Wesendonck Lieder* (to words by Mathilde), the 'Good Friday' theme from *Parsifal* and Act II of *Siegfried*, with its glorious woodland motifs.

Many famous visitors found their way to this lake-side retreat – singers, composers, pianists – as well as a very jealous wife, Minna Wagner.* The situation between the two women became intolerable, and, in order to seek a peaceful environment in which to complete *Tristan*, on 17 August 1858 Wagner fled his sanctuary: 'Red with shame the sun crept up from behind the mountains. Then I took one more lingering glance at the house opposite. . . .'

Auber, Daniel-François-Esprit (1782–1871)
Composer of *La Muette de Portici* (1828) and other operas which influenced the youthful Wagner. He was chiefly celebrated for his *opéras comiques*, the most famous of which was *Fra Diavolo* (1830).

Auerbach, Berthold (1812–82)
One of Wagner's Jewish friends. Auerbach was the author of a number of pastoral stories.

Avenarius, Cäcilie née Geyer (1815–93)
Wagner's half-sister, of whom he was very fond.

Avenarius, Eduard Brockhaus (1809–85)
The Paris agent of the Brockhaus publishing firm, Avenarius married Wagner's half-sister, Cäcilie.* He tried to help Wagner in his Paris days and in fact indirectly encouraged him to come to Paris in 1839 by his contact with the dramatist and librettist Augustin Scribe,* who had seen the scores of two of Wagner's early works, including *Das Liebesverbot*.

Bailey, Norman Stanley (b. 1933)
One of the leading English bass-baritones, specializing in the roles of Wotan* and Hans Sachs.* Bailey is an intelligent performer whose acting conveys enormous intensity. In gesture alone he is unrivalled. His voice, although not rich, is one of the most wistfully beautiful of recent years. His Wotans at Covent Garden and the Coliseum have been memorable, and he has sung Gunther*, Amfortas* and Hans Sachs* at Bayreuth.

Bakunin, Mikhail Alexandrovich (1814–76)
Russian revolutionary anarchist who emigrated in 1840. He settled in Dresden and soon afterwards came to know Wagner well. The two shared a common interest in anarcho-socialism and Romanticism. A lovable bear of a man, Bakunin still preached violent upheaval as the only path to social salvation. In 1849, Marx* and Bakunin shared the barricades of Dresden together, after which both were exiled from Germany. Bakunin retained his revolutionary Romanticism for life, accusing Marx, for example, of never transcending a Teutonic passion for authority. Wagner continued to follow the career of Bakunin in later life with great interest although their paths no longer crossed.

Baroncelli (Ri)
A Roman citizen, a representative of the fickle Roman crowd which is blown first this way by Rienzi's* promises of popular

power, then the other way by the price in blood exacted from the commons in the fight against their noble oppressors. Baroncelli stirs up trouble with the line 'What say you of our fallen kinsmen?' Then he accuses Rienzi of wanting a new alliance with the nobility in order to ally his daughter by marriage with Adriano Colonna* the surviving son of the patrician, Stefano Colonna.* Baroncelli later proposes that Rienzi be murdered during a solemn Te Deum, which he characterizes as 'yet another pompous fête to distract us from our wounds!'

Bartók, Béla (1881–1945)

Hungarian-born composer who attended the Bayreuth Festival of 1904 when he was twenty-three. He sent the following postcard home to his friend, Kálmán Harsányi, a poet: 'I am still under the spell of *Parsifal* . . . though it did not make such a tremendous impression on me as *Tristan*. . . . I feel disturbed by the continual praying on stage. . . . I found many innovations in the music. . . . It is amazing that a man of seventy could write anything so fresh as the Flower Maidens' love song. . . .'

Baudelaire, Charles (1821–67)

The French poet, most famous for *Les Fleurs du Mal*, was one of the few Parisian intellectuals to champion Wagner at the time of the 1861 *Tannhäuser* scandal. When Wagner was considered in France to be a brassy Teutonic joke, Baudelaire responded to his rich and innovative harmony as well as to the feeling of nostalgic regret which he expressed. Baudelaire was by no means a music critic, but the spontaneous and unsycophantic fan letter he wrote to Wagner after hearing only fragments of *Lohengrin* and *Tannhäuser* in a concert performance ranks as one of the finest of all amateur accounts of Wagnerism. While the rest of Paris jeered the full production of *Tannhäuser*, when it

was mounted by Imperial decree at enormous cost and after 163 rehearsals, Baudelaire saw through the fiasco to the highly attractive opera underneath. He rewarded Wagner with a second superb piece of intuitive criticism, *Richard Wagner and 'Tannhäuser' in Paris*, which was published in April 1861 in *La Revue Européenne*.

Bayreuth

City of northern Bavaria on the Roter Main River between the Fichtelgelbirge and the Franconian Jura to the north-east of Nuremberg. Wagner selected Bayreuth as the ideal location for his Festival Theatre since it was as dull and ordinary a Bavarian town as could be found. (It remains so today, except for the Wagner Festival.) His argument was admirably selfish. What, he argued, was the point of holding a celebration of one's works in a city which offered a host of rival attractions? How could the audience *concentrate* on the meaning of the operas if they had something else to do between performances?

Wagner first visited Bayreuth in 1835 on the lookout for promising singers to take to Magdeburg, where he was working at the time. He recalls happy memories of the town 'gloriously illumined by the setting sun'. After his financial alliance with King Ludwig II* in 1864, Wagner was even more drawn to the idea of establishing his dream theatre of the future in Bavaria. Skilful bargaining by the Bayreuth burghers, particularly Theoder Muncker and Friedrich Feustel,* persuaded him that Bayreuth might well be the place to choose. He was even keener after the municipality gave him a grant of land on the Bürgerreuth Hill, at a cost to the local community of no less than fourteen thousand guilders. With his architect, Gottfried Semper,* Wagner had previously drawn up plans for a theatre project in Munich. Now the whole project was moved north, although Semper was not retained and a new man, Otto Brück-wald, was eventually given the contract.

The Bayreuth Festspielhaus took four years to build. It was revolutionary in design and concept and nearly bankrupted Wagner several times over. The greatest innovation was the covered orchestra pit screened by a wooden deck (the *Schalldekke**) from the sight of the audience. This deliberately added to the mystery of the operas and gave a delightfully muffled tone to the orchestral playing. Unusually deep foundations were required to help hide the orchestra from view, and these periodically flooded during construction, nearly aborting the project. Money being tight, a timber-framed red-brick construction was selected. This excited scornful criticism a century ago, but today the Festspielhaus has a pleasing air of simple modernity because of its lack of lavish or redundant decoration. The final design was also unique in not including side boxes. The whole audience faces the stage and the whole stage faces the audience.

Finance for the theatre came partly from King Ludwig and partly from specially instituted Wagner Societies of Patrons*. Most major German cities contributed, as did some foreign capitals, such as London (where the Wagner Society was founded by Edward Dannreuther* in 1874). The funds were topped up by aristocratic patrons and by the hard-pressed Wagners themselves. The first Festival of 1876, at which the complete *Ring* was given its first performance, yielded a staggering deficit of 147,851 marks. The debt was eventually paid off, with government help. Wagner built his villa, 'Wahnfried',* at Bayreuth: five days after his death in Venice on 13 February 1883, he was brought back to his festival town for burial.

Since 1883, the Bayreuth Festival has preserved the works and memory of Richard Wagner, except for an interruption at the end of the Second World War (1944–51). Cosima Wagner* and Siegfried Wagner* ran the theatre until 1930; Winifred Wagner* and Wieland Wagner* until the war. Since Winifred, because of her political standpoint, could not be allowed to resume the directorship of the Bayreuth festival (whose assets she owned) after the war, reopening was delayed until 1953, when the management of the festival was placed in the hands of her sons, Wieland* and Wolfgang,* who were lessees. Wieland was in charge until 1966; Wolfgang Wagner, with contributions from Winifred, from 1966. Collaboration with Hitler* transformed Bayreuth into a Nazi propaganda centre, but brought tremendous tax advantages. Each year the 1,925 tickets put on sale in November for performances in the following summer are subscribed five times over.

Bayreuther Blätter
A Wagner Society periodical founded by Wagner in which he was wont to air his views on music, art, race, society and festivals.

Bayreuth, Le Petit
Parisian musical circle numbering Fauré, Duparc* and Chabrier* among its members, devoted to the memory of Wagner.

Beardsley, Aubrey (1872–98)
English artist and illustrator who perceived the profound sexual tendency of Wagnerian art (lust, incest and a metaphysical union which yet incorporated the physical elements). The Yellow Book movement of the 1890s embraced Wagnerism with indecent enthusiasm, Beardsley being the most explicit idolator. His most successful transposition of Wagner's eroticism does not depict Wagnerian personages at all, but simply the sensuality with which the audience listens to *Tristan und Isolde*.

In his gracefully obscene novella, *Under the Hill* (originally called *Venus and Tannhäuser*), Beardsley explores the Venusberg, the *mons veneris*, with an explicitness denied to Wagnerian art.

Beckmesser, Sixtus (M)

The town-clerk of Nuremberg – the comic baritone villain of *Die Meistersinger*, who schemes and plots his way to the very threshold of winning Eva's* hand in matrimony only to be exposed as a pompous ass by his guild-fellow, the cobbler Hans Sachs.* Beckmesser is one of Wagner's most vivid, neo-Shakespearean creations, a variant on the stock type of a petty bureaucrat who lusts after a pretty young wife in order to raise his prestige and libido during his declining years. He is a prey to his appetites, not without appeal even when he cheats, lies and steals to get what he wants.

In Act I, he tries to persuade Pogner* not to give his daughter Eva any say in the song contest which is to be held to select a husband for her. Beckmesser is confident that he can produce the best song, but not at all sure that he can obtain Eva's personal consent if she is afterwards consulted about his marriage proposal. Winking hard, he asks Pogner to 'put in a good word for him' anyway, since fathers have so much say in these matters.

Walther von Stolzing's* arrival disconcerts Beckmesser; the young knight is much too good-looking for his peace of mind; therefore the ever-crafty Sixtus tries to ensure that Walther cannot join the Mastersingers' guild by being as scornful as possible of Walther's application song. Alas for Walther, Beckmesser is actually the 'marker' appointed to list faults of composition and delivery, and he abuses his advantageous position as much as possible although it is undeniable that Walther's song is indeed quite unorthodox. To Beckmesser's relief, the song is rejected and Walther cannot even take part in the coming bridegroom selection contest.

Nevertheless, the town-clerk still leaves no stone unturned in his bid to find a way into Eva's affections. He attempts to woo Eva at night, but his serenade is skilfully sabotaged by that good angel Hans Sachs, who watches over Eva like a father,

cobbling noisily till Beckmesser cannot follow a note of his own score. To add injury to insult, Sachs' apprentice David* then beats Beckmesser up after a case of mistaken identity. It is therefore a self-righteous Beckmesser who steals Walther's song from Sachs' house, believing it to be Sachs' own composition; he thinks it is common justice for all the wrongs Sachs has heaped on his head – and on his feet, since even the shoes Sachs made for him are abominably tight!

Act III sees Beckmesser's comic undoing, since he cannot read Sachs' handwriting or blend Walther's song to its proper tune. Thus in the song contest he comes well and truly last, howled down by the crowd for delivering gibberish. His come-uppance is deserved – his sins are pride (in his post of marker), jealousy (of the musical skill of Hans Sachs) and skulduggery (in stealing Walther's song and then trying to ruin Sachs' own reputation by fixing the authorship on him). But Eva was a pretty prize, and Wagner allows us to feel some sympathy for a man who cuts a few corners when seeking to win the hand of such a companion.

Originally, the marker in *Die Meistersinger* was going to be called 'Veit Hanslich' not Beckmesser at all, after Eduard Hanslick,* the detested anti-Wagnerian critic.

Beecham, Sir Thomas (1879–1961)

This enormously influential and enterprising British conductor not only founded the London Philharmonic Orchestra and the Royal Philharmonic Orchestra, but also introduced the music of Richard Strauss into England. He championed Wagner even against the grain of his own more lightly framed aesthetics. According to the English critic, Neville Cardus,

He has no patience with a long stretch of Wagner. One night when I was at supper with him in Abbey Lodge, Lady Cunard called. She insisted that tomorrow night he should use a score for *Götterdämmerung*. 'You know very well that you don't know all the rhythmical changes.' With his incomparable blandness he replied: 'There are no rhythmical changes in *Götterdämmerung*, my dear Emerald. It goes on and on from half-past five till midnight like a damned old cart-horse.'

Beecham journeyed to Bayreuth in 1899 and heard the *Ring* for the first time but he was less than impressed by the 'inevitable crowd of cranks and faddists' who swelled the ranks of the idolators there. He found Siegfried Wagner's* direction feeble and, as ever, the conductors' tempi far too slow. Cardus again:

If Beecham, as a conductor, misses the tragic intensity of *Tristan*, the girth and amplitude of the comedy of *Meistersinger* and the gradual epic sweep of the *Ring*, he brings compensations; he mediterraneanizes Wagner, to use Nietzsche's term. He concentrates on the melody in Wagner and lends to the score as a whole a fineness of style that is fascinating even if it does reduce the stature and lighten the harmony and the rhythm. . . . In the *Ring* performances at Covent Garden between 1930 and the outbreak of war, Beecham persuaded people to listen . . . to the Wagnerian 'melos'. . . . When objections . . . were made to his tempi, Beecham produced metronomic evidence to prove he had conducted each music-drama in *The Ring* at much the same pace as Richter [Wagner's personal conductor]. Beecham artfully did not point out that an illusion of quicker movement can be created by the conductor who lightens the harmony. A fat man and a thin man walking side by side down the street do not proceed at the same tempo. . . .

Beecham was asked by Hitler to perform at Bayreuth in 1936 but the perceptive Briton turned him down flat.

Beethoven, Ludwig van (1770–1827)

Wagner's musical god. He said that, without Beethoven, his work would never have been possible. If he wished to praise a composer, he granted him 'a little of Beethoven'. His support for Bruckner was couched in the highest terms: 'He is the only one who approaches Beethoven!' He explained his thoughts on the symphonic master in a number of prose works (*Opera and Drama*,* 'On Beethoven', and in several of his letters ot Theodor Uhlig*). He recalled drawing inspiration from the Ninth Symphony, the work which first opened his eyes to the possibility of elaborating opera symphonically. In *Opera and Drama*, Wagner notes that when Beethoven wrote the simple melody for 'Freude, schöner Götterfunken', with its insistent beat, he was writing only as a musician, but in the 'Seid umschlungen, Millionen' he produces something quite over and above a mere musical setting of Schiller's words. Here, in this mutual reinforcement of words and music, lay Wagner's inspiration for *dramma per musica*. Ernest Newman* remarks,

Wagner was one of those dynamically charged personalities after whose passing the world can never be the same again. . . . Wagner is probably the only figure in the whole history of music of whom this can be said. Bach created no such upheaval. . . . We were not fit for Bach until Beethoven and Wagner – and Wagner, perhaps, even more than Beethoven – made us so.

Wagner, alone of his contemporaries, says Newman, perceived the 'poetic spirit' in Beethoven. Only Wagner could see that Beethoven was frustrated in his attempts to liberate a dramatic voice from his music. Ignoring tone poems (and some of his own work, which by music alone creates scenic and dramatic visions), Wagner flatly asserted that music by itself could not express the poetic imagination. He characterized the choral ending to the Ninth Symphony as the 'unconscious, instinctive cry of the musician for the redemption of music by poetry' (Newman's words). Great music must go deeper than a mere weaving of patterns, and 'the deeper it goes, the closer it comes to the heart; and our name for the necessities of the heart is poetry'.

Thus Wagner held Beethoven in a mixture of awe and compassion. He considered that Beethoven was trying to do the impossible: to express definite poetic ideas in uncongenial abstract forms. Newman continues, 'Beethoven's mistake according to Wagner, in one of the happiest and most famous of his analogies, was the same as that of Columbus, who, though merely trying to find the way to India that was already known, actually discovered thereby a new world. His vain effort was to achieve the artistically necessary in the artistically impossible.' What Beethoven really needed in order to deliver his imaginative message, said Wagner, was *words*, and it took eight-and-a-half symphonies for him to realize it. Ultimately Wagner was to reason that the form and content of words in opera must determine the form and quality of the musical utterance. Lyricism must not be imposed on the drama from outside. Thus, neither the chorus nor any of the characters is to make 'just music', whereas the orchestra, for the first time, acquires a 'capacity for speech' of its own. Rightly, Wagner credits Beethoven with setting him on this track, which in the end, after Wagner's lifetime, effected a revolution in all music, not just in opera.

Bellini, Vincenzo (1801–35)

Italian operatic composer with a wonderful gift of sensuous melody. In youth Wagner was entranced by the work of Bellini, particularly *I Capuletti e I Montecchi* (1830) and *Norma* (1831), publicly 'praying that Germans might emulate Bellini's melodic power'. *Das Liebesverbot* was his own attempt to do just that.

However, by 1871, Wagner had come to regard Bellini's contribution to art as 'insipid and threadbare', although by the 1880s the censure was modified to a cryptic 'Bellini! Bellini!' The truth is that Wagner loved good music. Bellini's creative gifts belied Wagner's artistic theories about 'Italian decadence' and so Bellini had to be damned along with the rest, but the condemnation was not wholly convincing.

Bennett, Enoch Arnold (1867–1931)

English writer whose laconic diary entry for Monday, 9 February 1914, reads, '*Parsifal* at Covent Garden. Putrid performance . . . poor orchestra. Appalling scenery. . . . Also long stretches of dull music. I never saw uglier scenery. I went to sleep in the middle of each act.' A few months later, German music was banned in Britain as part of the war effort. Given such standards of production, it possibly helped to raise morale.

Berg, Alban (1885–1935)

Self-taught Austrian composer who later studied with Schoenberg.* The author of the operas *Wozzeck* (1925) and *Lulu* (1937), he embraced Schoenberg's musical atonality and serialism. In 1909 he visited Bayreuth to hear *Parsifal*, but after the fine performances of Wagner he had heard in Vienna, under Mahler,* was completely unimpressed. The emphasis on eating and drinking between the acts disgusted him:

. . . The Bavarians drank beer, the Americans champagne. Siegfried Wagner had changed from his immaculate white tennis kit into a dark suit, but with all the autograph hunters hardly had any time to enjoy his 'Parsifal Steak' with rice and stewed fruit, before it was time to go back for Act III. . . . The whole place is a horrible exploitation of the Wagner idea. Extremely distressing to see what the 'German nation' had done to the greatest of all Germans.

Berglund, Joel Ingemar (b. 1903)

Swedish bass-baritone, who sang the Flying Dutchman* at Bayreuth (1942) and Sachs*, among other roles at the Metropolitan (1946).

Bergwerk von Falun, Das (The Mines of Falun)

On 25 May 1905, a sketch for a hitherto unknown libretto for an opera by Wagner was discovered by Hubert Ermisch among the papers of Wagner's Dresden friend,

Röckel*. It is dated 'Paris, March 5th, 1842' and three acts are complete. The story recapitulates elements from the legend of the Flying Dutchman on which Wagner had been at work in 1841. Falun is the Swedish town which houses one of the world's oldest mining enterprises, the Stora Kopparberg Mining Company, dating from 1347. The famous copper mine suffered a disastrous cave-in at the end of the seventeenth century. Wagner only referred to this work once, in a cryptic letter to Röckel.*

Berlioz, Louis-Hector (1803–69)

When in 1840 Wagner sought fame and fortune in Paris, one new French score above all others impressed him with its majesty and melody – that of the *Symphonie funèbre et triomphale* for military band, chorus and strings by Berlioz. Wagner waited on the composer who in turn assisted the struggling German by putting some musical journalism and other commissions in his way. But these two composing giants – the Fasolt and Fafner of the 1850s – were predestined to fall out over the musical spoils.

Berlioz believed in the creation of drama through music alone; Wagner wished to fuse symphony with opera. Berlioz was furious when the Paris Opéra mounted the 1861 production of *Tannhäuser*. Wagner responded by writing rude articles about Berlioz' incompetent use of harmonic polyphony. Their conducting styles were dissimilar to the point of contradiction and even at their moments of apparent personal rapport (for example in London in 1855) their contemporary creations – *Tristan* and *The Trojans* – brooked no artistic compromise. Eventually, Berlioz was to say of Wagner in opera, 'I am not sure that such music ought to be written', while Wagner commented that the music of Berlioz 'lacked a sense of beauty or coherent purpose'. Wagner believed Berlioz was in the pay of Meyerbeer.* However, both men remained mutually intrigued.

Wagner could not turn his back altogether on the composer of *Romeo and Juliet*, which revealed new possibilities for the orchestra, and Berlioz always acknowledged Wagner's remarkable musical colouring, 'despite his intellectual laziness and abuse of tremolo'.

Betz, Franz (1835–1900)

German baritone who made his début in Hanover in 1856 as Heinrich in *Lohengrin*, created the role of Hans Sachs,* and sang Wotan* in the first complete cycle of the *Ring* in 1876. His favourite role was Sachs, which he sang over a hundred times in Berlin alone. His other Wagnerian interpretations included King Marke* and Kurwenal* in *Tristan*, Telramund* in *Lohengrin*, Wolfram* in *Tannhäuser* and the Flying Dutchman* in *Der Fliegende Holländer*.

Bismarck-Schönhausen, Count Otto Eduard Leopold von (1815–98)

Bismarck became Prime Minister of Prussia in 1862 and Chancellor when the North German Confederation was established in 1867. On 21 March 1871, Bismarck was created a prince and appointed Imperial Chancellor of the new German Empire. Wagner was originally an opponent, but after 1866 and the Austro-Prussian War, resulting in the defeat of Austria, he gave Bismarck his general support. Nietzsche* was almost as horrified by this as by the Christian content of *Parsifal*. One of Wagner's greatest crimes in the eyes of his old radical friends was to write the *Kaisermarsch* (1871) in celebration of the Prussian victory over the French in the Franco-Prussian War.

Bispham, David Scull (1857–1921)

American baritone who sang Kurwenal* in London in 1892 and thereafter sang all the leading bass-baritone Wagnerian roles throughout the world. He himself claimed that his renderings of Beckmesser* were unrivalled.

Biterolf (T)

Bass Minnesinger at the court of Hermann, Landgrave of Thuringia,* who denounces Tannhäuser* violently during the Wartburg song contest because he blasphemes against Biterolf's unrelentingly spiritual conception of love. Tannhäuser taunts him with 'Prater – tis certain thou hast never gained the joys that I have often drained!'

Bizet, Georges (1838–75)

When Bizet, the composer of *Carmen*, first encountered Wagner's music he loathed it. Writing to his mother after reading two unspecified Wagner scores, he comments, 'There is absolutely nothing there! They are the work of a man who, lacking all harmonic inventiveness, has created eccentricity. . . . I like Verdi 100 times more!' However, by 1862, Bizet had changed his tune. 'Wagner', he announced in his quirky way, 'is Verdi with the addition of style!'

This change of heart caused problems for the up-and-coming Frenchman, since anyone praising Wagner in Paris at this time made himself many enemies. (For years the capital was riven between the Wagnerphiles and the Wagnerphobes!) In 1872, a respected critic such as Adolphe Jullien, reviewing Bizet's new work *Djamileh*, could simply rail against it for 'following the Wagner cult, that's where it leads, to madness, neither tonality, nor shape, nor rhythm. It's no longer music – it's macaroni!'

There are two ironies here. First, while Bizet was suffering for Wagner, Cosima was recording in her diary that she and Richard went to hear *Carmen* but found it 'glaring in the modern French manner' and 'tasteless'. Secondly, it is now recognized that Bizet, although not a revolutionary, achieved a real synthesis of music

and drama, in discrete form. Bizet wrote objectively; in this he differs from Wagner, all of whose operas are in essence about himself.

Bockelmann, Rudolf August Louis Wilhelm (1892–1958)

German bass-baritone who from 1926 onwards made regular appearances in leading Wagnerian roles. He gave the Flying Dutchman,* Gunther*, Kurwenal,* Sachs* and Wotan* at Bayreuth and at Covent Garden 1929–30, 1934–8, although his voice was better suited to the cobbler in *Meistersinger* than the Lord of the Gods in the *Ring*. He was a Nazi sympathizer.

Böhm, Karl (b. 1894–1981)

Austrian conductor with a wonderfully stable sense of tempo. Not a romantic interpreter of Wagner's music, but his build-up of dramatic tension is second to none. His memorable *Tristan*, with the Vienna Philharmonic Orchestra in 1933, cemented his partnership with the orchestra. He was at Bayreuth 1962–70.

Bohnen, Michael (1887–1965)

German bass-baritone who appeared at Bayreuth in 1914, singing Hunding* and Daland.* At Covent Garden he sang Henry the Fowler* in *Lohengrin*. His dramatic abilities were favourably compared to those of the great Russian bass, Shalyapin.

Borgatti, Giuseppe (1871–1950)

Italian tenor, who, from the early 1900s, concentrated on the music of Wagner, having sung Siegfried* and Tristan* at La Scala in 1899 and 1900.

Boulez, Pierre (b. 1925)
Outstanding French composer and conductor. As a conductor, he was entrusted with two Bayreuth productions: the 1966 *Parsifal* and the controversial 1976 *Ring*. His direction is characterized by an analytic clarity of sound, giving weight to each individual note.

Brabantine nobles (L)
A disaffected quartet who represent the opposition to King Henry the Fowler's* desire to use Brabantine soldiers in his struggle against the Magyars. They resent 'Protector' Lohengrin's* instant support for the German king's foreign policy.

Brahms, Johannes (1833–97)
The immense quality of Brahms' musical compositions was overlooked by Wagner, partly as a result of a clique-like feud between supporters of these two great German geniuses. Brahms was at fault in allowing his name to be added to a published attack on the Wagnerian 'Neo-German' school of music in 1860. But the Wagnerites could take care of themselves and they pretended that the music of Brahms was old-fashioned and retrograde, particularly through the medium of the writings of Hugo Wolf,* who regularly vilified Brahms in the columns of the fashionable weekly *Wiener Salonblatt* of which he was music critic 1884–7.

Brandt, Karl (1828–81)
Technical Director at the Darmstadt theatre. Wagner brought him to Bayreuth to help with the production details of the *Ring*.

Brangäne (T I)
Isolde's* mezzo-soprano maid, who, by disobeying her mistress, plays God in the central action of the opera and keeps both Tristan* and Isolde* alive to explore the extremes of their mutual passion.

Brangäne is well-versed in spells and potions since her original mistress, Isolde's mother, seems to have been something of a white witch. This being so, the two Irishwomen are accompanied on their voyage to the court of King Marke* of Cornwall by a bag of elixirs. Among these is an antidote for poison and two philtres – a love potion and a death potion. When Tristan does not pay Isolde any attention, nor atone for the 'crime' of slaying her former lover, Morold,* Isolde (really suffering from benighted love for Tristan) commands Brangäne to mix up the death potion, which both she and Tristan will drink together (he unwittingly). Brangäne, although never really understanding the full nature of Isolde's feelings, grasps enough of the situation to realize that her mistress cares for Tristan, so switches the philtres, making the frustrated lovers drink an amorous draught, not the bitter cup they had both expected. Thus the barriers to their passion are removed and Brangäne may take the credit or blame.

The maid is also perspicacious enough to see through the ruses of Melot* (Tristan's one-time comrade, but now bent on his destruction) right from the start, while Isolde is still taken in by the fellow, until the arrival of King Marke and the gloating Melot finally disabuse her.

Eventually, Brangäne has to confess her part in compelling the lovers to act out their emotions by telling King Marke about the switching of the drugs. She says she could not have handed her mistress the instrument of death – unaware that by releasing Isolde's inhibitions she did precisely that. The love of Isolde for Tristan and for death are but different roads to the same goal.

Branzell, Karin Maria (1891–1974)
A superb Swedish contralto, she sang Kundry* in Vienna and Fricka* at the Metropolitan in New York in 1924–44. In 1930–31 she sang Fricka and Waltraute* at

Bayreuth. Her Brünnhilde* (in *Die Walküre*) was always richly voluminous, the characterization enhanced by her height.

Braunes Buch, Das (The Brown Book)
A collection of annals, poems, sketches and *personalia*, written 1865–82 by Wagner to Cosima, primarily intended, one may guess, for posterity as much as for the Wagner family. It contains much of interest, especially the prose sketch for *Parsifal* showing that Wagner had completed the whole work in his mind 12 years before he started composing the music and that the heavy moralizing of *Parsifal* was always an integral part of the conception.

Breitkopf & Härtel
Publishing firm specializing in music, founded in 1719 by Bernhardt Christoph Breitkopf (1695–1777). For Wagner, they published *Tristan* and *Lohengrin*, but turned down the *Ring*. After 1859, Wagner's main publishers were Schott.*

Brema, Marie (1856–1925)
English mezzo-soprano of German-American parentage. In 1894, she was engaged by Cosima Wagner* for Bayreuth, so becoming the first English singer to perform there. She was Ortrud* in the first Bayreuth *Lohengrin* and also gave Kundry*. Thereafter she appeared as Fricka*, Brangäne* and Brunnhilde* (in *Götterdämmerung*), the last at Paris.

Brighella (Lt)
Captain of the watch and subordinate hypocrite to his master Viceroy Frederick. Brighella also betrays qualities of mild cowardice when threatened by the crowd in Act I Scene 1, and a desire to become a tyrant when allowed to judge the captives in jail during his master's absence later in the same act. His instant susceptibility to a pretty face and ankle involves him in professional, not to say moral, conflicts, for it is he who must enforce the Sicilian ban on responding to female charms. A 'bass-buffo' part.

Brilioth, Helge (b. 1931)
Swedish tenor who sang Siegmund* at Bayreuth in 1969, Siegfried* the next year at Salzburg and Siegmund at Covent Garden – where he has also sung Siegfried, Tristan* and Parsifal*.

Brockhaus family
A family allied by a double marriage with the Wagners. They gave Richard a considerable degree of personal support when he was a young man.

Bruckner, Josef Anton (1824–96)
Austrian composer, best known for his highly original symphonies. He disliked opera on the whole, despite his fervent admiration for all the work of Wagner, to whom he simply referred as 'The Master'.

Bruckner made Wagner's acquaintance in 1865. He followed up in 1873 by asking him to accept the dedication of one of his symphonies. Two works were submitted for approval. Wagner graciously gave his consent to the suggestion but the 'poor Viennese organist' (as Cosima called him) was so overcome that he forgot to ask which of the two symphonies Wagner favoured. He then sent an embarrassed note, referring to the third symphony in D minor, on which Wagner noted in reply, 'Yes, yes, warmest greetings'. Consequently this was the symphony which eventually carried the dedication.

Ten years later, Wagner was more specific: 'I know of only one who approaches Beethoven and that is Bruckner!' The latter in turn refused to eat in any house where Wagner was ever criticized and spent hours in solitary contemplation of Wagner's villa 'Wahnfried' whenever he made one of his frequent trips to Bayreuth.

Perhaps Bruckner's greatest tribute to Wagner is the adagio of his seventh symphony which was partly inspired by the sad realization, in January 1883, of Wagner's approaching death. He used to sit at Bayreuth for year after year in a seat with little view of the stage, or with his eyes closed, simply absorbing the music. He never had a clear idea of the plot of *The Ring* and is reported as once having asked; 'Why do they burn Brünnhilde at the end of *Walküre*?'

Bruckner, Max (1836–1919) and Gotthold (1844–92)

Brothers from the Coburg Court Theatre who were Wagner's favourite scenic designers. He entrusted them with the first productions of *The Ring* (1876) and *Parsifal* (1882) at Bayreuth. They continued their work at Bayreuth after Wagner's death.

Brünnhilde (W, S, G)

The fiery, red-headed soprano Valkyrie, daughter of Wotan,* Lord of the Gods, and Erda,* Mother of Earth. She inherits the wisdom of her mother and strength of will of her father. These combined qualities make her the ultimate force for moral good in the operas of the *Ring* cycle.

IN *Die Walküre*
Brünnhilde loves her father enough to carry out his many commissions, some of which are ignoble. For example, as a Valkyrie, she is his accomplice in filling up Valhalla with heroes 'deceived into a life of bondage'. Wotan boasts to her that 'together we have curbed mortals in their pride and bound them by treacherous treaties, shameful agreements, blindly to serve us'. Brünnhilde's role has even included 'arousing men to ruthless war till valiant hosts of heroes have gathered in Valhalla's hall'.

But Brünnhilde is young and has magnificent qualities waiting to be developed. She is perceptive, quick-witted, independent, loving and, if convinced of the rightness of her cause, capable of healthy rebellion. She is therefore fitted to take moral decisions, where Wotan seems only able to take self-interested ones.

In Act II, we learn that Brünnhilde is Wotan's favourite daughter and the 'child of his will'. This means that she represents that side of his divided 'will' which is devoted to martial and aggressive enterprises. However, Brünnhilde only carries out Wotan's warlike purpose (that is, she defends Siegmund* against Sieglinde's husband) because of her own remarkable emotional qualities. Until Siegmund appeals to her sympathies, she is intent on killing him in obedience to the commands of Wotan's 'legal' will. It is only because Brünnhilde is full of heart that she relents: 'I feel all your suffering', she tells Siegmund, 'I share all your pain.'

It is, in fact, Brünnhilde's patent *humanity* that makes her attractive to all who meet her. Wotan, himself, is drawn to take her into his confidence for this reason. And at the end of the opera, he is willing, for the self-same reason, to modify her sentence of punishment for having disobeyed his 'legal' instruction.

But Brünnhilde is as shrewd as she is sympathetic. She persuades Wotan to be merciful by showing him that through the birth of Siegfried,* an event which may enable a 'free' hero to restore the magic Ring to the Rhine, the gods can be saved from destruction. Would he not, therefore, like to ensure that the only man capable of awakening Brünnhilde from her enchanted sleep of punishment is none other than this hero Siegfried – so that together Brünnhilde and Siegfried can set the world to rights? Wotan, upon reflection, is certain that he would. And we leave Brünnhilde, at the end of *Die Walküre*, fast asleep on a fire-surrounded rock, waiting for her hero to awaken her to mortal life and love.

IN *Siegfried*

In Act III, Scene 2 of this opera, Wagner creates one of the greatest love scenes in opera, even though it takes place between two virgins: the man has never, until now, seen a woman in his entire life; the woman, who is his aunt, has never appeared in mortal form before.

Brünnhilde is duly grateful to Siegfried for wakening her from the enchanted sleep. Yet she rebels against him, filled with shame and disgust by the prospect of union with a common man, despite the fact that he is a hero.

However, Wagner reveals to her the lyrical compensations of mortality. Human love was denied to her when she was a goddess. Now it fills her newly-created mortal frame: she affirms human love in its entirety. There will be no 'renunciation' of love in this particular opera. Instead, the lovers will celebrate in full – 'feeling your heart beating beside me, joining our glances, sharing one single breath, eyes together, mouth to mouth'.

IN *Götterdämmerung*

Transformed physically and emotionally, Brünnhilde is now an adult personality. She alone has escaped the tangled web of the Ring curse and her half-sisters', the Norns,* tripping ropes of destiny. With love, she has gained that wisdom lost by her mother, Erda, and by the Norns. However, before she can use her wisdom to restore peace to the world, she must undergo a temptation from Wotan, a hallucination concerning Siegfried and a purgation by grief that will permit her to 'know all things . . . all things that must be . . . to have all things revealed . . . to cleanse the curse from the Ring'.

Her Valkyrie sister, Waltraute,* brings her the news that Wotan still desires his favourite daughter, Brünnhilde, to save the gods from death by tossing the Ring into the Rhine. At first, Brünnhilde hopes that the clock may be turned back, that Wotan has forgiven her rebellion, and that she might become a Valkyrie goddess once again. Yet when the Ring is mentioned, her true priorities prevail. Siegfried has given her the Ring as token of his love; for the new Brünnhilde, that is its primary significance. The symbol of power has been neatly transformed by Wagner into the mightier symbol of love. Brünnhilde has made this clear to Siegfried: 'In love I'm rich, though emptied of power!' And now she reiterates the message to Waltraute: 'The shine of this gold tells me that Siegfried loves me!'

Brünnhilde's metamorphosis by grief is born of the hallucination that Siegfried (who has been tricked by a magic potion into falling in love with Gunther's* sister, Gutrune*) no longer loves her. When he returns, his memory destroyed by Gutrune's drugs and his shape transformed by the Tarnhelm*, Brünnhilde cannot penetrate his disguise. She thinks she recognizes the flash of his eyes, but fails to understand his behaviour until it is too late. His death fills her heart with the saddest force in the universe – the grieving power of love denied. Accordingly, Brünnhilde finds it a simple task to restore the Ring to the river and pacify the heavens. By the end of the opera, power holds no temptation for her at all, but love, like a lure, wills her on even into a gesture of self-immolation. Brünnhilde dies in literal atonement for her share in a conspiracy to bring about the murder of Siegfried, whom she believed had forsaken her, yet commits *suttee* at the same moment for the greater glory of the god of love.

Brünnhilde's spell (G)

In order to protect Siegfried* in battle, Brünnhilde weaves a spell of invulnerability around his body. The only part of his anatomy that she neglects to charm is his back – but Brünnhilde knows he will never show that to an enemy. This oversight is responsible for Siegfried's death, when Hagen* distracts the hero and stabs him from behind with his spear.

Bülow, Blandine von (1863–1941)
Also known as 'Boni' or 'Bonichen', Cosima's younger daughter by Hans von Bülow.* She is the only member of the immediate family who concentrated on her own domestic life to the exclusion of any involvement with the affairs of Bayreuth. She married early, giving birth to four children between 1883 and 1896.

Bülow, Daniela von (1860–1940)
Also known as 'Loulou' 'Lulu', 'Lusch' or 'Luschen', Cosima's first child by Hans von Bülow.* Daniela spent most of her life helping her mother at Bayreuth. She married in 1886.

Bülow, Cosima: *see* Wagner, Cosima

Bülow, Hans Guido Freiherr von (1830–94)
A gifted pianist, conductor and journalist, Hans von Bülow had the double misfortune of worshipping Wagner while Wagner worshipped von Bülow's wife, Cosima. This led to a period of strain ending for von Bülow in tragedy. He wished it otherwise, but in parting from Cosima he also had to say goodbye to Wagner, although he continued to promote his music.

Bülow studied conducting under Wagner, 1850–51, and piano under Liszt in 1851. In 1853, he toured as a concert pianist and his repertoire is said to have included *every* major piano work. He married Liszt's daughter, Cosima, in 1857 but it was not a hot-blooded match (a year later, she wanted to commit suicide). In 1864 he became conductor of the court opera at Munich and thereafter arranged the productions of *Tristan* and *Die Meistersinger* which brought him into intimate contact with Wagner.

Cosima yearned to get away from her irritable, difficult husband and dedicate herself to a 'major' genius. Her affair with

Wagner began in 1864. By 1866, Bülow was consenting to Cosima's frequent visits to Wagner at Triebschen. His position was exceedingly painful. Self-interest counselled continued complaisance; his future was bound up with performances of Wagner's work at Munich. Gossip was becoming difficult to control, but von Bülow wished to do nothing irrevocable.

Wagner, however, did. In 1869 he bore off Cosima for good, and she never afterwards left his side. King Ludwig,* Wagner's patron, was sadly disillusioned. Cosima was his rival in Wagner's spiritual affections and, what is more, she had told him that there was no basis for scandal. He broke off all relations with her, while von Bülow filed a petition for divorce and, sending their two daughters to live with Cosima, retired to Italy to recover his shattered nerves and begin life again. He never met Wagner after that terrible summer of 1868, though he was deeply upset by the news of the composer's death, sending Cosima a telegram: 'Soeur, il faut vivre.'

Burgess, Anthony, (b. 1917)
English novelist and critic who supports the idea of widening Wagner's appeal by shortening his libretti:

It is no use . . . pointing to Wagner as a composer who approved of long libretti and justified them in the musical execution. Wagner thought of himself as a poet (he is, incidentally the poet most cited in the *Waste Land*) and wanted his audiences to admire the words as much as their setting, but there is not one of his operas which would not benefit by the lopping of about half the text.

Burgstaller, Alois (1871–1945)
German tenor who sang at Bayreuth 1894–1909. He incurred Cosima Wagner's* displeasure when, in 1903, he sang *Parsifal* in New York: the first performance of the work outside Bayreuth. (Wagner had expressed the wish that the opera should not be performed outside Bayreuth.)

Calderón de la Barca, Pedro (1600–81)
Gifted Spanish poet and playwright
(though Lope de Vaga is better known)
whose works Wagner highly esteemed.
The composer often read Calderón out
loud to Cosima in the evenings at Wahnfried.

Chabrier, Alexis-Emmanuel (1841–94)
French composer who initially qualified as
a lawyer and took a government post.
Deeply impressed by a performance of
Tristan und Isolde which he heard at
Munich, he resigned from his post in 1880
to devote himself to composition. He
joined a small group of musicians called
'Le Petit Bayreuth'.

In July 1889 he wrote: 'Yesterday . . . I
heard *Parsifal* for the first time. I have
never in all my life had an artistic experience at all comparable to this; it is overwhelming; one comes out after each act (I
do, at least) absolutely overcome with
admiration, bewildered, distraught, with
tears running down one's cheeks.'

**Chamberlain, Houston Stewart
(1855–1927)**
The English-born pseudo-philosopher
who married Wagner's youngest daughter, Eva, in 1908, thereafter settling in
Bayreuth. Chamberlain's most notorious
work *The Foundations of the Nineteenth
Century* (German edition, from 1899–
1935; English edition, 1910) seeks to show
that the Western Aryan *Volk* is entirely
responsible for the creativity of Europe,
whereas the Jews have contributed nothing and spoiled much. Educated in
France, Switzerland and Austria, Chamberlain became an early admirer of Wagner, not so much for the music as for the
ideal of a German aesthetic purity. His
first published piece, the article 'Notes sur
Lohengrin' (1885), reflects this interest. In
1892 he produced an analysis of Wagnerian drama and in 1896 a muddled biography of the master. During the First World

War, Chamberlain enrolled his pen in the
Kaiser's cause and became a naturalized
German citizen in 1916. After the war,
until his death, he eagerly espoused the
rising philosophy of fascism and in 1925
his last book bore the ominous title *Rasse
und Persönlichkeit (Race and Personality)*, expressing his continued belief in
Teutonic suprematism.

Chéreau, Patrice: *see* under Wagner,
Wolfgang Manfred Martin.

Christianity
For much of his life, Wagner was a
freethinker. His early encounters with the
works of Feuerbach* reinforced his poor
view of Christianity and his relationship
with Nietzsche confirmed his tendency
towards aesthetic atheism. But then came
Parsifal. Nietzsche was horrified. He accused Wagner of selling out to the pastors
– of continuing the line of life-denial with
which Luther had crippled the Renaissance. But was he right? It is exceedingly
hard to agree. If anything, *Parsifal* is
blasphemous and idolatrous. The message
is one of forgiveness by a Parsifalian
Christ who disdains to suffer on the cross;
instead, he redeems us all and yet lives on.
Thereafter, he directs our attention to a
pseudo-Buddhist ideal of self-negation
'beyond Nature'. This is hardly the doc-
trine of the Holy Trinity.

Wagner believed it was the function of
music to 'rescue the soul of religion', to
take symbols and to reveal the profound
truths which they conceal – to reveal, that
is to say, man's tragic knowledge of his
downfall, and bring about the sublimation
of his sinful lusts into selfless pity for his
fellows.

This makes Wagner an idiosyncratic
mystic but no true Christian.

Claudel, Paul Louis Charles Marie (1868–1955)

French poet, dramatist and essayist, famous for his *Cinq Grandes Odes* (1910) and his play *Le Soulier de Satin* (1922–4), whose works are pervaded by an immense nimbus of religious and mystical passion. Claudel had shared the Wagner fever of the Mallarmé circle of Symbolists, describing his own encounter with *Tristan und Isolde* as an experience 'only comparable to the taking of first communion'. In his 1926 essay *Richard Wagner – A French Poet's Reverie* (a title used by Mallarmé in 1885), Claudel hails Wagner as the hero 'who alone on the hill at Bayreuth, poised above degenerate Europe, above a Germany bloated with gold and material goods . . . gave witness to Christ in sacramental form. . . .'

Claudio (Lt)

A young noble of Palermo (tenor) who has loved one young Julia* not wisely but too well, and so fallen foul of Frederick,* the Viceroy's, decree against pleasure. The sentence is death. Only the machinations of his sister Isabella* prevent the decree being implemented with full rigour. Claudio reveals himself, quite naturally, to be reluctant to die. He would rather his sister went to bed with the Viceroy, a man she does not love.

Cobelli, Giuseppina (1898–1948)

Italian soprano who appeared as Sieglinde* at La Scala in 1925 and was also the Milan Isolde* and Kundry*.

She was a notable beauty whose career was brought to an unfortunate end by deafness in 1944.

Colonna, Adriano (Ri)

The son of Stefano Colonna,* Adriano is a mezzo-soprano principal boy who suffers tortures of anguish throughout *Rienzi* after falling in love with Irene*, sister of his father's enemy. His enthusiastic conversion to democracy never really replaces the ties and bonds of blood to his patrician family. His dilemma begins in the opening scene when he rescues Irene from the despoiling clutches of his father's men. He joins Rienzi's* cause out of love for Irene. He betrays his father's murder plot against Rienzi out of love for Irene. He begs Rienzi to spare his father's life when the plot is discovered – 'Make me not a murderer!' – and cites his love for Irene. Rienzi yields to his entreaty, but after a fresh insurrection Stefano Colonna has to be executed. Thereafter Adriano's predicament resembles Hamlet's: 'I must revenge my father, who from his grave must curse his son – Oh be at rest thou troubled shadow!' At the end, Adriano chooses death with his beloved Irene after she has chosen death with her beloved brother Rienzi.

Colonna, Stefano (Ri)

A Roman patrician, Colonna is a conventional and unredeemed villain who perishes by execution after a number of plots against the Roman ruler Rienzi.* He has nothing but contempt for the 'vile populace' and was previously responsible for the murder of Rienzi's younger but unnamed brother. He blasphemes against Holy Mother Church by calling her Papal Legate, Raimondo,* a 'tiresome babbler' even to his face.

Communication to my Friends, A

Autobiographical essay of 1851 in which Wagner describes his artistic evolution during the writing of *The Flying Dutchman*, *Tannhäuser* and *Lohengrin*.

Conducting, On

Pamphlet (1869–70) in which Wagner expounded his radical philosophy of conducting. The art had been in its infancy until Wagner came on the scene. His professional methods were a revelation to orchestras accustomed to feeling their way for a great deal of the time during a performance. Wagner was not a scientific metronomist. Indeed, he stated categorically that 'perpetual modification of tempo' – faster, then slower – was necessary for the conducting of any Romantic, post-Beethoven music, including his own. In other words, he asked for an explicitly subjective interpretation, but carried out 'imperceptibly' and sensitively.

This can be dangerous, but then Wagner nearly always was. He was ultimately rewarded by some fine, instinctive interpretations from Richter* and Furtwängler.* But, in his own day, Hermann Levi* inaugurated an era of exaggerated slowness of pace. During Levi's direction of the first performance of *Parsifal* (1882) Wagner called out from the stalls 'Quicker, quicker, the people will be bored', which makes his intention plain – he wanted his works to be given in a lively fashion. But with the arrival of Mottl* (1886), the movements got slower and slower. One critic called it the 'disease of exaggerated Adagios'. During the present century, the three acts of *Parsifal* lasted one hour and nine minutes longer under Toscanini* in the 1930s than they did under Pierre Boulez* in the 1960s.

Cornelius, Carl August Peter (1824–74)

A Wagner-Liszt protégé who wrote the comic opera *Der Barbier von Bagdad* (1855–8). His standing in Wagner's favour can be deduced from the list of Christmas gifts showered on him by the older man in 1863. They included a dressing-gown, a scarf, a cigar-case, silk handkerchieves, gold shirt-studs, pen-wipers, cravats, and an initialled meerschaum cigar-holder. Wagner first met Cornelius in 1853 but it is to the latter's credit that he never became a blind Wagnerian partisan, but always retained a grip on his Christian principles and light, distinctive musical style.

Crespin, Régine (b. 1927)

French soprano who sang Elsa* at Mulhouse in 1950 and then in Paris the next year, and later appeared at Bayreuth as Kundry* (1958–60) and Sieglinde* (1961). Wieland Wagner described her (as Kundry) as a 'mediterranean enchantress'. She also sang Elsa at Covent Garden and (in 1967) Brünnhilde* at Salzburg, although vocal problems led her to abandon the latter role.

Curse on Love; Curse on the Ring (R, but present throughout the *Ring*)

Alberich* the dwarf is able to steal the Rhinegold from its guardians because he alone is able to pronounce a terrible curse on love, foreswearing for ever the love of womankind. In return, he will be able to fashion from the gold a magic Ring* which will make him lord of all the world. Even though Alberich renounces love, it should be noted that, by *Götterdämmerung*, he has been able to father a son, Hagen.*

The curse on the Ring is uttered by Alberich after Wotan* has stolen all his gold. It runs, 'Let the Ring bring death; its wealth shall yield pleasure to none . . . care shall consume the man who commands it and mortal envy those who do not; he who obtains it shall find no joy; it will bring no gain to its lord; . . . while he lives all his days will be filled with fear; and all this shall be till the ring returns to Alberich.'

The victims of the curse of the greed for wealth and power are Wotan (who needs a direct command from Erda* before he will yield the Ring to the giants in *Rheingold*); Fasolt* (who is instantly slain by Fafner); then Fafner* (who is slain by Siegfried*); Siegfried himself (who for a time is safe from the curse because he is initially ignorant of the powers of the Ring); and, finally, Hagen and his half-brother Gunther,* who are both killed in attempts to get their hands on the Ring.

Brünnhilde* wears the Ring twice but she retains enough of the wisdom of Erda, her mother, to know how to countermand the curse of greed in one final gesture of self-renunciation. Thus Alberich's awful curse on love is finally transcended by a higher imperative – the predestined restoration of the Rhinegold to its river-bed by a child of nature who places a higher value on love than on power.

Daland (H)

The Norwegian sea captain who unwittingly introduces his daughter, Senta,* to the Flying Dutchman* and thus loses her for ever. A rich bass role to suit a somewhat mercenary character.

It is ironic that he should upbraid the Steersman* for failing to notice the arrival of the ghostly galleon of the Dutchman, when he himself fails miserably to perceive the Dutchman's unnatural eagerness to woo his daughter. Furthermore, a fine portrait of the Dutchman has been hanging for many a day on his own parlour wall. Presumably, Daland has had occasion to glance at the image from time to time. Senta has certainly a 'predestined' interest in the picture. Alas, Daland's eagerness to become wealthy (a telling Wagnerian theme) blinds his eyes to the likeness. The Dutchman dazzles him with gems. 'I hardly know whether I wake or dream! Could any son-in-law be more welcome?' Soon Daland is answering his own question: 'Ha! The prize for which all fathers strive, a wealthy son-in-law, is mine!' Daland becomes a rich man – conceivably at too high a price.

Dalmorès, Charles Boin Henry Alphonse (?1871–1939)

French tenor who was the 1908 Lohengrin* at Bayreuth. Later he gave the Tristan* in Chicago.

Daniella (Lt)

Inn-keeper and bass ring-leader in the crowd and chorus of Das Liebesverbot.

Dannreuther, Edward George (1844–1905)

English musician of German origin who championed the cause of Wagner in Britain, where he founded the London Wagner Society in 1872.

David (M)

Apprentice (tenor) to Hans Sachs,* who forms half of the sub-plot love affair (with Magdalene*) intended by Wagner to counterpoint the rather grander romance of Walther von Stolzing* and Eva*. David's other contribution to the tale (apart from providing laughs and boxing Beckmesser's* ears) is to show us a balanced view of Hans Sachs' character (he can be hard on David, his apprentice, and has been known to give him a whipping), as well as reminding us of the guild rules governing the translation of apprentices into journeymen (as happens to David in Act III).

Davison, James William (1813–85)

Wagner's contemporary, James Davison, was the influential music critic of The Times and a man who hated most of Wagner's music. The composer riposted by suggesting that Davison was in the pay of Mendelssohn, Meyerbeer and the 'press gang of Jews'. Certainly, despite the malicious childishness of this accusation, Davison was responsible for some of the tepidity with which Wagner's work was received when he visited London in 1855. Davison flatly asserted that a dramatic poem like Der Ring des Nibelungen could not possibly be set to music, and dismissed much of the Bayreuth offerings as 'pantomime' when he first attended the festival in 1876.

Debussy, Achille Claude (1862–1918)

One of the major influences on Debussy was undoubtedly what he regarded as 'Wagnerian sensuousness'. This pervades his composition *Prelude à l'après-midi d'un faune* in particular. The Wagnerian ideal of *Gesamtkunstwerk*, that all art can ultimately be synthesized into a unity, inspired Debussy with longings for social as well as metaphysical reform. Debussy supported himself by playing the piano on the Parisian soirée circuit – a fashionable if tedious existence for struggling musicians; for Debussy this was a Wagnerian initiation, since the constant demand in high circles was for Wagner, and still more Wagner. In 1888 and 1889 he journeyed to Bayreuth, where *Parsifal* impressed him most; its influence is plainly heard in *Pelléas et Melisande*. In 1914, Debussy was still telling André Caplet that orchestration should 'produce a colour like illumination from behind such as the wonderful effects in *Parsifal*', although for a while at this time he did rail against 'Old Klingsor' (as he called Wagner), whose profound impact made it hard for a composer to retain an individual style.

De Reszke, Jean (1850–1925)

Polish tenor, member of a well-known family of musicians. He gave Lohengrin* in London in 1887 (in Italian) and became almost legendary for his performances of Tristan* and Siegfried*.

Dernesch, Helga (b. 1939)

Austrian soprano who has appeared as Freia*, Eva* and Gutrune* at Bayreuth, as Brünnhilde* and Isolde* at Salzburg and as Sieglinde* and Isolde* in London. Since 1979 she has been singing mezzo-soprano roles.

Destinn, Emmy (1878–1930)

The Czech soprano who first sang Senta* at the age of twenty-three at Bayreuth. After the First World War, her powers are said to have declined, although her voice, in its prime, was famous for its rich, controlled clarity. A marvellous actress, she also wrote a drama, *Rahel*, and many poems. She has left over two hundred recordings.

Destiny of Opera, On the

Aesthetic pamphlet (1871) by Wagner, expounding his view that the orchestra must occupy the 'position of the ancient Greek chorus in carrying forward the dramatic and emotional action'.

Devrient, Eduard Philipp (1801–77)

Principal actor and producer at the Dresden Court Theatre, 1844–6, and director at the Karlsruhe Court Theatre, 1852–70. He was also a baritone, and in his spare time produced a history of German stagecraft.

Dietsch, Pierre-Louis-Philippe (1808–65)

French conductor and composer who conducted the sabotaged 1861 production of *Tannhäuser* in Paris. Wagner naturally accused him of malice, but it is probably more true to suggest simple incompetence; he certainly had no hand in the barracking. Fauré*, who studied under Dietsch, wrote that he had a 'cold nature and a methodical, reactionary mind'.

Donner (R)

A minor god in *Rheingold*; although a considerably more potent figure in wider Northern mythology. Donner is Wagner's bass-baritone version of Thor, god of thunder and lightning. When we see Donner it is as a figure of aggression: he offers violence to Fasolt* and Fafner* when they try to take away his sister, Freia,* in payment for their work on Valhalla*; he tries to attack Loge* when the sharp-tongued fire god attempts to wriggle out of the debate about how to protect Freia; and, most spectacularly, he clears up a patch of foggy weather at the end of *Das Rheingold* by calling forth a terrific musical thunderstorm, all the while swinging his gigantic hammer, and singing his defiant war-cry, 'Heda, Heda, Hedo!' The Gibichung* offer a sacrifice to Donner in *Götterdämmerung*.

Doré, Gustave (1832–83)

French painter and caricaturist who associated with Wagner during the Paris *Tannhäuser* period. Wagner always numbered him among his allies. They exchanged gifts: Doré sent his illustrations to Dante, Wagner the piano score of the *Ring*, which Doré hoped to embellish.

Dorella (Lt)

Former maid to Isabella* who was compelled to take up saloon-girl work in Daniella's* tavern upon the retirement of her mistress into a nunnery. She has life and fire to spare and her seductive wiles are far too powerful for Brighella's* weak defences.

Dorn, Heinrich Ludwig Egmont (1804–92)

Operatic conductor and composer in Hamburg who succeeded Wagner at Riga in 1839 only after 'stabbing him in the back', although Wagner and he were old friends from Leipzig days and Dorn had originally welcomed Wagner to Riga. Later he became conductor of the Royal Opera in Berlin, holding this post until 1869. After the *contretemps* with Wagner, Dorn became an irreconcilable opponent of his music. Dorn also composed *Lieder* and many operas – one of which was a setting of the Nibelung Saga!

Douglas, George Norman (1868–1952)

Scottish novelist and essay-writer, who claims in his memoirs to have discovered a new Wagnerian song. It turns out to be a piece of musical doggerel that Wagner once taught in German to a Neapolitan servant called Peppino, who later sang it to Douglas with more fervour than finesse.

Dove of the Grail, The White (L, P)

An executive agency of the Grail* which in *Lohengrin* arrives to release the boy Godfrey* from Ortrud's* wicked spell and in *Parsifal* hovers over the hero's head at the finale as a signal mark of favour. In the Grail legend, the dove appears each Good Friday to place a wafer in the Holy Cup and thereby replenish the Grail's power to nourish and inspire.

Dragon: *see* 'Fafner'

Note that Alberich* also turns himself briefly into a dragon when challenged to do so by Loge* and Wotan* in scene 3 of *Rheingold*.

Drolla (F)

Chamber-maid to Lora of Tramond*. She is in love with Arindal's ranger*, Gernot*, with whom she joins in teasing banter in Act II of *Die Feen*.

Dujardin, Edouard Emile Louis (1861–1949)

French writer, best known for his novel *Les Lauriers Sont Coupés* (1898), and founder of the *Revue Wagnérienne*, whose first number appeared on 8 February, 1885. It lasted some three years and was supported by Houston Stewart Chamberlain*; among the contributors were Mallarmé*, Verlaine*, Liszt*, Saint-Saëns* and Fauré.

Duncan, Isadora (1877–1927)

American dancer whose erotic style captured European audiences in the early 1900s. In 1904 Cosima Wagner* engaged Isadora's services for the *Tannhäuser* Bacchanal (Act I), but she caused much scandal in Bayreuth, falling into final

25

disgrace when she presumed to criticize the master. She was never asked to return.

Duparc, Marie-Eugène-Henri (1848–1933)
French composer of songs who supported the cause of Wagner in France from the late 1860s onwards. He met Wagner in 1869. In 1885 he gave up composition as a result of nervous trouble. He destroyed most of his work in hand, together with personal archives which had contained letters to and from Wagner.

Eckert, Karl Anton Florian (1820–79)
German composer, conductor, violinist and pianist, who in 1860 became Director of the Stuttgart Opera, whither Wagner fled from his creditors in 1864. It was from Eckert's house and hospitality that Wagner was summoned by King Ludwig II* of Bavaria to receive even more welcome hospitality and patronage.

Edda
Body of Icelandic literature contained in two distinct thirteenth-century versions: the Younger (*Prose*) *Edda*, and the Elder (*Poetic*) *Edda*. Wagner used them (in the editions of Karl Simrock (1851) and G. Lüning (1859)) as a supplementary source of material for his *Ring* cycle.

The *Prose Edda* was written down by the Icelandic chief and historian, Snorri Sturluson, *c*. 1230. Among the didactic and poetic material, Sturluson describes the visit of Gylfi, a king of the Swedes, to Asgard, the citadel of the gods. He is told about the origins of the world, the adventures of the gods and the fate in store for them in the *Ragnorök* (Doom, or Twilight, of the gods, that is, *Götterdämmerung**). The *Poetic* (Elder) *Edda* contains older, anonymous material, probably dating from the ninth to the twelfth centuries. It tells the heroic legends of gods, dwarfs and men from the birth of the world until their destruction. There is a collection of

the wit and wisdom of Odin (Wotan*), of a generally amoral and lawless kind. It was perhaps the *Poetic Edda* which finally encouraged Wagner to present Wotan in *Rheingold* as a lawman turned outlaw. This saga also includes the story of Thrym, the giant, who steals the hammer of the thunder god Thor (Donner*) then demands the hand in marriage of the goddess Freyja (Freia*) in exchange for it. A further saga describes the life of Wayland the Smith, and also of Sigurd (Siegfried*), including the latter's youth, marriage to Gudrun (Gutrune*), his death and the eventual fate of the Burgundians (Nibelungs*).

These same stories fill the German Mediaeval romance saga, the *Niebelungenlied**, which was Wagner's primary source for the *Ring*, but the original *Eddas* recount the events with a more authentic, pre-civilized stoicism. Wagner sketched outlines for a number of operas based on the Edda, including *Wieland der Schmied*.

Eisenach
City in the south-west of what is now Eastern Germany, on the slopes of the Thuringianwald at the confluence of the Hörsel and Nesse Rivers. It was founded by the Landgraves of Thuringia and chartered in 1283. J. S. Bach was born there. The action of *Tannhäuser* is set in the surrounding countryside, and also in the Wartburg castle above the city (where Martin Luther began his German translation of the Bible). There are both Bach and Wagner museums in Eisenach.

Eisslinger, Ulrich (M)
Mastersinger (a grocer by trade) who helps to swell the chorus of guild-members in the song-contest scenes.

Elisabeth (T)
Niece of Hermann*, Landgrave of Thuringia. Wagner based this character on St Elizabeth of Hungary (1207–31), whose

devotion to the poor made her an enduring symbol of Christian charity. The real St Elizabeth was in fact brought up at the court of Hermann of Thuringia, to whose son she was betrothed in early infancy. After his untimely death, she entered a severe Franciscan order and lived in extremes of poverty. She was canonised in 1234 and her feast day is 19 November.

Wagner's Elisabeth falls completely in love with Tannhäuser,* seduced by his brilliant singing voice, and during his unexplained absence (with Venus*) she languishes at the Landgrave's court. Her heart is overjoyed by his return, then crushed when the truth of his sins is discovered. She rallies quickly to save Tannhäuser when the rival *Minnesinger* makes as if to kill him, and then offers her own life to the Holy Virgin as an intercessional gesture to save his soul. God accepts her offering, she dies, Tannhäuser is saved, and then dies too. One is left wondering whether her sacrifice is not a little degraded by Tannhäuser's inability to spend a short while on earth contemplating and giving thanks for her sanctity.

Ellis, William Ashton (1853–1919)
English doctor who abandoned his medical career in order to devote himself to the labour of translating Wagner's prose works into (often inaccurate) English. George Bernard Shaw got him a Civil List Pension for his trouble.

Elsa (L)
Daughter of the Duke of Brabant. Before the action of the opera begins she has been struck motionless by a vision of a beautiful knight coming to help her in an as yet purely imaginary hour of distress. Soon afterwards, her younger brother Godfrey,* heir to the dukedom, disappears, and the dukedom is claimed by the regent, Count Frederick of Telramund. Thereupon Elsa is accused, before the assembled court of the visiting Henry

the Fowler,* King of Germany, of having murdered Godfrey. Elsa seems unable to speak in her own defence; she is still mesmerised by the memory of her vision. In an act of absolute faith, she consents to have her innocence tested in a trial by combat, thus venturing her very life on the blind assumption that a valiant champion will appear to defend her. He does. The heroic and lovely Lohengrin, the perfect knight of her dreams, steps forward anonymously first to save her and then to claim her for his bride. He tells her, however, that she must never ask him his name.

Elsa's strengths nourish her weaknesses. Since she is compassionate, Frederick's sister, Ortrud,* has no trouble in worming her way into her confidence and then betraying it by causing her to doubt Lohengrin's fidelity. For the noblest of reasons (she would like Lohengrin to need her help as well as her love), Elsa feels compelled to force him to identify himself: thus he will become vulnerable to her, and she can champion him. But in the attempt she violates the holy laws of a grail-knight's terms of service, and Lohengrin is forced to fulfil Ortrud's prediction that he will abandon his wife. She falls lifeless at his departure. In legendary terms, Elsa has proved to be unworthy of her brilliant knight's love. In human terms however, she is among the most attractive of Wagner's female characters.

Erda (R, W, S, G)
The Mother of Earth, the mother of the Norns* and the Valkyries,* and, for a time, Wotan's mistress. Also known as Wala.

IN *Rheingold*
Erda puts in a brief but dramatic appearance, pleading with Wotan* to hand over the bewitched and magical Ring to the giants Fasolt* and Fafner,* who demand it in payment for the building of Valhalla.* She rises from her natural element and

tells him, in a dread contralto voice, that of all the things she knows there is none more cursed than the Ring, so he must yield it, adding mysteriously that an evil day awaits the immortal gods. Then she vanishes.

Wotan is naturally intrigued and wishes to know more about his fate. He also wants to hear about her three daughters (the Norns), whom she says 'shape her visions' and can 'foretell the future'. But for the moment he must be content to bide his time.

IN *Die Walküre*

Erda is referred to as Wala in this opera. Wotan tells Brünnhilde* that he pursued Erda in order to discover if the fate she had predicted for the gods was avoidable: 'So I made my way down into the depths; by love's enchantment I conquered the Wala, humbled her silent pride, till she told me all she knew.' As a result of this sojourn, in addition to wise counsel, Wotan also gained a large family of daughters. Nine Valkyrie maidens she bore him, including his favourite, Brünnhilde. These are of service in raising a defensive army to protect Valhalla, since Erda has informed Wotan that Alberich* still plots to overthrow the gods, and – worse – if the Ring falls into his hands he will certainly succeed.

IN *Siegfried*

Wotan again summons Erda from the depths of the earth to ask her 'whether the swift-turning wheel of fate can be stopped'. Erda replies that he should ask Brünnhilde, because she was conceived in order to supply Wotan with information of that kind. Shamefacedly, Wotan explains that Brünnhilde lies chained in enchanted sleep on a high mountain top as a punishment for disobeying his orders. Erda is sorry, but she cannot help. Her powers of divination have been clouded and weak ever since she consented to make love to Wotan: 'Deeds of men have obscured my thoughts', she complains. 'My waking

leaves me confused'. Finally, it is Wotan who tells Erda what is to happen: if his hopes are fulfilled, Siegfried* and Erda's daughter Brünnhilde will inherit Valhalla. 'Then your wisdom's child will achieve the deed that will free our world,' he tells her. But Erda is no longer listening. She has already gone back to sleep. The significance is plain: nature no longer cares what happens to mankind. Men (and gods) must take responsibility for their own destiny. Mother Earth will no longer assist.

Erik (H)

An unfortunate youth who wishes to woo Senta,* the daughter of Daland,* but is crossed by misfortune. First, her father is eager to make a richer match for his child. Secondly, Senta is rather more impressed by the claims of tragic destiny in the person of the Flying Dutchman.*

Esser, Heinrich (1818–72)

The musician who discovered Hans Richter* for Wagner during his long career in Vienna.

Eva (M)

Soprano lead in *Die Meistersinger*, daughter of Veit Pogner,* who fervently wishes to marry Walther von Stolzing* and does everything in her power to try to bring this about. She is ready as a last resort to elope with him in Act II, but her old mentor, Hans Sachs, skilfully prevents this. Sachs loves Eva and Eva loves Sachs best after Walther, and so it is with much joy that, after an initial confusion, Eva realizes that Sachs is doing all in his power, despite his own passion, to make Walther hers. She clearly regards the song contest for her hand in marriage as little more than a ruse (that at first goes wrong) to get her father to agree to the desired match.

Fafner (R, S)

A simple bass giant from Riesenheim, who steadily becomes corrupted during the course of the *Ring*.

IN *Rheingold*

Initially, Fafner wishes to challenge Wotan's* power on earth. Together with his brother, Fasolt,* he helps build Valhalla* in return for the promised possession of Freia, goddess of Spring, because he knows that the loss of Freia* will harm the gods.

But when Loge* describes a Ring* which can confer universal power on its wearer, Fasolt immediately desires this new sovereign jewel instead of Freia. As soon as Wotan yields him the Ring, Fafner becomes subject to its curse. He kills his brother Fasolt with a single blow of his cudgel in order to keep all the gold for himself.

IN *Die Walküre*

We learn from Wotan that, with the aid of the magical Tarnhelm,* Fafner has transformed himself into a dragon and sits sleepily in a cave brooding 'on the gold he murdered his brother to gain'. In other words, Fafner shows absolutely no initiative whatsoever in using this power he schemed so hard to gain. The Ring has imposed on Fafner a fundamental curse of stupidity. However, while Fafner holds the Ring it is at least safe from Alberich,* who fears the dragon as much as Wotan does.

IN *Siegfried*

We hear from Mime,* the dwarf who has brought Siegfried up in the forest, about the dragon's powers: 'Poisonous foam,' he says to Siegfried, 'will pour from his mouth; if you are splashed by one single drop, it shrivels your body and bones. . . . A scaly tail he lashes around: and if you should be caught, he'll coil it tight. . . .' Siegfried remains undeterred. The fight which follows shows Fafner to have become utterly complacent in his cave-dwelling years. He cannot imagine defeat at the hands of this stripling. When Siegfried runs him through with the sword Notung*, he seems to die almost as much from surprise as from the cold steel in his heart. Before expiring, he reverts to his proper shape, but his final questions to Siegfried indicate no knowledge of world events (he has never, for example, heard of his conqueror). This simply goes to confirm that Fafner, the giant dragon, is one of nature's evolutionary dead ends. After the fight, Siegfried accidentally tastes Fafner's blood, which has the magical effect of making him wise. Not only can he suddenly understand the song of the woodbird, but when the time comes, he can divine Mime's murderous intentions towards him.

Fairy King, the (F)

A small bass part whose chief function is to explain the spells and curses confining Ada* to a solemn choice between love and immortality.

'Falparsi' (P)

Pun by Wagner, purporting to be the Arabic for 'the foolish pure one', or 'Parsifal' by another arrangement of the syllables. Kundry* tells Parsifal* that his father, Gahmuret*, was responsible for naming him thus during a trip to Arabia some months prior to his birth. By being so named, Parsifal can aptly fulfil the Grail's* prophecy that only a 'foolish pure one' will be able to overthrow the evil Klingsor.*

Farzana (F)

One of the fairy 'fates' who strongly resents the love between the mortal Arindal* and her immortal fairy queen Ada*. Together with her companion Zemina*, she decides to torment the already grief-wracked Arindal* in Act III of *Die Feen*. But she gets a swift come-uppance: the spells given Arindal by the magician Groma* are more powerful than Farzana's tricks. Arindal ends up by becoming immortal. It may be that Wagner developed the roles of Zemina and Farzana into the more sophisticated Norns* of *Götterdämmerung*, although the latter observe rather than act.

Fasolt (R)

A bass-baritone giant who helps his brother Fafner* to build Valhalla*, the palace of the gods. When the time comes to be paid for this work, Fasolt would clearly rather take Freia*, the agreed prize, instead of the re-negotiated fee in gold. He is susceptible to Freia's beauty whereas his brother, Fafner, craves power and wealth. Fasolt becomes the first victim of Alberich's* Ring-curse* when Fafner kills him in order to keep the Ring* to himself.

Feen, Die (The Fairies)

Opera in three acts, and the first that Wagner finished, written in 1833–4 but neither performed nor published as a whole in the composer's lifetime, although not for want of trying on Wagner's part. The full text became available only after the first production in 1888 at Munich under Hermann Levi. *Die Feen* ran to more than fifty performances between then and 1895.

Attending the 1981 Wuppertal revival of *Die Feen*, the reviewer of the *Financial Times* comments, 'This arch-romantic, magic opera, derivative in many respects (of Weber*, Marschner* and Meyerbeer*) is an amazing achievement for a young man of 21.' So it is (although, in fact Wagner was four months short of his twenty-first birthday when he completed the score). After his sister Rosalie Wagner's* unfavourable reaction to *Die Hochzeit**, the score of which he then destroyed, Wagner quickly wrote *Die Feen* while employed as *kapellmeister* in Würzburg in 1833. This time, Rosalie (and his friends) enthusiastically endorsed what was to prove, in essence, one of the least 'Wagnerian' of all his works. Wagner spoke 'very strongly' some fifty years afterwards 'against publishing these juvenile or occasional compositions'.

Ernest Newman* concedes that the 'construction is formal and cumbersome'. The two chief lovers in *Die Feen* have as foil 'two subordinate lovers, while set off against these couples is a third pair, who provide a sort of comic interest'. But Newman insists that

the music is decidedly interesting. The third act, in spite of a few strokes that get home, is much inferior to the other two, for which the fact that it was written in a month may be answerable. But the first two acts and the overture are full of striking things. . . . The opera has a poise which we do not find in . . . *The Flying Dutchman* . . . expressed without effort. . . . It is certain that there was not another young man in Europe capable of writing such a work at that time.

The plot is diffuse and deliberately borrowed. The central theme is Arindal's* indecision, a variant on the dilemma of Hamlet. What is fascinating about the opera is that so many of the themes of later works are here in embryo: forbidden inquiry, the fairy garden, magic weapons, final transfiguration.

Wagner tells us in *My Life** that he took the plot from Gozzi's fairy-tale 'La Donna Serpente', but chose the names of his heroes from Ossian's works and from similar 'fake Gaelic myths'. In the libretto, Arindal, Prince and later King of Tramond, together with his ranger Gernot*, have been enchanted by a magical doe who turns into a fairy queen, Ada*. She holds them in thrall for eight years, during which time she lives with Arindal and bears him a son and daughter. We learn that although this fairy is immortal, her father was an earthly man. This perhaps accounts for some of the consuming attraction she feels towards Arindal. Her sister fairies, Zemina* and Farzana*, are distressed by her infatuation and long to expel these mortal interlopers from their land. They are aided by a tough ruling from Arindal's father, the Fairy King, who enjoins the doe-queen not to reveal her name to Arindal for eight years, nor to let him ask her about it. At the expiry of the eight years she must also put Arindal's affection to a trial by torment, since her love-match with a mortal is an insult to fairyland.

In the eighth year, Arindal breaks the taboo by asking Ada her name, whereupon he and Gernot are banished from fairyland. Despite his piercing grief, Arindal is persuaded to return to his kingdom by Morald*, his ally, and by the sad news that his father is dead and that he is the new king of a land which is being besieged by the unpleasant neighbouring ruler, King Murold. Affairs at home are in a grave state. Only Arindal's warlike warrior-sister, Lora,* defending the last fortress in Tramond, stands between Murold and complete victory. Arindal looks forward to a 'warrior's death' in his homeland.

But Ada is now compelled to put Arindal to the trial by torment; even though he has asked her name and they are separated. Before the tests commence, she begs him never to curse her name however unpleasant things may appear.

After some comic banter between Gernot and the chamber-maid Drolla*, Ada makes Arindal believe she has thrown their two children to their deaths in a fiery chasm, that Morald his ally is dead, that his enemies have won a victory with Ada's help and that his country is lost. Accordingly, Arindal, as Ada foresaw, curses 'the beauteous witch'.

Ada now has a choice. According to the Fairy King's ruling, Ada may opt to remain immortal (after the eight years of anonymous bliss with Arindal she was due to assume mortal form) but if she refuses to renounce her love for him, she first has to endure a hundred years of being turned to stone. In resonant Wagnerian language she asserts that 'love conquers all – his love will one day break my stone fetters – my love shall him inspirit'. Arindal, however, goes almost mad on hearing that he has been deceived, that his children are well, his foes routed, and Ada more lost to him than ever.

In the third act, Groma*, the magician, contrives a happy ending by arming Arindal with enchanted weapons (a sword, a shield and a lyre) which break the spell of the fairy fates, releasing Ada from her lapidary prison. Arindal is now promoted to the full status of a fairy-king while his friend Morald succeeds him as King of Tramond. The final word in Wagner's first opera is prophetic. It was the lyre which ultimately freed Ada. It was melody which gave Arindal his opportunity to repledge his love: 'I know full well sweet music's magic might, / Which raises mortals to the ranks of gods . . . / In holy music's magic tones . . .'

Even in 1833 at the age of twenty, Wagner believed his chosen mission was both sacred and supernatural!

Ferris (P)
The name of a Knight of Klingsor* whom Parsifal* defeats before taking on Klingsor's mistress, Kundry*.

Feuerbach, Ludwig Andreas (1804–72)
German idealist philosopher who had a powerful influence over the leading German intellects of his day, including Marx* and Richard Wagner, although by 1880 Wagner was describing his early allegiance to Feuerbachian principles as 'mistaken'. The young Wagner was excited by Feuerbach's discussion *On Philosophy and Christianity* (1839), which suggested that 'Christianity has in fact long vanished not only from the reason but from the life of mankind' and is 'nothing more than an *idée fixe*'. He was equally stirred by its sequel, *The Essence of Christianity* (1841), which reduced religion to the status of a

'personal consciousness of the infinite', wherein God became little more than 'the outward projection of man's inward nature'.

Feuerbach's attacks on religious orthodoxy did much to inspire young idealists like Wagner during the revolutionary years of the late 1840s. But Wagner also found Feuerbach extremely useful for his artistic purposes, for if God was not in Heaven, then he might be found in man himself, and the immense musical and dramatic possibilities of that idea remained with Wagner for life. He frequently contemplated turning the life of Buddha into an opera, or even the story of Jesus of Nazareth, although on another occasion he did comment, 'What – Jesus as a tenor? God help us!' Wagner dedicated his *Artwork of the Future* (1850) to Ludwig Feuerbach.

Feustel, Friedrich (1824–91)
Bayreuth banker who helped Wagner establish the festival's finances.

'Fidi'
Nickname for Siegfried*, son of Richard Wagner.

Fischer-Dieskau, Dietrich (b. 1925)
Outstanding baritone, who has become one of the greatest *Lieder* singers of our time, Fischer-Dieskau sang at the Bayreuth Festival 1954–61; his Wolfram* was especially notable, and he also performed Amfortas* and Kothner*.

Flagstad, Kirsten Malfrid (1895–1962)
Norwegian singer, possibly the greatest Wagnerian soprano of this century. Born in Hamar, she performed in light opera from 1913. After a period of retirement due to her marriage, she found (in 1932) that her voice had become heavy enough to tackle the sternest Wagnerian tasks,

and in June that year she sang Isolde* for the first time, in Oslo. Recommended by Ellen Gulbranson* to Bayreuth, she sang Valkyrie* and Third Norn* there in 1933. Her 1935 Sieglinde at the Metropolitan Opera House and 1936 Isolde at Covent Garden were outstanding débuts. Thereafter, she sang Isolde and Brunnhilde* round the world to enormous acclaim. After the war, her husband was imprisoned for having collaborated with the Nazis but she was exonerated of all guilt. Returning to Covent Garden in 1948–51 she sang Isolde, Kundry*, Sieglinde and Brunnhilde, her farewell performance (June 1951) being as Isolde. Few women singers have been able to match Flagstad for sheer power and authority of voice. After her retirement, she became the first Director of the Royal Norwegian Opera.

Fliegende Holländer, Der (The Flying Dutchman)
Although he planned the opera in one act, Wagner was forced by contemporary theatrical convention to divide it into three acts. The text is by the composer, based on the *Memoirs of Herr von Schnabelewopski*, by Heinrich Heine*. The first performance took place at the Königlicher Hoftheater, Dresden, in 1843.

Wagner's fifth opera was written in 1841 under conditions of poverty, debt and near-despair by a composer who had no soles on his shoes and was living partly in Meudon, partly in Paris. His life was at crisis point. The dream of making a splendid Paris début had turned to absolute dust. His creditors in France were now added to those who vividly remembered him in Leipzig, Königsberg, Magdeburg and Riga. But from this low point he began to pull his career round and from the least auspicious personal circumstances to alter the course of European opera.

In *The Flying Dutchman* he turned his back on the extrovert manner of *Rienzi* and pursued a new and moody style. The music of the *Dutchman* is a sea symphony. One conductor, Franz Lachner, complained, 'Whenever you open the score, the wind blows out at you!' The leading theme is taken from Wagner's own experience: the near-shipwreck of the vessel *Thetis*, on which he had sailed with Minna* from Prussia to London in 1839 to avoid imprisonment for debt in Riga. After a storm off Norway, the *Thetis* put in to Sandwike, just as the Dutchman's ship does in the opera. There Wagner heard the 'brief, rhythmic cry' of the sailors hallooing ashore and working the sails, their voices re-echoing from the fjord walls, and it is this cry which forms the basis of the Sailors' song in Acts I and III.

The music anticipates the Leitmotiv* structure of the later operas, but the text is far more traditional. Indeed, at one point, Wagner sold a treatment of the story to Pillet, Director of the Paris Opéra, for a possible production in the Italian style. In other words, the opera is a transitional work, linking two operatic genres. The score is artistically far more satisfying than the libretto. Various versions of the Flying Dutchman legend exist.

The ghostly appearance of the ship, somewhere off the Cape of Good Hope, was always held to presage disaster. In the commonest version of the myth, the Captain (one Vanderdecken) is vainly trying to round the Cape by sail. This is a very difficult manoeuvre and in his frustration he rashly pledges his soul to the devil if only he can succeed. Like Faust, he gets more than he bargains for, and the devil compels him to go round the Cape for ever. In a Northern rendering, the Captain (now called Falkenberg) must sail for eternity through the Nordsee, playing at dice for his soul with the devil. This dice-game recurs in Coleridge's *The Rime of the Ancient Mariner* (1798), where the mariner sees two characters, Death and Life-In-Death, playing dice to win him.

Sir Walter Scott, one of Wagner's favourite authors, also adapted the legend for his narrative poem *Rokeby* (1813). Edward Fitzball and G. H. Rodwell wrote and set to music respectively a 'nautical burletta' called *The Flying Dutchman* which was performed at London's Adelphi Theatre in January 1827.

But it was to the German-Jewish poet Heine* that Wagner turned for his Dutchman, working up a version of the legend described in *The Memoirs of Herr von Schnabelewopski* (1834), a religio-philosophical work. Wagner identified at once with the 'Wandering Jew of the sea', who can only be released from the spiritual bondage of Satan's curse by finding one true and constant woman to offer him disinterested love. His own pretty wife, the actress Minna, had enjoyed all too numerous admirers in the Baltic towns where they had settled and her adulteries were painfully fresh in his mind: at one point she left him altogether. Wagner begged her to return, but when she did, the admiration resumed. Further, the high seriousness of this theme of 'redeeming love' must have contrasted very comfortingly at this time with the stage frivolities of the Paris opera – the establishment which rejected his work. Wagner was groping towards a discovery of his proper direction – towards myth, psycho-drama and Germany. His new work would be performed in the old country.

Thus *Der Fliegende Holländer* is a symbolic saga paralleling at the psychological level many of Wagner's own struggles. It speaks of a man who impetuously dared too much and incurred the wrath of fate. His only escape from his curse lies in finding some woman who will stand by him, come hell or high water. Such a role would be performed in Wagner's own life at a later date by Liszt's daughter Cosima (Cosima Wagner*). But in the opera itself, the task falls to the young Norwegian, Senta.*

The opera is set at some time in the eighteenth century. Senta is waiting at

33

home with her nurse Mary for the return of her father, Daland.* His ship, beset by storms, finally puts into port, closely followed by a second, the ghostly vessel of the Dutchman. Daland's Steersman* fails even to notice its unearthly approach. We hear that once every seven years, the Dutchman is released from his eternal voyage and allowed ashore. If he can win a maiden's love *even unto death*, the curse compelling him to wander will be broken and he will be free to regain salvation. But if a maiden swears before God to love him, and then refuses to join him and his devil-crew, she too will be damned. Satan is enjoying the joke, since no woman has yet proved constant even unto death, however far the Dutchman has travelled.

The Dutchman swiftly befriends Daland and there is an indecently hasty eighteenth-century agreement to let the visitor woo Daland's daughter for his wife. Daland is so taken by the Dutchman's offer of jewels that he fails to notice anything remiss about this hang-dog, melancholy suitor. Only Senta recognizes him right from the start as the legendary Flying Dutchman, whose portrait, significantly enough, has always hung in Daland's living-room. When Senta sees him, there is a long, Wagnerian pause – rather like the moment of first meeting between Siegmund* and Sieglinde* in Act I of *Die Walküre*. For Wagner, love has a universal power of transformation, carrying all the high hopes of European Romanticism, a true *Zeitgeist*.

Without entirely making it explicit that life with him could be abbreviated, the Dutchman wins Senta's promise of eternal constancy: 'Till death I pledge myself to you, yes, without reserve, till death. . . .' She is 'by powerful enchantment overcome' and wishes to show him the true grace of proper womanhood: 'I cannot help but be his means of grace.'

Her local admirer, Erik the huntsman, alarmed by these developments, reminds her that she is also promised to him. Like a cadet Siegfried, he recalls the day he 'braved all obstacles' to gain her favour. Senta, now very troubled, plays for time. But the Dutchman, having overheard Erik's outburst, proclaims his own despair, pronounces all is lost for another seven years, orders his ghostly crew and the ship with the blood-red sails to sea again, railing against women for their septennial perfidy.

But all is not lost. In a moment of selfless splendour (or subservient folly, depending on your degree of suspended disbelief), Senta sacrifices herself to the Dutchman, hurtling headlong over a cliff with the words 'Behold, till death I have been true' ringing from her throat. At once the spell is broken, the spectral ship vanishes and Senta and the Dutchman, magically entwining, emerge from the debris of the wreck, heaven-borne by gentle, resolving strains. The storm is over.

Flosshilde (R, G)

A mezzo-soprano, the least vacuous of the Rhinemaidens.

IN *Rheingold*

Flosshilde is mindful of her duty to guard the Rhinegold, wary of speaking to strangers and very alarmed by her companions' loose talk. But this still does not prevent her from taking part in the cruel treatment which all three Rhinemaidens mete out to Alberich.* Their heartless teasing may be intended to distract his attention from the gold. But there is no point in this, since shortly afterwards they tell him its secret.

IN *Götterdämmerung*

The Rhinemaidens reappear in the last opera of the cycle, united in an oracular trio, as an ironic device to show the audience how easily Siegfried* could have saved himself, if only he had returned the Ring to its guardians in the Rhine. In the finale, Flosshilde retrieves the Ring from Hagen* and holds it aloft in triumph, while her sisters drag him down to a watery grave.

Flower Maidens, Klingsor's (P)

Wagner asserted that these alluring assis-
tants of the magician Klingsor* should be
represented as flower nymphs and wood
spirits, not prostitutes, even though their
task is to seduce hot-blooded heroes from
the straight and narrow path to become
Klingsor's slaves. It is hard to understand
how this works in practice, since mere
dalliance with a wood nymph is not a
Christian sin – unless Wagner was offering
a sop to prim nineteenth-century morality
by denying their actual function. Clearly
they must be beguiling pixies, something
like the Rhinemaidens of the *Ring*, and
fully capable of knowing love. We know
they have captured a group of Grail
knights* in the past because these com-
prise the first 'shock troops' whom Klingsor sends out against Parsifal. The Flower
Maidens are Klingsor's second weapon
against virtue. They attract with their
half-clothed bodies, then stun with their
wild-flower perfumes. Despite Wagner's
pious protestations, their temptation is
spelled out for all to see: 'We do not play
for gold – We play for love's reward.' In
this sense, they are as lethal as the bacchantes of Venus* in *Tannhäuser*, as
seductive as the fairy visions in *Die Feen*.

Flying Dutchman, The (H)

One of Wagner's less successful hero-
figures, for despite a tremendous Romantic appeal, the Dutchman is also rather a
contrived and comical fellow. When he
sells his soul in return for rounding the
Cape of Good Hope, he does not make
the most imaginative use of the devil's
resources – but then the devil naturally
endeavours to get the best of his bargains.
In fact, the devil condemns him to sail on
for ever, with one proviso. Every seven
years, the Dutchman is allowed to halt his
ghostly vessel and try to win the heart of a
faithful maiden upon dry land. If she will
follow him even unto death, on board his
ship, then Satan's curse can be lifted.
Symbolically, his efforts represent that

dark side of male doubt and insecurity.
Can a woman *ever* be true? Wagner was
twenty-six when he first conceived *Der
Fliegende Holländer*; faced with professional disasters and domestic infidelities,
the question was vital and the answer
teased from the plot was probably reassuring.

In *Der Fliegende Holländer*, Daland's*
daughter Senta* fulfils the Dutchman's
dreams but not before he has almost
missed his opportunity because of exaggerated pessimism about the outcome.
We may speculate whether he could have
been successful in his quest for a loyal
woman sooner, but for his ever-ready
expectation that people would let him
down.

Foltz, Hans (M)

Bass mastersinger who is outraged by
Walther von Stolzing's* musical offering
in Act I: 'Who calls that a song?' he scoffs.
By profession Foltz is a coppersmith and
so used to hammering his point home.

Franck,
César-Auguste-Jean-Guillaume-Hubert
(1822–90)

Belgian-born composer, pianist, organist
and teacher who was one of the major
figures in French music of the period
1850–1900. Franck would have no part in
the adulation of Wagner common even
among his pupils. He wrote 'Poison!'
across his copy of the score of *Tristan*
(which he nevertheless kept close at
hand).

Frantz, Constantin (1817–91)

German political writer of federalist views
with whom Wagner became very friendly
in the Triebschen* period (from 1866).

Frederick, Viceroy of Sicily (Lt)
The 'Novice of Palermo' (bass), one of Wagner's earliest black villains. Curiously, Frederick is German and his German qualities are the butt of the entire opera.

While the King of Sicily is absent on affairs of state, his Viceroy attempts to stamp out sin in the realm by a proclamation against lechery. The penalty is death. This prohibition is particularly reprehensible because Frederick has secretly married and then abandoned his wife Mariana*, who languishes in a convent, heart-broken by his perfidy. Frederick is discovered to be a master of hypocrisy. When the saintly Isabella* pleads for her brother Claudio's* life, after he has offended against the love-ban, Frederick agrees – provided that Isabella comes to bed with him. To add Machiavellian insult to Borgian injury, he then orders Claudio's hasty execution. The most that can be said for Sicily's Viceroy is that he lacks redeeming features – which makes it all the more perplexing that in the dénouement he is spared to resume his hollow marriage to Mariana.

Freia (R, W, G)
The soprano goddess of Youth, also known as Holda. She is previously mentioned in *Tannhäuser* and *Lohengrin*. Freia's presence among the gods is vital, because she is the keeper of the rejuvenating golden apples which serve to keep them not only looking youthful but, in the last resort, alive. In this respect, her apples are symbolically paralleled in *Parsifal*, where the Grail Knights* must have regular contact with the Holy Grail,* or they too will die.

Freia is promised by Wotan* in payment to the giants Fasolt* and Fafner* for building his glittering palace of Valhalla.* When the giants claim her, the gods oppose the fulfilment of the contract. Wotan is therefore forced by his original greedy ambitiousness to find an alternative payment which the giants will accept.

Nothing will do but the Rhinegold and Wotan has to steal it for them. Freia is thus a key agent in enmeshing Wotan in immoral and lawless transactions. Eventually these will lead to *Götterdämmerung*, the gods' destruction, regardless of the fact that Freia is reprieved from submission to the giants.

As the goddess of Spring, Freia is presumably partially responsible for the incest of Siegmund* and Sieglinde* in *Die Walküre*, since they are intoxicated into passion by the loveliness of the spring night, as Wagner makes all too lyrically clear. Waltraute* refers to Freia (as Holda) in *Götterdämmerung* when she reveals that Wotan in his sorrow declines to eat any more of her golden apples. Later in the same opera, Gutrune* invokes Freia to preserve her happiness with Siegfried*.

'Freigedank, K.'
The pseudonym which Wagner used when he issued his anti-semitic pamphlet, *Judaism in Music* (1850). It stands for 'Freethinker'. An enlarged edition appeared in 1869.

Fremstad, Olive (1871–1951)
American-Swedish soprano, the illegitimate daughter of a Swedish immigrant to Minnesota. She trained under the legendary Lilli Lehmann* and sang in the 1896 Bayreuth *Ring*. In 1903, she gave Ortrud* and Venus* at Covent Garden, but thereafter her career centred on the Metropolitan Opera House, New York. For eleven consecutive seasons she was their star, giving Sieglinde,* Isolde,* Brünnhilde* and Kundry*. By all accounts, she was also a highly strung and difficult colleague, and so it was not a great surprise when her link with the Metropolitan ended in a row, after her final appearance as Elsa.*

Frick, Gottlob (b. 1906)

German bass who gave Daland* in 1934 in Coburg and then developed the full Wagner bass repertoire. He appeared frequently at Covent Garden 1957–67, where his rendering of Hagen* (in his big, dark-toned voice) was a memorable feature of performances of the Ring. Also, his Gurnemanz* is said to have equalled Ludwig Weber's*. He sang at Bayreuth 1957–64 as Pogner*, Hagen*, Hunding and Fasolt*.

Fricka (R, W, G)

The mezzo-soprano wife of Wotan,* Lord of the Gods. Her Nordic name is Frigga. She rides in a chariot drawn by two rams.

IN Rheingold

Fricka is the archetypal wife, defending the contract and morality of matrimony as perhaps defined by a nineteenth-century German middle-class *hausfrau*. (Her obvious model in real life would be Minna Wagner,* the composer's first wife.) She is a fine complementary companion to Wotan, since she shares his ambition to acquire power. But whereas Wotan seeks lawful rule over all the world, Fricka hopes for a conquest closer to home. Her husband is a philanderer and she would do anything, by fair means or foul, to force him into fidelity. That is why she supports the idea of building Valhalla.* She hopes that it will divert Wotan from his extramarital wanderings. And that is also why she is excited by Loge's* news of the fashioning of a magical Ring*: 'Could a woman use the golden ring for herself', she asks, 'and wear it to charm her lord?' If Fricka ever gets her hands on the Ring, Wotan will be sure to find himself domesticated.

It is amusing of Wagner to make this husband and wife team share a common desire for power and yet upbraid each other hypocritically. In *Rheingold* their domestic bickerings place their divinity on an earthly footing: 'Nothing is sacred,' nags Fricka; 'you harden your hearts when you men lust for power!' to which Wotan can only retort, 'And is Fricka free from reproach? Remember you begged for the palace as well!' As the guardian of family honour, Fricka is naturally outraged that Wotan should offer to sell her relation, Freia,* in return for the construction of Valhalla. She thus adds her weighty voice to those of the gods, who are instructing Wotan to steal Alberich's* Ring, in order to release Freia from this onerous contract. Fricka's intervention on behalf of conventional relationships reaches its climax in the next opera, *Die Walküre*.

IN Die Walküre

Fricka makes her mark in *Die Walküre* with a passionate emphasis. She is angry with Wotan for permitting Siegmund* to sleep with Hunding's* wife, Sieglinde.* Not only is this an offence against the laws which she holds sacred, it is also contrary to natural law, since Siegmund and Sieglinde are brother and sister. However, it is clear that Fricka is equally incensed by Siegmund's very existence, since he is Wotan's own bastard. She angrily exclaims, 'Your faithful wife you've always betrayed!' Wotan replies politically, 'Your concern is with things that have been; my thoughts turn to what is still to come.' Fricka, however, triumphs over Wotan's lofty dismissal by turning his own arguments against him. If the Lord of the Gods must live by law, then let him keep his word: 'Give Siegmund no help when he is called on to defend his life.' Wotan is quite vanquished, since he cannot deny that he is intending to aid Siegmund in an attempt to regain the magic Ring. And he is forbidden by his treaty with Fafner* to do this by any *personal* action.

The scene between Wotan and Fricka is one of the most human in the *Ring*; in writing it, Wagner may have recalled similar tussles between himself and Minna.

IN Götterdämmerung

The Gibichungs* offer a sacrifice to Fricka.

'Friedmund' (W)

The name (meaning 'peaceful') that Sieg-mund* in Act I of *Die Walküre* says he could never be called. This is his way of stressing the warlike nature of his past history.

Friedrich Barbarossa

Sketch for a drama originally made in October 1846, added to in the summer of 1848, but later abandoned, as Wagner explains in *A Communication to my Friends* (1851)*, since the Siegfried subject seemed to offer greater adaptability. Barbarossa (or Redbeard) was an Ottoman pirate who plundered shipping off the Barbary coast. His real name was Khayr Ad-Din (d. 1546).

Friedrich, Götz (b. 1930)

Marxist stage director who delights in radical interpretations of the Wagnerian classics. For example, in his 1972 Bayreuth *Tannhäuser*, the chorus gave the audience a clenched-fist salute, much to the distress of the conservative politician Franz Joseph Strauss, who was present. Writing in *Welt am Sonntag* on 30 August of that year, Dr Strauss protested:

The socio-political interpretation of this performance of Wagner was shown in an unabashed manner. Tannhäuser was no longer the hero . . . torn between earthly and heavenly love, but a social revolutionary who was expelled and punished by his society, and who was to herald the new age of a better society. . . . For the final chorus inevitably gave the impression that, in spite of its excellent vocal rendering, it was meant to represent the Workers' militia choir of the state-owned firm Rote Lokomotive in Leipzig. As far as I know, not even the Nazis attempted to render the final chorus as a sort of SA Song Society, and thus make Tannhäuser into a sort of higher SA leader.

Herr Strauss could not get the performances cancelled but the clenched-fist salute was suppressed. Friedrich claims that he really conceived Tannhäuser as a frustrated aesthete imprisoned by his art, not as a Trotskyite. However, his 1976 *Ring* design for Covent Garden, in collaboration with Josef Svoboda, emphasized heavily the Marxist message that the *Ring* is about the curse of corruption inherent in capitalist forms of socio-political power.

Fritzsch, Ernst Wilhelm (1840–1902)

Music publisher in Leipzig who brought out an edition of Wagner's collected works.

Froh (R)

A god with a modest tenor role.

IN *Das Rheingold*

As one of Freia's* brothers (the other is Donner*), he naturally seeks to protect her from the giants Fasolt* and Fafner*, who claim Freia as their reward for building Valhalla*, the home of the gods. Together with Donner, Froh offers violence to the giants, but is restrained by Wotan.* When the fire god Loge* speaks about the value of the Nibelung gold. Froh is harshly critical of him, saying that he is lying. But when Froh in turn applauds the idea of stealing Alberich's* ring as a solution to the problem of paying the giants, Loge gets his own back: 'Yes, that will be child's play – how simple!' he says.

Froh creates the rainbow over which the gods finally pass into their new palace, Valhalla. This work is said to symbolize hope for the future. In Norse mythology, his solid brother Donner was forbidden to cross the translucent bridge into Valhalla for fear that his weight might break it.

In the *Poetic Edda*, the god Frey (Froh) is described as the son of his own brother and sister, while Frey in turn had intercourse with his sister, Freya, who in some versions is herself wife to Odin (Wotan).

IN *Götterdämmerung*

The Gibichungs* offer a sacrifice to Froh.

'Frohwalt' (W)
The name (meaning 'joyful') which Siegmund in Act I of *Die Walküre* wishes he could call himself. This is his way of stressing his unhappy past history.

Frommann, Alwine (1800–75)
German painter, daughter of a Jena bookseller, who became one of Wagner's earliest fans. She wrote to him after seeing the Berlin production of *Der Fliegende Holländer* in 1844. It was the first real indication that Wagner had that the public were going to appreciate his works.

Fuchs, Eugen (1893–1971)
German bass who excelled as Beckmesser.* His Alberich* and Klingsor* were also products of a splendid musicianship, but he was asked to sing the thwarted suitor in *Die Meistersinger* throughout the world. His career at Bayreuth began in 1933 and lasted until 1961.

Fuchs, Marta (1898–1974)
German soprano who gave Kundry* at Bayreuth in 1933 and was the principal Bayreuth soprano for the rest of the decade in succession to Frida Leider*. She continued to sing at the Stuttgart Opera until 1951.

Furtwängler, Gustav Heinrich Ernst Martin Wilhelm (1886–1954)
One of Germany's greatest conductors, an outstanding exponent of the German Romantic composers, notably Wagner. Furtwängler was assistant to the dedicated Wagnerian Felix Mottl* at Munich (1907–9). He directed the Mannheim Opera (1915–20) and then succeeded no less a figure than Richard Strauss* as conductor of the Berlin State Opera concerts. During the 1930s he conducted at the Bayreuth and Salzburg Festivals.

The only cloud over his career was his alleged involvement with the Nazi party, although he never in fact supported it, merely seeing it as his duty, as a musician, to remain in Germany and continue to make music there. Feeling against him outside Germany, however, caused him to resign his post as Conductor of the New York Philharmonic in 1936 almost as soon as he had accepted it. For the same reason, after the war, his appointment as conductor of the Chicago Symphony Orchestra had to be cancelled by the orchestra's board, despite the fact that he was cleared of all accusations of complicity with Hitler at a hearing in 1946. Furtwängler was by far the most Wagnerian conductor of the operas, apart from Richter* and Wagner himself, and his recording of *Tristan and Isolde*, with Ludwig Suthaus and Kirsten Flagstad* in the title roles, is a gramophone classic. See 'Conducting, On'.

Gadski, Johanna (1872–1932)
German soprano who was the 1895 New York Elsa* and the 1899 Bayreuth Eva.* She gave Senta* at the Metropolitan Opera House in 1900 and until 1917 was their Brünnhilde* and Isolde.* Her career suffered when America entered the First World War, since her husband was, most unwisely, the representative of the Krupp armaments company. She left the USA in 1917.

However, she returned there in 1929–31, in a Wagnerian touring company which Sol Hurak organized and which was highly successful. Her career was cut short by her death in a car accident.

Gahmuret (P)
In Wagner's opera, Gahmuret is named as Parsifal's* father, and therefore Lohengrin's* grandfather. According to the text, Gahmuret died fighting in Arabia before Parsifal was born and with his dying breath asked that his son should be called Parsifal, the reverse of which is the alleged

arabic 'Falparsi'* ('foolish pure one'). In other legends, Gahmuret is listed as King of Norgals and Waleis, hailing from Anjou.

Gautier, Louise-Judith (1850–1917)
French writer, daughter of Théophile Gautier, who became Wagner's mistress. She was the spiritual inspiration behind the sensuous music of *Parsifal*. Although thirty years younger than Wagner, she fell in love with him at Bayreuth in 1876. Charles Baudelaire* and Victor Hugo had previously admired her. She had been friendly with Wagner since the Triebschen* days (from 1866).

Now, he found she could help him forget the 'sorrows' of the 'false fame' of the first festival at Bayreuth, which he felt was a failure. For Wagner, she was 'riches' the 'intoxicating luxury of my life'. Cosima* found out about their relationship probably in 1878. She tolerated it informally, but would not allow open correspondence to be passed between the lovers after February of that year.

Gawain (P)
The legendary Arthurian knight, whose fortunes rose or fell according to the inclinations of the poet who happened to be refashioning his myth. Originally he was the very model of chivalry, but in some later versions, for example the mediaeval prose *Tristan* and Malory's fifteenth-century *Morte D'Arthur*, he is even treacherous.

Wagner employs him in Act I of *Parsifal* as a benign force, rushing around trying to find medicine for his wounded master, Amfortas*, and so busy in fact that we never even catch a glimpse of his person on stage.

Gerhilde (W): *see* Valkyries

German Art and German Politics
Wagner's racist critique of German culture written in 1867, which deplored foreign influences on the German mind. He elaborated an argument put by Constantin Frantz* that 'developing our own culture would be the right propaganda for Germany and an essential contribution to the re-establishment of the balance of power in Europe against the French'. Wagner's views were further developed in the *Süddeutsche Presse* in September 1867. King Ludwig* loved the articles: 'By God', he exclaimed, 'whoever is not entranced by the spell of the words, whoever is not convinced and converted by the profundity of spirit revealed therein, does not deserve to live.'

Gernot (F)
King Arindal's* ranger who is compelled to share his master's eight-year sojourn in fairyland in the grip of the magic spell of Ada* and her handmaidens. Gernot is in love with Drolla* and when he finally returns home he teases her mightily about the 'beauteous maidens just ripe for the kissing', among whom he has passed so many delightful days of enchanted captivity. 'And since I'm quite handsome,' he adds, 'they all fell in love with me.'

In fact, this is simply intended as a comic device to relieve the heavy moods of Wagner's opening and closing passages in *Die Feen*.

Gervinus, Georg Gottfried (1805–71)
The great German historian whose *History of German National Literature* (1835–42) provided Wagner with most of the background material, plot and characters for *Die Meistersinger von Nürnberg*.

Gesamtkunstwerk (Whole Art-work)
An idea threading through most of Wagner's aesthetic writing and musical theory. He believed that the Greeks in the days of

Aeschylus had created a community festal art, uniting poetry, music, drama, dance and religion. This, ideally, conferred on the artist the status of priest, arbiter of morals and acknowledged member of the ruling elite. He argued that such an artist, transported to the nineteenth century, would never have suffered like him the slings and arrows of outrageous poverty in Paris.

Until Wagner came across Schopenhauer's works in the early 1850s, he endeavoured to express the ideal of a *Gesamtkunstwerk* in his own musical creation. The result was an alliance between libretto and score, where the music promised not to make gratuitous interruptions in the drama, while the drama promised to add the spirit of poetry to the music, giving it a new voice, just as Beethoven had given a voice to the climax of his Ninth Symphony. However, when Wagner read in Schopenhauer that music was the mistress of all the arts, he changed his mind. Henceforward, his music would take more and more charge of his dramas. The orchestra was to acquire a new independent voice of its own. Parts of the actual dramatic development would be expressed first and foremost in music. For instance, in *Tristan* there are times when the orchestra *is* Tristan, expressing what Tristan is feeling long before Tristan himself experiences it.

The Symbolist poets, like Baudelaire*, were attracted to the Wagnerian idea of the *Gesamtkunstwerk*, since it seemed very close to their own notion of correspondences and accordances between individual arts, especially between poetry and music.

See 'Art Work of the Future, The', 'Baudelaire, Charles'.

Geyer, Ludwig (1779–1821)
Perhaps Wagner's natural father (see entry on Richard Wagner) who was an actor, dramatist and portrait painter. He married Wagner's mother on 28 August 1814.

Geyer, Wilhelm Richard (1813–83)
Between 1813 and 1827, Wagner was known as 'Richard Geyer', after his stepfather, Ludwig Geyer.

Gibichungs (G)
The family of Gunther* and Gutrune* (the hall of the Gibichungs' is their home) in *Götterdämmerung*. Gibich was the name of their father. Their half-brother Hagen,* however, had an altogether different sire in black Alberich* (from *Rheingold* and *Siegfried*). Gunther is Prince of the Gibichungs, but Hagen has greater natural powers of command and authority. He runs events in the final part of Wagner's tetralogy of the *Ring* – until they catch up with him too.

Gide, André (1869–1951)
In his journal for 1908, the French novelist records his reply to an 'inquiry conducted by the German paper, the *Berliner Tageblatt*, on the occasion of the twenty-fifth anniversary of Wagner's death, to find out from the leading artistic and intellectual figures, especially in France, what was their opinion of the influence of Wagnerism'. Gide obviously enjoyed answering this question:

I reply:
I hold the person and the work of Wagner in horror; my passionate aversion has grown steadily since my childhood. This amazing genius does not exalt so much as he *crushes*. He permitted a large number of snobs, of literary people, and of fools to think that they loved music, and a few artists to think that genius can be acquired. Germany has perhaps never produced anything at once so great or so barbarous.

Glasenapp, Carl-Friedrich (1847–1915)
Author of *Richard Wagner, Leben und Wirken* (first edition, 1876–7), the first 'scientific' biography of the 'master' but really an obsequious piece of hagiography.

Gobineau, Joseph-Arthur, Count de (1816–82)

French diplomat who made a second career as the brilliant author of a number of obsessively racialist books. Wagner met him in November 1876 and embraced his doctrines enthusiastically. However, Wagner also made drastic modifications to Gobineau's theories and it would be more reasonable to indict Wagner as theorist than Gobineau for the use Houston Stewart Chamberlain* and Hitler* later made of the grand myth of 'aryan' supremacy. Wagner's music is not pro-Nazi, but in a very important sense his ideological lapse into racialism (see *Judaism in Music**) was proto-Nazi. Gobineau is now known only for his racist doctrines. But his *Essay on the Inequality of the Human Races* (four volumes, 1853–5) contains an original survey of the history of mankind, albeit from the racial point of view, covering a myriad of subjects. Even on the racial question, Gobineau 'affirms explicitly that every branch of mankind has elements of conscience and judgement which mark them off decisively from the beast' and he is not anti-semitic, which for a 'lazy public', is perhaps the biggest surprise of all. He actually wrote, 'The Jews became a people that succeeded in everything they undertook, a free, strong and intelligent people, and one which, before it lost, sword in hand, the name of an independent nation, had given as many learned men to the world as it had merchants. . . .' Contrast this with Wagner's view that the Jews were unable to make music at any profound level owing to debased blood!

Gobineau's friendship with Richard Wagner brought him a decisive share of fame and influence. The Master found in Gobineau's views on ethnic chaos a systematic treatment of elements in his own theory of cultural decay. After the death of the two men within months of each other, the Bayreuth circle infused further elements of anti-semitism into their presentation of Gobineau's system. As Gobineau's recent editor, Michael Biddis, remarks,

Modern Germans conveniently forgot that Gobineau had no praise for themselves but for the Teutons who had emerged from fifth century forests. They neglected Gobineau's assaults on vulgar nationalism and upon the imperialistic expansion which so encouraged blood-mixture. . . . By the time the Gobineau Society was founded in 1894, its hero's work had suffered a not too subtle metamorphosis.

This reinterpretation was carried out largely by Houston Stewart Chamberlain directly from Bayreuth.

Godfrey (L)

Elsa* of Brabant's younger brother (a non-singing part), entrusted by their father on his death to the care of Count Frederick von Telramund.* Unknown to Telramund, his witch-wife Ortrud* turns Godfrey into a white swan. It is on this metamorphosed creature that Lohengrin* arrives up in Antwerp to champion Elsa's cause against Ortrud's calumnies. Lohengrin hopes that the power of the Grail* will break Ortrud's spell over Godfrey, provided Elsa keeps her faith with him. Telramund, on the other hand, still believes Ortrud's lie that Elsa murdered Godfrey by drowning him in a pool.

All is revealed in Act III, when Lohengrin's intercessional prayers persuade the Grail to release Godfrey (who thus becomes the new Duke of Brabant). Elsa swoons and dies upon Lohengrin's return to Montsalvat*.

Goethe, Johann Wolfgang von (1749–1832)

Wagner's favourite poet. He and Cosima* read Goethe's entire canon between 1865 and 1883. As a youth Wagner had attempted to write dramas in the style of Goethe. In 1831, he wrote seven songs to words from *Faust* and in 1840 a *Faust Overture* on the same theme.

Gold, the Rhinemaidens' (R, but a theme throughout the *Ring*)
A treasure of gold lodged in the bed of the River Rhine, where it is guarded by three maidens. It has been there since the world began but conceals a hideous potential. For if a man shall foreswear love in its presence, he may steal the gold and fashion a Ring* which will make him lord of the world and master of its riches.

The river-gold is a token quantity. As we see in *Rheingold*, Alberich,* who steals it, can mine a great deal more by wielding the power of the Ring. It is this secondary gold which Wotan* eagerly offers to the giants Fasolt* and Fafner* in return for the building of Valhalla.* Unfortunately for the gods, the labourers will only be satisfied by a payment which includes the original Rhine gold, especially the magic Tarnhelm* and Ring. Thus the Ring gold – the treasure which must be restored to the Rhine if the world is ever to be set to rights – slips from the control of Wotan and the gods, ultimately to bring about their downfall.

The gold obviously symbolizes worldly wealth. When Alberich foreswears love for the gold, this also implies that money is a corrupting malignant force, a curse on men which Alberich makes explicit after Wotan has wrenched the Ring from his finger.

Good Friday music (P)
The beautiful and moving music heard after Parsifal* has blessed Kundry* in Act III. He gazes at the woods and meadows around him and they seem to abound with joy, on this day of the Lord's death. Gurnemanz* explains to Parsifal that nature does not weep but rejoices at her own rebirth, made possible by the Saviour's suffering. The inspiration for this music is said to have come to Wagner on the Good Friday after he had moved into 'Das Asyl'* (close to his mistress, Mathilde Wesendonck*). Here is music born of adulterous embraces pressed into the service of an opera preaching redemption through the denial of sexual love. Wagner himself referred to the Good Friday interlude as 'Field and Meadow Music' on a copy of the first score for the conductor, Hermann Levi*.

Goodall, Reginald (b. 1901)
English conductor whose interpretations of Wagner impressed British audiences from 1968 onwards. Goodall was on the staff at Covent Garden but tended to hide his light during the strenuous Solti* decade (1961–71), working as répétiteur. It was therefore a considerable surprise for the public to listen to Goodall's *Ring* at the Coliseum in 1973, with its sustained sense of movement, glorious flow and solid architecture. Comparisons with Furtwängler* and Knappersbutsch* were offered.

This was the first *Ring* in English for more than forty years and Goodall was its primary inspiration. It is fully preserved on records.

Götterdämmerung (*The Twilight of the Gods*)
Music drama in a prologue and three acts, being the fourth and final work in Wagner's tetralogy of the *Ring*. Text and music by Richard Wagner, based on a variety of Icelandic, Nordic and German poems and legends. *Götterdämmerung* was first performed as part of a complete *Ring* cycle in August 1876 at Bayreuth. The writing of *Götterdämmerung* occupied Wagner between 1869 and 1874.

Götterdämmerung is the climax, resolution and redemption of all that has passed in the previous operas of the mighty *Ring* cycle and it is also the culmination of Wagner's thinking and feeling about the nature of opera and drama. It is with *Götterdämmerung* that he returns, in a dialectically transformed style, to many of the traditions of grand opera – to the use of an introductory chorus, to the use of

43

set-piece orchestral interludes such as Siegfried's* Rhine Journey and later his Funeral March, and even to a conventional trio finale when Brünnhilde*, Hagen* and Gunther* stop 'acting' long enough to pool their vocal resources. However, there is nothing remotely Italianate about *Götterdämmerung*; all that he now borrows from traditional opera is grafted onto his own style of music drama. The sustained continuity of the *Ring*, its palpable circularity, is merely polished by these new elements, not fragmented.

The *Vorspiel*, or Prologue, introduces us to the three Norns,* spinning the Rope of Destiny. Their song grows increasingly troubled. Wotan* has cut down the World Ash Tree, the so-called Tree of Life, and piled its branches around the walls of his palace, Valhalla.* He is waiting for the destruction of the world and the end of the gods. Finally, he will kindle the wood in a dramatic conflagration. The Norns cannot see when this event is to occur, because their rope begins to fray, cut, as they explain, by the curse of black Alberich,* who is still aiming to regain the Ring* and rule the world. The times are certainly out of joint, for suddenly the Rope of Destiny breaks and the Norns can sing no more. However, this symbolic moment reveals that the curse of Alberich may be working against itself. For with destiny destroyed, it is possible that freedom will find new scope in the world.

We are hurried to Brünnhilde's mountain-top, where by contrast, everything seems delightful. The lovers are happy. Brünnhilde tells Siegfried she has no regrets for her lost divinity: 'In love I'm rich,' she says, 'although emptied of power.' Siegfried is strangely eager to be off into the world, performing heroic feats. She makes no objection. Before he leaves, they exchange presents. Brünnhilde lets Siegfried ride her fabulous horse, Grane,* while Siegfried gives Brünnhilde the magic Ring as a token of his love.

Act I opens in the hall of the Gibichungs.* Their lord is a weak and vain

fellow called Gunther,* whose sister, Gutrune,* is something of a mouse. Only Hagen,* their half-brother, is full of princely dignity. It is he who now proceeds to involve his relatives in a wicked plot that will destroy the marriage between Siegfried and Brünnhilde. Later we understand Hagen's motive, for he is the son of Alberich, the Nibelung dwarf, and devoted to his father's evil cause.

Gunther is troubled because he has made no mark in life and lacks a heroic reputation. Neither Gunther nor Gutrune is married. Hagen proposes to solve all their problems by giving Siegfried a drugged drink when he eventually arrives at their ancestral home. This will cause him to lose his memory and fall in love with Gutrune. Then, in order to obtain Gunther's permission for marriage to Gutrune, Siegfried will be obliged to capture Brünnhilde as bride for Gunther. Since Brünnhilde is the world's most famous woman, Gunther will gain both fame and wife and Gutrune an heroic husband. The weak and wicked pair agree to the plot, particularly when Hagen also mentions that Brünnhilde will bring the Nibelung Ring as dowry. The prospect of possessing this Ring attracts Gunther almost as much as the idea of possessing Brünnhilde.

Siegfried's journey towards the land of the Gibichungs is marked by a stirringly Romantic orchestral interlude. On arrival, he expresses mild jealousy of Gunther's position: 'No land or men have I,' laments Siegfried, 'No father's house or hall.' Hagen points out that he is rich in other ways, for he carries both the Ring and the Tarnhelm.* Siegfried protests that they are mere baubles, but Hagen carefully explains to him the wish-granting functions of the Tarnhelm, taking the precaution of *not* describing the superior powers of the Ring.

Hospitable drinks are prepared. Siegfried pointedly draws attention to his feelings for Brünnhilde; hers is the name on his lips as he swallows the drugged potion – and instantly forgets all about her and falls in love with Gutrune. In rapid succession, it is agreed that Siegfried shall marry Gutrune and that Gunther shall marry Brünnhilde with the aid of Siegfried and the Tarnhelm. Gunther is obviously unable to walk through the flames up to Brünnhilde's mountain dwelling, so therefore Siegfried, wearing the Tarnhelm, will impersonate Gunther and win Brünnhilde on behalf of his sworn blood-brother. Later, on his way down the mountain, he will change places with the real Gunther, so that Brünnhilde shall never suspect that any deception has taken place.

Scene 3 carries us to Brünnhilde's rock again, where she is joined by her sister, Waltraute.* Brünnhilde is delighted to have news of Valhalla and for a brief moment is tempted to hope that Wotan has summoned her home again; but no. Waltraute has disobeyed orders to mount a private mission, the purpose of which is to beg Brünnhilde to restore the Ring to the Rhine, since Wotan has said that, if Brünnhilde were to do this, the curse would be lifted. Brünnhilde delivers a negative; she is no longer concerned with the affairs of the gods, while the Ring, to her, is only a symbol and pledge of Siegfried's marital love. Waltraute shrilly calls her a traitor and withdraws.

The first Act now closes with a splendid ironic contrast to the foregoing scene. Siegfried in Gunther's form (wearing the Tarnhelm) arrives to claim Brünnhilde as Gunther's wife. Distraught and grief-stricken by this intrusion, Brünnhilde resists with all her might. She even commands the Ring to save her, but the Ring has little power to serve a prisoner against her jailor, and a prisoner is what Brünnhilde has now become. The disguised Siegfried rips the Ring from her finger and forces her into a cave. He swears that she *shall* be wife to Gunther. Therefore, during this one, pre-nuptial night the loyal sword, Notung,* shall separate them in the interests of the holy wedlock to come.

Act II restores Alberich to the drama.

He appears as a ghostly visitation to the sleeping Hagen. Alberich explains that the Ring is still waiting to be won by the Nibelungs. All Hagen has to do is kill Siegfried, since he is the current lord of the Ring and thus master of the world – although still in ignorance of the extent of his power. If Hagen does this, Wotan and all the gods of Valhalla will be destroyed. Hagen dreamily informs his father that he will do all that is required of him.

Siegfried now rushes back to the hall of the Gibichungs, making use of the Tarnhelm's power to transport its wearer instantly to any desired location. By now the complications of his position as proxy wooer become apparent, as Hagen always intended they should. The latter assembles the Gibichung vassals. Then Gunther leads in the submissive Brünnhilde, who is incensed when she sees Siegfried in Gutrune's arms; her protests are heard by all. She truthfully accuses Siegfried of being her husband in all senses of the term. He is compelled to utter a denial, since he retains no memory of the event. Then, swollen with jealous anger, Brünnhilde untruthfully accuses him of making love to her when he wooed her on Gunther's behalf in Gunther's form. Notung, she alleges, did *not* separate them on that fateful night, but hung on the wall in his scabbard. The Gibichungs grow angry and Gunther distressed. The contest becomes still more challenging for Siegfried when Brünnhilde demands to know how the magic Ring came to be on his finger, if, indeed, he was not the man who over-powered and tamed her will? Finally, in a moment of fateful and tragic irony, both Siegfried and Brünnhilde swear on Hagen's spear point that their *particular* account of events is the truth. Siegfried adds, 'and may this spear point strike at my heart if I have acted falsely!'

In Scene 5, Brünnhilde, Hagen and Gunther plot to murder Siegfried. Brünnhilde reveals to Hagen that she once wove a spell around her hero to protect him from all danger in battle. However, she knew he would never turn his back on any foe, and so his back is the one spot which remains unprotected. Hagen swears to make good use of her information. On that pregnant note, the curtain falls on Act II.

The final Act of *Götterdämmerung* (and of the *Ring*) brings us full circle: we have returned to the river bank of the Rhinemaidens whom we last met at the beginning of *Das Rheingold*. Siegfried is out hunting. He is led astray by a goblin and then finds himself beside the water where the three lusty Rhinemaidens are at play. They laughingly ask for his Ring as a present, then disappear. He offers it. They return and tell him all about the true nature of this awesome bauble. Then they *command* Siegfried to restore it to them, but he refuses to obey their orders, even though they tell him that, if he denies them, he is walking this very day to his death. With a fair degree of accuracy the Rhinemaidens announce that 'Siegfried is stupid and blind as a child!'

In the second scene Wagner offers us a long passage of ironic pathos. The Gibichung vassals, resting from the hunt, entreat Siegfried to sing of his many adventures. He does so. We hear again the saga of the death of Fafner and listen again to the happy song of the woodbird*. Hagen gives Siegfried a drink which contains an antidote to Gutrune's earlier potion. As Siegfried continues the story of his adventures, his voice grows increasingly troubled. He tells of a mountain top ringed by fire. He relates how the song bird told him to climb and claim his glorious bride for prize. When he mentions Brünnhilde by name, all his faculties are suddenly restored to him. But it is too late. At that intense and poignant moment, Wotan's black ravens* fly across the sky – awaiting Siegfried's imminent death. Hagen tells Siegfried to look up at them, and spears him in the back with a triumphant curse of vengeance as he does so. Siegfried, the hero, dies, murmuring his eternal love for Brünnhilde. The appalled

Gunther and his Gibichung vassals place Siegfried's body on his great shield and shoulder it in a solemn procession to their tribal hall to the strains of the grieving orchestral interlude of Siegfried's Funeral March.

The final scene of *Götterdämmerung* belongs to Brünnhilde. Her vision is now cleared. When Gunther and Hagen fall out over possession of the Ring, Brünnhilde hardly notices that Gunther is killed. When Hagen stretches forth his hand to remove the golden prize from Siegfried's hand, she watches indulgently. When Siegfried's lifeless hand rises accusingly in the air and Hagen and the chorus recoil, she simply advances towards the front of the stage and bids the turmoil cease. For all is now apparent to her: in her great grief for the loss of Siegfried, in her complete realization that he was never false to her but drugged into false-seeming actions, she understands the true disposition of the forces in the universe. What matters far more than power and war is mercy, pity, love and peace. When men are fearful or deceived, they must hold true to the bonds of love. Transcendance is a possibility. Any heart that fills with honest passion can renounce the Ring of cursed power. Such a heart can even renounce mortal life itself, as Brünnhilde intends to do in expiation of the crimes of Wotan and her own race.

The lord of the gods may rest. Loge* will light the fires in Valhalla, while, on earth, Brünnhilde stoops to ignite the funeral pyre of her husband, Siegfried. Then, mounted on her sturdy steed, Grane, she will ride to her death, certain that her sacrifice will bring peace to the gods and herself. So the Valkyrie rides into glory.

Hagen is now drowned as the Rhine overflows its banks. The Ring is returned to the Rhinemaidens, who joyously celebrate its repossession. Fire and flood fill the stage. The bodies of Gunther, Siegfried, Hagen and Brünnhilde are consumed by an inferno reaching up to the sky.

The mighty allegory is now finished. The meaning is controversial, and the *Ring* cycle will be reinterpreted as often as it is performed. But Wagner's message seems eternally to be one of hope, if only we can come to terms with those infernal fears that have brought Wotan and the gods to destruction.

It was the fear of Alberich which drove Wotan to his doom, and such fear is presented throughout the *Ring* as the quality which limits men's experience of love. Wotan's relationships with his fellow beings are *inauthentic* in proportion to his fear that the world will harm him. In reality, this fear is an internal phenomenon; Wotan is entirely afraid of himself, of his own Alberichian ego, and not without reason. His demented lust for power is an attempt to conquer and kill his own anxieties.

Fear is therefore a tyrant in the mind. Siegfried, the youth who is explicitly ignorant of fear, is the first 'free' agent in the *Ring* drama. This point is emphasized heavily – only a *fearless hero* can reforge the shattered fragments of the magic sword Notung, for example. Only a *fearless hero* can kill Mime.* Only a *fearless hero* can scale the fiery mountain top and claim Brünnhilde for his bride.

However, when Siegfried falls in love with Brünnhilde, then he learns what it is to fear, if only temporarily. He makes the critical discovery that fear, once recognized, can be counter-acted and it is this self-same cosmic power of love, of openness to love, that can calm all fears: 'In the fire our blood has kindled, in the flames that glow from our glances, in our burning ardent enchantments, I find again my boldness of heart. . . . I have failed to learn what fear is, not even you can teach me!'

Brünnhilde's final gesture of self-sacrifice in *Götterdämmerung* is only to be understood as her realization, born of grief, that love is the greatest power on earth and the only one able to conquer the fear driving men to lust after the fool's gold of ambition.

Grail, The Holy (L, P)

A sanctified cup, reported once to have contained the blood of Christ, which is the object of a quest by legendary Arthurian knights. It provided Wagner with the inspiration for two operas.

In the primary Grail legend, Joseph of Arimathea holds a cup to the side of the crucified Christ at the point where he has been wounded by the spear of Longinus,* and afterwards flees with the vessel of blood and the spear to place these most holy relics in the hands of a band of pious knights for safe-keeping. In some versions, the Grail-cup finds its way to Glastonbury, England; in others it returns to Heaven and is then re-issued miraculously to Titurel,* who founds a new Grail-Brotherhood at Montsalvat* to protect the relics.

Wagner's Grail works many wonders, possessing the power both to heal and to inspire. Men strive to reach it from the outside world. Parsifal*, for example, searches for Montsalvat after defeating Klingsor,* but the power of Kundry's* curse (with the consent of the Grail) keeps him roaming for many weary years. Such journeys are obviously spiritual quests for God and self.

In Wagner's story, the Grail-Knights* enjoy perpetual youth, granted by the arrival, each Good Friday, of the white Grail Dove which flies down and places a wafer in the Cup to confirm the continued virtue of the assembled company. However, unless the Grail is periodically unveiled and allowed to glow over the knights, they will lose their vigour just as surely as the gods in *Rheingold*, deprived of Freia's* magic rejuvenating apples, will wither. The sources of this legend begin with classical myths. The first extant text is by Chrétien de Troyes (*Perceval*, c. 1181–90). Thereafter, there are versions from France (Robert de Boron's poem *Joseph d'Arimathie*), Germany (Wolfram von Eschenbach's* *Parzifal* and *Titurel*) and England (Sir Thomas Malory's *Morte D'Arthur*), and this list is not exhaustive.

In several stories, the Grail is linked to the cup used by Christ at the Last Supper.

Grail knights, First and Second (P)
Two of the Grail knights (one tenor, one bass), who meet Gurnemanz* at the beginning of the opera in order to answer his questions (and ours) about what is happening to the stricken Amfortas.* They also describe the arrival of Kundry* for us, which they liken to that of a demonic Valkyrie.* Later, they serve in the Grail scenes.

Grane (W, S, G)
Brünnhilde's* horse, on which she ferries heros to Valhalla,* or rescues maidens in distress, such as Sieglinde.* Grane is put to sleep by Wotan* at the end of *Die Walküre* together with his mistress. When they awaken (in *Siegfried*) both have lost their enchanted powers. Brünnhilde is no longer a demi-goddess and Grane is no longer a sky horse. However, he is a perfectly serviceable mortal beast. Brünnhilde lends him to Siegfried (in exchange for the Ring*) for his Rhine journey to the hall of the Gibichungs;* and at the end of *Götterdämmerung*, Brünnhilde rides Grane into Siegfried's funeral pyre, where they both perish.

For many years, real horses were used on stage in the *Ring*. This led to a number of accidents and occasional hilarity.

Greindl, Josef (b. 1912)
German bass who first sang at Bayreuth in 1943 as Pogner,* returning often 1951–69, singing many bass roles.

Grétry, André Ernest Modeste: *see under* Saint-Säens, Charles Camille.

Grieg, Edvard Hagerup (1843–1907)
The Norwegian composer was so taken with Wagner that in 1858 at Leipzig he went to see *Tannhäuser* on fourteen consecutive occasions. Of the *Ring*, he wrote to his friend Bjørnsen, 'this strange work summing up the whole of our present culture has an added strangeness in being so far in advance of our time'. Grieg was another of those who attended the first performances at Bayreuth in 1876 on behalf of a newspaper in his own country, in his case the *Bergensposten*. He was very impressed by the whole enterprise and comments on people humming Wagner in the town. He also speaks of seeing 'Valkyries in the streets and gods and mortals disporting themselves in the shade of the trees'. Despite criticism of the 'ceaseless modulations of the score and the wearying chromaticism of the harmonies', Grieg concludes that Wagner is a true giant in the history of art, comparable perhaps only to Michelangelo. He likens the Nothunglied to parts of Beethoven's Ninth Symphony and the Siegfried Funeral March 'only to the Eroica. . . .'

Grimgerde (W): *see* Valkyries

Grimhild (G)
The mother of Hagen,* Gunther* and Gutrune* of the Gibichungs.* However, Hagen is the son of Alberich* and only half-brother to Gunther and Gutrune, Lord and Lady of the Gibichungs. In *Die Walküre* Wotan* hears from Erda* that Alberich has paid a woman gold to endure his sexual embraces and bear him a son. This is the same Grimhild, who therefore emerges from the plot of the *Ring* as an acknowledged prostitute.

Groma (F)
The first of Wagner's magicians, forerunner of Klingsor,* Loge* and Wotan,* those elemental agencies assisting plots to their curious and unpredictable ends. In *Die Feen*, Groma is but a voice and an

off-stage force alluded to by the other protagonists. He transcends the fairy curse and provides the weapons to defeat it. This crude theatrical device scarcely even hints at the subtle and elaborate handling of similar characters in Wagner's later operas – spell-binders on stage, who are not only bound by the spells of others, but also by the consequences of old spells uttered by themselves.

Grove, Sir George (1820–1900)

English engineer turned musicologist who compiled the famous *Grove Dictionary of Music and Musicians*, for which he was knighted in 1883, the year of Wagner's death.

Grove comments in a revealing letter to his friend Mrs Wodehouse,

I do think the tendency [of Wagner] to make music so long and ultra-earnest is wrong. If everything is to take the same road what amusements will the world have in the end? Music is turned from a relaxation into a study, but no other relaxation is put in its place. Surely this is wrong.

Gulbranson, Ellen (1863–1947)

Swedish soprano who was one of the second generation of Bayreuth singers, making her first appearance there in 1896, exactly twenty years after the Festival opened. She was Bayreuth's only Brünnhilde from 1897–1914.

Gundryggia (P)

One of the alternative names for Kundry,* which Klingsor* spits at her in derision, derived by Wagner from the heterogeneous collection of Grail* legends. In some of these twelfth- and fourteenth-century romances, Kundry figures variously as Cundrie, the Loathly Damozel, Orgeluse, or even as Parsifal's* wife under the name of Condwiramurs. Klingsor also calls her Herodias.

Gunther (F)

Gunther does little in *Die Feen* apart from attend and react to events as they develop. There is no active hint of his later embodiment in the person of Siegfried's* blood-brother, Gunther, the Lord of the Gibichungs in *Götterdämmerung*.

Gunther (G)

Baritone Lord of the Gibichungs* and half-brother to the villain, Hagen,* son of Alberich.*

Gunther's primary characteristic is inadequacy. He is an inadequate ruler (since Hagen is the real power behind his throne); an inadequate nobleman (since base plots are his stock in trade), and an inadequate friend (since he conspires to murder Siegfried,* his sworn blood-brother). Gunther is not so much black-hearted as faint-hearted, gullible and credulous. He lacks Siegfried's heroic qualities, while remaining envious of his fame. He would do anything to acquire a similar reputation, as long as it did not involve him in hardship or danger.

Very quickly Gunther agrees to fall in with Hagen's plot to trick Siegfried into falling in love with their sister, Gutrune.* He does this to try to motivate Siegfried into winning Brünnhilde* for himself. This is an explicit act of treachery, yet Gunther is undeterred. Siegfried will be drugged into losing his memory, as eventually he loses his life.

Gunther desires Brünnhilde as his wife for the same reason that modern millionaires marry film stars: she is the most famous woman of her day, and Gunther – realizing that fame is power – hopes some of the celebrity will accrue to him. He also plots to get his hands on the Ring.*

When Siegfried arrives, Gunther ignores several explicit hints that Siegfried and Brünnhilde are lovers. This is important, if only because Gunther later seems to receive this news with total astonishment: indeed, his 'discovery' of the previous connection between them will provide his main motive for assisting Hagen to murder Siegfried.

Gunther's thinking does not penetrate beneath the surface of events. He fails to probe for hidden reasons, with the result that he can only see Hagen in his true colours when it is all too late. Gunther offers feeble excuses for his own participation in the plot to kill Siegfried, although he does make some effort to deflect the fatal blow itself. Part of him, however, is very glad to see Siegfried dead, and it is that base ignoble part which plots to gain the Ring for himself while exorcizing the devils of jealousy which are eating his soul.

Brünnhilde accurately assesses Gunther to his face: 'Deep has sunk your glorious race, to bear such a coward as you.' His final act in the drama is to insult Hagen's heredity before fighting his first authentic battle on his own behalf with the Ring for prize. Inevitably, Gunther is the loser.

Gura, Eugen (1842–1906)

German bass-baritone who sang Donner* and Gunther* in the first complete Bayreuth *Ring* (1876). He sang there later as Amfortas*, King Marke* and Hans Sachs*. In England he sang Sachs and Marke in the first performances in that country of *Die Meistersinger* and *Tristan und Isolde* in 1882.

Gurnemanz (P)

A Holy man and knight (bass) of the Grail,* who combines many of the characteristics of fidelity and service seen in previous Wagnerian creations such as Wolfram* (T) and Kurwenal* (TI). Legend has it that the real Gurnemanz (or Gornemans) was Lord of Graharz, far distant from Montsalvat*, and that his function was to educate Parsifal.*

In *Parsifal*, Gurnemanz is part-narrator, part-spiritual guide, part-seer. He alone recognizes that Parsifal is poss-ibly sufficiently 'foolish' to fulfil the Grail's prophecy that Amfortas* will be saved by a 'bone-headed youth by pity made wise'. He it is who enforces the Grail's decree against blood sports under which all life is held to be sacred. He it is who grasps the truth that Kundry* must be bewitched, if her behaviour is to be explained. He it is who, like a respectful tourist guide, reveals the mysteries of the Grail to Parsifal in tones of absolute reverence, born of long, familiar service. He it is who tells us that Montsalvat is a kind of fairy-land. In a single economical phrase he informs Parsifal, 'You see, my son, time changes here to space.' Gurnemanz is also human enough to doubt the validity of Parsifal's election and kick him out of doors with a gentle curse, thus starting him on the journey to Klingsor's* enchanted castle, where his mission is made clear to him.

Gurnemanz gets his reward in Act III, because Parsifal returns at last to Montsalvat to succour all. Gurnemanz, like John the Baptist before him, is allowed to perform the joyous task of anointing his own saviour.

Gutrune (G)

A soprano role of restricted emotional scope. Gutrune is the daughter of Grimhild* and brother to Gunther,* Lord of the Gibichungs.* She is also half-sister to Hagen,* the son of the Nibelung Alberich.* Her mother, we hear, once prostituted herself to Alberich for gold. Her brother is a vain and weak-spirited creature, and Hagen is a villain. With this disadvantaged background, it is not surprising that Gutrune agrees to win Siegfried for her husband by lacing his drink with a cowardly love potion.

No good comes of it, and Gutrune is left at the climax of *Götterdämmerung* to reflect on Brünnhilde's* chiding words: 'You were never [Siegfried's] wife; only his mistress.'

Gutzkow, Karl Ferdinand (1811–78)

Novelist and dramatist who specialized in the 'social' novel. His works, particularly *Maha Guru, Story of God* (1833), a fantastic cynical romance, and *Wally, the Doubter* (1835), helped to radicalize young German intellectuals prior to the upheavals of 1848.

His books attacked the institution of marriage and questioned the citizen's duty of obedience to outmoded laws – with the result that outmoded laws sentenced Gutzkow to three months' detention and suppressed all his writings. On his release he wrote many plays and satires which were rather better received.

Wagner quarrelled violently with Gutzkow, who became dramatic manager of the Dresden court theatre (of which Wagner was *Kapellmeister*) in 1847, because the novelist did not share his low opinion of Halévy's,* *Les Mousquetaires de La Reine*, but actually wanted to have it performed.

Habeneck, François-Antoine (1781–1849)

Conductor and violinist who helped Wagner during his sojourn in Paris. He was director of the Paris Opéra 1821–4, and conductor there until 1846. He also founded the Sociéte des Concerts du Conservatoire in 1828, and introduced Beethoven's* music to France.

Hagen (G)

Son of Alberich,* the Nibelung dwarf, by an act of prostitution on the part of his mother, Grimhild.* In *Die Walküre*, Wotan* says, 'the dwarf [Alberich] has forced a woman; his gold bought her embrace; and she will bear Alberich's son'. This child turns out to be Hagen, the basso villain of *Götterdämmerung*.

However, Hagen is merely a device to allow Alberich to be represented as a force in all four operas of the *Ring* cycle. As Wagner makes clear at the beginning of Act II, Hagen has no will of his own,

but is dependent for motivation on the lust for revenge and power of his father, Alberich. This is doubly emphasized. Alberich explains that he first 'bred a deadly hatred into Hagen', afterwards feeding him on a diet of unhappiness. The boy was 'old in youth, gaunt and pale, hating the happy'.

Where Hagen differs from Alberich is in the high level of his intelligence. His father was a simpleton who fell for the circus tricks of Wotan;* Hagen is made of sterner stuff. He cleverly capitalizes on the weaknesses of those around him, including Gunther and Gutrune, until they unwittingly do his bidding. If Gunther wants fame and Gutrune a husband, then they shall have them – provided that Siegfried* suffers in the process. If Brünnhilde* is blind with jealousy, then she shall be offered the balm of revenge – as long as she reveals where Siegfried's vulnerability lies.

Hagen, in fact, does more than enough to gain the Ring* for the Nibelungs. He is only thwarted in the end by the combined forces of Siegfried's super-nature (the hero's corpse threatens him even after death), Brünnhilde's unprecedented gesture of self-sacrifice and a well-timed Rhine-flood which drags him down to a watery grave.

Cosima (Wagner)* records in her diary (7 February 1870), 'Discussion over such characters as Gunther and Hagen – the latter formidable, mysterious, stubborn, brusque. Over the simplicity we have lost; I find all these heroes like so many animals, lions, tigers, etc. they may prey upon each other, but no unpleasant convention, decorum or anything like that enters into it: they are quite naive.'

Halévy, Jacques-François-Fromental-Elie (1799–1862)

Franco-Jewish composer, for whose operas *La Reine de Chypre* and *La Guitarrero* Wagner had to prepare vocal scores as part of his hack-work in Paris in 1841.

Halévy's greatest success was with the grand opera *La Juive* (1835), which entered the full repertoire as soon as it appeared. Wagner held Halévy in esteem as a composer, whatever paranoid insults about the Jewish-Meyerbeerian stranglehold on the Paris Opéra he also uttered. 'For my part,' he wrote, 'I have never heard dramatic music which has transported me so completely to a particular historical epoch.'

Hanslick, Eduard (1825–1904)
The music critic whom Wagner later turned into a powerful enemy. Conservative by nature, Hanslick was unable to accept Wagner's innovations, but his problems were not assisted by Wagner's own gratuitous rudeness.

The men first met in 1845 and it was Hanslick's enthusiastic reviews of *Tannhäuser* in 1846 which got him established in the business of artistic criticism. He wrote music reviews for the *Wiener Zeitung* until 1850, then, after several years in the department of education, began in 1855 to write on music for the *Presse*. From 1856, for forty years, he gave lectures on music appreciation at the University of Vienna. Hanslick has been regarded by Wagnerians as a born trouble-maker. He is caricatured in *Die Meistersinger* as Beckmesser* (originally the character was to have been called 'Veit Hanslich'). But his accounts of the first *Ring* of 1876 were both perceptive and impartial. It is only later that he describes Wagner's music as 'tyrannized by leitmotivs' and a 'chromatic-enharmonic confusion'. However, as Ernest Newman* makes plain, Wagner told untruths about his relationship with Hanslick and it is these lies that have most strongly coloured the views of Wagner's supporters.

Harald (F)
Arindal's* traitorous field-marshal in *Die Feen*, who tries to use an enemy's army against his lord.

Hauser, Franz (1794–1870)
Bohemian singing teacher and one-time baritone who, in 1834, while he was director of the Leipzig theatre, rejected Wagner's opera *Die Feen* for performance there.

Heckel, Emil (1831–1908)
Piano-maker in Mannheim who conceived the idea of Wagner societies to help to fund the Bayreuth Festival Theatre.

Heine, Heinrich (1797–1856)
German-Jewish poet best known for his *The Book of Songs* (1827). Wagner used Heine's *The Memoirs of Herr von Schnabelewopski* (1834) as one of the sources for his treatment of the Flying Dutchman legend. Wagner had tremendous admiration for the older man, who defended but also satirized the excesses of the composer.

Helmwige (W): *see* Valkyries

Henry the Fowler, King of Germany (L)
In the opera, this character is nationalistic, grave and noble. It is an authoritative bass role requiring presence and dignity, but little besides. Henry offers justice to his subjects, deals fairly with Telramund* and welcomes Lohengrin.* But at no point does he intervene in the drama.

In real life, Henry I (876–936) was the founder of the Saxon dynasty and King of Germany from 919. In 924, Henry made peace with the Magyars, agreeing to pay tribute in return for a nine-year truce, at the expiry of which he destroyed their army at Riade in 933.

Henry the Writer (T)
Tenor *Minnesinger* at the court of Hermann,* Landgrave of Thuringia, who forms part of the choral ensemble accom-

panying Tannhäuser* and Wolfram von Eschenbach.*

Herald (Ri)
Small tenor role in *Rienzi.*

Herald, The King's (L)
A baritone master of ceremonies who adds dignity to the considerable mediaeval pageantry of *Lohengrin.*

Hermann, Landgrave of Thuringia (T)
The ruler of the land in which *Tannhäuser* is set is based on the historical Hermann of Eisenach, Count Palatine of Saxony (*c.* 1156–1217). In real life, Hermann's primary achievement was to oppose the attempt of the Emperor Henry VI to transform the German kingdom from an elective to an hereditary monarchy.

Wagner shows Hermann surrounded by a brilliant court of minstrel-singers and poets. As the bass figure of authority in the opera, Hermann offers only conventional commentaries on the action of the drama. He is totally shocked by Tannhäuser's* sojourn in the Venusberg.*

Herwegh, Georg (1817–75)
German poet of revolutionary sentiment and a kindred spirit to Wagner, who met him in 1851, during his exile in Switzerland. Herwegh was expelled from Tübingen Theological College, thereafter becoming a journalist. His *Poems of One Living* (1841–4) summarised the aspirations of German youth, causing the Prussian authorities to confiscate the book.

Herwegh was expelled from Prussia shortly afterwards for being rude to the King, so returned to Switzerland, then France. At the time of the Revolution of 1848, Herwegh went to Baden and personally led a force of eight hundred French and German workers in the local uprising. They met disastrous defeat and Herwegh

fled to Switzerland to nurse his wounded ideals in the company of Wagner and other exiles. Cosima was later godmother to Herwegh's son. Finally, in 1866 an amnesty permitted Herwegh to return to Germany.

Herzeleide (P)
Mother of Parsifal.* She is named 'Heart's Sorrow' because, like Sieglinde* before her, she is fated to lose her husband, Gahmuret,* in battle and afterwards give birth to his child. Herzeleide at least has the consolation of raising the boy, a pleasure denied to Sieglinde, but only at the price of renewed sorrows when, despite all her efforts, he too is called to a life of military vagabondage. Kundry* movingly narrates the tale:

I saw the child at its mother's breast,
Its earliest gurgles laugh still in my ear.
With sorrow in her heart, how even
Herzeleide did laugh then too,
When the delight of her eyes offered joy to her
  pain.
Softly couched in gentle mosses,
Caressing, she lulled him to sleep;
Fearful in care,
Her motherly yearning watched o'er his slumbers;
In the morning he woke
To the warm dew of his mother's tears.
All tears she was, child of sorrow,
Tears for the love and the death of your father.
To guard you against like perils
Was her highest duty's command.
Far from arms, the strife and fury of warriors,
She hoped to hide and shelter you in peace.
Ever caring she was and oh so fearful:
Ne'er must you learn anything.
Can you not still hear the cry of her lament,
When late and far you lingered?
Oh what joy and laughter it gave her
When, searching, she caught you!
As her arm fiercely clasped you,
Were you not frightened at her kisses?
Yet her grief you perceived not,
Nor the surging of her pain,
When at last you did not return
And all trace of you was lost.
She waited day and night,

Until her wailing ceased:
Her grief consumed the pain,
She courted silent death:
Sorrow broke her heart –
And Herzeleide died.†

Hesse, Hermann (1877–1962)

Celebrated German mystical novelist who wrote specifically about Wagner in *Klein and Wagner* (1920). The subject is a petty individual who leaves his wife. Thereafter, he experiences a series of raptures on the theme of Wagner. In his mind, the name 'Wagner' becomes synonymous with freedom and death (he has also heard of a certain Wagner – no relation to the Bayreuth clan – who has murdered his entire family. In a dream, Klein – the 'little man' – enters a theatre called Wagner where, journeying through his subconscious, he acts in many plays of relevance to himself and to us: 'Wagner was the collective name for everything oppressed, suppressed, neglected and despised in the former functionary Friedrich Klein.' Finally, seeking 'oblivion in rebirth' or 're-absorption in the Whole', Klein drowns himself.

Hitler, Adolf (1889–1945?)

Soon after his twelfth birthday, Adolf Hitler attended a performance of *Lohengrin*: 'It was the first opera I had ever heard,' he writes in *Mein Kampf*. 'My youthful enthusiasm for the Bayreuth genius knew no limits. Repeatedly I was drawn to his operas. . . .' One biographer says Hitler listened to *Tristan* no less than forty times during his years in Vienna (1907–13). The Hofoper alone at this time staged Wagner on no less than 426 evenings. In later life, Hitler claimed to have seen his favourites (*Tristan* and *Die Meistersinger*) at least a hundred times apiece, with *Götterdämmerung*, especially Act III, a close third. 'What joy each of

† Translation by Peggy Cochrane (Decca boxed score, 1973)

Wagner's works has given me,' said Hitler. 'The 10 days of the Bayreuth season were always one of the blessed passages of my existence.' Soon after the German reoccupation of the Rhineland in 1936, Hitler observed, 'I have built up my religion out of *Parsifal*. Divine worship in solemn form . . . without pretence of humility. . . . One can serve God only in the garb of the hero.' He went on to recall, 'The first time I heard the funeral march from *Götterdämmerung* was in Vienna at the Opera. I still remember as if it were today how madly upset I became on the way home when encountering a few slime-talking Yids [*mauschelnde Kaftanjuden*] I had to pass. I cannot think of a greater contrast – the glorious mystery of the dying hero and this Jewish garbage.'

Such 'heroism' has caused biographers like Joachim Fest to blame Wagner for Hitler's delinquencies: 'Because of Wagner, a whole generation was confused, misguided and alienated from the bourgeois world.' The English critic (of Jewish parentage) Bernard Levin replies, 'We can't blame Wagner for Hitler . . . but what have we to whom the music also appeals in common with the Führer?' The answer is more than we like to think. It is easy to clear the actual message of the *Ring*, for example, from any charge of fascism: Wagner states, 'the pursuit of power is incompatible with a life of true feeling,' and, 'the attainment of power destroys the capacity for love.' In the *Ring*, no one successfully lives by the spear or sword. But since the Wagnerian appeal is to the pre-moral *subconscious* as well as to the civilized faculties, anyone can enjoy him – whether democratic hero or fascist villain.

Hitler, of course, would have found this blasphemous. He held that the sole message of the 'Bayreuth genius' was to honour all things German. Hitler claimed Wagner for the Aryans just as the 1938 *Bayreuth Festival Handbook* claimed that the *Ring* principally serves as an illustration of 'the terrible seriousness of the racial problem'. Wagner, Hitler decided, was 'the greatest prophetic figure the German people has had'. When he first stood beside Richard Wagner's grave, Hitler's heart 'burst with pride'. A 'literally hysterical excitement' overcame him when he recognized his own 'psychological kinship with this great man'. He absolutely identified himself with Wagner's life – 'a life flowing into the glory of world-fame' – as well as with his art. It is typical that the Führer, without knowing the first thing about musical composition, should have decided to resuscitate an abandoned Wagnerian project by writing an opera about *Wieland der Schmied* (*Wayland the Smith*)*. Fortunately for art, his musical ignorance remained an insuperable obstacle.

It is generally contended that Hitler's appreciation of Wagner was unmusical: 'Music meant little more to him than an effective means to enhance theatrical effects' (Fest). It was the spectacular side of Wagnerian opera that Hitler loved. He rarely played records for pleasure or listened to symphonies or chamber works. His favourite moment was the stage-shattering *coup de théâtre* as Valhalla collapses in Act III of *Götterdämmerung*.

The Wagner family was a helpful agent in Hitler's early rise to power in Bavaria, above all in the English person of the eccentric Winifred,* née Williams. When Hitler moved house to the Obersalzberg, the Wagners were there to donate crockery and table linen, together with one page of the original score of *Lohengrin*. Previously, they had given money. The Bayreuth Festival reaped the rewards throughout the Hitler interlude. After 1933, the Nazi government provided an annual Bayreuth subsidy of sixty thousand marks, together with complete income tax exemption, so that the Festival Director, Heinz Tietjen, could afford to expand the Gibichungs'* chorus in *Götterdämmerung* from the required sixty-four to over a hundred singers. Hitler's summer visit to Bayreuth was an annual propaganda exer-

cise on behalf of the regime. Photographic records at the Bayreuth museum show Nazi soldiers blowing the traditional fanfare from the *Festspielhaus* balcony to summon the audience to their seats, rather than a section of brass from the orchestra. The Wagner-Hitler axis became so close that Winifred Wagner said in 1975 that she would be happy to see Hitler back again. She had cause to feel sympathetic to the sort of dictator who justified his 1933 Emergency Censorship Decree on the grounds that certain newspapers had criticized – Richard Wagner.

Hochzeit, Die (The Wedding)

Wagner's first opera, which he did not complete. He wrote the text in 1832; it is based on J. G. Büsching's *Ritterzeit und Ritterwesen*, a story of chivalry taken from a mediaeval poem, *Frauentreue*. Wagner destroyed the libretto, having written only a few sections of the first act; these fragments were performed at Leipzig in February 1938.

In 1832 Wagner, now aged nineteen, was anxious to produce something more dramatic than symphonies, sonatas and overtures. His mind was full of mediaeval legends and knightly tales. He also badly needed to earn some money, since the acting talents of his sister Rosalie contributed most of the household salary with which his mother strove to feed and clothe them. He had now to choose between making his next artistic move in the direction of poetry, novels, plays, libretti or even a full-scale opera. As he records in *My Life*,

My poetical efforts lay in the direction of a sketch of a tragi-operatic subject, which I finished in its entirety in Prague under the title of *Die Hochzeit*. I wrote it without anybody's knowledge, and this was no easy matter, seeing that I could not write in my chilly little hotel room, and had therefore to go to the house of Moritz, where I generally spent my mornings. I remember how I used quickly to hide my manuscript behind the sofa as soon as I heard my host's footsteps.

55

Not satisfied with this, Wagner then produced a novel. It tells the story of a young couple who were

going to be married, and had invited the friend of the bridegroom, an interesting but melancholy and mysterious young man, to their wedding. Intimately connected with the whole affair was a strange organist. The mystic relations which gradually developed between the old musician, the melancholy young man and the bride were to grow – the young man mysteriously killed, the equally strange sudden death of his bride's friend, and the old organist found dead on his bench after the playing of an impressive requiem, the last chord of which was inordinately prolonged as if it would never end.

Wagner goes on to say that he abandoned this excursion into fiction for an operatic project:

I never finished this novel: but as I wanted to write the libretto for an opera, I took up the theme again . . . and built . . . the following dramatic plot: Two great houses had lived in enmity, and had at last decided to end the family feud. The aged head of one of these houses invited the son of his former enemy to the wedding of his faithful partisans. The wedding feast is thus used as an opportunity for reconciling the families. While the guests are full of the suspicion and fear of treachery, their young leader falls violently in love with the bride of his newly found ally [presaging the Siegmund* plot in Walküre]. His tragic glance deeply affects her; the festive escort accompanies her to the bridal-chamber, where she is to await her beloved; leaning against her tower-window she sees the same passionate eyes fixed on her, and realizes she is face to face with tragedy.

When he penetrates into her chamber, and embraces her with frantic passion, she pushes him backwards towards the balcony, and throws him over the parapet into the abyss from whence his mutilated remains are dragged by his companions. They at once arm themselves against the presumed treachery, and call for vengeance; tumult and confusion fill the courtyard; the interrupted wedding feast threatens to end in a night of slaughter. The venerable head of the house at last succeeds in averting the catastrophe. Messengers are sent to bear the tidings of the mysterious calamity to the relatives of the victim: the corpse itself shall be the medium of reconciliation, for, in the presence of the different generations of the suspected family, Providence itself shall decide which of its members has been guilty of treason. During the preparation for the obsequies the bride shows signs of approaching madness; she flies from her bridegroom, refuses to be united to him and locks herself up in her tower chamber. Only when, at night, the gloomy though gorgeous ceremony commences, does she appear at the head of her women to be present at the burial service, the gruesome solemnity of which is interrupted by news of the approach of hostile forces and then by the armed attack of the kinsmen of the murdered man. When the avengers of the presumed treachery penetrate into the chapel and call upon the murderer to declare himself, the horrified lord of the manor points towards his daughter, who, turning away from her bridegroom, falls lifeless by the coffin of her victim.

One can readily see why Wagner's sister had her doubts about the advisability of staging such a gory and depressing gothic variation on the theme of Romeo and Juliet. As soon as she read the work, she advised Wagner to forget it. Despite the time he had already spent on it, he promptly tore up the libretto and filed away the score for an orchestral introduction, a chorus, a recitative and septet which were already completed. Years later, in May 1879, when he was well established and famous, Wagner was furious at not being able to buy at auction the manuscript score of this uncompleted first act, offered for sale as 'an unquestionably genuine manuscript by Richard Wagner, dated March 1, 1833'. The drama of Die Hochzeit, although wildly unrestrained, shows exactly where his imagination was tending towards: the conflict between passionate and moral love, nature and super-nature, impulse and bond.

Hoffmann, Ernst Theodor Amadeus (1776–1822)

German writer, composer, music critic and caricaturist, who wrote the Tales on which Offenbach based his famous opera.

Hoffman was one of the greatest influences on German Romantic art in the nineteenth century. (He changed his name 'Wilhelm' to 'Amadeus' in honour of Mozart.)

Wagner records that as a youth he was 'on fire with the maddest mysticism' because of his 'perusal of E. T. A. Hoffman's works'. This caused him 'to have visions by day in semi-slumber in which the "keynote", "third" and "dominant" seemed to take on a variety of mystical and ghostly forms'.

Hohe Braut, Die (The Heavenly Bride)

An opera Wagner sketched in 1836 and sent to the dramatist Scribe* for his consideration the following year. It was later offered to Reissiger. Wagner then turned it into verses, to which the composer Johann Kittl added some music, and it was subsequently performed in Prague in 1848 under the title *Bianca und Giuseppa, oder die Franzoson vor Nizza*.

Holtei, Karl Eduard von (1798–1880)

German actor and theatre manager, who appointed Wagner conductor at Riga in the late 1830s.

Hörselberg, the: *see* Venusberg, The

Hotter, Hans (b. 1909)

Austrian singer of German birth, the leading bass-baritone of his generation and a splendid Wotan* and Hans Sachs* – 'as Wotan towering physically, musically and dramatically over the dwellers of earth and heaven', according to one critic. He appeared as Sachs and Wotan at Covent Garden from 1948, in the same role at the Metropolitan in 1950 and again at Bayreuth from 1952 onwards. An eminent *Lieder* singer, Hotter has also worked as a producer, staging the Covent Garden *Ring* in 1961 under Georg Solti.*

Humperdinck, Engelbert (1854–1921)

German composer best known for his opera *Hänsel und Gretel* (1893), full of leitmotivs* and Wagnerism. A Mendelssohn scholarship enabled him to go in 1880 to Italy, where he met and became friendly with Wagner. The older man invited Humperdinck to join him at Bayreuth and assist with the production of *Parsifal*, 1881–2. He did so, copying the score and even composing six extra bars to facilitate a lengthy scene change. However, these bars were later dropped when modern methods permitted swifter backstage action.

Hunding (W)

The bass-voiced symbol of patriarchal marriage, the husband of Sieglinde*, a man for whom tribal honour and loyalty are the highest values. Wotan*, the Lord of the Gods, does not think much of him. He tells Brünnhilde* that Hunding would not be welcome in Valhalla,* that he is not even worth collecting from the battlefield after death.

For Hunding is both honourable and deceived. He takes care not to break the laws of hospitality when he discovers his enemy, Siegmund,* sheltering in his house. And he is willing to meet Siegmund squarely in battle when their enmity is discovered. On the other hand, Hunding only acquired Sieglinde as a wife through the violence of his kinsmen, who kidnapped her and murdered her mother. Sieglinde has never loved him. Perhaps this is Hunding's offence: he stands opposed to the Romantic Spirit and the Spirit of Spring. For him love is a question of contractual power. He pays the highest price for this crime, when Wotan kills him with a single angry glare.

Hunter, Rita Nellie (b. 1933)

English soprano with a vibrant dramatic voice, who made a powerful impression as Brünnhilde in the 1970 Coliseum *Die Walküre* (and the complete *Ring* cycle in 1973).

Huysmans, Joris-Karl (1848–1907)

French 'decadent' novelist and aesthete who pays tribute to the erotic power of Wagner's work in his *Ouverture de Tannhäuser*.

Suddenly in this musical scene, in this fluid and fantastic site, the orchestra bursts forth . . . the approach of Tannhäuser. The shadows spread rays of light, and the swirling clouds assume the forms of rearing haunches, of swelling breasts, throbbing and distended; the blue avalanches of space throng with naked forms, with cries of desire and appeals to lustfulness, with outbursts of the carnal life beyond . . . and no longer the antique Venus, the Aphrodite of old, whose immaculate form made men and gods bray as beasts during pagan orgies, but a Christian Venus, if such sin against nature and such coupling of words were possible! . . . It is the incarnation of the spirit of Evil, the effigy of omnipotent luxuriousness, the image of an irresistible and magnificent female satan. . . .†

Incest

For years, Wagner was notorious as the composer who promoted incest between Siegmund* and Sieglinde* off-stage between Acts I and II of *Die Walküre*. In the opera, Fricka* expresses her strong disapproval and her arguments have been echoed down the decades by a whole world of Mrs Frickas, including Karl Marx.* He suggests that Wagner inserted the incest for pornographic impact, 'pour épater le bourgeois'. In fact, Wagner was following his source material, where the love of brother and sister is a common theme, as well as trying to convey the idea of a primitive, un-peopled world before the rise of taboo. As Richard Capell writes in his book *Opera*, 'It is rare, in the sublime wilderness of the *Ring*, for human beings to meet; the early and unpopulated state of the world is indicated by (and excuses) the incestuous relations of its inhabitants. Not until the fourth evening of the *Ring*, when the tribesmen come out

† Translated by Raymond Furness, *Wagner and Literature*, London, 1982.

for Siegfried's wedding, do we learn that there are more than two or three families in the whole world.'

Indy, Paul Marie Théodore Vincent d' (1851–1931)

French composer and *Wagnérienne* who published a study of Wagner in 1903 and helped to reform French symphonic music along the lines indicated by César Franck.* D'Indy attended the 1882 Bayreuth *Parsifal* in the company of fellow enthusiasts from Paris. He shared Wagner's dislike of Jews (d'Indy came from an aristocratic military family, a breeding-ground for anti-semitism), which earned him the hatred of Saint-Säens* and others. D'Indy recounts the celebrated moment when Chabrier* was reduced to tears on hearing Wagner's music: 'I've waited ten years of my life to hear that A on the cellos during the opening bars of the *Tristan* prelude.' Among d'Indy's more important works are the orchestral variations *Istar*, the opera *Fervaal* and the *Symphonie sur un chant montagnard français*, for piano and orchestra, which reflects his interest in folk music.

Irene (Ri)

Rienzi's* loyal and stalwart sister (soprano), the 'fairest girl in Rome', who elects to share his death by fire 'like a true Roman' rather than join her lover, Adriano Colonna,* in amorous flight. Hitherto, her noble character was displayed to advantage when she pleaded for mercy on her prospective father-in-law's behalf, after his attempted coup d'état. Her presence is highly influential throughout the drama, since at one point it is enough by itself to prevent the crazed Adriano from murdering Rienzi and also to re-awaken Rienzi's courage after the excommunication scene: 'What – thou dost live – then Rome is not yet dead!' he says. She shares his fate with the glad boast, 'A Roman true I yet remain! – Leave me [to Adriano], I feel a giant's strength!'

Wagner obviously found the idea of such feminine metal inspirational, and in the later dramas we shall again encounter the strengths of Irene: in Senta,* in Elisabeth,* in Brünnhilde* – in fact, whenever love is heroically renounced for duty.

Isabella (Lt)

This soprano role calls for a dominant woman. She enters a convent on the death of her parents but soon leaves again in order to protect her brother (by conventional morality he ought to protect her) and to champion the rights of a wronged sister-in-God, Mariana.* Isabella makes a number of strongly feminist statements: 'That accursed man – God give me strength and I'll destroy him . . . what, fear you one weak woman? . . . Monster of hypocrisy!' It is Isabella who makes the central plea for passionate love between the sexes: 'The force of love is in every heart, only fools or liars pour contempt on the treasures and pleasures of love.' Frederick* is swiftly smitten to the quick: 'Her breath is warm.' He plays two unpleasant tricks on her – the first to win her body, the second to destroy her brother – but Isabella is equal to all his lordly wiles. She is even strong-minded enough to fall in love with Lucio,* but to keep it to herself until he shall have proved himself worthy of her sacrifice.

Isolde, an Irish Princess (T I)

Possibly the noblest of Wagner's legendary soprano lovers. The depth of her apparent hatred for Tristan* in Act I is really the measure of her underlying passion for him. She and Tristan have been spiritually betrothed ever since he slew Morold,* her former lover, and afterwards came to her door for magic medical aid. When Isolde realized that Tristan was Morold's killer, she raised a sword to slay him in turn, but was prevented by his startling gaze. Her arm was frozen and hate changed to love. He then wooed and won her – but, alas, only on behalf of his uncle, King Marke* of Cornwall. Tristan, too, is smitten with an equal love for Isolde, but fealty to his liege lord prevents him from acknowledging his feelings. On board ship, taking them both to Cornwall, Tristan does not even talk to Isolde.

Indeed, his loyalty to King Marke begins to erode even Isolde's female confidence – is she ugly? – and this is where she finds a sufficient surge of anger to reattempt murder. (Hers is the sudden fury of a Brünnhilde* who sees Siegfried* in the arms of Gutrune,* not the feebleness of an Elsa,* who swoons lifeless when Lohengrin* vanishes.) When her maid, Brangäne,* serves the couple with a love potion instead of the poison her mistress intended, Isolde begins to understand what Tristan has always known: that their love is deep, wide, eternal – and impossible. It cannot be realized, one brief night excepted, in this present life. But, at first, she rebels against this knowledge.

Her transfiguration is achieved in the mysterious *Liebestod* at the conclusion of the opera, when the vision of Tristan finally makes her aware that such a love can even transcend death. Perhaps there is no eternal hereafter (that is a chance Isolde will have to take), but by consenting to die for it, she affirms in the most absolute fashion love's inspiring victory over all.

Israel

An unofficial ban on the music of Richard Wagner (and also on that of Richard Strauss*) has existed in Israel since the Second World War. In Wagner's case, his theoretical anti-semitism is clearly the main reason. It has also been suggested that Wagner's music was played to Jews prior to their extermination in Nazi death camps. Certainly, the SS played records of Wagner, and also Mozart, after a day at their hellish task, but they refused to allow the Jewish camp orchestras to reproduce the sounds of Wagner at all. Instead, pieces by Franz Léhar (died 1948 – always a favourite of Hitler's), Johann Strauss and Franz Schubert were performed. The music of Carl Orff and Bruckner* was also much appreciated by the Nazis, yet remains unbanned in Israel. The English musicologist Hans Keller, who himself survived the death camps, comments,

To be sure, one does occasionally hear Wagner on Israeli radio – without his name being mentioned. On such occasions the bitterly ironical descent to the Nazi level is complete: in my lifetime, the only comparable miscarriage of musical justice happened early in 1938 when I turned on Vienna radio to chance upon Mendelssohn's Violin Concerto, played by the Nazi's single fiddling star, George Kulenkampff – and upon this closing announcement: 'The composer of the concerto is unknown.'

Keller adds that 'two groups of people, and two only, have ever Nazified Wagner – the Nazis and the boycotting Israelis.' Even so, his argument cannot entirely ignore Wagner's ominous remark, recorded by Cosima in her diary for 19 December 1881: 'He makes a drastic joke to the effect that all Jews should be burned at a performance of *Nathan*!'

Janssen, Herbert (1892–1965)
German baritone who excelled in the lighter Wagnerian roles at Covent Garden (1926–39) and Bayreuth (1930–37): Wolfram,* Kurwenal,* Kothner,* Gunther* and Amfortas.* But his Sachs* and Wotan,* called into service in New York on the retirement of Friedrich Schorr,* were less successful.

Jesus von Nazareth
Opera projected by Wagner in 1849, but never finished.

Jews, The: *see* Anti-semitism;
Chamberlain, Houston Stewart; Gobineau, Joseph-Arthur, Count de; Halévy, Jacques-François-Fromental-Elie; Hitler, Adolf; Indy, Paul-Marie Théodore Vincent d'; Israel; *Judaism in Music*; Mehta, Zubin; Meyerbeer, Giacomo; Mendelssohn-Bartholdy, Jakob Ludwig Felix.

Jones, Gwyneth (b. 1936)
Welsh soprano who gave such a highly-praised Sieglinde* at Covent Garden in 1965 that comparisons were made with the immortal Lotte Lehmann.* From 1966 she has sung at Vienna and at Bayreuth, where she gave Sieglinde, Eva,* Kundry,* Elisabeth*/Venus* and Senta*. In 1974, she was chosen as the *Götterdämmerung* Brünnhilde for Bayreuth, then sang Brünnhilde there throughout the centenary *Ring* of 1976. Her voice is a *lirico spinto*, which stands up well to the bruising of the heavier roles. Dramatically, she is a generous and compelling performer.

Joukowsky, Paul (1845–1912)
A painter of Russo-German parentage, who became a close friend of the Wagners in the composer's last years, designed the scenery for *Parsifal* and was a pall-bearer at Wagner's funeral.

Joyce, James (1882–1941)
Irish writer who pushed verbal experiment to its furthest degree in *Finnegans Wake* (1939) makes fun of *Die Walküre* in the Circe episode of his earlier and more accessible novel *Ulysses* (1922). In defiant parody of the raising of Notung* from the tree by Siegmund,* Joyce's hero, Stephen Dedalus, raises his ashplant to shatter a lampshade in a Dublin brothel. Joyce had borne a childish grudge against Wagner ever since a friend suggested that Wagner was a better musician (in music) than Joyce was in words. The Irish author

found 'nothing to admire' in *Götterdämmerung*. He regarded *Die Meistersinger* as 'pretentious stuff' and dismissed *Tannhäuser* as 'ridiculous': 'What sort of a fellow is this Tannhäuser* who, when he is with Saint Elizabeth [Elisabeth*], longs for the bordello of the Venusberg,* and when he is at the bordello of the Venusberg longs to be with Saint Elizabeth?'

Judaism in Music

Wagner's pseudonymous antisemitic pamphlet which he unwisely published in 1850 and even more unwisely reissued under his own name in 1869. See 'Antisemitism'.

Julia (Lt)

She does not appear on stage but Julia's reported premarital incontinence with Claudio* offends Viceroy Frederick's* Ban on Love. As a result both Claudio and Julia are condemned to death, a sentence which is only forestalled by the deft intervention of Claudio's sister Isabella.*

Kalergis, Marie: *see* Muchanoff, Countess Marie

Kappel, Gertrude (1884–1971)

German soprano who gave the 1912–14 Covent Garden Brünnhilde.* She was also a memorable Isolde*, at the same house (1920s), being endowed with a beautifully rounded delivery and powerful dramatic sense. She sang at the Met from 1928–36.

Karajan, Herbert von (b. 1908)

A child prodigy at the piano, Karajan has risen to become one of the most influential, not to say autocratic, figures in twentieth-century musical life. From 1938 he conducted at the Berlin State Opera and he remains a celebrated exponent of Wagner. A member of the Nazi Party from 1934, he was later exonerated of complicity by an Allied Tribunal. Even so, his American début in 1955 led to public protests. He has held appointments with the Vienna State Opera, the Salzburg Festival, the Vienna Philharmonic, the Berlin Philharmonic and the London Philharmonia. He was at Bayreuth 1951–2. His recordings of the *Ring* are noted for their subjective, free-flowing approach.

Kareol

The seat of Tristan's* castle in Brittany, where the faithful Kurwenal* takes his master after the fatal fight with Melot.*

Kemenate (L)

The name given to the women's quarters in the Castle of Antwerp.

Kemp, Barbara (1881–1959)

German soprano who gave Elsa,* Isolde* and Kundry* in New York and Senta* and Kundry* at Bayreuth 1914–27. She was married to the composer Max Von Schillings.

Kietz Gustav Adolf (1824–1908)

A Dresden sculptor and one-time companion of Wagner. His brother, the painter Ernst Kietz, was friendly with Wagner in the Paris years.

King, James (b. 1925)

American tenor who gave Siegmund* and the more 'spiritual' Wagnerian roles (Lohengrin* and Parsifal*) at Bayreuth from 1965–75. His voice is very bright and clear.

King of Sicily, The (Lt)

A purely processional part: the King appears on stage at the opera's climax, but does not speak.

Kipnis Alexander (1891–1978)

American-Jewish bass of Ukranian origin who was compelled to give up his career at Bayreuth in 1934 after the rise of the Nazis. His performances of Pogner*, King Marke* and Gurnemanz were outstanding.

Klindworth, Karl (1830–1916)

German pianist and conductor who studied under Liszt.* He ran his own Berlin music school. He met Wagner, for whom he prepared vocal scores of the *Ring*. Klindworth's house sheltered the young Winifred Williams [Wagner]*, who eventually married Siegfried Wagner.*

Klingsor (P)

The bass-voiced magician Klingsor is a mixture of Fallen Angel, Alberich* and Wotan*. He wants power, since, like Alberich, he has had to renounce love, and in the course of Act II of *Parsifal* he very nearly obtains it. There are also echoes of Wagner's previous stage magician Groma* from *Die Feen* and the sorceress Ortrud* in *Lohengrin*.

According to legend, Klingsor was the merlin-like magical guardian of the Grail.* In other stories, it is suggested that he was the first Grail Knight to be taken in adultery, the punishment for which was castration. This involved a very profound 'renunciation of love' indeed, and the mutilation was believed to confer increased wisdom as a small consolation. Certainly, this is the case in Wagner's story.

In his tale, Klingsor has committed some unnamed sin and by way of atonement he wishes to join Titurel's* Brotherhood of the Grail. As Gurnemanz* relates, Titurel showed no indulgence to Klingsor and 'however much he toiled, it was always to him denied'. Just as Alberich had failed to ingratiate himself with the Rhine-Maidens in *Das Rheingold*, so Klingsor was excluded from the warmth of

the Grail's fraternity. To prove the high seriousness of his application, Klingsor had even unmanned himself. But still Titurel would not accept him, and the knights were asked to drive him hence from Montsalvat.*

His rage and castration engender wisdom. He learns the arts of sorcery and decides that if he cannot have the Grail, nobody else should either. As Gurnemanz relates, 'The wilderness he made into a garden of bliss, wherein there grow women of devilish grace.' These sirens he still employs to trap straying Grail Knights. If they succumb to lust, they fall under his spell and must do his bidding, just as the magic ring in *Rheingold* enthralls the Nibelungs to Alberich. He also controls Kundry,* whom he has bewitched.

When Titurel's son, Amfortas,* came to destroy him, Klingsor transformed Kundry into the most enchanting siren and even Amfortas had to succumb. This put the Holy spear of Longinus* into Klingsor's evil hands and he gave Amfortas a bitter wound with it, a wound that would not heal until the spear should return to the Brotherhood. But Klingsor holds the spear fast and it cannot be liberated by force. Only a 'pure fool made wise by suffering' can achieve this end, says the Grail, which is why Amfortas and the Brothers will have to await the arrival of Parsifal* in person.

Klingsor's visionary powers tell him that Parsifal will prove the most potent threat to his kingdom, but will also represent his greatest opportunity of controlling the Grail once and for all. But the 'shield of foolishness protects him', just as Siegfried's* ignorance of fear protected him in *Siegfried*. Klingsor therefore decides to employ an even more beautifully apparalled Kundry, bride of the devil, to deflect Parsifal from his rightful path, since 'only against Klingsor is Kundry's power as naught' (for of course, Klingsor is a sexless creature).

Like Alberich, Klingsor is amused by

the sufferings of those who serve him, so that when his knight-slaves are put to rout, he simply chuckles. A destructive urge comes over him: 'May thus the whole breed of knights slaughter themselves!' he growls. Defiance is his dominant mode, and adds to his attractions. Courage and strength are as admirable in Klingsor as in Milton's Satan, despite the palpable contradiction of perceiving good in one so evil. But unlike Alberich and Satan, Klingsor is not even to see the partial realization of his master-plan. While Alberich, through Hagen,* destroys Valhalla,* and while Satan, through Eve, evicts the human race from Paradise, Klingsor, through Kundry, fails dismally to achieve his end. The fatal dart aimed at Parsifal's head is arrested in flight, the knight improvises the sign of the cross and Klingsor and all his works are vaporized, as if he were a cinema vampire.

Klingsor seems to get less than justice from Wagner. He did not become wicked by renouncing love in a pettish fit, like the villain of the *Ring*, but strove hard and single-mindedly to serve his maker before Titurel arbitrarily sent him to the Devil.

Klose, Margarete (1902–68)
German mezzo-soprano with a rich voice and dignified stage presence. She sang in the Paris Wagner season of 1930 and gave Ortrud* at Covent Garden in 1935 and Fricka* in 1937. She was at Bayreuth from 1936 to 1942.

Knappertsbusch, Hans (1888–1965)
German anti-Nazi conductor who assisted both Richter* and Siegfried Wagner* at Bayreuth, where he was principal conductor 1951–64 and one of the greatest Wagnerian exponents since the war.

Knüpfer, Paul (1866–1920)
German bass who performed regularly at Bayreuth 1901–12 and delivered an impressive Gurnemanz* and King Marke* at Covent Garden 1909–13.

Kobbé, Gustave (1857–1918)
American musicologist who compiled a famous *Complete Opera Guide*, although it is incomplete and sometimes misleading. His entries for Wagner ignore the youthful works but he does provide an interesting personal description of the composer:

In 1849, *Lohengrin* still not having been accepted by the Dresden Opera, Wagner took part in the May revolution, which, apparently successful for a very short time, was quickly suppressed by the military. The composer is said to have made his escape from Dresden in the disguise of a coachman. Occasionally there turns up in sales as a great rarity a copy of the warrant for Wagner's arrest issued by the Dresden police. As it gives a description of him at the time . . . I will quote it –
'Wagner is 37 to 38 years of age, of medium stature, has brown hair, an open forehead; eyebrows brown; eyes greyish blue; nose and mouth, proportioned; chin, round, and wears spectacles. Special characteristics: rapid in movements and speech. Dress: coat of dark green buckskin, trousers of black cloth, velvet vest, silk neckerchief, ordinary felt hat and boots.'
. . . I saw Wagner several times in Bayreuth in the summer of 1882, when I attended the first performance of *Parsifal*, as correspondent by cable and letter for one of the large, New York dailies. Except that his hair was grey (and that he no longer wore his spectacles on his chin) the description in the warrant still held good, especially as regards his rapidity of movement and speech, to which I may add a marked vivacity of gesture.

Kobbé was killed in 1918 when a seaplane landed on his sailing-boat.

Kollo, René (b. 1937)
German tenor who initially sang lyric roles such as Froh* and the Steersman*, in which he made his début at Bayreuth (1969). Since then he has sung Parsifal*, Erik*, Lohengrin*, Siegfried*, Tristan*, and Walther*.

Kothner, Fritz (M)

One of the journeyman-mastersingers, a baker (baritone), who calls the roll of the guild-meeting in Act I since he is the 'last elected man' in the company. During the debate to fix the rules of the forthcoming song-contest, it is the traditionalist Kothner who loudly opposes Hans ‚Sachs'* suggestion that the people be allowed to select the winner: 'Nay, Sachs! indeed that plan has no sense, Ruled by the folk, all art goes hence.' The cobbler continues to argue, but Kothner reiterates his opposition: 'But shame will fall upon our art If in our work the crowd have part.' Eventually, a compromise is reached, and Sachs gives up the appeal to the people, provided that Eva,* who is to be the contest 'prize', can still veto her marriage to the winner if she is not inclined to fancy him.

Kothner continues to administer the proceedings during Walther's application to become a Mastersinger, and is very ready to have him disqualified for his unruly verses: 'I understood none of it, I must admit!' Kothner is particularly upset that Walther,* carried away by the passion of his lyric, should have risen from his seat during the rendition. He resumes direction of affairs in Act III when Walther's fine new song, amended by Hans Sachs, sweeps all before it, even the objections of the pettifoggers.

Kundry (P)

One of Wagner's most alluring characters because of her complex double nature. In previous operas, Wagner has created two separate entities to represent the saint and sinner in woman. But in Kundry he unites both the Madonna and the Magdalen. In strict Wagnerian terms, Kundry is an amalgam of Holy Elisabeth* and Venus.* This naturally increases her dramatic significance because, with a change of clothes, a crazy wild woman becomes an attractive harlot; with a second change, she becomes a drab and placid servant. Moreover, for the first two acts at least, we

are aware that she may be under a spell. This potential for transformation makes Kundry very exciting. Thus until the second curtain, none of her actions, except some kindness to Amfortas,* are of her own volition. When we see Kundry, for the most part we are actually watching her puppeteer – Klingsor.*

And yet the real Kundry manages to make herself known, giving hints of a finer nature. Does she not indeed have some compassion for Parsifal's* bereavement? Her song would indicate so. Does she not perhaps genuinely believe that there is some secret comfort in the sexual love she offers Parsifal during the beautiful temptation scene? Perhaps.

Her wildness in Act I is partly due to guilt. The awful truth is known to her alone: she has been the agent of Amfortas' ruin and she is forbidden to communicate this to others. Her repeated protest that 'Kundry never helps' is both a cry of despair and a cryptic warning.

But does she deserve her burdens? Why was she bewitched? Because she once laughed in the Creator's face. By our own rational standards, this smacks rather more of a social gaffe or rank bad manners than a serious sin against the Godhead requiring such drastic retaliation, and we are reminded yet again that the world of *Parsifal* is a closed one. We have to bear in mind the rules issued by the composer or squirm uncomprehendingly in our seats. Kundry, like so many Wagnerian sopranos before her (Elisabeth, Elsa,* Isolde*), has to die, simply because it is written, according to Wagner.

Kundry's character contains elements of Brünnhilde,* Erda,* Fricka* and Sieglinde,* whom Wagner had recently created for the *Ring*. She is a 'wild rider' like Brünnhilde; full of pregnant wisdom like Erda; fired with anger like Fricka (when denied her womanly rights), and maturely erotic like Sieglinde. Unlike Wagner's early cardboard characters, she is therefore nearly a normal woman.

In mythology, Kundry was also known

as Condwiramurs, Cundrie, the Loathly Damozel and Orgeluse. Klingsor calls her Gundryggia and then Herodias, as if to suggest that she is a long-lived devil who has threatened Christianity from its inception. In one legend, she is Parsifal's legitimate wife, which perhaps adds piquancy to her predicament in this opera. Her action in washing Parsifal's feet underlines Wagner's desire to see in her the bride of Christ. This is the 'good' Kundry's crowning moment.

Kurt, Melanie (1880–1941)

Austrian soprano who gave Sieglinde* and Brünnhilde* to acclaim at Covent Garden (1910). She also sang at the Metropolitan Opera House from 1915–17, her début as Isolde* being highly praised. Her voice was rich and extremely powerful.

Kurwenal (T I)

Tristan's* loyal servant (baritone) who really has no idea of the true nature of his master's feelings. His fidelity is so precise that he cannot comprehend Tristan's ultimate longing to be united with Isolde.* At first, Kurwenal regards Isolde with hostility as little more than a captive princess, rather than as Tristan's ideal love. Even after the lovers swallow their potion, he fails to grasp the real import of their exclamations. And in the third Act, he sends for Isolde, not because he thinks Tristan is dying of love, but because he knows Isolde has medical skills which she can apply to wounds that will not heal. He never really understands what is happening around him (he even attacks those who have come to aid and forgive Tristan, and thus is mortally wounded himself), but his regard for Tristan is good and pure.

Lammers, Gerda (b. 1915)

German soprano who gave the 1955 Bayreuth Ortlinde* and later Brünnhilde* at Kassel. She was the Covent Garden Kundry* in 1959.

Larsén-Todsen, Nanny (1884–1982)

Swedish soprano who sang 1927–31 at Bayreuth in the roles of Isolde,* Kundry* and Brünnhilde*. She had a beautiful voice with a powerful, slow beat.

Laube, Heinrich (1806–84)

German journalist, dramatist and minor novelist who befriended Wagner in his early Leipzig days, although later they fell out. Laube was the editor of the *Zeitung für die elegante Welt*, and published in it his review of an early symphony by Wagner in 1833. Laube went on to become an important theatre director in Vienna and Leipzig, but failed to gain Wagner's support in his application to take over the Munich Opera in 1867. Laube took revenge by writing a spiteful review of *Die Meistersinger*.

Laubenthal, Rudolf (1886–1971)

German tenor who many claim was the best Siegfried* of the 1920s. He also played Erik,* Walther* and Tristan.*

Laussot, Jessie *née* Taylor (b. *c.* 1829)

A young, charming and wealthy Englishwoman, married to a Frenchman, with whom Wagner had a passionate affair in 1850. She had studied music at Dresden, then married a Bordeaux businessman. She helped Wagner financially and, since her private life was unhappy, reciprocated the love he freely offered. However, Minna Wagner* became suspicious. So, too, did Jessie's mother, who forced from her a full confession. Wagner's letters to Jessie were intercepted and M. Laussot offered to blow the composer's brains out. The Laussots finally told Minna that Wagner had seduced Jessie. Minna behaved so stoically and lovingly that Wagner realized that he might have made a mistake in neglecting her. The Laussot episode strengthened the Wagners' marriage (for a time), although for the Laussots it ended

65

in divorce. Jessie later married the German historian, Karl Hillebrand, setting up home in Florence.

Lawrence, David Herbert (1885–1930)

English novelist and poet, who owed a considerable debt to the music of Wagner in his early novel *The Trespasser* (1912) and in his stories 'The Primrose Path' (1922) and 'The Witch à la Mode' (1934), which explore respectively the themes of erotic ecstasy (*Die Walküre*; the alternative title for *The Trespasser* was *The Saga of Siegmund*), love and death (*Tristan und Isolde*) and immolation *Götterdämmerung*).

Lawrence's respect for Wagner was never excessive nor did it influence his most important fiction. Indeed, on occasions he held Wagner in some scorn, dismissing *Tristan* as 'long, feeble, a bit hysterical, without force or grip . . .'; *Siegfried* as 'good, but it did not make any terrific impression on me' and the entire Wagnerian canon as damnable: 'Damn Wagner, and his bellowings at fate and death. . . . I like Italian opera. . . .'

Lehmann, Lilli (1848–1929)

German soprano who sang Woglinde* and Helmwige* in the first performances of the Bayreuth *Ring* in 1876 and returned as Brünnhilde* in 1896.

Cosima Wagner* asked her to appear in the 1886 *Tristan*, but as Brangäne*, not Isolde,* which Lehmann, now a star, declined. Twenty years later, in her memoirs, Lehmann described at length what it was like to be directed by Richard Wagner: 'The big notes,' he said, 'will take care of themselves; the little notes and the text are the chief thing – do not address the audience but always each other – in monologues, look up or down, but never in front of you' (advice not always followed by present-day performers). She recalls Wagner's 'tears of joy' as she and her colleagues sang their Rhinemaiden trio by heart without a single mistake for the first time. She shows movingly what it was like to participate in the heady, revolutionary days of Bayreuth, when both buildings and performances were brand-new. She offers a number of criticisms of Cosima's direction of the 1896 *Ring* cycle, which involved departures from Wagner's own intentions but were always justified by Cosima questioning young Siegfried Wagner* thus: 'You remember, Siegfried, do you not, that it was done this way in 1876?' The hapless lad, thus consulted, was all of six years old in 1876, when his father's Nibelung operas were first performed.

Lehmann, Lotte (1888–1976)

German soprano, famous for her Marschallin in *Der Rosenkavalier*, Lotte Lehmann was also a justly celebrated Elisabeth,* Elsa,* Eva,* Sieglinde* and Gutrune* in the Wagnerian canon. No one sang a sweeter Sieglinde,* but there was reportedly just a hint of cosmopolitan worldliness about Hunding's* hut whenever she was in it.

Her voice was large and wistful, although she never failed to triumph with the phrase 'Mein armer bruder' in *Lohengrin*.

Lehrs, Samuel (1806–43)

Learned but tiresome individual whom Wagner caricatured in a short story, 'Eine Ende in Paris' written in the early 1840s.

Leider, Frida (1888–1975)

German soprano with a dark, ample voice. She made her début at Halle as Venus* in 1915 and gave the 1924 Covent Garden Isolde* and Brünnhilde,* two roles of which she was the outstanding interpreter during her years at Bayreuth (1928–38).

Leitmotiv (leading motive)

A term which simply means 'recurring musical theme'. Wagner employs leitmotivs throughout his mature operas, the best examples being in *Tristan* and the *Ring*. This is the key to his hold over the audience. By repeating these motives at unexpected moments in subtly altered forms, Wagner can make the listener feel two conflicting emotions simultaneously or reinforce the dramatic action at any stage of its development. In his earlier works, the motives are just 'tags' which do not undergo extensive transformations; but in the *Ring*, the entire score is an interweaving of motives which 'symbolize now one aspect, now another' of persons, objects, emotions or events in the drama. Wagner's own term for a leading motive was 'melodic moment of feeling'. It allows the composer to suggest emotions to the audience without actually stating them in the libretto. This inevitably gives the listeners a psychological insight into the meaning of the play unfolding before their eyes.

Equally interesting is the fact that it gives members of the audience an insight into themselves. The *Ring* is constructed according to the principles of the 'stream of consciousness' technique in literature. These convolutions more clearly represent the actual way in which people think – with numerous messy recapitulations, loops, asides, flashbacks and conflicts of feeling – than does the linear development of a formal libretto or story. By thus mimicking the internal movements of the mind, Wagnerian opera engages more than the surface, rational faculties of its listeners. Our composer disturbs the sediments underneath and invokes what may with literal accuracy be called 'gut responses'. He wants to tap our passions and our instincts.

It is the richness of Wagnerian leitmotivs that attracts the hearer. For example, the horn call in the second act of *Siegfried* is changed in *Götterdämmerung* from 6/8 to 4/4 time, becoming the theme for the married and mature Siegfried*. Later, it undergoes textural and rhythmic modifications to form the basis of the great orchestral elegy after his death.

Allusive or untransformed leitmotivs were previously used by Mozart in *Così Fan Tutte* and by Weber* in *Der Freischütz*, with which Wagner was well acquainted. Liszt* and Berlioz* had both used transformational motives prior to Wagner. Rimsky-Korsakov, Debussy* and Richard Strauss* would develop the full use of leitmotivs after Wagner's death.

Lemnitz, Tiana Luise (b. 1897)

German lyric soprano who sang Sieglinde* during her years at the Berlin State Opera (1934–57) and Eva* at Covent Garden (1936), Elsa* and Sieglinde* (1938). She also gave lovely performances of the *Wesendonck Leider*.

Lenbach, Franz-Seraph von (1836–1904)

Fashionable German portrait painter who made a study of Cosima Wagner.*

Leubald und Adelaide

A five-act tragedy by the fourteen-year-old Wagner, written under the influence of William Shakespeare. Forty-two people died in the course of the drama; in order to produce speeches for the final act, the author had to bring back most of them as ghosts.

Levi, Hermann (1839–1900)

Despite his Jewish origins, Levi was one of Wagner's favourite conductors. To him Wagner entrusted the 1882 première of *Parsifal*. Levi was Director of the Munich Opera 1872–96.

Liebestod (T I)

Isolde's* triumphal vision in song at the end of *Tristan* in which she seems to see Tristan, who has just expired in her arms, resurrected and transformed, wafted on perfumed airs, which envelop her, and her alone of the company on stage, until she asks the final question: shall she surrender to their irresistible perfume and join her love in highest bliss?

Liebesverbot, Das (The Ban on Love)

Wagner's second completed opera, and his only opera in two acts; it has a subtitle, *Die Novize von Palermo* (*The Novice of Palermo*). Text based on Shakespeare's *Measure for Measure*. The first performance was given on 29 March 1836 at the Magdeburg theatre, where no further performances were given. Early in 1840 the work was accepted for performance at the Renaissance Theatre in Paris – which, however, went bankrupt and closed down before rehearsals could begin.

It is fascinating to speculate just what kind of work Wagner might have gone on to produce, had fortune smiled on *Das Liebesverbot*. Wagner craved popular and financial success. (His creditors craved the same on his behalf.) He had decided to throw in his lot with the Italian-French operatic tradition more completely than ever. His desire to marry Minna Planer [Wagner*] made it imperative to acquire cash and more career security. And it was to *Das Liebesverbot* that the young Wagner looked to bring this worldly reward. If a decent production had been mounted to public applause – who knows, Wagner might never have read another German saga but spent the next decade in Paris collaborating with Scribe* and comparing flourishes with Meyerbeer*. He almost certainly would not have become the bitter, damaged personality he did, always eager to see persecution where none existed until he generated it.

By the standards existing at the time, this is a well-crafted opera. The story has intrinsic merit, being taken from Shakespeare's *Measure for Measure*, and its Bacchanalian spirit should have appealed to sophisticated audiences. In the 1830s there was money to be made from transforming Renaissance morality plays into tracts for rebellion against authority. Wagner's was a contemporary liberalism: 'Our epicureanism', he wrote, 'is pure and strong.' But this moral radical is also fired by an underlying desire to justify his socially unconventional arrangements with Minna prior to their wedding. The affair was never a 'vulgar amour', he tells Apel* in a letter, but the world's tongues had jabbered: what better riposte than a musical melodrama which proved the world to be a resounding hypocrite? In these two senses, professional and personal, the rejection of *Das Liebesverbot* is a key event in Wagner's psychological development.

He began the libretto in May, 1834 (being much influenced by Johann Heinse's novel *Ardinghello* 1785) and completed the score early in 1836. In later years, he was to dismiss much of the music as 'horrible, execrable and disgusting'. Cosima Wagner* rather liked the overture 'in which the banning theme seemed to me very good – soulless, legal, harsh, dramatic'. Wagner agreed that it was well orchestrated, but '*That* I could do in my mother's womb – the overture is all thunder and lightning'. Deryck Cooke has pointed out that several of the motives from the *Ring* can be traced in juvenile form in *Das Liebesverbot*, particularly the titular 'ban on love theme' itself. Ernest Newman* believes the music 'almost invariably fails when it aims at expressing serious feeling; but the gay and humorous scenes are admirable, and the youthful gusto of the whole thing is irresistible. . . . Wagner has every trick of the trade at his fingertips, every recipe for froth and foam and sparkle'. Other critics note the use of the 'Dresdner Amen' in the Nuns' Chorus of Act I which Wagner cared for sufficiently to exploit again years later in *Tannhäuser*.

The tale is set in fifteenth-century Palermo. The King is absent and in his place a puritanical German Viceroy, Frederick*, holds temporary sway over the pleasure-loving Sicilians. The wild orgiastic opening shows Palermo at carnival time. Pleasure-booths outside a tavern are being attacked by the gentlemen of the Watch, under the command of Brighella*, and the populace are putting up opposition to this intrusion. The tavern-keeper and his servants, Dorella* and the curiously named Pontius Pilate, are arrested, but have no idea on what charge. Three young nobles, Lucio*, Angelo* and Antonio*, fight their way to the front of the mêlée. Dorella appeals to Lucio for help with the offer of a bribe: 'To marry me you once did vow – I'll set you free if you free me now!' Lucio replies – 'A stroke of luck!' It is clearly an ill wind that blows this fellow no good.

The 'liberally-minded' nobles demand to know on what orders Brighella is acting. He reads the Viceroy's Ban on Love:

In the name of the King we, Frederick, Viceroy of Sicily, being deeply distracted at the grievous growth of lustful living in this our godless and corrupt city of Palermo, are resolved to bring about a more pure and godly way of life, and to that intent, as well as to the hindrance of further abominations, to cut off and destroy with all severity the original root of these evils. We do therefore in virtue of our office hereby ordain that the feast of extravagance and vice called CARNIVAL be abolished and every custom thereof forbidden on pain of death; that all taverns and houses of pleasure be done away with and that every person who shall be taken in drunkenness or lechery be put to death!

One of the high spots of Act I has been reached, since the crowd greets this stern-minded, Cromwellian tract with manic hoots of derision, laughter, cries, cackles, shrieks and jeers. It is possible to perceive from the score that the youthful Wagner was enjoying his work, for the message of his *Liebesverbot* (if not of Shakespeare's)

is that unremitting Puritanism is only pure in its idiocy. Even more telling is the fact that the scorn is acutely directed at a *German* national characteristic: 'We'll laugh this German back to his snows – he'd best be gone to sober life and chastity.'

Matters turn more serious with the arrest of young Claudio* for having sex before marriage (shades of Wagner and Minna) with Julia*, contrary to the final paragraph of Frederick's decree. Although Claudio (and the rest) had no idea of the existence of the decree at the time of their merry-making, German retrospective justice is about to catch up with them. Claudio proclaims that only his sister Isabella*, at the Convent of St Elizabeth, can save him, which is a pious hope rather than a sober judgement, and the scene ends with the prisoners being led away, despite the protests and jostlings of the crowd.

The action now moves to the Convent of St Elizabeth, where, after the prayer of the Nun's Chorus, Isabella learns from one of the nuns, Mariana*, that the only reason Mariana has taken the vows is because her husband, recently promoted, had decided that she would be a hindrance for him in his work. 'It is the cause of every woman's grief – a man broke his word. That is why I have been here for three years!' Who is this husband who marries in secret, and then denies his own wife? Frederick, Viceroy of Sicily! Isabella waxes vengeful, but before she can show much mettle, Lucio enters to deliver Claudio's plea for help. Instantly, Isabella and Lucio are smitten with love for each other. The difference between them is that while Isabella conceals her passion until the finale, Lucio makes a clumsy declaration of lust, even in the convent, and is rebuffed. Dorella, who was previously betrothed to Lucio, is put out. Isabella resolves to aid Claudio by trying to see Frederick.

The scene changes to Frederick's reception room, where, in the unexplained absence of his master Brighella decides to try the prisoners in the light of the Love-Ban Law. He first sees the inn boy Pontius Pilate and, in trying to fit the punishment to the crime, considers the merits of crucifixion before deciding on banishment. The next prisoner is his undoing. In a foretaste of the scene yet to be played between Isabella and Frederick, Brighella finds that the seductive attractions of Dorella easily overpower the written word of law: he 'hotly lusts to use Dorella in that kind for which the law would whip her'. He articulates the comic dilemma, 'Love tempts me – duty calls', for many a line, before lust is temporarily abated by the chilling arrival of Frederick in full panoply.

The crowd petitions for the restoration of the Carnival, but Frederick merely snarls that he is appalled by their 'degraded souls given over to filthy vices'. The heroic populace, mouth-piece for the composer, cat-call in reply that he is full of 'devil-prompted pious unction'. When the double sentence on Claudio and Julia is confirmed, Isabella breaks in, begging for a private audience. This is granted, and Frederick is quickly swayed by her eloquent advocacy on behalf of amorous indulgence: 'The force of love,' she says, 'is in every heart – only fools or liars pour contempt on the treasure and pleasure of love.'

Frederick naturally responds, 'She speaks with passion and her breath is warm – I am a man – oh she has shaken me!' Isabella asks him redundantly (in view of the situation) if he has 'never felt the breath of passion?' Frederick concurs, and promises that her brother will be freed, provided she has sex with him, at a time to be appointed. Isabella, shaken rigid, calls back the crowd so that she can denounce this 'monster of hypocrisy', but he shrewdly suggests that they will never believe her, since his coldness is legendary. Act I closes with Isabella seeming to agree to his bargain, but secretly aiming to trap him, while aiding Mariana. The drama is well poised, with Frederick threatening lust, Isabella revenge.

The much shorter second Act begins with a scene between Isabella and Claudio, the former getting angry when Claudio is none too eager to die to save his sister's honour. Accordingly, she does not tell him straight away what she plans to do. The infatuated Lucio enters and hears with anger of Frederick's monstrous designs. Isabella sends a letter to Frederick telling him that, if he would claim his prize, he must come masked to the carnival – both actions being contrary to his own proclamation on 'lustful living'. Brighella puts Pontius Pilate in charge of the watch and he himself goes masked to the carnival, in pursuit of Dorella. Isabella, now also masked, goes to the carnival, together with Mariana, who is dressed identically with the heroine. Isabella intercepts Frederick's letter commanding the execution, not the promised reprieve, of Claudio. Incensed by this latest instance of treacherous double-dealing, Isabella summons the chorus, and then the grand hypocrites – Frederick and Brighella – are unmasked in all their villainy, with Frederick fondling Mariana.

To the end, Wagner maintains his impulsive, Italianate air of irreverence: when Frederick pronounces himself 'ready by my own law to perish' the crowd responds with a flat 'No – all your laws are here abolished – you are condemned to live!' The lovers pair off in procession: Isabella now declares for Lucio, Dorella for Brighella, and even Frederick makes incongruous peace with Mariana. Carnival ensues, and the rightful King returns.

Das Liebesverbot is impregnated with simple healthy desires. Sexual energy is the royal hero of the piece. ('The force of love is in every heart') and the true monarchs are the commons. Wagner will be taking a diametrically opposite line in *Tannhäuser*, which preaches redemption for the devilish sins of lust through a holy courtly love, even unto death. Musically, the later work will be incomparably superior; psychologically, its theme far more profound. But it is not given to all of us to make an ultimate sacrifice of self for the beloved; whereas the force of sensual love *is* in every heart. Wagner lost touch with this aspect of reality, partly because *Das Liebesverbot* did not succeed, and he continued to require the gratuitous deaths of heroines – indeed this is the central Wagnerian theme for several operas to come, until he resolved his insecurity in the *Ring*. At least in that work, the gods die for man: Siegmund* dies saving Sieglinde*, and Brünnhilde* has a genuine guilt to expiate (she is an accessory to murder) – unlike, for example, Elsa* in *Lohengrin*, who only wished to know whom she had married! Elsa's fate makes us look back at the more open world of *Das Liebesverbot* with some regret.

Liszt, Blandine (1835–62)
Cosima Wagner's* elder sister. She married the French politician, Emile Ollivier, but died a few years later when giving birth to a son.

Liszt, Daniel (1839–59)
Cosima Wagner's* only brother. The child of Liszt* and the Countess d'Agoult*, Daniel died in Hans von Bülow's* house in Berlin.

Liszt, Franz (1811–86)
Romantic composer, virtuoso pianist, promiscuous lover, masterly conductor, brilliant teacher, appalling parent, Catholic clergyman – these are just a few of the attributes of Liszt's genius. When Wagner finally married Liszt's daughter Cosima* in 1870, he gained a formidable father-in-law in addition to a formidable wife.

Liszt was born in Hungary. By the time he was nine, he was giving public concerts as a pianist. He studied under Czerny, who had been a pupil of Beethoven*. In 1824, he made a sensational début in Paris. The world was for many years thereafter literally at his feet. So were some of the loveliest women in Europe. Nevertheless, despite this worldly success, his serious commitment to composition, conducting and performance as a pianist was never in doubt. He invented the symphonic poem, in which he developed his concept of the metamorphosis of themes which was related to Wagner's idea of the leitmotiv*, and his influence helped to launch many composers on their careers, notably Brahms* and Grieg*.

Liszt had many love affairs, and the French Countess Marie d'Agoult was not the first or last to listen or succumb to his rhapsodies. Their affair, which lasted for a few years, yielded inspiration not only for his music and her novels but the person of Cosima Liszt, later Cosima von Bülow, and, ultimately, Cosima Wagner, Richard's second wife. She was born in 1837.

Liszt met Wagner eleven years later, when he had just taken up a post as Director of Court Music at Weimar. His new mistress was the Princess Sayn-Wittgenstein*, errant wife of the Prince. In 1849, after the failure of the uprising in Dresden, Liszt helped Wagner to escape from Germany and accommodated him in his house at Weimar. He also mounted the first performance of *Lohengrin* in 1850.

The two men corresponded a great deal, although Liszt was always alienated from Wagner by the latter's views on the Jews, which Liszt could see were silly and deranged. He was considerably more upset a few years later when his 'difficult' daughter Cosima left her respectable husband von Bülow to set up house with none other than Richard Wagner. Liszt strongly disapproved – which, considering his own record as a womanizer, was monstrous humbug. But the two great composers remained seriously estranged between 1868 and 1872. The period was prolonged for months after Wagner's marriage to Cosima in 1870 because, in 1869, Wagner had reissued his unpleasant pamphlet, *Judaism in Music*. Nevertheless, from 1872 the hatchet was buried and relations became far more friendly. Liszt was a frequent guest in Wagner's Bayreuth house 'Wahnfried'*, where a room was kept prepared for him. However, Liszt never really grew close to Cosima. She could not forgive him for neglecting her as a child nor for letting his other mistresses, such as the Princess Sayn-Wittgenstein, come between them. When Liszt died, it was in Bayreuth, close to Cosima. Yet Cosima did not bother to attend her father on his death-bed, since organizing the festival of her husband's works claimed the first loyalty on her time.

Litvinne, Félia Vasil'yevna (1860–1936)

Russian soprano who was the first Paris Isolde* in 1899 and Brünnhilde* in the first complete *Ring* in Paris in 1911. She sang at Covent Garden several times from 1899 to 1910.

Loge (R, but present throughout the *Ring*)

The firegod, also known in Scandinavian legend as Loki.

IN *Rheingold*

Loge is aloof yet omnipresent – by the very nature of his function he must be on call anywhere in the world, even in Nibelheim, land of dwarfs. In fact, wherever oxygen and sparks touch combustible material, there will the god of fire be found.

In Wagner's characterization, there are further reasons for Loge's sense of isolation. First, apart from Wotan*, the gods dislike him because he is sharp-tongued and deceitful. Accordingly, they never give him any of Freia's* rejuvenating apples to eat. This proves to be a blessing in disguise for Loge when the giants subsequently take Freia hostage. Whereas the other gods wilt and fade, having no food, Loge is unaffected. But at the opening of the opera, Loge is a social outcast in some danger of having his head knocked off by Donner*. Certainly, he is a spirit who must survive very much on his own resources.

Loge has been forcefully 'persuaded' into Wotan's service because of his ability to solve problems. In his travels, Loge sees and hears almost everything. This, allied to a sharp intelligence – his keen, ingenious flame – helps him become a subtle psychologist. Thus, when Wotan needs to resolve the dilemma of how to pay the giants for the building of his palace, Valhalla*, *without* parting permanently with Freia, it is from Loge that he expects the answer. He is not disappointed. Loge suggests that the giants might be interested in a great fortune of gold that the Nibelheim dwarf, Alberich*, is even now amassing through the power of the imperious Ring* of the Rhine. The giants agree. But perhaps Wotan is hasty in clutching at this solution because Loge does not suggest to the Lord of the Gods that he should win and permanently keep this Ring for himself, but merely steal it from Alberich before returning it to the Rhinemaidens.* Wotan wilfully misunderstands Loge's meaning, because his mind is blinded by dreams of power, but there is also an ambiguity in the word 'gold' as used in the drama. The 'gold' to be paid to the giants is the gold that Alberich has mined from the earth, using the power of the Ring. The 'gold' that must be returned to the Rhine is the magical metal of the Ring itself. And 'deceitful' Loge is the only god who always says he's in favour of returning this piece of property to its rightful owners!

After helping to trick Alberich into custody, relieving him of his riches, Loge is also the only god to show a measure of remorse towards the Rhinemaidens, still bewailing their loss in the depths of the river below. The other gods are happy to pay for their palace of Valhalla in stolen goods; Loge feels a little disgusted and wonders to himself whether he should not catch fire now and burn them all up.

IN *Die Walküre*

Loge does not sing again in the *Ring*, but he is invoked on a number of occasions. In Act II of *Die Walküre*, for example, we hear Wotan still blaming his predicament on the firegod's 'crafty counsel'. 'He lured me on,' complains Wotan, 'then left!' The truth, of course, is a great deal more complicated than that. Loge told him to give the Ring to the Rhinemaidens. Wotan said he would rather keep it for himself. Erda* 'forced' him to hand it over to the giants. Loge is not to blame for the result.

At the climax of Act III of *Die Walküre*, Wotan is still able to command Loge to encircle Brünnhilde's* rock with fire, even though the firegod escaped from Wotan's control shortly after the events described in *Das Rheingold*. It seems that he must obey when Wotan calls on him for specific purposes.

IN *Siegfried*

Loge is still present on Brünnhilde's rock but powerless to prevent Siegfried's* passage to the summit.

IN *Götterdämmerung*

The Norns* tells us that Wotan has again trapped Loge and is waiting to spear him to the heart when the time comes for the final burning of Valhalla.

Lohengrin

Three-act opera, text by the composer, based on a large number of mediaeval German poetic sources, chiefly Wolfram von Eschenbach's* *Parzifal* and the mediaeval German epic, *Lohengrin*. The opera was first produced at Weimar on 28 August 1850 under the direction of the composer's future father-in-law, Franz Liszt,* but Wagner did not see his work performed until May 1861, after his sentence of exile had been rescinded.

Wagner went to Marienbad in 1845 at the age of thirty-two, to take a cure. He describes in his autobiography how the idea for the prose draft of *Lohengrin* first came to him during the course of his treatments:

It was a marvellous summer, almost too hot, and I was therefore in high spirits. I had intended to follow the easy-going mode of life which is a necessary part of this somewhat trying treatment, and had selected my books with care, taking with me the poems of Wolfram von Eschenbach . . . as well as the anonymous epic *Lohengrin*. . . . With my book under my arm I hid myself in the neighbouring woods and, pitching my tent by the brook in company with Titurel* and Parsifal*, I lost myself in Wolfram's strange, yet irresistibly charming poem. Soon, however, a longing seized me to give expression to the inspiration generated by this poem, so that I had the greatest difficulty in overcoming my desire to give up the rest I had been prescribed while partaking of the water of Marienbad.

The result was an ever-increasing state of excitement. *Lohengrin* . . . stood suddenly revealed before me, complete in every detail of its dramatic construction. The legend of the swan, which forms such an important feature of all the many versions of this series of myths that my studies had brought to my notice, exercised a singular fascination over my imagination. Remembering the doctor's advice, I struggled bravely against the temptation of writing down my ideas . . . but no sooner had I got into my bath at noon than I felt an overpowering desire to write out *Lohengrin*, and this longing so overcame me that I could not wait the prescribed hour for the bath, but when a few minutes had elapsed, jumped out and, barely giving myself time to dress, ran home to write out what I had in mind. I repeated this for several days until the complete sketch of *Lohengrin* was on paper. The doctor told me that I had better give up taking the waters and baths, saying emphatically that I was quite unfit for such cures.

The music was written during the following three years, starting with the climax of Act III, the struggle between Elsa's* doubts and Lohengrin's* hopes that their marriage will succeed. This shows Wagner beginning to see the drama in psychological stages. The height of passion is more important to him now than the historical setting, so the height of passion is where his composition will begin (just as in the *Ring*, Wagner is first inspired by the pathos of Siegfried's* death, not the loss of the Rhinemaidens'* gold). The first performance of *Lohengrin* under Liszt made a considerable impact, but the opera was generally regarded as a failure until it began to be taken up by the small German opera theatres. Finally, says Charles Osborne, it was hailed as the 'apotheosis of the German romantic opera'. *Lohengrin*, he suggests, stands at the cross-roads:

Romantic in its almost pre-Raphaelite purity and static, two-dimensional characterization, it also anticipates the direction Wagner was to take in his next completed work, *Tristan und Isolde*, by its delicate balance, though not yet fusion, of music and drama. Already the music was being made subservient to the drama whenever Wagner felt a tension of interests. . . . By the time Germany applauded *Lohengrin*, its composer had left German romantic opera far behind.

In *Opera and Drama* (1851), which was finished soon after *Lohengrin*, Wagner repudiates choruses and traditional vocal ensembles as destructive of dramatic effect. The new 'singer' in his future conception of opera is to be the orchestra, which will carry forward the moods and events, as they are registered. In *The Flying Dutchman*, *Tannhäuser* and now *Lohengrin* Wagner had tried to implement his new theories but succeeded only in fits and starts. *Lohengrin* did not become a music drama because Wagner could not yet do without standard devices: the introduction to Act III and the Wedding Chorus, for example. He had not yet found out how to sustain a full opera without 'numbers'.

Thus, musically, *Lohengrin* is Wagner's major stepping-stone towards the further shore of nineteenth-century opera, away from the country of pastoral melodramas and one-dimensional political tragedies. It also represents, as Newman* remarks, rather more than the 'story of a virtuous first soprano, a noble tenor, a wicked second soprano and a baritone of good intentions but easily led astray by his wife'. The tale which follows is only to be understood in the light of history and psychology.

The action of *Lohengrin* opens near Antwerp on the banks of the River Scheldt. Henry the Fowler,* King of Germany, is recruiting among his Brabantine subjects for soldiers to fight against Hungary, since the nine-year truce with the latter is breaking down. Wagner emphasizes the east-west conflict in *Lohengrin*, a conflict between German consciousness ('Wherever is German soil raise troops, then none shall dare insult our German realm,' says Henry) and the threat of barbarism from the east. This was appreciated by nationalistically-inclined members of his audience from 1850 to 1945 and beyond.

Interfering with Henry's recruiting drive is a dispute over the succession to the Brabantine ducal throne. Count Frederick von Telramund* is claiming the title, since the late Duke's daughter, Elsa, has, he believes, murdered the only other rightful heir, the boy Godfrey*. When Ortrud* (who has since become Telramund's wife) told him she saw Elsa commit this fratricide, he naturally broke off his engagement to Elsa, married Ortrud and accused Elsa of her brother's murder.

Elsa has refused to answer the charge. She seems 'empty-headed and lost in dreams,' says Telramund. Morever, he is especially glad to have terminated their engagement, since she has given him cause to think she has another paramour. The King decrees that a trial of Elsa and of Telramund's claims to the throne shall be instantly convened – as well as Elsa's examination on the charge of murder.

When asked what answer she can offer her accusers, Elsa becomes Cordelia – at first she can only mouth the word 'Nothing!' Then she recounts a dream: 'Arrayed in shining armour a knight approaches more virtuous and pure than any yet seen . . . sent to me from heaven . . . that knight will defend me and be my champion!' Frederick stands impassive: 'Here is my sword! Which of you will venture to contest the price of my honour?' We are obviously going to see a trial by combat.

But first, Elsa's champion must appear. When the Herald* trumpets the last call to arms, and Elsa promises that any successful defending knight will acquire both the dukedom and her hand in marriage, a wondrous sight staggers the eyes: 'A swan is drawing a boat here,' murmurs the crowd, 'A knight is standing upright in it . . . the swan draws him by a golden chain. . . . A miracle. . . .' Telramund's wife Ortrud is meanwhile visibly struck with dread by the miraculous approach of the dazzling, armoured visitor.

Lohengrin (for it is he) announces that he is sent to 'stand champion for a maid calumnied by a grievous charge!' Can Telramund, then, be lying? Elsa exults in time-honoured fashion: 'My hero, my rescuer, take me! I give myself wholly to you. . . .' Lohengrin proposes marriage as soon as he shall have disposed of Telramund; he is accepted, but then commands his new fiancée 'never to ask me or be at pains to discover from whence I journeyed here nor what is my name and lineage!' (We are back at the court of Queen Ada* in *Die Feen*, when she required the same promise of her beloved Arindal.*) Elsa swears, 'My lord, never shall this question come from me!'

So far so good. Lohengrin declares he now loves Elsa. Telramund and Lohengrin engage in single combat and after a furious battle Telramund is defeated and dishonoured. Lohengrin declines to take his life, even though it is forfeit. The new Protector of Brabant (he refuses to become a worldly Duke) is carried shield-high into the citadel of Antwerp, there to be feasted and praised.

Act II opens in Antwerp castle and descends at once to a very human, very modern exposition of greed, envy, jealousy and revenge. We are confronted by a seething Ortrud and a shell-shocked Telramund. In disgust, Telramund repudiates the 'companion of his shame. . . . Did you not lie to me . . . that you saw the crime committed, how Elsa herself drowned her brother in the pool? And did you not seduce my proud heart with your prediction . . . that our . . . ancient royal race would soon flourish again and rule in Brabant?' Ortrud retorts that he is a coward: 'Ah if you knew how to oppose him (who now brings us this misery) you would find him weaker than a child!' Swiftly, Ortrud gets Telramund to believe that, contrary to the noble rules of chivalry, Lohengrin only defeated him in battle by using magic spells. Not only that, but Lohengrin can therefore be defeated by the same tokens that gave him his strength in the first place: 'If he loses but a tiny part of his body, he will be revealed in all his weakness!' she promises. And still further: 'Were he forced to disclose his name and race, all his power, which a spell alone lends him, would be at an end!' Ortrud can only know these things because she has studied the 'secret arts', and thus reveals herself to be a witch. She also reveals that the secret of Lohengrin's defeat may lie with Elsa, since Lohengrin is bound to reveal his identity to Elsa – and Elsa alone – if she should ask. With all this in mind, the Telramunds defy the sentence of banishment imposed on them by King Henry and plot to overthrow Lohengrin by force as well as by guile, exploiting any disaffected Brabantines and, if possible, Elsa herself to accomplish their end.

First Ortrud insinuates herself back into Elsa's favour by displaying her wretched condition, professing contrition and exciting true pity. That accomplished, she releases the worm of suspicion into Elsa's soul: 'Have you never reflected that he of such mysterious lineage might leave you in the same way as by magic he came to you?'

Frederick meanwhile is gaining support among the nobility, who resent Lohengrin's decree (in his capacity as new Lord of Brabant) that all the Brabantines who can bear arms will help King Henry fight the Hungarians in the east.

Then, when Elsa appears gorgeously arrayed for her marriage to Lohengrin, Ortrud steps forth, stops the festal procession and challenges her to name her husband-to-be. Elsa perceives that Ortrud is not at all sorry for her former plotting, but can only shout 'slanderer!' by way of a somewhat feeble reply. She is well aware that her own doubts about the durability of Lohengrin's fidelity are growing.

The King and Lohengrin press forward to hear what the commotion is about. Frederick adds to the confusion by unmasking himself and angrily calling Lohengrin a cheating sorcerer: 'Loudly, before the whole world, I ask his name, rank and lineage!' Lohengrin refuses to answer, adding that, were the request to come from Henry himself, he would deny it: 'There is only one to whom I am bound to reply: Elsa . . .' and she, of course, has sworn never to ask the question. Frederick gets close enough to Elsa to feed her doubts further: 'Trust in me, let me tell you a way of obtaining certainty [about the identity of your betrothed] . . . Let me but wound the smallest part of him, a finger tip, and I swear . . . he will be faithful and never leave you!' (Shades of Hagen* playing on Brünnhilde's* desires for greater fidelity from Siegfried* in *Götterdämmerung*.) Elsa refuses, or so it seems, and rejoins Lohengrin. The latter, instead of having Telramund and Ortrud arrested and instantly executed, as common sense and the law would prescribe, merely tells them to leave, thus guaranteeing a store of trouble to follow in Act III.

Now we approach the climax of the opera and the music which interested Wagner most. It is the brilliant bridal chamber scene wherein Elsa's doubts about Lohengrin will destroy all hope of a lasting union between them. Elsa notices how sweetly her name glances from his lips, whereas she is for ever forbidden to utter his. Lohengrin has truly saved her life, but what can she do in return? 'O could I know you too in need! Would that I knew a danger threatening you so that I might courageously share your cares!' We move swiftly towards the inevitable and awful question: 'Let your secret be revealed to me, that I may fully know who you are!' And again a little later: 'Tell me without demur from whence you came – let me prove my power of silence' – all her 'female' wiles are employed to learn the truth. Finally, in the grip of dreadful fantasies (that Lohengrin will be taken from her by the same mystic swan that brought him hither), Elsa spells it out in words of one syllable: 'Tell me your name!' and tell it he must.

Before Lohengrin can impress upon Elsa the gravity of her action, Frederick von Telramund and four disaffected nobles burst in to see if assassination can succeed more swiftly than Ortrud's psychological manipulation of Elsa's inner doubts and fears. Lohengrin slays Telramund with a single blow. And so the scene ends with Lohengrin agreeing to give Elsa her answer, but only before the King's judgement seat.

Thus, in the next scene an extremely perturbed Henry the Fowler is told that Lohengrin will no longer lead the Brabantines to war, but is abdicating from his position altogether. His reason is that 'the wife whom God gave to me let herself be misled into betraying me'.

Lohengrin explains the facts restricting his freedom of action: how he is the grail-servant and son of Parsifal* sent from the castle of Montsalvat* by holy orders to champion Elsa for the cause of virtue. However, only if he 'remains abroad unknown can he keep his holy power – now alas I must be parted from you!' Before taking his leave, Lohengrin prophesies that Henry will enjoy a great 'German' victory over the Magyars. When the swan arrives to bear him back to Montsalvat, Lohengrin recalls with deep regret that the swan, who is really Elsa's enchanted brother Godfrey, has not been freed from the curse which trapped him – as would have happened had Elsa not asked Lohengrin his name.

Ortrud stands forth to boast that it was she who put the spell on Godfrey in order to try and gain the throne of Brabant. Lohengrin has an inspiration and sinks down in prayer. At once, the white dove of the Grail* flies in, hovers over the swan and transforms him back into – Godfrey. The power of Christian prayer conquers all. Ortrud is thus vanquished, Godfrey will become the new Duke of Brabant, and Elsa feels overjoyed to see her relative restored. But she is heart-broken by Lohengrin's departure, and, thus torn between delight and despair, she expires.

What does *Lohengrin* really mean? It is based on a miscellany of legends (Lohengrin and the Swan, the 'Jungere Titurel', 'Le Chevalier au Cygne', Zeus and Semele – possibly Orpheus and Eurydice as well), but these are less important in themselves than for what they represent. Why do such myths grow? Why do they have such power to stir us? Why does a composer like Wagner experience an 'ever-increasing sense of excitement' when confronted by them?

One answer is that they allow us to project our inner fears by supplying appropriate symbols. If an artist can manipulate these symbols in obedience to his will, he may then satisfy an internal longing of his own. If a sufficient number of his fellow-creatures also enjoy his creation, then his satisfaction increases and something of his personal condition is shown to be endemic in us all. In the same way, when large numbers of children identify with fairy-tales it proves the universal validity of their spectres of good and evil. There is a bogeyman, if we enjoy reading about him – but he is part of us, and not part of objective reality. The same applies to the gods, the Nibelungs, the Grail servants, noble, holy Lohengrin and passive, earthly Elsa: they acquire existence when human beings recognize their truth and grant them meaning.

Wagner was more drawn to mythologizing his inner world than most because he was a neurotic man who subconsciously doubted that he could ever be loved. Any profession of faith by a woman seemed to him to threaten, more than promise, happiness. Imagine, then, the artist's intoxicated attraction towards a symbolic heroine who agrees to love absolutely a man whom she cannot even identify by name. Wagner sees Elsa as a type of earthly Grail. She is the female who offers a man everything in return for nothing except the champion's act of defending her *own* good name. We share the artist's excitement since we, too, have not escaped all psychological damage and similarly yearn for a love that requires no guarantees, payment neither in coin nor in kind.

Writing his operas was obviously cathartic for Wagner, just as hearing them is catharsis for us. But we can widen the terms of his favourite subject-matter to suggest what his notion of triumphant spiritual love can include: any sense of religion, human solidarity, art, or higher consciousness – even the collective unconscious if we feel Jungian, or will-lessness, if we follow Schopenhauer. And we can narrow the notion of temporal passion over which he elevates spiritual love to mean only the ugly desire of an Alberich* to rape away the psychic pain of his own self-loathing. This would leave uninfected both the healthy sexuality of ordinary folk and what might be termed royal lust. When we look at the operas in this wider framework, we can begin to appreciate the vast scale on which Wagner attempts to exploit his themes, and offer him our applause. The great pity is that too many warm-blooded men and women have rejected *Lohengrin* (and *Parsifal*) simply because they think Wagner is yet another tedious evangelical offering frigid clichés of no value in helping them to conduct their modern, post-Freudian lives.

In *A Communication To My Friends* (1851), Wagner tries to elaborate the psychological dynamics of *Lohengrin*: 'Elsa,' he says, 'is the unconscious, the un-volitional, for which Lohengrin's conscious, volitional being yearns. . . .' Charles Osborne says there is a much simpler way of understanding this opera: 'Lohengrin . . . represents Wagner, the misunderstood genius. The tension . . . is also that which existed between Wagner the artist and his audience.' In other words, Wagner descends to earth like Lohengrin, to daze our eyes with beauty. For the last word I quote Osborne:

The libretto of *Lohengrin* is not simply a peg for the music to hang upon. Despite the fact that its philosophical meaning is open to question, it works magnificently in purely dramatic terms. Upon two-dimensional mediaeval fear of the unknown world, Wagner has superimposed a drama which is modern in its psychology and unerring in its poetic instinct. Thus he retains the best of not two worlds but three, the spiritual, the psychological and the aesthetic. It is the inter-penetration of these worlds upon one another, in Wagner's music and words, which makes *Lohengrin* a great opera.

Lohengrin (L)

The tenor knight of the swan, drawn from a plethora of mediaeval legends and the epics of Wolfram von Eschenbach,* whom Wagner transforms into a psychic symbol of the artist-hero – and, some would say, even of himself.

Lohengrin is the son of Parsifal* and a knight of the Holy Grail.* When he arrives, swan-borne, from Holy Montsalvat* (the castle of the Grail) the crowd is dazzled by his sparkling display: 'What sweet blissful awe seizes us! What gracious power holds us in thrall! How handsome and noble of aspect he is!' This is echoed by the rest of the nobles at King Henry's* court, and even by the King himself. Elsa* above all is swept off her feet by the appearance of this gallant champion. Instantly she offers him her lands, life and love. Almost as instantly, Lohengrin falls in love with her; this is later explained as god's will. He only enjoins her never to ask who he is or where he comes from.

Obviously, in human terms this is completely unrealistic, but we are not dealing in purely human terms. Perhaps Lohengrin should have realized (even in supernatural terms) that he was in no position to offer Elsa matrimony, since a higher duty would always call him and a man may not serve two such outstanding mistresses as Elsa *and* the Grail. However, Lohengrin is positively intended to represent the dual nature of man struggling between exalted and base loves. For a while in the bridal scene, Lohengrin even sounds like an eager Tannhäuser* in the Venusberg* (or Frederick* bewitched by Isabella* in *Das Liebesverbot*): 'Oh grant me the rapture of breathing your breath; let me press you ever closer to me, that in you I may find my happiness!' However, this mood gives way in Act III to the higher love he bears for the Mystery of the Divine Chalice.

Lohengrin is a courtly and noble knight in every respect, one worthy to have sat at any King's round table. He grants Telramund* mercy after the trial by combat in Act I. He sticks to his letters patent by denying even King Henry himself the right to question him about his origins. He is un-Machiavellian enough not to eliminate Telramund and Ortrud* once and for all after their public denunciation of him as a sorcerer, during the scene of the processional.

But he is also too unworldly to succeed as an earthly husband. It is folly to tell Elsa she may not know where he has come from and then to add that he was deliriously happy there anyway. Of course, she might begin to suspect that one day he will break his oath and return thither since it cannot be too painful to re-enter paradise.

Loki

Scandinavian form of the name of the fire-god Loge*.

London, George (b. 1920)
American bass-baritone who was the 1951 Bayreuth Amfortas* and the 1962 Cologne Wotan* both under the direction of Wieland Wagner*. London was involved in the staging of the *Ring* in Seattle in 1965 in a setting described as 'story-book realism'.

Longinus (d. AD 58)
Roman soldier who, according to tradition, thrust his spear into the side of the crucified Christ. The blood from the wound was caught in a cup later called the Holy Grail*. Longinus' spear is the 'Holy Shaft' given to Titurel* by a miracle; it subsequently passed through the hands of Amfortas*, Klingsor* and Parsifal*.

Lora (F)
Sister to Arindal*, King of Tramond, Lora is a doughty warrior-woman in love with Morald*, her brother's best friend. She defends the 'last fortress' in the kingdom when all seems lost to the ravaging attacks of the neighbouring King Murold. There is a strong element of 'Walküre spirit' about Lora, since she refuses to listen to counsels of despair and goes on trying to save the future.

Lorenz, Max (1901–75)
German tenor who for nearly three decades was a prominent Wagnerian in the roles of Tristan,* Walther* and Siegfried*. He appeared at Bayreuth from 1933–39 and again in 1952. An intensely dramatic interpreter.

Lortzing, Gustav Albert (1801–51)
German light operatic composer to whom Wagner was more indebted than he would ever admit. Lortzing composed *Hans Sachs* (1840), which Wagner characteristically belittled (almost always a confession of indebtedness) and *Undine* (1845), in whose finale a palace crashes into a rising river (a premonition of *Götterdämmerung*).

Love, redemption through
Wagner's transcendental operatic belief. A man (usually) can be saved if he finds a woman willing to love him, by negating herself even to the point of death. A man can also acquire power by denying love's claims, as is the case with Alberich* in the *Ring*, but only by inflicting on his spirit a deathly sense of grief. In *Das Rheingold*, Loge* reports that in the earliest days of the world, Alberich alone was prepared to renounce love for power: all other beings esteemed 'woman's love and beauty of greatest worth'. This seems to suggest a pre-historical Wagnerian vision of a golden age when love, not gainful greed, governed men's actions. The last act of *Götterdämmerung* shows Brünnhilde* attempting to restore this noble philosophy to the world by committing suttee on Siegfried's* funeral pyre, thus redeeming her own previous unfaithfulness. She thus becomes the penultimate Wagnerian heroine (with Kundry* yet to come) who chooses death as her means of redeeming the world's woes. *See* 'Schopenhauer, Arthur'; 'Sex'.

Lubin, Germaine Léontine Angélique (1890–1979)
French soprano who sang Sieglinde,* Kundry* and Isolde* in Paris before giving the two last-named roles at Covent Garden and Bayreuth 1938–9. She was a pro-Nazi friend of the Wagner family and welcomed the arrival of the Wehrmacht at the time of the fall of Paris. This and subsequent acts of 'fraternization' earned her a three-year prison sentence (1944–7) for collaboration.

Lucio (Lt)

Sicilian noble (tenor) formerly engaged to Isabella's* maid Dorella:* 'He hath pestered every maid in Rome with promises of love.' However, he does fall in love for good with Isabella and his character improves throughout the opera. For example, at the beginning of Act I he wriggles out of his commitment to Dorella by suggesting that he will release her from the clutches of the Watch – which he does not do. Then, when he meets Isabella, he makes a rather crude pass at her. Thereafter, however, he manages to control his behaviour. At the end, he shows true valour in championing Isabella's cause both against Frederick* and her own brother's weakness: 'I'll go tell him he must die at once that you may be saved!' Isabella becomes his by the final curtain.

Ludwig, Christa (b. 1928)

German mezzo-soprano who includes the roles of Brangäne,* Fricka,* Waltraute* and Ortrud* in her repertoire. She has recorded Venus* and Kundry*.

Ludwig II, King of Bavaria (1845–86)

Perhaps only such a Gothic earthly lord as Ludwig could really enjoy Wagner on his own terms. Fairy grottos were Ludwig's domestic furniture; Valhalla* just another palace on the list. Wagner suffered in life from enormous delusions of grandeur. For King Ludwig, delusions of grandeur were a feasible way of life.

Little did Wagner know, when he published his poem of the *Ring* in 1863, that a copy would find its way into the hands of the young Bavarian Crown prince. How clever of him, then, to have described in the preface a dream of turning the *Ring* into a mighty opera cycle and to have asked if any royal patron might like to step forward and finance it: 'Will this Prince ever be found?', he wrote, more in hope than in faith. But the words acted like electricity on the young Ludwig's soul.

Yes, he *would* be that Prince if he ever got the chance. Nothing would please him better than to dedicate his kingdom to the production of the noblest Romantic operatic art. He had already listened in rapture to *Lohengrin*, whose swan motif was a part of his personal armorial pedigree. And to one of his dreamy reclusive temperament, the works of Wagner sounded like a statement of innate sympathy and understanding.

In 1864, Ludwig ascended his ancestral throne. At once he sent word to Wagner to join him in his philosophic kingdom (he was only eighteen). At first, Wagner could not believe his luck. Being on the run from his creditors, he actually refused to see the royal messenger, fearing that he was the police. His spirit was at its lowest ebb. His marriage was on the rocks. He could no longer find the will to put pen to paper. Now, out of the blue, came this sudden summons from a monarch to a pauper minstrel to share both palace and unlimited purse. Things like this, Wagner might justly have reflected, can only happen in operas. The point is crowned by one witty critic who says that Wagner's greatest achievement was to make life conform to the demands of art. When only the arrival of a fairy prince with a blank cheque book could have saved him, Wagner 'invented' King Ludwig.

Wagner duly journeyed to Munich. His debts were cleared for the first time in twenty years and he was free to work. As a result, he in due course managed to finish *Die Meistersinger* and compose the *Ring* and *Parsifal*, as well as to build the Bayreuth Festival Theatre. Without Ludwig's assistance, none of these achievements would ever have been possible.

In June 1865 von Bulow* conducted the first performances of *Tristan und Isolde* at Munich. Events now turned against Wagner. For his extravagance, and the scandal of his affair with von Bulow's wife, Cosima [Wagner*] were used against him by the King's cabinet, who realized that

Wagner (whose arrival in Munich they had not originally opposed) would not be useful to them in negotiations with the king to further their political ends. As a result, the king felt obliged to ask the composer to leave the country for a few months.

Ludwig continued to support the exiled composer for the rest of his days, but his personal bond was now broken. In later years, the king continued to worship the Master from afar, and his government helped pay off the huge debt incurred by the first Bayreuth festival in 1876. But these were only indirect contacts. It was some comfort to Ludwig to be able to enjoy the specially commissioned performance of *Rheingold* in Munich in 1869, given contrary to Wagner's wishes. And Ludwig must be the only man in history for whom a private performance of *Parsifal* has ever been given, an event which he enjoyed in solitary splendour in 1884. Yet the monarch mourned the absence of the Master.

In later life, Ludwig's behaviour became that of a lost soul in torment. He could not bear company, which was one reason why he wanted *Parsifal* to be given in private. He was racked with guilt by his sexual preference for boys. He was bored to death with state business. He inwardly yearned to create an edifice to protect himself from worldly cares and intrusions, one which might even reach up to the heavens and touch God. Since he could not do this in musical art, he would choose to build a fantasy palace. In this residence, he could turn himself into a luxurious hermit, surrounded by pinnacles of unfulfilled desire. His palace of Neuschwanstein, decorated with scenes from Wagner's operas, is the culmination of this melancholic craving. Alas, the Bavarian burghers were unimpressed. On 10 June 1886, Ludwig was declared insane by a specially convened tribunal and forced to abdicate. Nobody knows how he died, but three days later, his body was found floating face down in a lake, and it is

supposed that he took the Romantic Roman way out: suicide in that brief moment of clarity between fits of depression.

Lüttichau, August, Baron von (1786–1863)
Director of the Dresden Opera during Wagner's time there in the 1840s.

Lytton, Edward George Earle Lytton-Bulwer, 1st Baron (1803–73)
English writer and politician whose romantic and historical novels entertained Wagner greatly. He adapted Lytton's *Rienzi* (1835) for his own operatic purposes (1837–40), eliminating the character of Walter de Montreal, the unscrupulous but heroic *condottiere*, as well as Rienzi's ambitious wife Nina. Wagner also discussed Lytton's *Eugene Aram* (1832), which was based on an actual murder, with his family and friends in 1878 (see Cosima Wagner's *Diary*).

McIntyre, Donald Conroy (b. 1934)
New Zealand-born bass-baritone and the first British singer to be invited to give Wotan* in a complete cycle of the *Ring* at Bayreuth (1973). His voice is a powerful *heldenbaritone*, heard again in the role of Wotan at Covent Garden on many occasions.

Magdalena (M)
Nurse (soprano) for Eva*, who serves her mistress in neo-Mozartian fashion, impersonating her as desired, and who also turns off her own lover's food supply whenever he fails to carry out commissions satisfactorily. The love between David* and Magdalena parallels that between Walther von Stolzing* and Eva.

Magnan, Bernard Pierre (1791–1865)
French officer who admired Wagner's operas and helped obtain the Emperor's support for the 1861 Paris performance of *Tannhäuser*.

Mahler, Gustav (1860–1911)

Austrian composer and conductor, whose principal works are nine symphonies and the orchestral song cycle *Das Lied von der Erde*. As chief conductor at the Vienna Imperial Opera (1897–1907) he established himself as an outstanding interpreter of Wagner, of whose music he had always had a profoundly sympathetic understanding.

Maier, Mathilde (1833–1910)

Wagner's mistress in 1862, described as a well-bred, serious girl, whom he would have married if he could. His wife Minna (Wagner*) was so disparaging of this relationship that Wagner actually became angry and asked for a divorce. Minna refused. Yet Mathilde declined to marry her composer-lover in any case, because she suffered from a hereditary deafness which she felt made it impossible for her to marry a musician.

Mallarmé, Stéphane (1842–98)

French Symbolist poet, celebrated for 'L'Après-midi d'un faune', later set to music by Debussy, who was converted into an enthusiastic Wagnerite by the novelist and critic, Édouard Dujardin*.

Mallarmé venerated what he called the 'religious spirit' of Wagnerian opera. He praised the composer for 'rehabilitating theatre's sacred function' and for 'cleansing it with the great musical water of the Temple'. But Mallarmé principally responded because, in his early aesthetic writings, Wagner seemed to be saying that poetry was the most important of the arts. Thus Wagner's youthful championship of the *Gesamtkunstwerk*, of the unity of all arts, excited the French Symbolist, not the Wagner who later came to agree with Schopenhauer that the music must predominate.

In *Richard Wagner, A French Poet's Reverie* (1885), Mallarmé defines Wagner's genius as a 'fusion of Music with Drama' until a state of poetic reverie, 'richer than any air on earth', entrances the listener. The 'authentic dramatist', he concedes, 'must obtain the assistance of the other arts to stir up the otherwise inert and nonexistent miracle of the stage . . . [but] . . . only poetry is really capable . . . of performing this miracle itself'. In a private letter to René Ghil, Mallarmé stated this even more plainly: 'the duty of poetry is to take everything back from music . . .'

Aesthetic theory, however, did not prevent Mallarmé from producing that beautiful but difficult poem, 'Hommage à Wagner', in 1886. In this, the poet describes the composer as a 'pillar' of art whose death three years before has somehow added to the sacred mythifications of his music.

Malten, Therese (1855–1930)

German soprano. Wagner heard Malten sing Senta* at Dresden in 1881 and invited her to sing Kundry* at Bayreuth in the first season of *Parsifal* the following year. She sang Kundry in King Ludwig's* private performance of *Parsifal* in 1884, and in the same year gave Kundry, Isolde* and Brünnhilde* at Dresden. At Bayreuth again she sang Isolde, Eva* (1888) and Kundry (1894).

Mancinelli, Luigi (1848–1921)

Italian conductor and composer. He gave the 1889 London Covent Garden *Meistersinger*, having visited Bayreuth the previous year to hear the performance there. He conducted much Wagner in London and New York, but after 1900 (when it became customary to sing Wagner in German, and engage Germans to conduct it) Mancinelli was excluded from the German repertoire. Bernard Shaw* noted that Mancinelli's Italian tempi conflicted with Wagner's German mood and spirit, but Weingartner* insisted it was possible to give an Italianate rendering of the operas, idiosyncratic as this opinion may seem today.

Mann, Thomas (1875–1955)

Outstanding modern German novelist, whose *The Magic Mountain* (1924) is consciously constructed on the principles of Wagnerian leitmotiv* technique. Writing to the Austrian Social Democrat, Ernst Fischer, in 1926, Thomas Mann simply declared: 'Wagner was my strongest and most formative artistic experience.' This is as evident in his writing on *Tristan* (1903) as in his novel *Buddenbrooks* (1901). Since Mann was Germany's leading progressive, but also Romantic, novelist, he was both repelled and attracted by the total Wagnerian output – being repelled above all by the philosophy. In 1942, he sent this explanation to Agnes Meyer of the *Washington Post*: 'My way of talking about Wagner has nothing to do with chronology or development. It is and remains "ambivalent", and I am capable of writing about him one way today, another tomorrow.' Mann first wrote about Wagner in his *Sufferings and Greatness of Richard Wagner* in 1933; Wagner's fiftieth but Hitler's first anniversary. Mann apologizes for Wagner's reactionary traits; he stresses his fundamental nature, 'conditioned through and through by renewal, change and liberation'. By 1937, four years of Hitlerism and Mann's own enforced exile from Germany have tempered the message, although he still stresses Wagner's 'real prophecy that not goods, nor gold, nor lordly pomp, nor sad compacts of lying bonds' will ever satisfy man's inner hunger. After the war, influenced by the German critic Theodor Adorno*, Mann wrote of a 'poison' in Wagner which can only be neutralized by awareness of the 'will-to-power' in all of us.

Mannerlist grosser also Frauenlist, oder die Gluckliche Barenfamilie (Women's Wiles Outsmarted, or The Happy Bear Family)

One of Wagner's abandoned operatic projects, dating from 1837.

Mariana (Lt)

Viceroy Frederick's* milk-and-water wife, who departs to a nunnery as soon as her husband, promoted to regal status, considers her superfluous to his requirements.

It is only with a great deal of prodding that she is induced to practise a deception on her mighty master to re-trap him into matrimony – and all this after she has allowed him to marry her in secret and then go on pretending to be a bachelor. No Brünnhilde* here.

Marke, King of Cornwall (T I)

A king possessed of all the graces except perspicacity. He loves Tristan* paternally, and has even made arrangements for the young knight to succeed him, but his eyes are blind and his trust doting and total. He cannot see what is under his nose, something that the baser Melot* appreciates as soon as the ship bringing Isolde* from Ireland docks at his port: that Tristan and Marke's beloved Isolde love each other.

When the scales fall from his eyes, even his act of forgiveness arrives too late to help Tristan and Isolde in this life. His personal tragedy is to possess a perfect quality: an unimpaired and extreme trust (such as Lohengrin* wished from Elsa*); on earth the possession of such a quality must lead to disillusion.

Marker (M)

That member of the guild of Mastersingers elected by his brethren to enter the *Gemerk* and penalize prize songs for technical errors. Originally, the Marker in *Die Meistersinger* was not going to be called

Beckmesser* but 'Hanslich', after Eduard Hanslick,* the music critic whom Wagner most detested.

Marschner, Heinrich August (1795–1861)

Presided for almost three decades as conductor at the Court Theatre in Hanover. Marschner composed the Romantic opera *Hans Heiling*, as well as *The Vampire* and *The Templar and the Jewess*. As conductor at the Court Theatre, Marschner flatly refused to have anything to do with Wagner or his works. In bitter terms (only echoed by Wagner himself in his less pleasant correspondence about composers like Meyerbeer) Marschner wrote of the 'Mendelssohn,* Schumann,* Wagner clique' which he claimed was attempting to annihilate him through indifference. Wagner, for his part, praised Marschner's music for its individuality and melodic sensitivity and it is beyond doubt that he was considerably influenced by *Hans Heiling* (1831–2) which stands stylistically between Weber's* *Der Freischütz* and Wagner's own *Der Fliegende Holländer*.

Marx, Karl Heinrich (1818–83)

Marx had little time for his musical contemporary, whom he dismissed as 'The Government band-leader'. He complains indignantly that he could not find lodgings in Weiden in 1876 because of the tides of Wagner fans flowing to the first Wagner Festival at Bayreuth. (Marx had to sleep on a bench at the railway station.) 'Everywhere you are pestered,' he wrote to his daughter Jenny, 'with the question: What do you think of Wagner?' In framing his own answer, the totally unmusical Marx found it hard to separate political from moral analysis:

He is the very characteristic of the Neo-German, Prussian Reich's musician: he and his spouse (the one who is separated from Bülow*) the cuckold Bülow and their common father-in-law Liszt* are living together, all four, in perfect harmony; they embrace kiss and adore

one another and thoroughly enjoy themselves. If, apart from that, you keep in mind that Liszt is a mad Roman monk and Mme [Cosima] Wagner* . . . is the 'natural' daughter of Mme d'Agoult* (Daniel Stern), then you could not imagine a better libretto for Offenbach than this family group with its patriarchal relations.

Ironically, the two men had far more in common than either could have suspected. They had shared the barricades of 1848–9 (Marx in Paris, Wagner in Dresden); had shared the friendship of Mikhail Bakunin;* shared an acute love for the plays of Shakespeare,* family life and unremitting intellectual toil, and it might be fair (if cynical) to suggest that only differences of income and geography kept them from establishing a closer rapport, especially in their younger days.

Mary (H)

Senta's* nurse and one who leads her astray by constantly harping on the story of the mysterious Flying Dutchman,* whose portrait adorns the walls of Daland's* house.

Materna, Amalie (1844–1918)

Austrian soprano who sang Brünnhilde* in the first complete performance of the *Ring* at Bayreuth (1876) and sang Kundry* in the first performance of *Parsifal* (Bayreuth, 1882).

Matzenauer, Margarete (1881–1963)

Austro-Hungarian soprano and contralto who sang at Bayreuth in 1911 and was the 1914 Covent Garden Kundry.* Later she gave Brünnhilde* and Erda,* which indicates her extraordinary vocal compass.

Mayr, Richard (1877–1935)

Austrian bass whom Mahler encouraged to take up music after an early career in medicine. He was the Bayreuth Hagen* in 1902 and later specialized as Pogner* and

Gurnemanz.* He was, however, most famous as a legendary exponent of Baron Ochs in Richard Strauss's *Der Rosenkavalier*.

Measure for Measure

Comedy by William Shakespeare (probably written 1603–4). The plot is taken from Cinthio, and thereafter Wagner borrowed it from Shakespeare* for his early opera *Das Liebesverbot*. In Shakespeare's version, the Viceroy is called Angelo, not Frederick*, and he is Italian, not German, also, the Duke, Vincentio, plays a crucial part in saving Claudio from death, whereas in the opera the sole agency for grace and salvation is Claudio's* sister, Isabella.*

Mehta, Zubin (b. 1936)

Indian conductor, whose early success led to appointments as principal conductor of the Montreal Symphony Orchestra (1960–67) and musical director of the Los Angeles Symphony Orchestra (from 1962). He has also been much associated with the Israeli Philharmonic Orchestra. Mehta broke the unofficial Israeli ban on performances of work by Wagner when he conducted the prelude to *Tristan* at a Tel Aviv concert on 15 October 1981. Many in his audience booed and hissed. Four days later, a repeat performance was stopped after demonstrations in the concert hall. Mehta justified his action in the following words:

There are over 60,000 Volkswagens in Israel, 80 per cent of Israeli taxis are manufactured by Mercedes-Benz and one in two Israeli homes is equipped with a West German-made TV set. I have the support of 113 out of the 115 members of the orchestra as well as thousands of subscribers to our concerts throughout Israel. We must destroy the anti-Wagnerian myths. It is vital that we perform the music of the nineteenth century's greatest musical revolutionary after Beethoven.* If an orchestra can-

not play Beethoven and Wagner, it might as well not exist. Wagner was basically a second-class human being, but I do not think Beethoven was a terribly nice person. At some point a man's creativity transcends his real character. Bruckner* was a naive idiot. Mahler* a towering intellectual giant. But if you put *their* music side by side they are equally great cathedrals.

Mein Leben: see My Life

Meistersinger

Name used by certain German poets and musicians, usually otherwise employed as artisans or craftsmen, from the thirteenth to the seventeenth centuries. They claimed artistic descent from a dozen old masters, whose leader was Neinrich von Meissen, called Frauenlob. In a sense, they might claim to be heirs of the courtly *Minnesinger* ('singers of love') but their true antecedents were more probably lay church choristers. Later on, music and singing qualified as 'crafts', and so the mastersingers formed song-school guilds whose principal activity was the holding of competitions.

With time, composition became a more restricted activity, governed by a strict *Tablatur* of rules. These ossifying restrictions led to a small revolution under Hans Folz (*c.* 1515), who persuaded the leading song-school at Nuremberg to permit a wider range of subjects and more novel tunes. The grades through which a novice now had to pass included *Schuler*, *Schulfreund*, *Singer* and *Dichter*, until he was admitted as a full *Meister* upon having a melody of his own commended by the adjudicators. It was in this setting that the real-life Hans Sachs* flourished, although some scholars suggest the song-guilds were already in decline by his day (he died in 1576).

Musical form and subject-matter remained remarkably constant down the centuries. The songs, derived from Gregorian chant and folk sources, had their music determined by the metre (*Ton* meant metre and melody); each composition consisted of two identical *Stollen* – the *Aufgesang* (pre-song) followed by an *Abgesang* (aftersong) – with its own distinct metrical form. A verse was determined by syllable-counting, regardless of stress, and there were complex rhyme schemes. There were three verses (or any multiple of three) per song (also known as a *Bar*), generally given as unaccompanied solos. Subjects were religious until the sixteenth century; thereafter secular themes were permissible. (At the beer-hall late at night, the songs were frequently obscene.)

Contrary to Wagnerian propaganda, the Mastersingers were not popular, and produced little in the way of lasting music. Their importance consists in a fine effort to inculcate civic virtue during troubled times, and sheer longevity. The last guild closed at Memmingen only in 1875.

Meistersinger von Nürnberg, Die (*The Mastersingers of Nuremberg*)

Opera in three acts, text by the composer, based on various historical sources. It was first performed at the Royal Court Theatre, Munich, on 21 June 1868. The conductor was Hans von Bülow*. Wagner sat in King Ludwig's* royal box. The audience received the work with enthusiasm, but Wagner's enemies in the press attacked it mercilessly.

After the daunting experience of completing *Tristan und Isolde* (1857–9), there were a number of reasons why Wagner was glad to select the Mastersingers of Nuremberg as his next operatic subject. He wished to extend his 'holiday' from the seemingly endless unfinished score of the *Ring*. He had temporarily sated even his own exalted appetite for tragic artistry and now wished to give expression to his contrasting capacity for comedy. *Tristan* had raised too many questions in his head about the purpose of art, so what better solution than to write an opera, albeit a comedy, containing some of the answers?

Moreover, there was no immediate possibility of a production of *Tristan*. *Die Meistersinger* was in any case an old project. If *Tristan* had interrupted the writing of the *Ring*, then the *Ring* (as well as *Lohengrin* and *Tristan*) had already interrupted the writing of *Die Meistersinger von Nürnberg*.

Wagner produced the first draft of his poem on this theme as early as July 1845, soon after he had read about the cobbler-poet Hans Sachs* in Gervinus'* *History of German National Literature*. 'Immediately after the conclusion of *Tannhäuser*,' he told his friends in 1851,

I was fortunate in being able to visit a Bohemian bathing place [Marienbad] for the benefit of my health. Here, as on all occasions when I have been able to withdraw from the air of the footlights and from my official duties in such an atmosphere, I soon felt in a light and joyous mood. For the first time, and with artistic significance, a gaiety peculiar to my character manifested itself within me. Almost without premeditation I had a short time previously resolved that my next should be a comic opera. . . . As among the Athenians of old tragedy was followed by a merry satirical piece, there suddenly appeared to me, during this journey for my health, the picture of a comic play, which might suitably be made to serve as a satirical supplement to my 'Battle of the Bards at the Wartburg' [*Tannhäuser*].

Having prepared this first sketch, Wagner did not return to the project for sixteen years. He produced a second sketch in Vienna in October 1861, and this time pressed on, for the reasons explained above. By this time he had consulted more source material, including Jakob Grimm's study of the sixteenth-century Mastersingers*, *Uber den altdentschen Meistergesang* (1811) and – even more important – J. C. Wagenseil's *Nuremberg Chronicle* (1697). Most of this work is devoted to a history of Nuremberg, but the concluding part gives an account of the Mastersingers, their art and the rules which they followed, on which Wagner was to rely heavily. Wagenseil's list of twelve 'old Nuremberg masters' corresponds almost exactly with the characters in the opera, although Wagner has used his own imagination in attributing different occupations to them. The original Mastersingers were probably not artisans (as Wagner represents them) but prosperous businessmen, whose purpose was to raise the cultural level of the community by supplying a highly developed and disciplined form of art, in their case the formal song set to a very precise classical programme of some thirty-two rules. Here was an updated version of the *Minnesinger* tradition adapted to industrial civilization. But although Wagner represents them as in the main comic characters, mere amusement was not on his mind. He put into the mouth of Hans Sachs all those questions about the purpose of art which had been nagging him in the intervening years. Moreover, his spirit of political revolution was changing direction. Now he no longer looked towards a liberal class of democrats to energize society; instead, he wanted a better defined national people (the *volk*) to energize art. The last lines of *Die Meistersinger* warn of the dangers of foreign cultural domination: 'Honour your German masters, if you would shun disasters; let each hold them deep in his heart; then may depart the pomp of holy Rome, no change will come to holy German art!'

Wagner, incidentally, was not the first composer to write an opera on this subject. Albert Lortzing's *Hans Sachs* (1840) anticipates Wagner's masterpiece in a few details, and was based on a play of the same title (1827) by J. L. F. Deinhardstein, which Wagner had probably read but which could only have been of slight use to him for his own far more ambitious purposes.

Musically, Wagner's opera represents an about-turn for the composer of *Tristan* and its revolutionary post-Beethoven* chromatic motifs, but it is by no means a 'French' opera in the style of *Rienzi*. Wagner 'cheated' a little by writing yet again about a song-contest; this gave him

licence to feature set operatic numbers: the prize song, marches and choruses. He also returns to the use of vocal melody of the traditional kind, sometimes elaborated in the spirit of Bach.

More than one critic has noticed that Wagner also wrote the opera to give his opponents a music lesson. They wanted traditional forms? All right, *Die Meistersinger* is a three-act opera about a classical prize song, constructed so that the opera itself follows the prize song's classical form. As we shall see when we have discussed the libretto, Wagner was also promoting his own anti-conservative philosophy of art in the very classical forms which his enemies held dear.

Die Meistersinger is set in mid-sixteenth century Nuremberg, a prosperous mediaeval city famous for the beauty of its buildings. Unlike any other of Wagner's fully mature operas after *Tannhäuser*, it opens with a full-scale overture (or prelude, as Wagner calls it), in which many of the work's dominant themes appear. The overture leads without a break into Act I. The scene is the interior of St Catherine's Church. A service is in progress, and in the congregation is Eva*, the daughter of a wealthy goldsmith, Veit Pogner*. A young knight, Walther von Stolzing*, who is in love with her, stands apart from the congregation, gazing at her in adoration. His love is returned by Eva, who desires to marry him immediately, but her father, while not opposing this desire, simply stipulates that she must unite with a colleague of her own choosing from his guild of Mastersingers. Unfortunately Walther, although fond of singing, does not know the first thing about the guild's complicated entry regulations or fastidious rules of musical composition. Eva's nurse Magdalena* instructs her lover David*, Hans Sachs the shoemaker's apprentice, to acquaint Walther as rapidly as possible with the various guild requirements.

Walther cannot hope to become a singing 'master' in a single afternoon. Every song by an applicant that the mastersingers hear is judged by one of their number, who takes upon himself the role of 'Marker'*. If a composition breaks the guild's rules of musical emphasis or development, each transgression will be marked against it. If more than seven black marks accrue, both song and singer are rejected. Moreover, the singer has to be intimately familiar with all the prescribed modes ('the tender, the dulcet, the rosy-toned, the passing passion, the forgotten-tone', and so on), the correct pitches, coloratura, grace notes and breathing intervals. David himself is still a beginner, even after months of effort.

We now meet Pogner talking to another guild singer, Sixtus Beckmesser*, who is the moderate villain of this civilized opera. Pogner makes his stipulation regarding his daughter's marriage crystal clear: he would like her to marry the winner of the annual midsummer song contest of the Mastersingers' fraternity, but only if she herself also consents to the match. The arrival of Walther, with his obvious good looks, upsets Beckmesser, the oldest of Eva's admirers, who resolves to serenade her from the street at night with his new song – which must surely capture her heart and vote.

The Masters assemble for the guild session. We learn from Pogner that their purpose is to promote art and thus disprove suggestions that burghers only dream of amassing treasure and gold. Pogner repeats his pledge concerning Eva and the St John's Day song contest. The Masters discuss the vital subordinate question of how to judge the event if Eva is to be the main prize. Hans Sachs wishes the 'people' (the *volk*) to decide. Others oppose him ('Ruled by the mob, all art goes hence'), and there is a considerable discussion of aesthetic principles, until Sachs withdraws his suggestion, provided that Eva retains the right to veto any proposed marriage with the winner: 'Leave the maiden free and I give in!'

Beckmesser does not approve of this, but has to accept it.

We can easily detect that a great fondness for Eva makes Sachs protect her and that he and Beckmesser are natural operatic opposites destined to duel vocally over Eva and other prizes in several scenes to come.

Sachs now introduces Walther to the company, vouching for his parentage and sponsoring his application to join the guild. Beckmesser jealously casts doubts on his noble lineage, dismissing him as a 'raw, toothless coxcomb', but Sachs reminds him that members of the guild leave their rank at the door, for 'lord and peasant alike we hold'. Walther, lapsing into anachronism, tells the company that his singing teacher was 'Herr Walther von der Vogelweide'*, the famous *minnesinger* who died *c.* 1230, on whom Wagner had already based a character in the original Wartburg song contest (*Tannhäuser*). Beckmesser rightly points the irony. Sachs: 'A goodly master!' Beckmesser: 'But long since dead; from him I wonder what rules could be learned!' Now Walther clarifies his position by saying that his singing tutor was von der Vogelweide's book of poems, and also the rural bird-song implicit in the mediaeval poet's name. Again Beckmesser sarcastically comments that this time it must have been the 'finches and titmice taught you our Master-singing!' The comedy flows fast and free until Walther takes his place to sing his entrance song.

He has two problems. He is ignorant of most of the guild regulations and he is about to be marked by none other than Beckmesser. Although Walther's song is inspiringly fresh and lovely, it offends in many ways against the Masters' rules and, gleefully observing the letter of the law, Beckmesser clamours for its rejection. Only the thoughtful Sachs, commenting on this 'new piece of German art' (compare Wagner's music), 'found it new, but free of fault, though from our courses turning, his step was firm and did not halt.

If you by rules would measure what does not with your rules agree – find out first what its rules may be!' But he is shouted down: Walther is judged to have failed. Pogner privately deplores the outcome, since he clearly wishes Walther to marry Eva; moreover, he suspects that the mid-summer song contest will be an anti-climax, since Eva will not marry any winner who is not Walther! The act closes in confusion and ill-regulated argument.

Act II takes place on a beautiful summer's evening. Magdalena hears from David that Walther has failed to gain the guild's favour, so punishes him by not letting him have the food she has prepared for him. Sachs chases away a crowd of apprentices who make fun of David, then Pogner and Eva turn out for an evening walk. Magdalena tells Eva the bad news about Walther. Pogner retires and Eva tries to talk to Sachs. But he is in an unattractive, bantering mood, or so it seems to Eva, and she leaves him. Before she goes, Sachs challenges her feelings: If Beckmesser is her chosen lover why not select him, Sachs, if she must have an old fogey? Sachs simply wishes to find out if she truly cares for Walther. If so, he means (in spite of his own desires) to help Walther as much as he can.

The action grows ever more complicated and exciting. Beckmesser arrives to serenade Eva. Walther arrives to persuade Eva to elope with him. Eva persuades Magdalena to impersonate her, so that she can run away with Walther during Beckmesser's egregious serenade. Sachs, cobbling very late a pair of shoes for Beckmesser to wear to the song contest, tries to frustrate both the serenade and the elopement. He throws up his shutters, so that the street is too well-lit for nocturnal flight, and comically destroys Beckmesser's vocal wooing by 'marking' his song with noisy hammer-strokes on his shoemaker's last whenever a turn of phrase irritates his master-ear, which is far too often for Beckmesser's comfort. Beckmesser is convinced that Sachs is only

trying to destroy his confidence in his song entry in order to win Eva for himself. Eva thinks the same, but she will be disabused long before Beckmesser is. Gradually, Sachs' banter grows more and more blunt and impolite. He stands up and sings jeeringly in competition with Beckmesser. Roused by the noise, David looks out and (misunderstanding the situation) thinks that Magdalena is being wooed by Beckmesser, whom he then thrashes. The neighbours are roused, more voices join the throng, the on-stage business turns into a riot, in which apprentices and journeymen cheerfully take part – until the Nightwatchman* blows his curious wooden alphorn and the street empties as rapidly as it had filled.

After a quiet and moving prelude (whose themes embody Sachs' sadness and disillusionment with the world), the curtain rises on the first scene of Act III, set in Sachs' workshop the following morning (the day of St John's festival). Sachs is seated by himself; David appears and tells him about the beating he gave Beckmesser the previous night, and the reason for it. Sachs now delivers an important monologue on the nature of art and illusion: if illusion surrounds us, and all art is illusion, then surely it would be better to direct illusion to nobler ends! That is what Sachs will attempt by educating Nuremberg to appreciate Walther von Stolzing's unorthodox poetry (just as Wagner hoped to persuade Europe to accept his own music as not only valid, but supreme).

Walther enters and tells Sachs of a beautiful dream he has had during the night, which Sachs encourages him to express in a song. He then instructs Walther in the proper fashioning of a master song. It has to 'walk a tightrope'. 'A song simply full of poet's passion [like *Tristan*?] might turn our maids' minds in evil fashion'. But, equally, a song from an old Master might lack youth's inspiration. No, Walther must begin by remembering last night's wondrous dream, which he described as 'of beauty rare and filled with love'. Then he must make firm compositional rules and keep to them, all the while pondering on his vision's beauty. Gradually, Walther's unrestrained memories are balanced and extended into three perfect but original stanzas and he proceeds safely from one end of the narrow tethered rope of art to the other without a slip. Sachs copies down the song as Walther sings.

After these two songsters have retired inside Sachs' house, Beckmesser happens to come by (the shoes which Sachs made for him pinch abominably) and spies the completed song on the table. He assumes that it must be Sachs' own trial piece, intended to enable Sachs to win Eva himself, and immediately steals it. Sachs comes out, sees the song is missing, but lets Beckmesser keep it. He knows at once that it is too revolutionary a composition for the conventional Beckmesser to master, and so actively encourages him to use Walther's song, not his 'serenade' to Eva, in the forthcoming competition. He reassures Beckmesser that he is not a rival for Eva's hand. Hardly believing his luck, Beckmesser makes Sachs agree that he will never publicly claim the song as his own, even if it should carry off the victor's prize, to which Sachs merrily consents.

Exultantly, Beckmesser disappears to look at his new lyric and Eva arrives because her new shoes pinch as well (in all this fuss, Sachs is obviously not keeping his mind on his job). When she overhears Walther's wonderful song, she realizes that Sachs is trying to help and must have been doing so all along. 'Were my heart free of Walther,' she tells him, 'it is you who would be my choice.' Sachs ironically alludes to the story of Tristan* and Isolde*, saying that he would not endure King Marcke's* woe, meaning that he understands that his own deep, longing love for Eva must be denied.

David and Magdalena now appear, dressed for the festival. Sachs promotes David from apprentice into full journeyman, in order that Walther's song may be properly attested (mere apprentices not being eligible attesters) and it is accorded a fitting mode: 'The mode of the "Morning Dream-Story" be it named!' Eva now sings of her happiness, and of her expectation that Walther will win the song contest, thus beginning the great quintet. The other characters present (Walther, David, Magdalena and Sachs) each join in, singing of their own thoughts and hopes. After the quintet, a short orchestral passage leads without a break into the second and final scene.

Scene 2 is set in a meadow just outside the town, where the song contest is to take place. The people of the town and the neighbouring countryside are flocking in; the members of the various guilds appear in procession as, finally, do the Mastersingers. Sachs is greeted by the crowd with a great chorus in which they sing of their love and admiration for him. Deeply moved, he thanks them and says that he is to be their spokesman in the contest. Kothner*, one of the Mastersingers, declares the contest open, and Beckmesser, as the oldest entrant, is asked to sing first.

Beckmesser duly stands forward to sing Walther's song, but, to the amusement of all the onlookers, manages to transpose the words into pure gibberish. For example, 'Morgenlich leuchtend in rosigen Schein, von Blüth und Duft geschwellt die Luft' ('Bathed in sunlight at dawning of day, while blossoms rare made sweet the air') becomes, in Beckmesser's version, 'Morgen ich leute in rosigems Schein, von Blut und Duft' ('Bathing in sunlight at dawning of day, with bosom bare'), and so on, with even less continuity than this farcical opening couplet. Beckmesser furiously accuses Sachs of having composed nonsense. Sachs denies it, but says that the real composer will be able to sing the song to the complete admiration of all hearers, without having to glance at text or score. And the climax of the opera is reached as Walther von Stolzing steps forward and sings his heart-thrilling ballad. The people applaud in wonder, and by unanimous acclamation declare him to be the contest-winner. Pogner makes Walther a Mastersinger guild-member. Eva gets the husband of her choice and Walther reminds his audience to be prepared to accept new works of art, always remembering that they should still fall within the broad German tradition. In these words Wagner commended his own innovative, but native, style of opera to his German audience.

The composer could congratulate himself on this joyous revel of a score, which cheers up anyone with ears to listen; but it often goes unnoticed that he could also congratulate himself on a succinct discussion of the problems of art and opera. In a nutshell, Sachs suggests that all art is illusion, and by no means as satisfactory an illusion as it should be. Too often it is traditionally hide-bound. Therefore, those who strive to break the mould should be praised, not condemned. Or, at least, before they are condemned, it should be asked if they have not in fact devised aesthetic workable rules for their compositions in a new style. If these rules do indeed work, and preserve the composer's inspiration, the resulting creation, far from being condemned, deserves applause.

In *Die Meistersinger*, Wagner also comments on *Tristan und Isolde*, that preceding work which had puzzled so many of his friends as well as the German musical world. The function of a work of art, he suggests, is to create a temporary illusion which endows the audience with the experience of major and minor passions otherwise denied to them. By surrendering to the illusion, you can feel what it is like to be Tristan, without suffering all the tragic consequences. This teaches exact lessons about your own feelings. In short, art can actually bestow wisdom.

In a sense, Wagner was debating an old question. Should art be used for educational purposes and is there any danger in the process? If the truth is dangerous,

what are the limits of the artist's responsibility, and should his medium be controlled? Wagner was very concerned about this, both as a victim of censorship himself (*Das Liebesverbot*, for example, had to be re-named *The Novice of Palermo** before it could be licensed, in case the audience thought it was too lascivious), and also as the composer of music in *Tannhäuser* and *Tristan* which he genuinely thought might drive people insane.

His answer comes with *Die Meistersinger*. This opera suggests that there are myriads of artists and art-forms. Each creator sees life from a different viewpoint at different times. Each work of art therefore yields a very specific, highly particular vision. The same artist might support contradictory views in succeeding works of art, just as Wagner himself offered very different ideas of 'redemption' in *Die Meistersinger* and in *Tristan*. Tristan cannot deny his passion for Isolde. Hans Sachs simply swallows his feelings for Eva to persevere with the business of living. To passive members of the audience who welcome the destructive urge in *Tristan*, Wagner now says, 'Wait; you must also consider the corrective counsel of *Die Meistersinger*.' Not only are there other solutions besides that greedily adopted by Tristan and Isolde; the same world of art, of illusion, that encompasses *Tristan's* tragic grandeur also includes the counter-sermon of Hans Sachs; there are more things in heaven and earth than can be dreamed of in any one music drama.

Melchior, Lauritz (1890–1973)
The leading *Heldentenor* of the century. Melchior was born in Denmark, making his first appearance as Tannhäuser* in 1918 at Copenhagen. Thereafter he was given financial help to study the remaining Wagnerian tenor roles by the English novelist, Hugh Walpole, and other patrons. In 1924, Melchior sang Siegmund* at Covent Garden, then later that same year gave Siegmund and his first Parsifal*

at Bayreuth, regularly returning there until 1931. He appeared annually at Covent Garden 1926–39, notably as Siegmund, Siegfried* and Tristan*. From 1929 he sang mainly at the Metropolitan, New York. In all he sang each of the main Wagnerian leads (except Walther von Stolzing*) over a hundred times each, and sang Tristan at least two hundred times. He alone was still fresh and vigorous in the third acts of *Tristan* and *Götterdämmerung*, when most tenors flag. His voice always produced the lusty high C in *Siegfried* over the shrieks of the Rhinemaidens, as well as a true baritone warmth in the lower registers. There were doubts about his sense of rhythm, which is why he tended to avoid the part of Walther, and also his acting, but none about the beauty of his voice.

Melot (TI)

Tristan's* former comrade who sets a trap to destroy him, possibly out of love for Isolde*: 'Your glance, Isolde, also dazzled *him*,' says Tristan. Isolde's maid Brangäne,* sees what Melot is up to but Isolde is convinced that Melot has cleverly arranged a midnight hunt to get rid of the rest of the court so that she and Tristan may be together. Melot meanwhile has told King Marke,* on pain of losing his head if he is mistaken, that Tristan is betraying him with Isolde and that he, Melot, will lead Marke to where the lovers are trysting – if only Marke will organize a nocturnal hunt.

Melot is simple-minded enough to believe that by exposing Tristan and Isolde he has saved King Marke's honour, but he fails to reckon with Marke's own estimation of Tristan as the very 'fount of honour'. If Tristan errs, then honour itself is lost and cannot be 'preserved'. The honour system itself is wrong. Tristan allows Melot to wound him fatally in the ensuing battle. In Act III, Tristan's everloyal servant, Kurwenal,* slays the unimaginative tenor upstart, but not before

Melot has also fatally wounded Kurwenal, who dies shortly afterwards.

Mendelssohn-Bartholdy, Jakob Ludwig Felix (1809–47)

German-Jewish composer and conductor who was a notable victim of Wagner's hysterical anti semitic attacks in *Judaism in Music*.* The triumph of Wagner's view (which became state policy under the Nazis), led to the serious eclipse of Mendelssohn's music for a generation or more in modern Germany.

Originally, the two had been friends: 'My dear, dear Mendelssohn,' Wagner was writing in 1843, 'I am really happy you like me. If I have come a little closer to you it is the nicest thing about my Berlin expedition.' When the older man became conductor of the Leipzig Gewandhaus Orchestra in 1835, Wagner sent him the score of his Symphony in C major for performance, to read, but Mendelssohn never conducted it. Perhaps this rankled with Wagner more than Mendelssohn ever realized. Later, Wagner alleged that Mendelssohn had 'turned Leipzig into a Jewish metropolis of music'. He also suggested that Mendelssohn, as conductor, had always 'rushed his tempi' – in part, of course, because 'Jews lacked true creativity'. It is all the more remarkable, therefore, that Wagner probably got some of his inspiration for the opening bars of *Rheingold* from Mendelssohn's overture, *Fair Melusine*. Indeed, some critics go so far as to suggest that Wagner actually stole from Mendelssohn here.

Messengers of Peace (Ri)

A chorus in Act II of *Rienzi* to mark the temporary cessation of hostilities between Rienzi* and the Roman nobles.

Method for the Cornet à Pistons

To earn some money on his first unhappy sojourn in Paris, Wagner undertook in 1841 to write a handbook for players of the *cornet à pistons*. He did so with his usual energy, but, alas, his exercises could not be played on the instrument, since his understanding of its pitch was incorrect.

Metternich, Princess Pauline *née* Countess Sandor (1836–1921)

Granddaughter of a famous statesman, Princess Pauline was wife of Prince Richard Metternich, the Austrian ambassador to the court of Napoleon III in Paris. It was largely through pressure from the Metternichs that Napoleon commanded a performance of *Tannhäuser* at the Paris Opera in 1861.

Meyerbeer, Giacomo (1791–1864)

German-Jewish operatic composer who established a craze for spectacular romantic productions. He was wealthy in his own right, so early failures did not cause him distress on the scale experienced by Wagner in his young days. Meyerbeer's first French opera, written to a libretto by Augustin Scribe*, was *Robert le diable* (1831). It appealed to the voguish taste for lavish treatments of mediaeval legends, with supernatural and gruesome catastrophes. Its success was total, and the style immediately became *de rigueur*. He wrote several other, equally successful, operas.

In the light of their later disputes, it is interesting to note that Meyerbeer helped Wagner quite considerably at the outset of the younger man's career. Meyerbeer prompted the first German production of Wagner's *Der Fliegende Holländer* (1843) and wrote numerous letters of introduction for Wagner when he came to Paris. But Wagner, who originally celebrated Meyerbeer's style by adopting it in *Rienzi*, conceived a totally irrational hatred of the man and all his works. Meyerbeer became Wagner's transcendental 'enemy' symbol; anyone who liked Meyerbeer was immediately accused of conspiring against Wagner. The fact is that Wagner could not accept his own failures in Paris and therefore cast around for someone to serve as scapegoat.

This personal discontent is the sad origin of Wagner's public anti-semitism, and of his offensive pamphlet *Judaism in Music**.

Meysenbug, Malwida von (1816–1903)

German writer and feminist, she was expelled from Berlin in 1852 on account of her democratic writings and settled in England, where she met Wagner in 1855. She met him and his wife Minna* in Paris in 1860. She later published *Memoirs of a Female Idealist* and became friendly with Wagner and his second wife Cosima.*

Mime (R, S)

Alberich's* tenor brother, a skilled worker in metal, who fashions the magic Tarnhelm* from the Rhinegold.

IN *Das Rheingold*

Mime's basic characteristic is deceit. So far, he has obviously found this to be a successful way of dealing with the world. But it fails to work on Alberich, once he has acquired the power of the Ring.* He can see through his brother's guile and Mime's lies now earn him a sound fraternal whipping.

Mime also shares the family lust for power. He is attracted to the Tarnhelm because of the opportunity it presents to overthrow Alberich and make himself lord of the Nibelungs. This desire for glory on the part of the otherwise un-heroic dwarf will lead him into terminal trouble during the course of *Siegfried*.

IN *Siegfried*

Mime has raised and sheltered Siegfried* from birth for the sole purpose of preparing him to fight the giant Fafner.* Mime hopes that this will allow him to take the golden Ring from Fafner's cave. Thus every action of Mime towards Siegfried is fundamentally hypocritical. These three qualities of Mime's – deceitfulness, lust for power and hypocrisy – do not make him particularly likeable. And yet the unprovoked bullying meted out to him by Siegfried, not to mention his semi-racial slurs on Mime's appearance ('I saw my face in the stream, it was not like yours'), quite often makes us feel more sympathy for the unappetizing dwarf than for his heroic tormentor.

Mime shows little astuteness during the guessing game with Wotan*/Wanderer. Perhaps the presence of the Lord of the Gods makes him feel too intimidated. Yet, for all his crafty scheming, the last thing he remembers to do when the chance presents itself is to further his own ambitions. One tends to feel that if Mime did become lord of the world, some regions of the globe might not need to take a great deal of notice.

Clearly his ambitions outmatch his abilities. Mime's principal contribution to the operas is comic: his twenty-year plot to exploit Siegfried's abilities is frustrated by a woodbird and a dash of dragon's blood. This truly galling outcome ends in the hilarious scene where, for once, Mime is compelled to tell *only* the truth. Siegfried finds this much too provoking and silences Mime for ever, a piece of black comedy that Alberich finds even funnier than we do.

Minne, Frau (T I)

Isolde's* name for Venus, or the Goddess of Love, whom she apostrophizes at the beginning of Act II. Her maid Brangäne* is upbraided for not recognizing Frau Minne's hand in events: 'Did you not recognize the work of the Goddess of Love?' demands Isolde, after Brangäne has tried to take the blame for making Isolde* and Tristan* declare their love for each other. It should be noted that Wagner's wife at this time was of course called Minna [Wagner*].

Minnesinger

German poet-musicians of the period *c.* 1170–*c.* 1230. Primarily, they were troubadours singing of courtly love. They used to sing extempore as well as painstakingly composing both words and music in advance. Most were members of the lower nobility, but some were peasants and others kings. The musical roots of their songs lie in the pentatonic scale and follow the Gregorian chants and popular melodies of the day.

The greatest of the poet-*Minnesinger* was Walther von der Vogelweide,* who appears as a character in Wagner's *Tannhäuser*, as do other famous real-life minstrel-knights. Tannhäuser* himself has a basis in historical reality. *Minnesinger* should not be confused with the *Meistersinger*,* although the latter retained something of the folk spirit of the former.

Minton, Yvonne Fay (b. 1938)

Australian mezzo-soprano who appeared at Bayreuth in 1974 as Brangäne.* She returned two seasons later to sing Fricka* and Waltraute.* Her highly successful career is assisted by commanding dramatic presence and lithe physique – different from so many potential and past Brünnhildes.*

Mödl, Martha (b. 1912)

German soprano with a warm and beautiful lower register and tremendous acting talent. Wieland [Wagner]* and Wolfgang Wagner* both gave her personal coaching in the interpretation of Kundry,* Isolde,* Brünnhilde (in *Die Walküre*),* Venus,* Sieglinde* and Gutrune.*

Montsalvat (L, P)

The mountain and castle of the Holy Grail* which Wagner locates somewhere 'facing Moorish Spain'. As the critic William Mann observes, 'From AD 711 this could have been anywhere in the country except the northern tip around Bilbao.' The name is probably French ('Mont sauvage'), since the proper Spanish rendering would be 'Montsalvaje'.

Moore, George Augustus (1852–1933)

Irish novelist, dramatist and autobiographer. His early novel *Evelyn Innes* (1898) is an examination of the impact of the spirit of *Tristan* on the lives of aristocrats and singers who challenge the Victorian bourgeois conventions to forge their own destinies. In the story, Evelyn* an aspiring soprano, the daughter of a church organist, falls under the sway of Sir Owen Asher, Wagnerian nonconformist, who sweeps her off to Bayreuth where she is a triumph in the major Wagnerian roles. The tale ends unhappily, however, with Evelyn turning to the Catholic Church for comfort when her spirit of rebellion is exhausted.

Moore's great autobiography *Hail and Farewell* contains a detailed account of a visit to Bayreuth where he was warmly welcomed by Cosima [Wagner]* and Siegfried Wagner*.

Morald (F)

Blood-brother to Arindal,* King of Tramond, and boy-friend of Lora,* Arindal's sister. He seeks out Arindal to beg him to return and save his kingdom from devastation. His alleged death is also part of Arindal's 'ordeal by torment' in Act II, since the loss of so dear a friend would obviously be painfully felt. However, Morald lives to wed Lora and succeed to the throne of Tramond upon Arindal's translation first into a condition of insanity, and then into one of immortality in fairyland.

Morold (T I)

Legendary Irish hero, betrothed to Isolde,* whom Tristan* slays prior to the action of Wagner's operatic drama. His death is of the utmost significance, since not only does it leave Isolde free to be wooed by kings, such as Marke* of Cornwall, but it also permits that first fatal 'look' from Tristan at Isolde, when Tristan seeks shelter in Isolde's Irish fastness soon after Morold's decease.

Isolde is enraged to notice that Tristan's sword has a great sliver missing which is the exact fit for the splinter she had to remove from Morold's skull. But when Isolde tries to stab Tristan in revenge, her hand is stopped by the force of his loving gaze, and she heals his wounds instead of adding to them, so losing the chance to avenge her dead fiancé.

Thus the ground is prepared for the fatal reunion of the legendary lovers, when Marke* – by a coincidence – sends Tristan to win Isolde's consent to marriage with him.

Moser, Augustin (M)

A tenor Mastersinger (tailor by trade) who adds his voice on the side of conservatism when Walther von Stolzing* makes his application to join the guild.

Mottl, Felix Joseph (1856–1911)

Austrian composer/conductor who assisted in the preparations for the first Bayreuth festival in 1876, and conducted *Tristan* and *Parsifal* at Bayreuth in 1886–94 and the *Ring* in London in 1898. He had catholic tastes which did not always please Wagner or Cosima, including a liking for the music of Berlioz*.

Muchanoff, Countess Marie (1823–74)

Russo-Polish pianist (a pupil of Chopin), who appears in Wagner's autobiography, *My Life*, under the name of Mme Kalergis* – the name of her Greek husband, whom she married at the age of sixteen and from whom she separated a year later. She recognized Wagner's genius at an early stage, travelling a long distance to

Dresden to hear the first performance of *Tannhäuser* in 1845. She played an important part in Wagner's life, as friend and helper, at a later stage, after his marriage to Cosima [Wagner].*

Muller, Maria (1898–1958)
Czech soprano who made her début in 1919 as Elsa* at Linz and 1930–44 appeared regularly at Bayreuth, singing Senta*, Eva*, Elisabeth*, Elsa* and Sieglinde*. After the war she was heard as Sieglinde and Elisabeth in Berlin. She died in Bayreuth.

Music drama: *see Gesamtkunstwerk*

My Life
Richard Wagner's highly unreliable autobiography, written at the request of King Ludwig* and ending with his summons to Munich by Ludwig in 1864. Wagner began to write it in 1865; the first three parts were published privately 1870–75, but the fourth and final part was not published until 1881 and the first edition for the general public did not appear until 1911. *Mein Leben* is one of the most devious apologies in autobiographical history. For a corrective view of actual events, the lives of Wagner by Newman* and Westernhagen are to be preferred. *Mein Leben* is, however, of great interest to students of psychology. Wagner stands revealed as a self-deceiver and liar on the largest scale: a man of greatness who was yet troubled by a cosmic sense of inferiority. Newman writes:

The autobiography is simply the last and longest of a thousand speeches for the defence. . . . I shall try to show that the account he gives of the episode with Madame [Jessie] Laussot* in 1850 does not square with his letters to Minna [Wagner]*. . . . He deliberately tries to mislead the reader with regard to his relations with Frau Wesendonck;* everyone who has read Wagner's ardent letters to her must have gaped with astonishment to find him glossing that long and passionate love-dream as . . . 'friendly relations'. . . . He is plainly guilty of serious sins both of omission and commission in his account of his dealings with Von Hornstein . . . and Franz Lachner . . . and Eduard Hanslick. . . .*

Nachtigall, Konrad (M)
Tinsmith (tenor) and conservative member of the Mastersinger's guild who does not support Hans Sach's* motion that the Midsummer's day prize-song should be judged by the people of Nuremberg instead of by trained 'Markers' (such as himself). Nachtigall disapproves strongly of Walther's* unruly singing.

Neidhöhle (S, G)
Named as the place where Fafner* the giant has taken the Rhinegold. It is said by Mime* to be 'at the edge of the wood to the east'. Brünnhilde* describes it as 'eastward' and Siegrune (one of the Valkyries*) says it is 'hard by a gloomy forest'. Wotan* visits Neidhöhle in the guise of the Wanderer in *Siegfried*, although in *Die Walküre* Brünnhilde has already informed us that 'father fears it and never goes near'. Both Hagen* and Siegfried* refer to Neidhöhle in *Götterdämmerung*.

Neidlinger, Gustav (b. 1912)
German bass-baritone who was an established figure at Bayreuth 1952–75. His Alberich* is still remembered as the finest since the last war and he sang the other major Wagnerian bass-baritone roles: Kurwenal,* Klingsor,* Hans Sachs* and Telramund.*

Neumann, Angelo (1838–1910)
German-Jewish baritone who later took up theatre directing. In 1882–3 he travelled over half of Europe, from Königsberg to Amsterdam, with his Wag-

ner Theatre, giving 140 performances of the *Ring* alone and 58 other Wagner concerts.

Newman, Ernest (1868–1959)

One of the finest of all Wagnerian critics, Newman belonged to the 'scientific' school of criticism. He believed that writing on music must be raised from the traditional 'hit and miss affair' to the level of 'certainty'. This is obviously an impossible task, but his contribution to Wagnerian studies was certainly a splendid antidote to Wagner's own mischievous and unreliable account of historical events.

Newman was born in Everton, Lancashire, and educated at Liverpool College and Liverpool University. After spending fourteen years as a bank clerk, he began writing music criticism for the *Manchester Guardian*. Thereafter, he worked for the *Birmingham Post*, the *Observer* and the *Sunday Times*, of which he was music critic from 1920 (with only one brief interruption) until he retired in 1958. Among his books one may mention *The Unconscious Beethoven*, *Wagner as Man and Artist*, *Wagner Nights* (containing invaluable accounts and synopses of Wagner's nine repertory operas) and, above all, the *Life of Richard Wagner* (4 volumes, 1933–47) which, despite the appearance of much new material, has yet to be superseded. In this biography Newman writes:

About the polemics of the would-be critics of Wagner . . . there is nothing more to say. One might have thought these people would have finally asked themselves how it could happen that in the entire world more had been written about this man, whom they try to calumniate, than about anyone else in the whole history of art. . . . The simple truth of the matter is that today, when we can survey his work from sufficient distance in time, we recognize Wagner as one of the three or four genuinely original spirits in the entire history of music; indeed, in a certain sense, even as that one of them whose effect has been most fruitful and transforming.

Nibelheim (R)

The underground land of the Nibelungs, black and noisy from the fires of Alberich's* gold-smelters.

Nibelungen Kanzlei (Nibelung Bureau)

A group of musicians who from 1872 until 1875 helped Wagner prepare for the première of the *Ring* at Bayreuth. Its members included Joseph Rubinstein,* Anton Seidl* and Hermann Zumpe.*

Nibelungenlied, Das (The Song of the Nibelungs)

A Middle High German poem, written *c.* 1200 by an unknown Austrian poet, preserved in three thirteenth-century manuscripts, and a major source for Wagner's *Ring* cycle. No text has provided greater inspiration for German Romantic artists. The poem is full of inconsistencies. In one place, the Nibelungs are referred to as Burgundians; in another, as the people of Siegfried's* land.

The poem traces the love story of Siegfried for Kriemhild, Princess of Worms, a tale sadly complicated by the sudden news of the arrival of a beautiful queen, also willing to be wooed, called Brunhild. The plot introduces us to the characters of Gunther* and Hagen* and also to a treasure which is sunk in the Rhine.

Together with *The Völsunga Saga* and the texts of the *Edda*, the *Nibelungenlied* is primary background material for any study of the *Ring* in depth.

Niemann, Albert (1831–1917)

German tenor who gave Tannhäuser* at the first Paris performance in 1861 and sang Siegmund* during the first complete cycle of the *Ring* at Bayreuth in 1876. Both in this role and in Tristan,* Niemann, who was heroic of voice and immensely tall, was recognized as having no rival in his lifetime.

Neitzsche, Friedrich Wilhelm (1844–1900)
German philosopher who, when he was
twenty-four, became acquainted with
Wagner at Leipzig. 'Every nerve in me
quivers,' he wrote, 'when I hear this man's
preludes to *Tristan* and *Meistersinger!*'
Between 1868 and 1872 the young Nietzsche (who became Professor of classical
philology at Basel University in 1869) was
welcomed more than twenty times as a
guest at Triebschen*. In one letter he
wrote, 'Wagner is the living illustration of
that which Schopenhauer* calls a
genius. . . . The world does not know at
all the human greatness and singularity of
his nature.' The Wagner-Nietzsche
friendship developed, deepened and took
firm root. When the time came to dis-
agree, it caused intolerable pain to them
both. The schism did not occur before
Wagner had literally inspired Nietzsche to
write his *The Birth of Tragedy out of the
Spirit of Music* (1871). This combined
Schopenhauer's metaphysics, Dionysian
aesthetics and Wagner's own theory of art
into a challenging unity. Wagner gave
Neitzsche immense help, including the
run of his priceless library. Perhaps it is
fitting that the conclusion of the book –
calling for a new artistic Socrates to stand
forth – could be applied to either of them.

Before long, however, their friendship
was in trouble. Neitzsche could still write,
'It is an incomparable good fortune for
someone who has groped and stumbled on
dark and strange paths, gradually to be led
to the heights, as you have done with me,
for which I cannot honour you otherwise
than as a father' in his birthday greeting of
1874, but his private thoughts were becoming sceptical. When they began to
appear in print, relations deteriorated.
Wagner did not enjoy that part of Nietzsche's essay on *Richard Wagner in
Bayreuth* (1873) which seemed to question
the relevance of his operas to everyday
concerns. A few years later, when Nietzsche brought out his collection of deeply
anti-Romantic aphorisms, *Human, All
Too Human* (1878), dedicated to Vol-
taire, the friendship really did end. In
August that year, Wagner attacked Nietzsche in an unsigned article in the
Bayreuther Blätter. Shortly afterwards,
Neitzsche denounced Wagner for selling
out to Christianity and the new German
Empire. Some scholars even suggest that
Wagner is the evil genius against whom
Nietzsche inveighs in his greatest work,
Thus Spake Zarathustra (1882–4). Cer-
tainly the funny and furious *The Case of
Wagner* (1888) was intended to bury once
and for all his one-time friend – by now, of
course, dead.

Yet a note of ambiguity remains. It is
true that Neitzsche disapproved of
Wagner's anti-semitism; that he loathed
the Christian inspiration behind *Parsifal*;
that he hated Wagner's conversion to an
'affirmation of death'; that he was pained
to discover Wagner had mocked his own
musical compositions by excessive insin-
cere praise in the Triebschen days; and
that he could write in cold blood, 'Is
Wagner a human being at all? Is he not
rather a sickness? Everything he touches
he makes sick – he has made music
sick. . . .' Nevertheless, Nietzsche could
also write, in an unpublished note for *The
Case of Wagner*, 'I loved and honoured
him more than anyone else – him – the
most profound and most daring and also
the most misunderstood of those who are
hard to understand today.'

Nightwatchman (M)
Bass representative of the long arm of the
law, who helps Wagner clear the stage
when the chorus threatens to spill over
and get out of hand at the end of Act II. A
necessary device in a very populous and
high-spirited opera.

Nikisch, Arthur (1855–1922)
Austro-Hungarian conductor. As a young
man, Nikisch played violin under
Wagner's baton during the performance
of Beethoven's* Ninth Symphony for the

foundation ceremony at Bayreuth. He conducted the London *Ring* of 1913 and Sir Adrian Boult (who was influenced by him) recalls with some humour his 'flexible tempi' – once for example taking twenty minutes off Richter's* time for the spear-scene in *Siegfried*. Nikisch, who excelled in Romantic music, was the leading conductor of his time.

Nilsson, Birgit (b. 1918)
Swedish soprano who succeeded Kirsten Flagstad* as the queen of Wagnerian opera. Her pure, free-ringing voice delighted audiences around the world, beginning in her native Stockholm in 1946. She made her début at Bayreuth in 1954 as Elsa,* and, from 1957 onwards, was the first choice for Isolde* and Brünnhilde*. She often gave Venus* and Senta* as well.

Nissen, Hans Hermann (1893–1980)
German bass-baritone who was among the best Wotans* of his day. He was the 1943 Bayreuth Hans Sachs* and sang the Wagnerian bass-baritone repertoire in all the world's leading opera houses.

Nordica, Lillian (1857–1914)
American soprano who was the Bayreuth Elsa* in 1894 and later gave Brünnhilde* and Isolde* at Covent Garden.

Norns, The Three (W, S, G)
A trio who spin the rope of destiny, telling in a song the story of the world. The first, second and third Norns are contralto, mezzo-soprano and soprano respectively. They are mentioned by Hunding* in *Die Walküre* and by Erda* in *Siegfried*. Since Erda is their mother, they are half-sisters to the Valkyries.* They make their only formal appearance in *Götterdämmerung*.

The Norns serve as a type of Greek chorus, bewailing the world's woebegone state. They inform us that the World Ash-tree* (*see* Yggdrasil) has died and that Wotan* has cut the branches into 'holy' firewood. He has ordered this to be stacked around the walls of his palace, Valhalla,* where he sits in state, waiting for the final conflagration of the Gods. Unless some miracle occurs, this will obviously be soon, but the Norns cannot tell when. Their rope of destiny is breaking, the curse of Alberich* is cutting into the thread and their wisdom comes to a literal end when the fibres finally part.

Notung (W, S, G)
The magic sword which Wotan,* in *Die Walküre*, thrusts into the ash-tree in the middle of Hunding's* hut, in order that Siegmund* should find a weapon in his 'hour of need'. The same sword is shattered by Wotan's spear after Fricka* has persuaded him to keep his word to punish Siegmund's incest with Sieglinde.* Hunding is allowed to kill Siegmund, but Brünnhilde* gathers up the shattered fragments of Notung, so that they may be of use to the offspring of the pregnant Sieglinde.

IN *Siegfried*
Mime* has obtained Notung, together with the infant Siegfried,* son of the now dead Sieglinde. He has also heard the prophecy that the one who reforges Notung shall slay Fafner,* the dragon guarding the Rhinegold. But Mime cannot forge it. When Wotan, in the guise of the 'Wanderer', meets Mime, the latter misses his chance in a guessing contest to ask him who can refashion Notung. In fact, the answer, gratuitously supplied by Wotan, is 'the one who has never felt fear' – which is virtually Siegfried's code-name. When Mime has digested the meaning of this, he watches with impatient rapture as Siegfried melts the fragments of Notung into a new sturdy

blade, strong enough to shatter the anvil on which it was forged. His rapture ceases when, after Siegfried has killed Fafner with Notung, he also gives Mime his quietus with the same blade.

Thereafter, the trusty Notung breaks the runic spear of the lord of the Gods himself, after Wotan has barred Siegfried's way to Brünnhilde on her fire-bound rock. (Symbolically, this shows the world-order created by Wotan being destroyed by the weapon Siegfried has made for himself.)

IN *Götterdämmerung*

Siegfried, in Gunther's* form, captures Brünnhilde on her high rock and then (ironically) lays Notung between himself and Brünnhilde, as a pledge that there will be no immoral activity overnight between the pair in Brünnhilde's cave. Later, when Hagen* is in control of Brünnhilde's will, she tells the lie that Notung did not separate her from Siegfried but hung on the wall in its scabbard. This starts the train of events that even the faithful Notung, strong but mute, is powerless to arrest. Siegfried is slain by Hagen, and Notung is buried with his master in the flames of Valhalla.*

Notung is symbolic of most of the manly virtues – above all, courage and phallic virility. In *Die Walküre* it works as a symbol of rebirth, permitting the illicit but fruitful union of Siegmund and Sieglinde. In *Siegfried*, it shows a conservative craftsman like Mime that the new age is dawning, since Siegfried scorns old-fashioned processes of welding. In the same opera, it literally represents Siegfried's rite of passage into adulthood, and few males have so obviously forged their own manhood. In *Götterdämmerung*, Notung symbolizes chivalric chastity, but in an inverted situation (separating true husband and wife), so that evil consequences follow.

Novice of Palermo, The: *see Liebesverbot, Das*

Odin

Alternative Norse form of Wodan, or Wotan.*

Ohms, Elisabeth (1888–1974)

Dutch soprano, who sang Brünnhilde* and Isolde* at Munich, appeared in the 1931 Bayreuth *Parsifal* and then sang at the Metropolitan Opera House in New York from 1930–32, where she gave all the important Wagnerian roles, except for Senta.*

Onegin, Elisabeth Elfriede Emilie Sigrid, née Hoffmann (1889–1943)

German contralto and mezzo-soprano, who gave Fricka* and Brangäne* at the Metropolitan Opera House, New York, in the 1920s and Fricka, Brangäne and Erda* at Covent Garden in 1927. She sang Fricka, Erda and Waltraute* at Bayreuth 1933–4.

Opera and Drama

Wagner's massive treatise on the nature of his art, on which he began work in 1850 and published in 1851. In this book he describes the function of leitmotivs.* These significant themes would be presented by means of the orchestra. But they would not merely recur when the action became heightened: they would permeate the entire opera. Instead of pointing the text, the orchestral accompaniment would emphasize the emotion behind it. Harmonic and rhythmic variations would constantly modify these feelings. The result would be a 'drama-symphony'. There would be no 'numbers' and no chorus.

Wagner had conceived his mature idea of the music drama. The only problem remaining was a practical one. There was no existing European theatre capable of staging such a work, no orchestra capable of playing such a work and no singers capable of delivering the text of such a work to proficient standards. Before Wagner could reform the writing of operas, he would have to reform their production. Eventually he realized this, and the Bayreuth Festival Theatre was his ultimate answer to the problem.

Orchestra, Concerning the Royal

Wagner's 1846 report on the state of orchestral playing (as represented by the orchestra of the Dresden Court Theatre). An extraordinarily thorough document, it is full of practical suggestions for reform, both musical and financial, which the theatre authorities were unwise enough to reject. The result was that Wagner realized that he must either suppress his artistic ideals, or wait until he could himself create the proper musical and theatrical conditions for their realization.

Orsini, Paolo (Ri)

A patrician, member of the princely family which historically has supplied Italy with a number of Popes and papal officers. Orsini plots with his traditional foe Stefano Colonna* to strip Rienzi,* the Tribune of the People, first of power and later of his life. For his presumption he is executed.

Ortel, Hermann (M)

A soap-boiler Mastersinger (bass) who is as shocked as the rest by Walther's unconventional attempt to fashion a 'Master' song. Ortel helps swell the conservative chorus in the guild scenes, but plays no independent part in the action.

Ortlinde (W): *see* Valkyries

Ortrud (L)

Daughter of Radbod, Prince of Friesland* and wife of Frederick, Count of Telramund,* Ortrud is one of the most human of Wagner's conceptions in *Lohengrin*, and by far the most wicked.

Primarily an ambitious witch, Ortrud has disposed of Godfrey,* the rightful heir to the throne of Brabant, by turning him into a swan. Then, in order to get rid of Elsa,* his sister, she tells Telramund (who, initially, is betrothed to Elsa) that she actually saw Elsa drown Godfrey in the local pool. Telramund therefore renounces Elsa and marries Ortrud, and both of them put in a bid for the ducal throne of Brabant.

The plan goes wrong, thanks to Lohengrin's* supernatural intervention, but not before Ortrud has used sound psychological skills to undermine Elsa's sudden love for Lohengrin.

Her lines are magnificent: 'Would you threaten me, threaten me, a woman?' she fumes at Telramund. 'Coward! If you had so fiercely threatened him who now brings this misery . . . victory, not shame, would have been yours. . . . Give *me* the power and I will show you plainly how feeble is the god who protects him.' It becomes more and more plain that Ortrud is allied with Satan. Telramund acknowledges this by calling her a 'heathen sorceress' but she seduces his continued support with her promise to initiate him fully in the arts of 'the sweet bliss of vengeance'. Full of art and deceit, she easily beguiles Elsa into pitying her, and into believing her malicious suggestion that Lohengrin will soon depart, irrespective of his wedding promise.

Ortrud remains consistent throughout the drama, never asking for pity and never faltering in the commission of crime. Both Goneril and Regan would have been impressed by her.

Pages (T)
Tiny parts (for mixed sopranos and altos)
in the court scenes of *Tannhäuser*.

Parsifal
A 'Stage Dedication Festival Play' in
three acts; text by the composer, based
on the poems of Wolfram von Eschenbach and many other literary sources. It
was first performed at Bayreuth on 26
July 1882, at the height of Wagner's fame
and success, and was the final and
crowning achievement of his life.

Many people find *Parsifal* impossible
to approach because they are so alienated
by its religiosity. It can even be argued
that *Parsifal* has no place in the operatic
theatre. There are many operas about
theology, but not so many that could so
easily pass muster as High Mass. Inevitably, the subject-matter recommends
itself to Catholic Christians, such as the
French mystical writer Paul Claudel.*

Since 1848 Wagner had been toying
with the idea of writing an opera about
Jesus of Nazareth. He was also drawn to
the Eastern philosophy of Buddha and
the stoic asceticism of Arthur
Schopenhauer.* The *Ring* had been
Wagner's synthesis of these influences in
a pagan setting. Now he hoped that
Parsifal would do as much within a more
traditional Christian framework. He
would not have time, he realized, to write
separate operas about the Messiah or
Buddha. *Parsifal* would be his parting
shot. This may help to explain why it
sways back and forth from the source
legends to the spirit of the *Ring*, glancing
at the life of Christ and ending up at a
Catholic cathedral with an Eastertide
service of thanksgiving.

Wagner first read the story of Parsifal
in the mid-1840s, and he made a prose
draft for an opera on the subject as early
in 1857. In 1854–5 he had toyed with the
idea of introducing Parsifal into Act III
of *Tristan*, since both the knight of the
Grail* and the heroic Tristan* renounce

the 'desire before their eyes' for the
'desire beyond their grasp' – Tristan
renouncing life for passion; Parsifal,
passion for life. He also felt that Tristan
might be able to advise Parsifal on a cure
for wounds that refuse to heal, since he
was an authority on the subject, and
thereby assist the tortured Amfortas.*
But happily these ideas were dropped.

Parsifal had been briefly alluded to in
Lohengrin (1850). It was idiosyncratic to
write an opera about the son (Lohengrin)* before the father (Parsifal*), but
Wagner was practically addicted to upset-
ting proper chronologies. He sometimes
found it artistically important to 'place'
one opera by going on to write a
'complementary' work set in the period
preceding it. Be that as it may, by 1858 he
was telling Mathilde Wesendonck* of his
wish to set to music the theme of a Good
Friday miracle, and in 1859–60 the
characters of Kundry* and Amfortas*
took shape in his mind. He finally wrote
the score in Bayreuth 1877–82. King
Ludwig* guaranteed to fund a performance (apparently he felt this pious gesture
might in some sense expiate his own 'sin'
– homosexuality?) and all the omens
boded well.

However, Wagner's health had never
been less cooperative than while he was
at work on the music of *Parsifal*. Hoping
to find a female antidote to his troubles,
Wagner took to bed Judith Gautier,*
with whom he had enjoyed a brief
relationship at Bayreuth in 1876. He
bombarded her with requests for the
perfumes and satins with which he had to
surround himself in order to compose
sensuous music 'that must have the
softness and shimmer of silk, like layers
of cloud which continually separate and
rejoin together'. Wagner felt the need to
fall in love when tackling a great new
opera. Where else was he going to find
the erotic inspiration behind Kundry and
the perceived suffering of the sexual
sinner Amfortas? The matron Cosima,
like a Wagnerite who has learned the

virtues of renunciation, looked on all-comprehending. She carefully made the best of her remaining domestic and managerial tasks. Thus the opera was cosseted into being by female help-mates.

Parsifal is the tale of the Grail, the vessel held by Joseph of Arimathea to the side of Christ when He had been cruelly wounded by the spear* of the Roman centurion, Longinus.* The Grail thus becomes the most holy relic in Christendom. Joseph is reputed to have carried the Grail and spear (now the second most Holy relic) to a group of saintly knights who found in the Grail a source of perpetual nourishment, replenished every Good Friday by a white dove* which fluttered down and dropped a wafer into the cup. Some sources say that the Grail made its way to Glastonbury, England; others, that it ascended into Heaven and then, by a miracle, came back to earth, before becoming the object of a second Grail cult (as in Wagner's version) at Montsalvat* ('Mont sauvage'), which this opera firmly places in Spain.

Thus Act I opens in the sacred precincts of Montsalvat, which is also a grand nature reserve, for all forms of life are held sacrosanct within the Grail's domain. An old holy knight, called Gurnemanz,* tells two squires (and therefore the audience) that the Grail leader, Amfortas, is still suffering from a wound that will not heal and recent remedies brought from abroad have failed to ease his pain. We meet a wild, dishevelled woman called Kundry, who has also brought something she hopes might ease the leader's suffering. She claims to have fetched it from Arabia. The squires are put off by her appearance, although they note her ability to ride like a Valkyrie, brave and free.

Amfortas is carried forth on a litter. He is obviously in pain. We hear that Sir Gawain,* who brought one recent draught of medicine, has now gone away to seek another, but we also hear that

Amfortas places his confidence in the power of the Grail's own prophecy, not herbs. He believes that he will only be relieved of his agony when a 'pure fool', one 'by compassionate suffering gaining knowledge' shall arrive in Montsalvat. Amfortas is so disconsolate that he feels this prophetic stranger might prove no more mysterious a visitor than Death.

Kundry now offers her balsam and she is thanked. Amfortas notices that this is not the first time she has served him. This is a more profound remark than he thinks. Kundry, bewitched by the magician, Klingsor,* can be transformed with enchanting ease into the most ravishing seductress, as we shall see in Act II, and in this guise was the original agent of Amfortas' downfall. How did this happen?

At an earlier stage in the story, Titurel,* who received the Grail from Heaven, passed on his duties to his son, Amfortas. Like all new rulers, the latter wished to make his mark and so was particularly anxious to purge the pleasure palace of the magician, Klingsor, hard on the borders of his own demesne. And so to another question. What was a wicked magician doing in such close proximity to the holy land of the Grail?

Klingsor was once an ordinary mortal who attempted to join the Grail brotherhood. Titurel rejected his application, even though Klingsor went so far as to castrate himself as a proof of his dedication. Still Titurel was adamant, and so Klingsor turned to devilry. He acquired the art of sorcery, set up his rival establishment and now swears to destroy the band of Grail-servants from which he has been excluded. To this purpose, he fills his pleasure-gardens with nymphs and bacchantes who offer themselves to any straying Grail knight. If the young devotee dallies, he falls into Klingsor's power.

This is what had happened to Amfortas when he sallied forth to destroy Klingsor's pleasure-dome. Kundry, condemned to serve Klingsor (because she once laughed at the Saviour, Jesus Christ), was compelled by the sorcerer to waylay and beguile the noble Amfortas. Amfortas thus not only lost the spear of Longinus to Klingsor but was also wounded by it with this stubborn wound that still refuses to heal.

And so it is that Amfortas thanks Kundry for her medicine, totally in ignorance of her full identity and earlier role in his story. Only Gurnemanz half realizes that she is possibly under a spell. He defends her against the squires' detractions, recalling that misfortune has always befallen Montsalvat whenever she is absent. Only Kundry knows what damage she does, which is why she insists, in an often repeated phrase, that she 'never helps'.

Gurnemanz tells the young squires and knights the complete story of Klingsor's rise to power. He has just repeated the Grail prophecy about the arrival of a 'pure fool', able to overthrow the evil magician, when a white swan, pierced by an arrow, flutters down onto the stage and expires. This shooting, of course, is a crime (Wagner was a passionate anti-vivisectionist and animal-lover), for the Grail protects all forms of life, apart from those which are wicked. Who, we wonder, can have been responsible?

A young man, clad in hunting gear, sporting a bow and arrow, comes looking for his prey. He boasts that he can 'hit anything in flight'. Gurnemanz reproves him heavily. The lecture is taken so much to heart that the youth, on impulse, breaks his bow and remaining arrows, swearing never to go hunting again. He is asked his name and where he comes from. He says he does not know. He can recall his mother's face, but she always refused to tell him his family history.

This rouses Kundry from the undergrowth where she is muttering to herself, to offer, spontaneously, some bitter information unknown to the youth himself. She says his mother, heart-broken

by his absence, has just died.

The unnamed youth forgets his recent pacifist vows and attempts to throttle Kundry until restrained by Gurnemanz' warning: 'She spoke true; for Kundry never lies, whate'er she's seen.' Both Kundry and the young man sink to the ground, the former because her Alberichian master Klingsor wills her to demonic sleep; the latter out of grief.

Gurnemanz, meanwhile, has noticed that this boy might well be 'foolish' enough to fulfil the terms of the Grail's saving prophecy, and so instructs him further in the Grail mysteries. The youth wishes to know where he is, for, while travelling, he has hardly moved, and yet 'so far I seem to have come'. Gurnemanz sets him straight in one perfect, crucial phrase: 'You see, my son, time changes here to space.' Now we know we are firmly fixed in the symbolic world of fiction, but one containing the most potent images of Christianity.

After a linking orchestral passage Scene 2 opens, to reveal the stately ritual of the supper of the Grail knights and the awesome unveiling of the Holy Grail itself. Gurnemanz permits the youth to witness the proceedings, in the hope that he will somehow be able to bring comfort to Amfortas. We hear the ghostly, moribund voice of old Titurel begging Amfortas to uncover the Grail, which alone grants the gift of life, but he is understandably hesitant, since the worst of Klingsor's wounding curse is that his pain becomes intolerable whenever the Grail is exposed to view. And yet how else shall the knights survive?

The Grail is uncovered; the knights are reinvigorated; Amfortas writhes in pain, his wounds flowing with fresh blood; the prophecy is chanted around the room; a blessing and prayer are spoken by all; food is ritually distributed – and yet still the unnamed youth stands silent. Gurnemanz berates him for being 'Nothing but a fool', which is a subtle variation on 'pure fool', and pushes him out of the hallowed precincts. A voice repeats the prophecy as the curtain descends, but, unknown to Gurnemanz, the youth has now been set upon the right path.

Act II opens in Klingsor's magic castle. We see the master magician seated before a mirror showing him what is happening beyond the grounds. He can glimpse the 'foolish' youth approaching, so rouses Kundry – a Kundry, however, transformed from the dishevelled creature of the first act into a beautiful houri, clad in rich oriental garments. He mocks her as no better than a sexually abused beast. His bitterness towards women becomes apparent. She craves for peace. (Not for the first time in Wagner's work we find ourselves listening to a spirit who might find death preferable to life.) Klingsor tells her that the youth will be the most difficult of all the Grail favourites to subdue. Therefore she must put on her most lubricious robes and lascivious smiles. She protests, but is compelled. Klingsor is confident. Kundry's power is invincible. Only a castrate such as he can resist. With high hopes, he goads her to her task. Can the youth win?

First Klingsor sends out inferior knights – those who have fallen under his previous erotic spells – to attack the ignorant youth. They are bloodily repulsed when the youth seizes the sword of Ferris,* one of their number, and turns it on them all. Klingsor, however, is gratified rather by the scene: he wishes all his lowgrade knights could be eliminated as swiftly. But now it is time for more significant defensive weapons to be deployed.

The light fades, and Kundry vanishes into the darkness. Then the tower of Klingsor's castle disappears – and Klingsor with it – and a magic garden rises in its place. Parsifal, standing on a wall, gazes in wonder at this lovely grove, which is suddenly filled with semi-naked nature spirits – the Flower Maidens* – who attempt to woo him and entice him to smell them, like the flowers they appear

to be. They quarrel for his attention like children but do not directly seek to make love to him. (Wagner emphasized that they were not prostitutes.) But since the youth remains unimpeded in his progress by these distractions, Klingsor has to resort to his big gun: Kundry. Her firm voice rings out across the stage: 'Parsifal, stay!'

He is at once stopped in his tracks. 'My mother once called me that in a dream,' he exclaims. He turns to see by whom he has been named. There, lying on a bed of flowers, is the most beautiful woman imaginable, erotically attired, calling him by his name, and giving no hint that this could be the formerly bedraggled hag, Kundry, whom he had previously attempted to strangle.

Kundry sets out to seduce him. She uses psychological wiles to reinforce formidable physical attractions. She repeats his name, then says it backwards: 'Falparsi'.* She says that this means 'the foolish pure one' in Arabic. She tells him his family story. His father, Gahmuret,* was slain fighting in the Holy Land before he was born. His last wish was to have his son christened Parsifal. His mother, Herzeleide,* heart-broken, brought up her son as a fool, so that he should never learn the profession of arms nor perish in battle like his father. However, when soldiers passed their house one day Parsifal followed them and Herzeleide died of grief. Ever since Parsifal has been impressing the world with his strength and courage.

Parsifal is filled with dread. This woman seems to know far too much about him. He feels the fear of Siegfried when beholding the womanly Brünnhilde* for the first time. The pain of his mother's death hits him afresh. The parallel with Siegfried continues. He is suddenly drenched with guilt, calling on his mother and exclaiming to her, 'Your son has to be your murderer' – just as Siegfried had assumed responsibility for the sorrow of Sieglinde.*

At the mention of pain, however,

Kundry sees her chance: 'Now atone for this distress in the comfort which love offers you,' she says, and opens her arms to receive him. He still resists. She repeats her offer: 'Learn to know the love that enveloped Gahmuret when Herzeleide's searing passion seized him!' This is subtle psychological pressure, but Parsifal is a properly repressed youth, and declines to take her. Thereupon, Kundry impresses his lips with one of the longest stage kisses in the repertoire. Parsifal finally jumps back, as if stung. He feels a sympathetic wound in his side, exactly like that of Amfortas. He sees exactly what this man must have suffered when he, less wary than Parsifal, succumbed to the temptations of Kundry's gentle flesh. His mind is flooded with knowledge of his sacred mission. He pleads aloud for rescue from stain, from guilt, from all those lusts of the flesh that have so bedevilled Puritans down the ages, but he at least pleads to some purpose. It is one of the main points of *Parsifal* that if the youth makes love to Kundry, then he cannot serve the Grail and fulfil his destiny.

The 'good' side of Kundry begins to perceive that Parsifal could be her saviour as well as the Grail's champion. Parsifal underscores the point: 'If for one hour I were to forget my mission in your embrace, for all eternity you would be damned! For your salvation too I am sent if you will but turn from your desire!' But Klingsor has not yet given up. He makes the 'wicked' Kundry say, 'Then it was my kiss that made you see so much, so clearly? The full embrace of my life thus aids you to reach the godhead!' She invites him to pursue the theological discussion more intimately: 'One hour be mine! And one hour let me be yours. . . . And you shall be shown the way.'

But all Kundry's wiles fail, and she can only call on Klingsor to help. The climax of the opera has now been reached. The magician appears, holding the sacred spear. Kundry curses Parsifal. Her final black act is to doom his feet never to find the path in the world that they seek – especially the path leading back to the Grail. Klingsor shouts that he can threaten to more purpose: 'His master's spear shall fix the fool!' He flings the spear straight at Parsifal's head, but – miraculously – it is halted, hovering inches from the target. Parsifal takes the holy shaft and makes the sign of the Cross, thus instantly destroying Klingsor and his sorcery for ever. Kundry collapses with a shriek and the curtain falls.

The final act begins with a prelude, after which the curtain rises to reveal a pleasant landscape in the environs of the Grail. It is a spring morning. Gurnemanz emerges from a hermit's hut. Much time has passed since the last Grail ceremony and he is now very old. Kundry is discovered, groaning like a beast in a thicket, and Gurnemanz revives her. She is completely transformed. Gone is the fabulous raiment, gone her defiance. As soon as her strength allows, she adopts the role of Gurnemanz' serving-maid. There is an absolute passivity about her.

A black-clad knight with sealed visor enters, carrying the spear of the Grail. Gurnemanz inquires if he has lost his way. Obtaining no reply, Gurnemanz protests that it is not seemly for him to be dressed in arms on this, Good Friday, the Lord's Triumphal Day. The knight opens his visor, and both Kundry and Gurnemanz recognize Parsifal.

Subject to Kundry's curse, he has wandered far, all the while seeking his path back to the Grail. He has had many adventures and fought many battles – keeping the spear, however, unused at his side, in order to bring it back, undefiled, to the Grail, where he is to employ it to heal Amfortas' wounds. He has always striven to fulfil his foreordained duty, but not till today has the Grail let his feet wander in the correct direction.

Gurnemanz urges haste, since Amfortas has been in such unremitting pain that now he 'lusts for death' – even asking that the Grail remain concealed in its shrine, lest the sight of it prolong his life. The Grail knights have fallen on evil days. They no longer receive pleas to take part in holy wars in the world outside, and their morale is low. Titurel is dead – 'A man as all men' – and no longer a servant of the Grail.

Parsifal is ritually bathed with cleansing water from the holy spring and anointed. The redeemer has come. Kundry washes his feet and dries them with her hair. Parsifal baptizes Kundry, granting her blessing and absolution for all her sins.

Parsifal gazes on the forest and meadows lit by the morning light, and the orchestra plays the wonderful Good Friday music.* Gurnemanz says that this is the magic of Good Friday, with nature rejoicing at its rebirth through the agony of God's suffering.

The scene dissolves back into the hall of the castle of the Grail. The knights reassemble. Titurel's coffin is opened. Amfortas pleads for someone to end his misery – even for a Grail knight to run him through with a sword. Parsifal, Gurnemanz and Kundry enter. Amfortas again prays aloud for death. Parsifal steps forward, saying, 'One weapon will suffice!' and, touching Amfortas' wound with the tip of the sacred spear, makes him whole. The miracle restores all the company, except Kundry, who, like Elisabeth* (*Tannhäuser*), Elsa* (*Lohengrin*) and Isolde* (*Tristan*) before her, sinks lifeless to the ground. Parsifal, the new leader, uncovers the Grail, the holy Dove hovering above his head. And so the final curtain falls.

It is a long opera, but ritual cannot be hurried. If you dislike ritual, *Parsifal* probably is not the opera for you. But, as with sermons of old, there is much to be said for unhurried pondering on durable religious myths. If you object to the content, take it as allegory. Most men and women seek some kind of a Grail, whether it is called God or Om or Dialectical Materialism. Others are content simply to quest. Still others pursue a kind of immortality through parenthood. *Parsifal* may be full of cranky moralizing, but it succeeds as a source of spiritual invigoration. Heroism may be out of date, but the spirit is still served by the story of a raw boy, no less than a fool, being sent out into the world with a solitary purpose: to gain compassionate wisdom through the experience of suffering, and thus in the end to achieve his spiritual aim.

Did Hitler* learn the wrong lessons from *Parsifal*? Parallels are invidious, but some have seen them. Hitler experienced suffering while fighting for the Kaiser in the First World War, winning the Iron Cross, First Class, only to go on to the pursuit of an ultimate aim which was the implementation of a bestial social programme. Hitler would perhaps have enjoyed the comparison, but he failed to understand Wagner's allegory. He claimed, 'I have built up my religion out of *Parsifal*. Divine worship in solemn form without pretence of humility. . . . One can serve God only in the garb of the hero. . . .' But whatever Hitler built upon him, Parsifal was instructed in the arts of peace. He was enjoined to lay aside weapons of power. He was forbidden even to shoot a swan, for the Grail holds all forms of life sacrosanct. The opera said as much to Hitler when he watched it, but the Führer naturally saw only what he wanted to see.

Wagner originally wished *Parsifal* to be performed, at no charge, to selected Wagnerites only, but this proved impossible. He laid down strict instructions that this *Buhnenweihfestspiel* ('stage dedication festival play') should only be produced at Bayreuth, but this too proved impossible. The first New York production was mounted in 1903, and ever since then *Parsifal* has been included in the repertoires of the world's leading opera houses, as if to confirm that in this work, so loaded with esoteric theology, grand opera will nevertheless insist on being sung in the world; Wagner's great music will out.

Parsifal (P)

Siegfried's* *alter ego*, who makes a spiritual journey in the course of the opera from unreflecting fool to Christ-like shaman. By coming to perceive completely the amount of pain suffered by Amfortas* when he lost sight of the Grail* in the seductive arms of Kundry,* Parsifal is transformed from a brash knight into the Grail's redeemer. The Christian parallel is more than clear: by understanding how Christ died on the Cross, how he must have loved mankind to endure such pain, the sinner knows he is redeemed. Parsifal acquires similar knowledge by treading the path of Amfortas, but without succumbing to a like temptation.

At the commencement of the opera, Parsifal (or Parzifal; the character is taken from the poems of Wolfram von Eschenbach* and other legends) is the child of the woods. He has run away in search of adventure after being inspired by the sight of some passing soldiery. Having arrived at Montsalvat,* his first act is to break the holy law forbidding unlawful killing by shooting a wild swan with his bow and arrow. His offence is made clear. With startling suddenness, he agrees to renounce all forms of hunting.

Then he tells us that he is the Knight of No Name, utterly ignorant of his origins, because his mother, Herzeleide,* refused to give him any information. The bewitched Kundry interrupts to inform him that his mother has died of grief since he abandoned home. Intemperately, Parsifal attacks Kundry, as though she were a goblin-like Mime.* He even tries to throttle her, until it is pointed out to him that Kundry, whatever she looks like, always speaks the truth.

And so Parsifal's education begins. He experiences almost the same grief for his mother's death as she must have felt at his reckless departure. Gurnemanz* rouses him from his sorrow and tries to instruct him in the mysteries of the Grail; for he hopes that Parsifal is the Messiah who has come to save the Grail brotherhood and heal Amfortas' wound, according to prophecy. Although Parsifal is impressed by the Grail ceremonies, he has no immediate conception of a mission, until Gurnemanz inadvertently sets him on the right path to Klingsor's castle by ejecting him from Montsalvat.

The evil magician, Klingsor,* well aware of the role Parsifal is destined to play, despatches knights, Flower Maidens* and finally the comely Kundry herself to destroy the youth before he can understand that his preordained purpose is to dispose of Klingsor.

After beating off the knights, Parsifal is delayed only briefly by the Flower Maidens before facing the serious problem of Kundry's offer to love him and make him a man. Even Parsifal is forced to admit how near he is to succumbing, and he is terrified.

But that is precisely the higher purpose of the temptation; he must open his eyes to the delights and sorrows of the world in order to transcend them. Only then will he be the Grail's man, fit to become the Grail brotherhood's true leader. Kundry does her best to outwit him, dwelling sympathetically on his mother's death, yet subtly stressing the fact that he is to blame for it. The parallel with the life of Siegfried is again underlined. Parsifal is moved to exclaim; as if to his mother, 'Your son has to be your murderer!' and almost drops his guard in his distress.

Kundry has made a formidable start. She has already named him (and we learned from *Lohengrin* that anyone who names an anonymous knight gains a hold over him). Now she plays on his guilt and desire. All goes well until the very moment of attempted consummation, the long stage kiss. Parsifal jumps away, as if stung. He has suddenly seen the light of the Grail. He perceives what Amfortas desired in Kundry and feels the price in pain he had to pay for his lust. Through sympathetic imagination, he even feels pain in his own side from the wound that Klingsor inflicted on Amfortas with the sacred spear.* He also realizes much more. He comprehends that the Christian world is sinful and man a fallen creature merely befouling his nest. The true purpose of his mission is manifest: he must save the Grail from Klingsor's wicked grasp, in order to preserve the island of virtue which is Montsalvat. And this is what he achieves, redeeming Kundry and healing Amfortas at the same time.

If Parsifal sometimes seems a cold youth, it remains clear that the opera is written in praise of obedience to one's vows as much as of asceticism for its own sake. Parsifal has a hidden religious vocation and it would be inappropriate to expect him to behave in anything but a disciplined fashion.

Parsifal Cross, The
Wieland Wagner's* elaborate shorthand symbol for the dramatic contrasts in *Parsifal* – for example, the chaste but corruptible Grail knights* are counterposed with the unchaste but redeemable Flower Maidens* in a thoroughgoing system of oppositions.

Patronat, The
The subscribers to the first performance of the *Ring* at Bayreuth in 1876, who, in return for an advance cash payment, obtained a *Patronatschein* ('certificate of patronage'), which served as entrance ticket.

Pecht, Friedrich (1814–1903)
German portrait painter and friend of Wagner, whom he met in Paris when both men were in their late twenties.

Pegnitz, River
River in Bavaria which rises in the uplands of Franconia and flows through Nuremburg. It is mentioned in *Die Meistersinger*.

Pilate, Pontius (Lt)
Whimsically named ostler who rises during the course of the opera from the status of condemned prisoner to acting Captain of the Watch.

Planer, Minna: *see* Wagner, Minna

Plaschke, Friedrich (1875–1951)
Czech bass-baritone, who sang Pogner* at Bayreuth in 1911 and was the 1914 Covent Garden Kurwenal,* Hans Sachs* and Amfortas.* He was a great actor as well as singer.

Pogner, Veit (M)
Bass-voiced goldsmith-Mastersinger of Nuremberg, whose daughter, Eva,* wishes to marry the young Franconian knight, Walther von Stolzing.* Pogner's main ambition is to ensure that any future son-in-law of his shall be drawn only from the select Guild of Mastersingers. But this is no ruthless ambition, since Pogner would also like to see Eva married to a man of her own choosing. He looks with favour upon Walther, and is wise enough to perceive that Eva is besotted with the young man, and so the problem is really this: how can Walther be secured a Master's seat in the Guild?

Pogner never addresses this difficulty himself, preferring to leave the future in the hands of fate. Fortunately for him, Hans Sachs,* the shoemaker, is a man used to manipulating events to suit himself, and it suits him very well to see Eva married to the man she loves, both to frustrate Walther's elderly rival Beckmesser,* and to challenge the ancient rules of the song school in the process. Pogner emerges from the opera as a kindly enough man, if somewhat eccentrically obsessed with the life of the ancient Guild.

Praeger, Ferdinand (1815–91)

German composer, a London friend of Wagner who published a book of supposed reminiscences (*Wagner as I Knew Him*, 1855), later exposed as fictions.

Pringle, Carrie

English singer who was one of the Flower Maidens* in the first production of *Parsifal* at Bayreuth in 1882.

According to one recent newspaper report (*Sunday Times*, 1 November 1981), she was also Wagner's mistress, having proved to be 'irresistible'. It is further alleged that a row between Wagner and Cosima [Wagner]* over Carrie Pringle precipitated his fatal heart attack on 13 February 1883, and that this is why Cosima's diary entries cease the day before.

Prohaska, Jaro (1891–1965)

Viennese bass-baritone who made his Bayreuth début in 1933. For the next eleven years he sang at Bayreuth almost every year. His greatest role was that of Hans Sachs*. His other Bayreuth roles were Wotan,* Gunther,* Telramund,* Amfortas* and the Flying Dutchman.* He retired in 1953.

Proust, Marcel (1871–1922)

French novelist who was an ardent Wagnerite. He compared the interconnected structure of his own writings to the similarly interlinked operas of Wagner. His favourite musical work was perhaps *Tristan*, given often at the Paris Opéra during the Third French Republic, but he was equally moved by *Parsifal*, which he first heard at the Colonne concert on 14 January 1894. In *Le Côté de Guermantes*, the Duchess's lady guests are compared to Klingsor's* Flower Maidens*, 'their flesh appearing on either side of a sinous spray of mimosa or the petals of a full-blown rose'. Elsewhere in Proust's long novel, Wagner provided musical inspiration, particularly in connection with the famous 'Vinteuil Sonata' theme, which the author hinted was based partly on the prelude to Act I of *Lohengrin* and the Good Friday music* from *Parsifal*. Much to Proust's disgust, Wagner's music was banned throughout France during the First World War. When Proust complained about this to the great actress Madame Réjane (the model for Berma in his book), she called him a filthy Boche and nearly pushed him into a rose-bush, a suitably Proustian fate. However, the support in France for Wagner remained undiminished since so many composers (Débussy,* Chabrier,* Saint-Säens* and Fauré) had forcefully acknowledged his genius.

Puccini, Giacomo (1858–1924)

Italian composer, who had catholic tastes in opera, as befitted a man coming from a long line of ecclesiastical musicians. His twin gods were Verdi and Wagner.

He visited Bayreuth in 1889 to see if *Die Meistersinger* could be cut and adapted for the Italian stage. It was, and a performance was mounted at La Scala in December of that year.

Puccini was so fond of *Tristan* that it is reported that he had to keep his copy of the score closed while he was writing *Turandot*. 'Enough of such music. We are mere mandolin-players, amateurs. Woe to him who gets caught up in it!' His favourite piece of Wagner was *Parsifal*, which he studied so intensely that in 1923 he booked seats on three consecutive occasions, in order to be able to take in the work, just one act at a time. The spell proved irresistible: he ended up staying for the entire performance on each occasion.

Pusinelli, Anton (1815–78)
One of Wagner's oldest and most trusted supporters. From the composer's early thirties onwards, Pusinelli was both doctor and friend to the Wagners.

Rackham, Arthur (1867–1939)
Fanciful but talented English illustrator of the *Ring of the Nibelungs* (issued in two parts in 1910 and 1911).

Radbod, Prince of Friesland (L)
Referred to by Telramund* as the father of his wife Ortrud,* although Radbod does not take any part in the action of *Lohengrin*. He is based on the real-life Radbod (d. 719), whose daughter was in fact called Theutsind.

Raimondo, Papal Legate (Ri)
Small bass role, which allows little scope for dramatic expression, apart from the splendid malediction against Rienzi in the excommunication scene.

Ravens of Wotan, The
Two birds, called 'Thought' and 'Memory', whom Wotan* commands daily to scour the world and bring him tidings of events. We hear in Act I of *Götterdämmerung* that Wotan has stirred himself from his depression to send forth the birds to discover whether Brünnhilde* has at last restored the ring to the Rhinemaidens.* The ravens report that she has not. They are also the harbingers of doom to Siegfried* in Act III, since it is their arrival above his head which causes Siegfried to turn round, thus presenting his vulnerable back to Hagen's* spear.

Reichmann, Theodor (1849–1903)
German baritone, who sang the Wanderer* (*Siegfried*) in 1878 at Munich. He gave all sixteen performances of Amfortas* in

the first production of *Parsifal* at Bayreuth in 1882, then repeated the role regularly each year until 1902. In 1888 he added Hans Sachs* to his Bayreuth repertoire and in 1891 sang Wolfram* there. He appeared 1884–92 at Covent Garden and for thirty years his rich warm voice showed no signs of failing.

Remedios, Alberto (b. 1935)
English tenor, born in Liverpool, who came to prominence as Walther* in 1968. His unfaltering line and wonderful ringing clarity made him an unforgettable Siegfried* in the 1973 *Ring* at the London Coliseum.

Renoir, Auguste (1841–1919)
The great French painter who gave robust and tender life to his human subjects, especially women. He sketched Wagner, an atypical choice of physiognomy, at Palermo in 1882, later completing a portrait in full colour. Cosima [Wagner]* used to spell his name 'Renouard'.

Rethberg, Elisabeth (1894–1976)
German soprano, famous as Elisabeth,* Elsa,* Eva* and Sieglinde.* Eventually she also sang Brünnhilde* in *Siegfried* but this was not an ideal role for her voice.

Revolutions of 1848–9
In the wake of the downfall of King Louis Philippe of France, and against a background of economic depression, there were in 1848–9 a number of sympathetic social revolutions across the continent of Europe, including that which excited Wagner to action in Dresden. Rebellions broke out against the Habsburgs in Bohemia and Northern Italy, while uprisings took place in many of the main German towns.

Wagner had actively supported the previous revolution of 1830, also a Continent-wide movement. Now he again risked life and fortune for the ideals of 1848. The King of Saxony, when confronted by democratic demands, suspended the constitution. The people revolted. The King called on Prussian troops to assist in putting down the rebellion. The citizens took to arms.

In Dresden, Wagner was joined on the barricades by Mikhail Bakunin,* the Russian anarchist, August Röckel,* musical director of the Court Theatre, who later spent thirteen years in prison for his activities, and Gottfried Semper,* the architect of the new Dresden Opera House. The singer Wilhelmine Schröder-Devrient* offered aid and comfort to the rebels. Semper built the street barricades, which were described as the best ever made for a revolution. Wagner obtained hunting rifles from the tenor Tichatschek* and apparently ordered a supply of hand grenades from a weapon-smith. He risked his life several times in attempts to win over the soldiers of Saxony to the rebel cause. But it was all in vain. Bloodily, the rising was quashed.

By the end of 1849, the same was true of the other risings in Europe. All were suppressed. The only apparent difference made by this revolutionary upsurge was to the immediate lives of individual revolutionaries. Some were punished at home; others, like Wagner, fled into exile abroad (Wagner obtained a false passport, with the aid of Liszt,* in Weimar). Born agitators, such as Bakunin, did not lose faith in direct action, but Romantic dissidents, like Wagner, were ultimately tamed. By 1860, Wagner had made peace with the authorities and his exile was revoked.

In 1848–9, different classes of revolutionary had different aims: the workers wanted bread and freedom, but many middle-class intellectuals were primarily interested in greater liberty of thought, as well as a measure of political democracy. Wagner certainly belonged to the second group.

Rheingold, Das

Prologue in four scenes, without interval, to the trilogy The Ring of the Nibelungs; text and music by Richard Wagner, based on a variety of mediaeval Icelandic, Nordic and German poems and legends. At the insistence of King Ludwig,* Rheingold was first sung in Munich on 22 September 1869, to Wagner's intense annoyance. He had always stipulated that the four operas of the Ring were only to be given as a complete cycle; but in 1869 Siegfried and Götterdämmerung were still incomplete. However, as the King's pensioner, Wagner had to give way and allow Rheingold to be given in this isolated performance. The first full Ring cycle was presented at Bayreuth in 1876.

Das Rheingold is the most glorious prelude in the history of music and a touchstone for the Wagnerian novice. If you can listen to the unbroken sweep of Rheingold's magnificence without pleasure, then it is highly unlikely that you will ever develop into an enthusiastic Wagnerite. In this 'preliminary evening' of the Ring, we hear without interruption the mightiest Wagnerian music: the chilling motive of the renunciation of love; the amusing percussion to mark the entrance of the giants; the bewitching hammer tunes of Alberich's* slaves in Nibelheim; and the subtle, dancing menace of the ironic firegod, Loge.*

The opera starts by slowly recreating the River Rhine from source to mouth in rising arpeggios of the chord of E flat major. By the time the curtain falls, some two hours afterwards, Rheingold has flooded its ideal listener with an awareness of the Ring's three great modern themes: the choice in politics between tyranny and law; the choice in relationships between power and love; the choice within oneself between tendencies towards egotism and altruism. Rheingold presents these choices in the most complex mixture of allegory and symbol. To take just one example, the life and death struggle between Alberich and Wotan, in addition to being a fairy tale about dwarfs and gods, may also be understood in terms of a contest between two halves of the same personality. The whole of the *Ring* can be seen as the clash of the forces of the mind within one human being's consciousness. In this case, the outcome of the *Ring* has implications not only for society, but for personal sanity, and it is to this compelling subject, in all its levels of richness and mythic allegory, that the 'preliminary evening' directs our attention.

The whole of *Rheingold* takes place in the first days of life on earth. The only creatures so far in existence are those whom we meet in the course of the drama. They are the Rhinemaidens* swimming in the River Rhine, guarding a precious treasure of sunken gold; Alberich,* one of a race of dwarfs living in an underground land called Nibelheim; the giants, a simple but strong-minded folk, who occupy the earth itself; Erda,* Mother of Earth, who is the source of all worldly wisdom; her daughters, the three Norns* (whom we do not meet till *Götterdämmerung*), busily spinning the Rope of Destiny, attached to the Tree of Life (see Yggdrasil) beside the Fountain of Wisdom; and a group of beings residing above the earth (in a palace built for them by the giants) who have evolved into gods, the chief among whom is Wotan. There are no ordinary human beings present in this pagan world. None will be created until the period of the next opera, *Die Walküre*.

During the course of *Rheingold* Alberich is going to attempt to conquer the world. He will be opposed by the more legally minded Wotan, but he, too, will seek world supremacy. Their conflict will sow the seeds of a future discord that will crack the surface of this primitive world order. It is always helpful to remember the many different levels of interpretation possible when considering Wagner's intentions in the *Ring*. At the level of personal allegory, we shall be shown what

happens when the human mind 'attempts to practise more than earthly power permits'. *Rheingold* may be summarized as a picture of the breakdown of society when cursed with a lust for gold; or it may be seen as the breakdown of the human self when dominated by any overriding material obsession.

Water is the first element encountered in the *Ring*. We meet the three frivolous Rhinemaidens, presumed daughters of Wotan, who are called Flosshilde,* Wellgunde* and Woglinde.* Frolicking in the river, they immediately let it be known that their job is to guard a treasure of gold lodged on the river-bed. Alberich, the dwarf from Nibelheim, enters. He is very attracted to the Rhinemaidens' beauty and asks naively if he can make love to them. They decline, but in the most graceless fashion, mocking him as a 'scaly, spotted lecher of small stature.'

Sunrise interrupts the trio's teasing, striking the full face of the gold and filling the river with a glorious light. The music paints the picture for us. Alberich asks the maids what glory is dazzling his eyes and they foolishly tell him all about their secret hoard and how it is protected. They reveal 'that the world's wealth can be won by any being who seizes the gold and fashions from it a magic Ring*. That "man" will then become lord of the world.'

We are not told why this gold is lying in the Rhine in the first place. But it is made completely clear why the treasure has to be guarded from passing danger. The gold symbolizes world power against the day that money shall rule men's minds. One further security device possibly the most powerful of them all, guards the gold. Woglinde explains 'that the man who would master the gold must first pronounce a curse upon love and renounce love's joys for ever'. World power extorts this as the fee. Wellgunde adds, as if to reassure her sisters, 'And such a man will surely never be found since all men need to love.' Woglinde agrees, pointing to the dwarf: 'He, least of all, will endanger the gold since lechery, judging by our experience, rules his actions.'

At this moment in the development of the drama, we have no clear idea of what Wagner means by 'love'. Alberich goes on to terrify the Rhinemaidens by telling them that – contrary to their suppositions – he is indeed willing to curse love in return for world power, but *what* has he renounced? Is it sex play with Rhinemaidens that he is giving up for ever? Or is he renouncing the future possibility of any deep, spiritual bond with womankind? Would it in any case be possible for Alberich, as so far characterized, to enter into such a Romantic bond? In other words, when Alberich denounces love, is he in fact offering to pay a far lower price than would have to be paid by another character in the same situation who had finer sensibilities? It is interesting to look forward to *Götterdämmerung*, in this respect, where we discover that Alberich has begotten a son. It obviously follows that Alberich's curse on love does not include a curse on the considerable consolations of sexual intercourse. Therefore, it is unclear, to say the least, exactly what sort of a bargain Alberich is striking. To some commentators, he seems only to be promising to give up what he is unlikely to have, if, indeed, his actions are 'ruled by lechery', not by love, as Woglinde suggests.

Be that as it may, the Rhinemaidens are horrified when Alberich, now grown authoritative, pronounces the damning curse on love and steals their treasured hoard. The contrast between the sunny themes of the gleaming gold and the bleak blackness which follows Alberich's terrible utterance could not be more complete. When the gold vanishes, the light of the world goes with it, and all we hear are the Rhinemaidens' woebegone wails.

To the music of a masterly transitional theme, we ascend from the Rhine high into the clouds and land on a mountaintop. In the background there is a brand-new fortress, called Valhalla.* On the mountain we see Wotan lying asleep, while his wife, Fricka,* stares in wonder at her glorious new home. She wakens Wotan. He, too, gives Valhalla a long, hard look, but his eye is full of pride, since this house is the 'work of my will'. That is all very well, rejoins his wife, but how *will* it be paid for? The giants still want their fee.

This raises a serious problem for Wotan, and one which he would rather not think about. In return for constructing Valhalla, he has promised to the giants, Fasolt* and Fafner*, possession of his sister-in-law, Freia*, goddess of Spring. Unfortunately, Freia is the one price he cannot afford to pay, since, through the agency of her golden apples, Freia keeps the gods youthful. If she departs, they will quickly die (except for Loge, who does not get any of the fruit, and therefore can survive on his own resources). Fricka tartly reminds Wotan of all this, critically pointing out that 'You harden your hearts when you men lust for power!'

Their domestic bickering is interrupted by Freia herself, fleeing from the giants who have come to collect their prize. Wotan plays for time, asking what wage for their work they have in mind. Surely, he prevaricates, they did not think he was being serious about Freia, because that, of course, was a joke?

Alas for the gods, the giants have a primaeval sense of humour. They point to Wotan's staff, where the bargain is recorded. Fasolt is motivated by Freia's great beauty, but his brother is hoping to cause Wotan's downfall by removing Freia's rejuvenating apples from the gods' control. Freia's brothers, Donner* and Froh,* arrive, and threaten the giants with violence. However, killing the giants cannot resolve Wotan's dilemma. He is bound by his oath to strike an acceptable bargain with them. If he breaks his oath, all his power will be dissolved anyway. There must be another solution.

At long last, Loge the firegod arrives. Wotan at once blames him for the problem. Was it not really Loge who got him into this trouble, says Wotan, by agreeing that Freia could be promised to the giants, since they would never want to claim her? Loge shrugs, then explains that he has been delayed by a long journey to find something in the world the giants might realistically be expected to prefer to Freia's charms. 'But in all the wide world,' he confesses, 'nothing at all is of greater worth to a man than a woman's beauty and love.' The gods begin to despair.

But Loge is only indulging in crafty salesmanship. He casually announces that he did find one creature, a dwarf called Alberich, who seems to have discovered something far more ravishing than any female smile, and that is the Rhinegold's magic Ring. Wotan and Fafner are immediately excited by the talk of the Ring's fabulous power to confer authority. And Loge's ruse works.

Eventually it is agreed that Wotan will seize the gold from Alberich to give to the giants. Fasolt and Fafner take Freia hostage until the evening, by when, they insist, the gold must be available to pay them off. Loge stresses to Wotan that the Rhinegold (as distinct from the gold Alberich is mining with the aid of the Ring) ought to be returned to its maiden guardians. But Wotan has decided to bend, if not to break, his own rules. It cannot, he argues, be theft to steal from a thief. No, says Loge, provided that the gold is then returned to its rightful owners. Wotan does not reply, and the dilemma is left unsolved, while Loge and Wotan descend through a cleft in the rocks to Nibelheim, leaving their fellow gods, deprived of Freia's magic presence, to wilt and fade before our eyes.

Now we discover what use Alberich has made of the Rhinegold. He has fashioned the Ring and turned the Nibelheim dwarfs into slaves, forcing them to pass weary days mining gold for his treasury. Even his brother, Mime,* has lost his liberty. Alberich compels Mime to fashion a magic Tarnhelm,* or wish-helmet, which enables the wearer to assume any shape he pleases or not to be seen at all. Mime attempts to use the Tarnhelm on himself, to escape from Alberich's brutality, but he does not know the spells which make it work. Alberich grabs the helm from Mime's hands, puts it on, pronounces the correct spell, then chastises Mime for telling him the lie that the Tarnhelm was not finished. In the middle of this comic episode, Wotan and Loge arrive. It now proves laughably easy for them to capture Alberich. He has recognized Wotan, but his new power emboldens him to make a show of his strength. When Loge plays on his vanity, the black dwarf eagerly agrees to demonstrate the Tarnhelm's versatility. First he turns himself into a dragon; Wotan and Loge cower in mock terror. Then he obligingly assumes the form of a toad. Wotan puts his foot down hard, traps the toad, removes the Tarnhelm and ties up the struggling, cursing Alberich. As Robert Donington tells us, '[Alberich] . . . makes no attempt to turn the tables by brandishing the Ring at his captors; it seems he is enough of a realist to know that it can have no power against destiny, in other words against the underlying purposes of the self, for which the Ring is primarily a symbol.' This is perhaps so, but Wagner is also telling us that the Ring is a commanding agency only when two conditions are fulfilled: firstly, the owner must be aware of its functions; secondly, he must not be in thrall to the power he wishes to use the Ring against. The Ring is certainly a symbol of destiny, but only when its wearer has enough 'freedom' to follow that destiny. And Alberich does not. He is led back through the cleft of rock to the mountain-top, where the gods keenly await his return.

Alberich is first told that the price of his freedom is the gold his slaves have mined in Nibelheim. He reluctantly agrees, since as long as he keeps the Ring he can always mine more of the precious metal. The Nibelungs are commanded by the power of the Ring to bring all the gold from the mines to the mountain-top. Loge then increases the price by demanding retention of the Tarnhelm, and Wotan breaks Alberich's heart by adding his demand for personal possession of the Ring. Alberich offers anything, including his own life in a bid to appease his tormentors, until he realizes that death would also deprive him of the Ring. Wotan seizes the jewel from his finger. Alberich asks in a sarcastic voice if he can now consider himself to be free. Wotan says yes. In that case, retorts Alberich, accompanied by a crescendo from the orchestra, 'I hereby pronounce my fateful curse on the Ring – everyone shall desire it, every owner shall be terrified of losing it, and all into whose possession it comes shall meet a violent death until the Ring returns to Alberich, its lord.' With a murderous glare, Alberich vanishes from the stage, together with his followers.

The other gods now drag their weary bones into the stage light, but visibly recover when Fasolt and Fafner return with Freia. The giants insist that the gold must be piled high, until it completely hides Freia from sight. Their great greed is not sated until both the Tarnhelm and the Ring are added to the stack. Wotan at first refuses to yield the Ring. However, Erda, the Earth Mother, dramatically rises from the ground to warn him that he must part with it, since the gods are not fated to be rulers of the world for ever. Reluctantly, Wotan surrenders to her decision.

Fasolt and Fafner immediately fall victims to the Ring curse, the first of many to experience its maledictory power. Fasolt is slain by Fafner in an outburst of hot temper over the division of the golden spoils. Then, while Fafner carries off his booty, Freia is fully restored to the bosom of the gods.

Donner then clears the mist surrounding Valhalla by creating a mighty musical thunderstorm, and his brother, Froh, conjures up a rainbow bridge over which the gods may walk into their new palace – into Valhalla, the curse and cause of all this struggle. Loge stands to one side, ashamed to walk beside these so-called 'gods', and even more ashamed of his part in depriving the Rhinemaidens of their gold. Their voices rise up in sweet beseeching to Wotan, but he has made himself virtually powerless to help them by lawlessly spending their gold on Valhalla. He is irritated by their outburst and abruptly commands Loge to silence them. To a final, magisterial theme, the gods proceed into Valhalla, the hall of false glory, now peopled by dishonourable deities.

And so, the Prelude now ended, the stage must be redressed for the beginning of the *Ring* proper: for a complete description of the conception and birth of Siegfried* into a world riven by competing factions and energies. The events leading up to the conception of Siegfried are the subject of the next opera in the cycle, named after Brünnhilde,* his bride-to-be, whom Wagner calls *Die Walküre*.

Writing to his friend August Röckel* on 25 January 1854, Wagner says,

The composition – now complete – of the difficult and momentous *Rheingold* has brought me once again a great sense of certitude, but I perceive anew how much there is, by the very nature of my poetic intent, that can be revealed through the music alone. I can no longer look at the poem without music. In time I think I shall be able to tell you about the composition. For the present, only this much – that it has become a close-knit unity; there will scarcely be an orchestral note which does not proceed from a preconceived motive.

He was right. With the possible exception of *Tristan*, *Rheingold* is the greatest tissue of inter-connected sound with which the world has been filled.

Rhinemaidens (R, G): *see* Flosshilde, Wellgunde, Woglinde

Richter, Hans (1843–1916)

Austro-Hungarian conductor, an out-standing exponent of the works of Wagner. He studied in Vienna. With a recommendation from Wagner, he conducted the Munich Opera. He was principal conductor of the Bayreuth Festivals for many years, commencing with the première of the complete Ring in 1876. He assisted Wagner in conducting the 1877 Wagner Festival in London and in 1882 and 1888 gave the first London performances of *Die Meistersinger* and *Tristan*. From 1879 until 1897 he directed the famous 'Richter' concerts in England; thereafter he took over the Hallé orchestra at Manchester, retiring from this post in 1911. He was at Covent Garden regularly from 1903–10. His last performance (*Die Meistersinger*, 1912) took place at Bayreuth.

Ridderbusch, Karl (b. 1932)

German bass who appeared at Bayreuth in 1967 and subsequently as King Henry,* Titurel* and Fasolt.* In the same year he gave a fine account of Hunding* in New York and was the 1971 Covent Garden Fasolt, Hunding and Hagen.* He was heard as Sachs* in Salzburg in 1974–5.

Rienzi, der Letzte der Tribunen (*Rienzi, the Last of the Tribunes*)

Wagner's first successful opera, in five acts. Text by Wagner, after Lord Bulwer Lytton's* recent novel, *Rienzi* (1835). Wagner finished the score in 1840, and the opera was first performed at the Dresden Hofoper on 20 October 1842. The success of the work led to a production of *Der Fliegende Holländer* on 2 January 1843 at the same theatre and to Wagner's appointment as conductor there in succession to Weber*.

Whereas Bulwer Lytton, in his novel, kept well to the historical facts, Wagner simplified and refined the tale. The true historical Rienzi is actually Cola di Rienzo (1313–54), a messianic popular leader sometimes dubbed the 'Mazzini of the fourteenth century' because of his efforts to unite the Italian states under democratic government. Petrarch wrote sonnets to Rienzo to encourage him in his ambition: it was, after all, somewhat bizarre that the 'Holy Roman Emperor' should be a German dwelling outside Italy. Rienzo championed the cause of the people of Rome against the nobles and stemmed an aristocratic rebellion against his authority by executing eighty of the titled ring-leaders. This created a lingering bad feeling against the self-styled 'Last of the Tribunes' and he had to go into exile after 1347. Returning in 1354 as a senator, Rienzo was ironically slaughtered by the great Roman mob, the same civic-minded folk who had cheered his elimination of the nobles.

Wagner was genuinely excited by this personage: 'with his grand thoughts living in an era of rudeness and depravity, he attracted all my sympathy and imagination'. This was clearly the sentiment of the radical Wagner who would welcome the barricades of 1848 with an eager heart. In the same spirit, Wagner wanted to produce a grand opera far too magnificent for the petty theatrical stages of the Northern Prussian towns where he had hitherto eked out his living. He read Lytton's novel in 1837 in Dresden. In summer of the following year he began his musical treatment of *Rienzi* with such an utter disregard of the means which were available (in Riga) for its production, 'that my desire to create it would force me out of the narrow confines of this puny theatrical circle to seek a fresh connection with one of the larger theatres. . . . For *Rienzi* I had dreamed of the most magnificent theatrical conditions. . . .' He finished the composition of the whole on 19 November 1840, in France. 'I had in Paris the example of the Grand Opéra before me,' he writes, 'and my ambition was to surpass all that had gone before in brilliant finales, hymns, processions and musical clang of arms. . . . I wished to display introductions, duets, trios etc etc with all possible splendour.'

As we know, Paris was a cold climate for the young German upstart. *Rienzi* was not performed there: in operas it was possible to make a tribune out of a man of the people; in real life, self-styled musical tribunes were offered no golden key to the kingdom of fame. Not until Dresden agreed to stage the first performance of *Rienzi* did Wagner's luck change. Then it was towards Germany that he was pulled, away from the sensuous seductions of Paris (his Venusberg?) and into a career at last yielding fame and security. After 1842, his national *volk* became the audience of the future.

Rienzi is perhaps most influenced by Auber's* *La Muette de Portici* (1828), in what Wagner called this 'vast chaos of sound . . . this monster'. Ernest Newman* hated the work: 'To put it familiarly, the youthful Wagner had been obviously shaping up for some years for a bad attack of the musical measles; he had to get it out of his system, and *Rienzi* was the illness that enabled him to do so. To me it is the least satisfactory of all his works – far less enjoyable than *Die Feen* or *Das Liebesverbot* . . . one expects a composer to show more indubitable signs of originality at twenty-six or twenty-seven. . . .' The piece is over-long, says Newman (Wagner agreed) and, on the harmonic side, excites a 'strange impression of pretentious poverty. . . . No one lives except Rienzi. . . . In this opera, Wagner's voice was loud but his imagination was at a virtual standstill.'

Some of this is nonsense, for if *Rienzi* is an uneven work, it has always been popular and remains in the repertoire. The overture is hackneyed, but vivid. The drama is hurried on by rattling strokes of excitement at key points – for example, by Rienzi's 'Roman Battle-cry' and by the soprano aria 'Just and upright God' after the battle is done. This is at least the score of an independent master, even if it is not that of an innovator. Newman may have

disliked the florid style, recalling Auber,* Spontini* and Meyerbeer,* in which *Rienzi* is written, but dislike is the lowest form of appraisal.

Wagner writes of complete pandemonium at the first performance. Rehearsals, as ever, were inadequate, and the astounding enthusiasm of the Dresden audience for every note of the stirring novelty on that first night – with constant cries of 'author' or 'composer' – caused delays after every scene. *Rienzi* is a long poem at the best of times: the first performance began at six, and by ten Wagner was in despair when he realized that they had only completed three acts. The evening ended at a quarter past eleven, and it was triumph all the way. The next day Wagner hurried round to the singers, armed with cuts to trim the operatic monster to civilized proportions, but the silver-tongued tenor, Tichatschek,* was adamant: 'I will have none of my heavenly part removed', and the rest concurred. The company may have a lot to answer for, since Wagner goes on to record, 'At last I came round to Tichatschek's view – if he could stand it, the audience could stand it!'

Rienzi, described on the title page as a 'Grand Tragic Opera', is set in mid-fourteenth-century Rome. The opening scene shows the rebellious aristocrats breaking into Rienzi's house, in order to make off with his sister Irene* and spoil her virtue. The ringleaders are Orsini* and Colonna,* but their attempt is foiled from an unexpected quarter: Colonna's own son Adriano Colonna* (a mezzo-soprano role in male attire) takes Irene back – 'Touch her who dares,' he shouts, 'My life for hers!'

After further struggles, Rienzi enters and his commanding presence alone is enough to quell the uproar. We learn that the nobles had previously disposed of his younger brother violently. Now they have tried to snatch away his sister: 'Rome is made a robbers'-nest,' he laments. Colonna sneers at Rienzi for being a 'babbling lawyer', then sullenly retires with his comrades.

Provoked beyond endurance, Rienzi primes the people for an uprising against the nobility, hoping for the support of the Church, in the form of Raimondo,* the Papal Legate. Irene praises Adriano's conduct to Rienzi, who is a little surprised to find a Colonna who would wish to 'preserve a maiden from dishonour!' However, Irene talks him round; then Rienzi persuades Adriano to join his side in the coming troubles: 'Rome shall be great and free! Those that in the dust are trod shall rise free citizens of Rome!' Adriano agrees to oppose his father, and students of this type of libretto will by now be well aware that not a whit of good can come from this tussle between blood and ideals. Adriano and Irene intemperately fall in love.

At the beginning of Act II, the splendid song of the Messengers of Peace* is heard. Rienzi is now clad as an antique Roman Tribune, an indulgence on his part which the people of Rome accept in return for their liberty. The nobles, on the other hand, take this as a further personal affront. Rienzi claims that they must 'acknowledge law and freedom, not my person'. They do neither. A plot is quickly concocted to remove Rienzi: 'Cut off Rienzi,' says the elder Colonna, 'and the vile mob and rabble will be what they always were.' Young Adriano Colonna overhears all this talk. His father dares him to betray his own kin; Adriano tells the audience that he will.

Ambassadors from abroad enter and join a festal procession which hails 'a united Italy!' Adriano tells Rienzi that the Orsinis, who are in league with his father, will shortly attempt to assassinate him. But Rienzi has donned a chain-mail undergarment, so that when Orsini stabs him, the dagger-point is turned aside. The nobles are taken prisoner and the law decrees that they should be beheaded.

If Rienzi had now executed the leading nobles (and prepared an accident for Adriano), his reign might have continued untroubled on its way, but he grants Adriano's desperate appeal for clemency for his father. The nobles now swear renewed fealty to the state in the guise of Rienzi, but they are not sincere in this: 'The haughty mercy which he gives,' says the elder Colonna, 'abases us, while yet it spares. And every noble, while he lives Yes, unto death, resentment bears!'

The people are angry that Rienzi has not carried out the executions, and even more so when the nobles rise again, necessitating a new battle and much bloodshed among the common soldiers. The Song of Liberty is heard.

Adriano, torn between ties of blood and politics, soliloquizes 'Where can I turn my sword, the noble's pride – on my lover's brother? On my father's head?' before deciding to ask Rienzi for yet more indulgence for his erring family.

Rienzi quite firmly replies, 'Ere thou again shalt move my heart, Let all the world in ruins fall' – and accordingly, when the nobles are conquered yet again, their ring-leaders, including the elder Colonna, are put to death.

It only remains, in this long evening, for Adriano Colonna to seek his revenge, now having decided that the claims of blood far outweigh the pull of political ideology. He spreads rumours among the commons that Rienzi is no longer in favour with the Church (which is, as it happens, true), while reminding them how many of them died unnecessarily in the recent war. A new assassination is plotted, but before it can be put into operation, the Papal Legate excommunicates the beleaguered Rienzi: 'Vae, Vae, Tibi Maledicto.' Irene stands by Rienzi in this hour of need, telling Adriano to go: 'A Roman true,' she asserts, 'I will remain.'

Somewhat prophetically, we slip forward a few years into the fire-moods of *Siegfried* and *Götterdämmerung*. Adriano tells Irene, 'Nay, thou art mine! E'en through the flames I'll find my way to thee!' The mob begins to set fire to the Capitol, and while this Valhalla of the Mediterranean is burning around his ears, Rienzi quite rightly tells the people that they have not been worthy of his rule.

This is your thanks. What? Are ye Romans!
Degenerate folk! Unworthy of that name!
The last of Romans – curses you!
Accursed, destroyed, be Rome again –
Let death, yes, death and destruction come!
So wills the Roman folk once more!

Rienzi, Irene and Adriano all perish together.

Thus is a young man's drastic solution to the world's problems thrust in all its extravagance into the audience's collective face. It is an unreflecting, pseudo-anarchist explosion. Later, in the mature catharsis of *Götterdämmerung*, it will not be the people who will destroy the world, but the Gods who bequeath human beings the choice of setting the world to rights or allowing it to rot, Rhine-sodden and charred, for ever.

Rienzi, Cola, Last of the Tribunes (Ri)

A character taken from Lord Lytton's* novel of the same name, based on the historical Cola di Rienzo (1313–54).

In Wagner's opera, Rienzi is a figure of enormous presence. The mere fact of his arrival quells civil disturbance in the opening scene. The tenor gets by far the best music in this marathon drama, which perhaps helps to explain his impact.

Early on, we hear his democratic catechism: 'overthrow the nobles, resurrect the popular constitution, let the people decide – Rome shall be great and free – those that in the dust are trod shall arise liberated citizens!' And in honesty he should have added that they will be saddled, for their pains, with Cola Rienzi as their overweening Tribune.

His tragic flaws are arrogance, vengefulness and an ill-timed act of clemency. The attempted assassination of his person is seen as an attack on Rome herself. Rather like Louis XIV or General de Gaulle, Rienzi seems to assume that 'l'état c'est moi!' Rather more serious is the fact that his political judgement is inferior to the demands he makes upon it. If a man wishes to change the course of history, he must consider all the consequences, as Machiavelli enjoins, and in particular must set aside his personal feelings. But Rienzi, desperate to avenge his murdered brother, pushes his revolution against the nobles who were responsible for it too far and too fast, with the crucial result that Mother Church eventually fails to renew her alliance with him, which is his ultimate undoing. He even presumes to influence the election of the next Emperor of Charlemagnia: 'Let Rome elect him if she will – For Rome is free – All hail to Rome.' This endangers the security of the papacy.

Rienzi's most significant mistake is to yield to Adriano Colonna's* pleas for mercy after the failure of the Orsini-Colonna coup d'état. The law prescribes death. Rienzi is merciful because Adriano loves Rienzi's sister, Irene,* and because he gave advance warning of the attempted assassination by Orsini,* so saving his life: One feels, however, that a true, historical Machiavelli would not, like Rienzi, have stayed his hand, but would have eliminated the troublesome Adriano while he could. The irony is that, after a new aristocratic uprising, Rienzi will be compelled by the people to kill the nobles in any case.

The result is chaos and conflagration. Rienzi dares the fates to do what they will and, dutifully, the fates oblige. Raimondo,* the Papal Legate, excommunicates Rienzi, the common people rise and set light to the Capitoline buildings, and Rienzi perishes in the fire, together with Irene and Adriano.

Rienzi's most admirable quality is courage and defiance even unto his Roman death.

Riesenheim (R, S)

The home of the giants, Fasolt* and Fafner,* and their people, situated 'on the earth's broad surface', according to Wotan* (*Siegfried*).

Ring (R, but present throughout the *Ring*)

A magic band of gold which Alberich* fashions from the Rhinemaidens'* treasure and which was supposed to make its master lord of the world. However, Wotan* tricked Alberich out of the possession of the Ring, and so the latter cursed all those who subsequently came to possess it, wishing on them a life of fear and death by violence (see 'Curse on Love').

This curse is actively at work throughout the drama of the cycle bearing the Ring's name, until Brünnhilde* changes the course of destiny in the redemption scene at the close of *Götterdämmerung*.

The Ring is not a simple agent of command. Those who remain initially ignorant of its function, such as Siegfried,* are free from the curse for as long as that ignorance lasts. However, they are quite able to use the Ring's subsidiary powers, as mediated through the magic Tarnhelm.* Brünnhilde finds herself powerless to use the Ring against Siegfried in *Götterdämmerung*, when the bewitched hero comes to woo her in Gunther's* form. This seems to be because the Ring will not function against one who has bound its wearer in chains of submission. This is why Alberich cannot use the Ring to free himself from Wotan's physical ropes in *Das Rheingold*; while Brünnhilde is bound by chains of love to Siegfried in *Götterdämmerung*.

Thus, for much of the drama, the Ring is hedged about by the forces of destiny and curses, until it truly becomes a great prize of no intrinsic value, although strongly contended for. This helps Wagner to make his symbolic point about worldly riches, which often reduce men to spiritual poverty.

Ring Des Nibelungen, Der

A Stage-Festival Play for Three Days and a Preliminary Evening; text by the composer, based on the thirteenth-century Icelandic sagas the *Poetic Edda** and the *Prose Edda**, together with the *Völsunga Saga** and the German mediaeval poem *Der Nibelungenlied* (*Song of the Nibelungs*). The four parts of the *Ring* are *Das Rheingold* (written 1853–4); *Die Walküre* (written 1854–6); *Siegfried* (1856–69; last few pages, 1871) and *Götterdämmerung* (1869–74). Wagner's original conception was of a work to be called *Siegfried's Death* (see *Siegfrieds Tod*), but the project grew in his mind until he found himself committed to describing Siegfried's* life, together with the lives of his parents and the lives of the gods, their progenitors. The whole twenty-odd hours of the complete *Ring* (including intervals) was intended to be heard in just four evenings, but the work is now rarely given on consecutive nights. The first complete cycle was performed in Bayreuth on 13–17 August 1876 (over five nights, with one day, 15 August, intervening).

Resumé

The four operas of the *Ring* tell us the story of the struggle between Wotan* and Alberich* for mastery of the world. Wotan, the Lord of the Gods, would like to crush Alberich by force, but is prevented because his own authority depends on respect for the rule of law, including the law of destiny. Alberich, by contrast, suffers from no such inhibition, although he, too, is aware that destiny does not always conform to his exact wishes. Alberich steals the Rhinegold and fashions from it a magic Ring,* which will bring him world power unless Wotan can trick him out of it. In order to get the gold, Alberich had to pronounce a curse upon love, renouncing its joys for ever. In attempting to defeat Alberich, Wotan also begins to lose touch with his true nature, eventually sacrificing both his power and his life for the sake of his ambition.

In *Das Rheingold*, Alberich loses the Ring to Wotan. Wotan then immediately loses the Ring to the giant, Fafner,* but not before Alberich has pronounced a terrible curse on the Ring and all who possess it: they shall meet a terrible death.

In *Die Walküre*, we meet Siegmund* and Sieglinde,* children of Wotan, the first human beings to appear in the *Ring*. The Lord of the Gods is unable to rescue the Ring and destroy Alberich directly. But until it is done, the gods are threatened with potential overthrow. Therefore, the cunning Wotan has engendered a 'free spirit' in the form of Siegmund, not bound by laws or treaties but hero enough to wrest the Ring from Fafner and noble enough to return it to its lawful guardians in the Rhine. Wotan's jealous wife, Fricka,* aborts this plan by proving to Wotan that Siegmund is not free at all. He is the creature of Wotan's will. After making Sieglinde pregnant with the child who will become Siegfried, Siegmund is killed.

In *Siegfried*, Wotan makes a second attempt to create all the circumstances in which a 'free' hero can carry out his purposes. Siegfried fulfils the first part of Wotan's plan, but, as a free agent, destroys Wotan's own power in the process. He also falls in love with Brünnhilde.* With the advent of Siegfried, freedom has appeared in the world.

In *Götterdämmerung*, we see Siegfried tricked and killed by the forces of Alberich, but these cannot secure the Ring before the world is set to rights by Brünnhilde. Since her marriage to Siegfried, Brünnhilde, too, has been a free agent. Accordingly, Brünnhilde countermands the curse of the Ring, sacrificing her own life in a symbolic renunciation of power, by restoring the Rhinegold to the Rhine. Wotan, his kin and his ambitions finally perish in the fires of Valhalla.* (For detailed accounts of the plot, see the entries on each opera.)

General Analytical Introduction

Although set in the remotest pre-dawn of history, the *Ring* is for many Wagner's most accessible work. The greatest art always functions at a multiplicity of levels, and this is as true of the *Ring* as of Homer's *Odyssey*, Cervantes' *Don Quixote* or even Proust's *Remembrance of Things Past*. The Nibelung operas may be regarded as nothing more than sophisticated musical fairy tales or interpreted as the most perceptive modern allegory of mental and social breakdown. They appeal to us today because they seem to address our special problems (and in this respect the *Ring* is obviously superior to its successor, *Parsifal*). First, there is a welcome escape from nineteenth-century theology: the *Ring* makes no statement about man's *guilty* relationship with God. But, secondly, the *Ring* busies itself with an examination of the equation, 'Power minus Love equals Chaos' – and no problem formula has greater modern relevance.

We are all aware, for example, that power politics since the Second World War have threatened the human race with extermination at the pressure of a button. This fact alone should recommend to our attention a great modern drama-cycle which seeks to explain why the human race finds itself in this situation of such absolute self-contradiction. The men whose fingers have access to those doom-buttons are all lawfully appointed. But the drive which places many of them, albeit lawfully, in their horrific positions is a primitive force well understood by Wagner: the wish to conquer inner fear by asserting the self, thus shoring up the ego. It is the dual nature of such power – part legal, part primeval – which Wagner deals with in the characters of Wotan and Alberich in the *Ring*. The only difference between them is that Wotan's egotistical lusts are compromised by inconvenient legal contracts. In the musical dramas which unfold, we are asked to sit and watch what happens to these representative power-seekers when their ambitions are tested to the point of destruction. *Götterdämmerung* is, after all, only a Teutonic conception of Armageddon.

And yet Wagner's argument may be taken right down to the level of the ordinary individual. He is saying that anyone with an over-developed desire for self-assertion, an excessive power-drive, is compensating for inner deficiencies. The desire to obtain a position of authority *for its own sake* betrays the impulse of a frightened person. And yet the action is self-defeating, since internal inadequacies can never be remedied from the outside. Any power obtained by these means is an illusion. What such men have in common is the wish to armour themselves against feelings, to renounce what Wagner summarily calls 'love'. Without love, without pity, without ties or bonds of any kind, the cold political animal may hope to obtain his goal, but at what price? The price, says Wagner, is an excess of anxiety, a cosmic sense of despondency very often resulting in a complete nervous collapse. The *Ring*'s central message is plain: each man must keep himself open to the possibility of emotional acceptance *and* rejection, or he will begin to die from the inside.

There were good reasons why Richard Wagner became preoccupied with these moral and psychological issues during his late thirties. He had just participated in a social revolution which had failed abysmally. He had given up his secure career as a purveyor of public entertainments to the Dresden bourgeoisie and he was broke. He had come to realize that his marriage to Minna Wagner* only scratched the emotional surface of his needs and desire. And he felt piercing inner discontent with his own relationship with humanity (although this could be admitted only indirectly through his art). Therefore, he decided to embark on the most ambitious and costly project in the history of opera – one which would not be completed until 1874, which would not be in proper production until 1876 and, even

then, would make a record financial loss.

Rejecting the themes of Jesus of Nazareth and Frederick Barbarossa as 'insufficiently grand', Wagner, as I have mentioned, first composed a poem called *Siegfried's Death*. This contains most of the events now recounted in *Götterdämmerung*. As his conception developed, Wagner realized that he would have to create a preceding drama, recording the details of Siegfried's life. Therefore, in 1851 he wrote a new poem, called *Young Siegfried*,* corresponding to the opera now simply known as *Siegfried*. Even this additional work did not satisfy him. He next decided to explain the circumstances surrounding Siegfried's birth in a poem called *Die Walküre* (1852), and was not finally satisfied until he had added a prelude in the form of *Das Rheingold* (written later in 1852), to take the story back to the first days of the world and the origins of the gods. His original essay of October–November 1848, *Siegfried's Death* – preceded by a prose draft, *Die Nibelungensage (Mythus)*, written earlier in October – thus became a trilogy of operas, preceded by a prelude called *Das Rheingold*. The text of the four operas was printed privately in 1853 as *Der Ring Des Nibelungen*, comprising a prelude and three dramatic poems.

It was perhaps insane even to contemplate such a gigantic project; even Wagner's vast energies were almost defeated by it. Half-way through the composition of *Siegfried*, he broke off to write *Tristan* and *Die Meistersinger*, because the *Ring* literally seemed endless, a circular Herculean labour. With its completion in 1874, however, Wagner could rest content that these four operas, with their complex interweaving of almost a hundred separate musical motives into nearly twenty hours of sustained sound, were by far and away his greatest achievements, and possibly the outstanding artistic undertaking of the entire nineteenth century.

Ritter family

Julie Ritter befriended Wagner during his Swiss exile, lending him money from 1849. Her son Karl continued the association. The Ritters rejected Wagner after the publication of his pamphlet *Judaism in Music* under his own name in 1869.

Röckel, August (1814–76)

Austrian conductor, composer and writer who was the musical director at Dresden 1843–9. Wagner became one of his closest friends. Röckel was heavily committed to the revolt of 1848. After the uprising was quelled, he received a sentence of life imprisonment. Wagner wrote him a number of artistically significant letters describing his early conception of the *Ring* cycle. Röckel was released in 1862 but he and Wagner later fell out in Munich, when Wagner grew to believe – rightly or wrongly – that Röckel was spreading gossip about himself and Cosima [Wagner]*, not long before Cosima's final break with her husband, Hans von Bülow.*

Rode, Wilhelm (1887–1959)

German baritone and (during the 1920s and 1930s) one of the finest exponents of Sachs* and Wotan,* whose Nazi sympathies finally ended his career in 1945.

Romanticism

The early nineteenth-century artistic and philosophical movement which had an overwhelming impact on Wagner's mind. He, in turn, poured his huge energies into the music of Romanticism. Among the defining ideals of this vast and diffuse shift in sensibility we may list a love of nature in the face of the beginnings of industrialization; an allied reverence for inspiration and imagination, and hence for imaginative art; a nostalgia for preindustrial history and the mythical aspects of, for example, mediaeval chivalry; a rejection of received religion or authoritarian politics; a compensating interest in personal psychology, personal expression and 'sincerity'; and an overriding desire to 'feel' rather than 'deduce' as a way of acquiring information. Romanticism produced a rich yield of talents in all the arts, from poetry to painting. Famous romantic musicians include Beethoven,* Weber,* Liszt,* Berlioz,* Richard Strauss* and Mahler.* Wagner himself suggested that Beethoven's Ninth Symphony, the 'Choral', was the seminal Romantic work.

Richard Wagner's entire life was Romantic, so, too, is his art, in form and content. No greater egotist had ever walked the European stage, except in the theatre of war. Wagner was the Napoleon of opera. He conquered the world with his music, capitalizing on the early campaigns of Beethoven and spreading Romantic revolution wherever there was an opera house. No one today can be a true devotee of Wagner and remain unaffected by the desire for self-expression which runs Romantically throughout the operas.

It should be noted that Germany has in some respects remained a land of romance. As late as 1944, six out of every nine children were christened Sieglinde or Edeltraud, Gunther or Ekkehard – and occasionally the authorities had to prevent over-enthusiastic parents from choosing names so mediaeval that they were scarcely pronounceable. On the other hand, Germany's quest for material wealth since the Second World War has created such high levels of industrial pollution that some experts fear that the country's brooding forests will all be dead by 1990. 'One third of the country is covered with the superb, ancient forests which are so much a part of the German soul. For centuries, they have inspired poems, songs, music and literature. Many Germans like to hike in them for days on end and 40 per cent of the population goes for a forest walk at least once a month' (*The Times*, London, 1982).

Rossweise (W): *see* Valkyries

Roswaenge, Helge (1897–1972)
Danish tenor of warm sonority who was the Bayreuth Parsifal* in 1934 and 1936. His career continued until the late 1960s.

Rubinstein, Anton Grigoryevich (1829–94)
Russian composer who was acquainted with Wagner and Liszt*. He wrote many operas and directed orchestras in St Petersburg, Vienna and on tour in America.

Rubinstein, Joseph (1847–84)
Russian pianist who in 1872 asked Wagner if he could come and work for him. He was appointed musical assistant at Bayreuth, but became unpopular because of his efforts to monopolize the 'master'. He became so depressed by Wagner's death that he committed suicide shortly afterwards. Rubinstein made a notorious attack on Schumann* in the *Bayreuther Blätter*. He also repudiated his own Jewishness, mysteriously beseeching Wagner to 'deliver him from his deficiencies'.

Russell, Anna
English musical cabaret parodist whose targets include Wagner's *Ring of the Nibelungs*. Accompanying herself at the piano, Russell recapitulates the story of the *Ring*, paying special attention to the 'domestic life of Mrs Fricka* Wotan* and the relationship between Siegfried* and his aunts' (the Valkyries*). She notes that Gutrune* is the first woman Siegfried has ever met who is *not* his aunt. A recording of her parody was issued in 1953.

For an exhaustive list of other Wagnerian parodies, from the 1850s to the present-day, see Raymond Furness, *Wagner and Literature* (Manchester University Press, 1982), chapter 4, 'Parody and Persiflage'.

Rysanek, Leonie (b. 1926)
Austrian soprano, who made a sensational impression as Sieglinde* at the first post-war Bayreuth Festival in 1951. Her voice has a thrilling upper register. She has also sung Senta* and in 1982 appeared at Bayreuth as Kundry*.

Sachs, Hans (M)
Wagner's warm and human character, the journeyman artist, based on the real life Hans Sachs (1494–1576) who composed over four thousand master songs and six thousand poems. The original Sachs enjoyed long life, great fame, and creative satisfaction, punctuated by moments of tragedy, with the death of his seven children and, in 1560, of his first wife. For a short time he ceased to compose, but after a second marriage in 1561 he resumed his work. Sachs became a master at the Nuremberg song school in 1517, a master cobbler in 1519 and head of the Nuremberg group in 1554. After his death, he was virtually forgotten until Goethe* rediscovered his poems; today his songs and occasional plays are enjoying a revival.

For Wagner's purposes, Sachs is a foil to Tristan.* In *Die Meistersinger*, we see an ordinary but gifted human being, not particularly good-tempered, who is able to forget his unfulfilled love for Eva because of his commitment to his larger task as artist and leader of the Nuremberg community. Wagner thus suggests to his audience that forbidden love (Sachs is far too old for Eva) does not necessarily end in tragedy, and it is amusing to note that, the real-life Sachs did (at the age of sixty-six) marry a seventeen-year-old 'Eva' after his first wife's death.

Sachs is one of Wagner's greatest bass-baritone roles, partly because of the generosity of his nature. He keeps an open mind about Walther von Stolzing's* revolutionary master-singing and reflects that the purpose of art is to ennoble rather than degrade. He also endears us to him with his impish sense of fun. The teasing of

Beckmesser* in Act II is practically un-rivalled on the operative stage.

Wagner was indebted for several aspects of the characterization of Sachs to Lortzing's* treatment (1840) of Johann Deinhardstein's play of the same title (1827).

Sailor (T I)

The owner of the tenor voice which, singing of Ireland and an Irish maid, awakens Isolde* from her sleep on board Tristan's* ship at the outset of Act I. Isolde mistakenly believes that she is being mocked, whereas the young sailor is in fact singing of his own love, left behind in Ireland.

At a deeper level, the sailor is another voice adding to the orchestral symphony which at this point conjures up the atmosphere of departure. The music speaks of separated lovers and of the violent longing for reunion which fills Isolde's soul, as well as that of the audience.

Saint-Saëns, Charles Camille (1835–1921)

Leading French composer and Wagner-phile who visited Wagner and Liszt* at Wahnfried* in 1876. His enthusiastic championship of Wagner's operatic innovations caused consternation in Paris. Wagner had made his feelings about France and French Art unacceptably clear in his farce Eine Kapitulation, published in 1870 at the height of the siege of Paris. Paris, after all, had laughed the first French performance of Tannhäuser off the stage in 1861. Thus, when Saint-Saëns reported that Wagner had returned to the original intention of the operatic art form, 'in which music and words go together so that one talks while singing and sings while talking . . . in which the music would not be forced on the verse . . .' he was castigated by his fellow-countrymen, who preferred the florid feats of vocalization and embellishment which were popular with French opera-goers at that time. Saint-

Saëns' reviews were reprinted in Harmonie et Mélodie (1885), when French Wagnerphilia began to replace Wagnerphobia and the Revue Wagnérienne was founded, with contributions from Verlaine,* Huysmans* and Mallarmé,* among others. Saint-Saëns was the first to point out that Wagner's idea for Bayreuth was in many ways presaged by the Belgian essayist and composer Grétry, who wrote in 1797,

I would like to see a hall which is rather small, seating not more than a thousand persons, with only one kind of seat throughout, with no boxes, neither large nor small. I would like the orchestra to be out of sight so that neither the musicians nor the lights of the music desks can be seen by the audience. This would create a magical effect as no one would expect the orchestra to be there.

Saltzman-Stevens, Minnie (1874–1950)

A fine American soprano who gave Brünnhilde* under Richter's* direction in 1909 at Covent Garden, where she also sang Sieglinde* and Isolde* (1910–13). She sang Kundry* and Sieglinde at Bayreuth, 1911 and 1913. Her career was cut short by illness.

Sandwike

Small Norwegian fishing village, where Wagner and his then wife Minna [Wagner]* sheltered on board the ship Thetis after a Baltic storm in 1839. Daland* and the Flying Dutchman* both shelter at the same spot in Act I of Der Fliegende Holländer.

Sarazenin, Die (The Saracen Woman)

Grand opera projected by Wagner (to follow Rienzi) in 1842, and rapidly abandoned by him when he became interested in the Tannhäuser legend.

Sayn-Wittgenstein, Princess Carolyne: see Wittgenstein, Princess

Scaria, Emil (1838–86)

Austrian bass, who sang Wotan* in the first *Ring* cycle given in Berlin (1881) and London (1882), both presented by Angelo Neumann*. During the latter cycle he lost his memory and broke down in Act III of *Die Walküre*. Later in 1882 he sang Gurnemanz* in the first performance of *Parsifal* at Bayreuth, and he produced the work at the first festival there (1883) after Wagner's death. He died insane, a few months after a mental breakdown.

Schalldekke

The deck screening the orchestra pit from the audience at the Bayreuth Festival Theatre. In adopting this device, Wagner was following an idea of the eighteenth-century composer Grétry, who wrote in an essay (1791), 'I would like the orchestra to be out of sight so that neither the musicians nor the lights of the music desks can be seen by the audience. This would create a magical effect . . .'

Scheidemantel, Karl (1859–1923)

German baritone, who performed at Bayreuth annually 1886–92 as Klingsor,* Amfortas,* Kurwenal,* Hans Sachs* and Wolfram von Eschenbach.* He was appointed Director of the Dresden Opera in 1920 and produced two volumes on the art of singing, with reference to Wagnerian roles.

Schleinitz, Marie, Countess von (1842–1912)

Confidante of Cosima Wagner* and wife to Count von Schleinitz (1807–85), the Prussian Minister of the Royal Household. She later became a tireless worker on behalf of the Bayreuth Theatre.

Schlesinger

Berlin publishing firm which established a Paris office in 1834. It was this company which commissioned Wagner's abortive *Method for the Cornet à Pistons.**

Schmedes, Erik (1866–1931)

Danish tenor and an excellent actor who was the Bayreuth Siegfried* and Parsifal* in 1899–1902 and 1906.

Schnabelewopski, Herr von: see Heine, Heinrich

Schnorr von Carolsfeld, Ludwig (1836–65)

German tenor, whose premature death greatly upset Wagner. Schnorr was a plump giant with a good voice (although not the equal of Tichatschek's*) and marvellous dramatic abilities. He sang Tannhäuser* and Lohengrin* and studied the part of Tristan,* although he always entertained a superstitious fear of this role.

However, he managed to overcome his reservations in 1862, when he and his wife sang *Tristan and Isolde*, before Wagner. Three years later, they took part in the first public performance. Schnorr thereafter dedicated himself to Wagner's works, and the master entertained the highest hopes that Schnorr's sympathetic understanding would produce a perfect Siegfried.* Unfortunately, Schnorr caught a chill while rehearsing Tristan for a second time, and died shortly afterwards. He was not yet thirty. Wagner wrote, 'In him I lost the great granite block needed to raise my building – I am now left with a pile of rubble.'

Schoenberg, Arnold (1874–1951)

Austro-Hungarian composer, born in Vienna. Schoenberg was strongly influenced by Wagner in such early works as the string sextet *Verklärte Nacht* (*Transfigured Night*, 1899) and the huge *Gurrelieder* (1900–13) for soloists, chorus and orchestra. In due course he evolved the system of serialism, becoming one of the key figures in the development of twentieth-century music. He said: 'For me Wagner is an eternal phenomenon, quite independent of how the currents of fashion regard him. One cannot even call Wagner's world of ideas obsolete or antiquated.' Among Schoenberg's most celebrated pupils were Berg* and Webern.

Schöffler, Paul (1897–1977)

Austrian bass-baritone who was a great Hans Sachs* and sang at Covent Garden in 1934–9 and 1949–53.

Schopenhauer, Arthur (1788–1860)

The 'pessimistic' German philosopher whose work Wagner practically idolized. He said reading Schopenhauer had been 'the most important event of my life'. The compliment was not returned. After hearing *Der Fliegende Holländer*, Schopenhauer remarked that Wagner 'did not know what music was'. He preferred the classical, early nineteenth-century models to Wagnerian luxuriousness. The composer sent him a presentation copy of the poem of the *Ring* in 1854, dedicated with 'reverence and gratitude', but Schopenhauer did not regard the book as any sort of German literary landmark.

Tristan is the work of Wagner's which is most directly influenced by Schopenhauer. In some ways, it is a musical setting of Schopenhauer's *The World As Will And Idea* (1818), but all of Wagner's mature operas are pervaded by Schopenhauer's central notions, even the commonsensical *Die Meistersinger*. This is not just because the philosopher accorded music the highest status of all the arts, although Wagner was obviously flattered to agree. But what he really valued in Schopenhauer was the belief that man is responsible for his own destiny.

In this respect, there is an affinity between Schopenhauer's basic teachings and twentieth-century existentialism: we can only perceive the world through our perceptions; therefore, we create the world for ourselves, even though we can only know it at second-hand, since it lies outside us. Of all the things in the world,

said Schopenhauer, there is only one which can be known in two ways, from the inside and the outside, and that is ourselves. This inside 'self-knowledge' is called 'will', and it reveals to us our primary drives.

Perception tells us that the world is full of will, that there is a restless mass of energy in all creation, from the simple strivings of plants to our own aggressive lusts. This striving is opposable by death. Annihilation stands ever ready to sap the energy of natural will.

Active willing, in other words, is a restless, exhausting compulsion. Schopenhauer accordingly sees death not as doom, but as liberation. Trapped in our bodies, fated to strive for unrealizable goals, we can only master our destiny by learning to regard life as an illusion. Men are victims of circumstances so long as they believe in the efficacy of egotistical self-assertion.

In art, the greatest models are therefore heroes and saints, those figures who accept death and transcend it by renouncing earthly desire for the sake of a noble love. Man's finest achievements, in fact, have been the arts; his greatest achievers are artists, since they summon us to willlessness through catharsis. They cleanse us of that redundant tempest which would otherwise overwhelm the material world in a rage of discontent. However, this state lasts only a short time after each performance. Ultimate wisdom is attained by that tiny chosen band of people who can negate themselves in life, either by identifying with the sufferings of others or by personal asceticism.

Why Wagner was so profoundly stirred by these Romantic notions of sacrifice and heroism is obvious, even if he was no ascetic himself. What he found especially useful in Schopenhauer was the command to look *within*. Self-analysis and self-knowledge, at unconscious as well as conscious levels, could give rise to rich artistic expression.

In a letter to Mathilde Wesendonck,

written in Venice on 1 December 1858, Wagner gaily explains that he has been modifying some of the precepts of the great philosopher, 'friend Schopenhauer', and now suggests that there *is* 'a sacred path towards the complete pacification of the will and this is through love, and certainly not an abstract love of humanity, but real love, a love which springs from sexuality, the attraction of man and woman'.

Schorr, Friedrich (1888–1953)

The leading bass-baritone of his day, Schorr was an exceptional Wagnerian specialist. Born in Hungary, Schorr made a stupendous début at Graz in 1912 in no less a role than Wotan,* which few can contemplate at thirty-four, let alone twenty-four.

From 1924, his fame rested on fine interpretations of the Flying Dutchman,* Wolfram von Eschenbach,* Wotan, Telramund,* Gunther,* Kurwenal,* Hans Sachs* and Amfortas,* Sachs and Wotan being his most famous roles. He was the Wotan at Bayreuth 1925–31 and was the first choice for this part and Sachs at the Metropolitan 1924–43. The majesty and clarity of his voice are preserved on record. He once said, 'When I sing Wagner I try to bind the phrases and spin them just as if it were Verdi.'

Schott

Music publishers at Mainz. Franz Schott (1811–74) took over Wagner from Breitkopf & Härtel* in 1859 and in due course published the *Ring*, *Die Meistersinger* and *Parsifal*.

Schröder-Devrient, Wilhelmine (1804–60)

German soprano, whose acting talents and wondrous voice swept Wagner off his feet and filled his breast with the passion to compose music especially for her. Schröder-Devrient sang in Bellini's* *I* *Capuletti e I Montecchi* as Romeo. It is now thought that it was her performance in 1834 in this opera which particularly inspired Wagner. For Wagner, she gave the first performances of Adriano Colonna (*Rienzi*),* Senta* and Venus,* although she was not happy as Venus and did not sing the role well. 'What on earth am I to wear?' she wailed. 'I can't just put on a girdle!' The first performance of *Tannhäuser* was, in any case, a failure for reasons beyond Schröder-Devrient's control – not least the non-arrival of the scenery and the hoarseness of the leading man, Tichatschek.*

It is significant that Wagner was attracted to this soprano – dubbed 'The Queen of Tears' – because of her dramatic abilities; his philosophy of the *Gesamtkunstwerk*,* a union of music and drama, always required of singers that they should also know how to act.

Weber* shared Wagner's enthusiasm for Schröder-Devrient, as did Schumann,* although Berlioz* deplored that very quality which Wagner praised: her acting, indeed her over-acting. It is generally agreed that from about 1837 onwards the singer's voice declined. Like Wagner himself, Schröder-Devrient was known for her numerous love affairs, which would explain why she became the heroine of a collection of spurious pornographic memoirs.

Schumann, Robert (1810–56)

One of Wagner's *bêtes noires*. Wagner admired Schumann, but the admiration was only returned to a limited extent. Although Schumann, having seen *Tannhäuser* performed, admitted its power as a stage piece, he insisted that Wagner was 'not a good musician' and that his music was 'often quite amateurish'. Moreover, Wagner believed that he was not given his due by the journal, *Neue Zeitschrift für Musik*, which Schumann founded in 1834 and edited for ten years.

Schumann-Heink, Ernestine (1861–1936)
Austrian contralto and mezzo-soprano who, in London in 1892, gave Erda,* Fricka* and Brangäne* under Mahler's* direction. She sang Erda in nine cycles of the *Ring* at Bayreuth from 1896. In 1914 she left Austria to pursue her career in America.

Schwarz, Hans (M)
A stocking weaver (bass), one of the Mastersingers, who helps to condemn Walther von Stolzing's* attempt to make a master song in Act I and swells the numbers on stage in Act III.

Schwarzkopf, Olga Maria Elisabeth Friederike (b. 1915)
Preeminent lyric soprano of her day, who sang the Bayreuth Eva* in 1951. Her talent has been primarily devoted to the art of *Lieder* and latterly to teaching.

Schweizerfamilie, Die (The Schweizer Family)
An opera (1809) by Joseph Weigl (1766–1846), which Wagner considered rescoring during the late 1830s.

Schwertleite (W): *see* Valkyries

Scott, Sir Walter (1771–1832)
One of Wagner's favourite authors. We know from Cosima's diaries that he read Scott's *Count Robert of Paris*, *The Fair Maid of Perth*, *Ivanhoe*, *Quentin Durward*, *Woodstock*, *The Heart of Midlothian*, *Kenilworth*, *The Life of Napoleon*, *Old Mortality*, *The Pirate*, *The Presbyterians* and *Waverley*. It may seem strange that such a colourful Romantic novelist did not provide Wagner with anything but material for diversion. However, it must be remembered that a century ago the novels of Scott supplied a wide audience with the light entertainment which today is provided by television, and so Wagner merely reflected the prevalent judgement of his day.

Scribe, Augustin Eugène (1791–1861)
French dramatist who wrote popular libretti for the composers Meyerbeer*, Verdi and Auber*. In 1837, while Wagner was Director of Music at the Court Theatre in Königsberg, he sent Scribe the score of *Das Liebesverbot*, in the hope that Scribe might adapt a libretto to it for a production in Paris. Discovering that Scribe had at least looked at the work, Wagner was in due course encouraged to come to Paris in 1839.

Seidl, Anton (1850–98)
Austrian-Hungarian conductor, who worked with Angelo Neumann* on his extensive Wagner tour of 1882–3. In 1885 he moved to the United States. He conducted the first American performances of most of Wagner's major works, as well as the first London *Ring* in 1882.

Semper, Gottfried (1803–79)
German architect, with whom Wagner planned his 'theatre of the future'. He was involved with Wagner's building and other schemes in Dresden, Zurich and Munich. He produced designs for an unbuilt Wagner Theatre in Munich, but was not retained to design Bayreuth. He was later among those involved in planning the South Kensington Museums in London.

Senta (H)
Senta is the daughter of the Norwegian sea captain, Daland,* and one of Wagner's archetypal soprano leads, born to sacrifice herself to save a hero (albeit a modest one, the Flying Dutchman*).
At the beginning of Act II, we find her in the living-room of her father's house,

together with a nurse and other maidens. She is apparently engaged to Erik,* a local huntsman, and her thoughts run from time to time on the claim he has laid to her heart. More often, however, she sits brooding over a curious portrait hanging on the wall. This shows a Spanish gentleman whose bizarre story Mary* the nurse has often told her. It is, in fact, a likeness of the Flying Dutchman, dressed in Iberian style because he first set sail when Holland was still under Spanish rule. Senta cannot get him out of her thoughts; in fact, she is bewitched and beguiled by the tale of his accursed wanderings.

Like so many of her kind in prose and verse, Senta would obviously like to do something important with her life. The Flying Dutchman holds such powerful sway over her imagination because of his obvious need for a love which is not ordinary – perhaps a love for herself? Here, then, is Romantic passion of a very nineteenth-century order, set in eighteenth-century Norway. Goaded on by the music as much as by her companions, Senta leaps to her feet, begging, 'Let me that woman be whose constancy redeems you! May the angel lead you to me!'

Right on cue, as it were, in stalks the Dutchman. He is already being urged by her father into precipitate matrimony with Senta. The promises to her former suitor Erik are predictably set aside. Senta recognizes her fatal lover at once: 'He comes for me!' she exults.

Wagner seeks to explain much of the attraction in terms of Senta's compassion for the Dutchman's predicament. But the true agency is her own desire for drama. She loves him because he needs her and therefore 'by powerful enchantment' (of her own making) she is overcome. Not all the promises she has made to Erik can restrain her from the grand gesture of suicide. When she sees her demon lover sailing away, she jumps over the cliff to join him in his ocean prison. Love *can* redeem, as we eventually learn from the *Ring*, but Senta's example is less than irreproachable, although for Wagner she represented the very type of the 'woman of the future'.

Sex

On 20 August 1871 Cosima Wagner* records in her diary the following pronouncement by Wagner: 'I remember that when I was at Dresden I told Röckel* I hoped to have written all my works before I was forty; I assumed that the sexual urge, with which all productivity is connected, would last until then.' Thirteen years earlier, Wagner was writing to his mistress, Mathilde Wesendonck*, that 'there *is* a sacred path towards the complete pacification of the will – a path recognized by none of the philosophers, not even Schopenhauer – and this is through love, and certainly not an abstract love of humanity, but real love, a love which springs from sexuality, the attraction of man and woman'.

The sexual act released Wagner's artistic energies; sexual possession gave him ideas which he metamorphosed into music. This is what happened with Mathilde Wesendonck (Isolde*), with Cosima (Brünnhilde*) and with Judith Gautier* (Kundry*), to take only three examples. All three of these women were married to Wagner's close friends or acquaintances, and, in the first two cases, to men who either supplied the cash to keep his domestic household afloat or helped him in other significant ways. Thus a primitive kind of 'wife-stealing' had its appeal for the composer, as is evident in his work when Gunther* 'steals' Brünnhilde from Siegfried* in *Götterdämerung*, or when the hero claims Isolde from King Marke* in *Tristan*. In real life, Wagner seems to have had a need to claim a woman *from another man*, and this need proved conducive to the creative process. It was an act of free assertion against man-made rules and was therefore liberating. More than that, it enhanced Wagner's own sense of potency. To win an unattached woman was a coup, but to divert the love of a female soul *away* from a friend and *towards* himself was an essential act of self-affirmation. The woman was desirable because others desired her. The act was intrinsically attractive, because it testified to Wagner's capacity for betrayal and showed the dimensions of his personal power. Only a man with divine self-belief could have written Wagner's works. Only a man suffering from an incapacitating lack of self-confidence could have needed both to write the works and to stage the real-life dramas which sustained them.

If Wagner's private muse was erotic, it is characteristic that he should have wished others to live by different rules. There was one law for Wagner, and it included sexual love. For those hearing *Tannhäuser*, *Tristan*, *Lohengrin* and *Parsifal*, however, the message was chastity and celibacy. Nevertheless, Wagner's message is ambiguous because his music retains the mood of its original sensual inspiration. In general, the amorous motives are more artistically convincing than the themes of renunciation (with the possible exception of Alberich's* lovedenial in *Rheingold*). This is the source of D. H. Lawrence's* remark that *Tannhäuser* is 'pornographic'; he thought it promoted sex by denying it. See also 'Incest'.

Wagner as Therapy
One Wagner-lover complained recently in a letter to the *Guardian* that a performance was interrupted when a woman in the audience protested loudly, 'Will you keep your hands to yourself?' For some people, Wagner's work seems to provide a release from social tension and taboo; it operates at a deep, primeval level, stirring passions. English critic Bernard Levin says that he has never succeeded 'in sitting through the end of the *Ring* without weeping', and the leading Wagnerian soprano, Gwyneth Jones,* comments:

I suppose what people get out of the *Ring* is a kind of ersatz religion, I mean not ordinary Christianity or any other formal religion, but they get something which puts them in touch with the essence of religion. I feel this when I'm singing the *Ring* or *Parsifal*, the music is so sacred that I sense a great closeness to God, what I call God. By the third act of *Parsifal* with the Good Friday music* I am always crying my eyes out on the stage.

Shakespeare, William (1564–1616)
One of Wagner's most revered authors, all of whose plays and poems he read eagerly and often aloud. At the age of fourteen, Wagner wrote a drama under the influence of Shakespeare, called *Leubald und Adelaide*.* Specific use was made of *Measure for Measure** for the libretto of Wagner's youthful opera, *Das Liebesverbot*. Wagner said that Beethoven* was the only mortal who could be compared with Shakespeare. Shakespeare's use of thematic imagery strengthened Wagner's theory of the leitmotiv*; he valued too the history plays, with their strong sense of 'historical process working itself out through the drama'.

Shaw, George Bernard (1856–1950)
This prolific Irish playwright wrote a great deal of music criticism and was particularly attracted to Wagner. Shaw visited the Bayreuth festivals sending back despatches signed, facetiously, 'By Reuter'.

In December 1898 he published *The Perfect Wagnerite* in an attempt to explain the ideas of the *Ring* in simple terms to his untheoretically minded English readership. However, the book also offers an interpretation of the *Ring* as a parable on the collapse of capitalism and the emergence of a classless society. He thought, however, that in *Götterdämmerung* Wagner had lost control of his design, resorting to the histrionics of grand opera. The book ran through three further editions but this useful commentary has not been reprinted since 1922.

Shaw's Wagnerian criticism is peppered with a fine wit: he wonders for instance in one article why the Bayreuth Rhinemaidens* wander about in 'muslin fichus and tea-gowns', and he criticizes the use of steam on stage: 'it cannot be denied that from the very first it carried with it the flavour of washing day, totally irreconcilable with the magical strangeness of the Wishing Cup or Tarnhelm.'* He also wrote, more provocatively:

I must also admit that my favourite way of enjoying the *Ring* is to sit at the back of a box . . . with my feet up . . . and listen without looking. The truth is, a man whose imagination cannot serve him better than the most costly services of the imitative scenepainter, should not go to the theatre . . . In planning his Bayreuth theatre, Wagner was elaborating what he had better have scrapped altogether.

Shepherd (T)

Small soprano role, introduced to provide colour in the supposedly mediaeval landscape of *Tannhäuser* and to show us the mixture of pagan and Christian beliefs among the peasantry: the shepherd sings as freely of Holda, the pagan goddess of Spring, as of the Virgin Mary.

Shepherd (T I)

A Breton character (tenor) who sings a song at the outset of Act III, to the music of which Tristan* awakens, but only to remember that the song the shepherd sings has always presaged trouble and death. Tristan dies soon afterwards.

Sibelius, Jean (1865–1957)

Finnish composer whose work won him the status of national hero. He visited the Bayreuth Festival in 1894 and wrote these words to his friend and teacher, Martin Wegelius, immediately after hearing *Parsifal* for the first time: 'Nothing in the world has ever made so overwhelming an impression on me. All my innermost heart-strings throbbed. I was beginning to think of myself as a dry old stick but it is not the case. . . . I cannot begin to tell you how *Parsifal* transported me. Everything I do seems so cold and feeble by its side. *That* is really something.'

Sieger, Die (The Conquerors)

Title for a projected opera about the life of Buddha, for which Wagner wrote a brief prose sketch in 1856 and which he had still not given up hope of composing twelve years later, but which he ultimately abandoned. He obtained the idea from reading Émile Louis Burnouf's *History of Buddhism*.

Siegfried

Music drama in three acts, being the third work in Wagner's tetralogy of the *Ring* cycle and the second in his poetic trilogy, *Des Ring des Nibelungen*. Text and music by Richard Wagner, based on a variety of thirteenth-century Icelandic, Nordic and German poems and legends. The writing of *Siegfried*, begun in 1857, was interrupted for a number of years in the early 1860s in order for Wagner to turn his hand to *Tristan* and *Die Meistersinger*. The opera was completed in 1869 (except for the last few pages of the full score, which were written in 1871), and was first performed as part of the first production of the complete Ring cycle at Bayreuth in 1876.

With this opera, Wagner at last introduces the hero tenor who is central to his whole conception of the *Ring*. Siegfried* is a valiant freethinker, fearless and uninhibited, a character influenced by Nietzsche's superman, Rousseau's noble savage and the athletic spirit of nineteenth-century German nationalism. He is the Romantic paradigm: the creature who lives in harmony with nature, who can tame bears and talk to birds in their own language. Siegfried was born to break the mould of the old world, to do away with mediaeval superstitions and provide an example to the human race of how they can survive on their own resources. He is the archetypal lover, tall and strong, who beats a path to the enchanted dwelling of his paramour, reckless of the dangers from spear or fire.

Siegfried was certainly the character who most caught Wagner's imagination. But there are moments when the composer seems to regard him as a little too light-headed, a little too aggressive, a little too determined to seek the power of fame in the world. For example, when we first encounter Siegfried in Act I he is terrorizing his foster-father, Mime*, by trying to get him bitten by a wild bear. This is by no means the first occasion on which Siegfried has acted callously. Mime tells us he has almost come to expect it.

Siegfried and Mime have lived in the forest together ever since Siegfried's birth. One day in the woods, Mime (who is the Nibelung brother to Alberich*) chanced to encounter the heavily pregnant Sieglinde*. Mime brought her to his cave to shelter her, and served her as midwife. Siegfried was safely born, although the mother perished at the birth. Before she died, Sieglinde had shown Mime the fragments of the magic sword, Notung*, which her husband had worn when he was killed. Then she revealed the heroic destiny of her offspring-to-be. Mime has taken the trouble to raise Siegfried as if he were his own son, yet always for a black, ulterior purpose. He hopes Siegfried will kill Fafner* (who, with the aid of the Tarnhelm*, has turned himself into a dragon, in order to guard his gold) and win the magic Ring* for him, after which he proposes to use the magic to make himself lord of the world.

Mime, therefore, has personal motives for cherishing Siegfried, whom he carefully brings up to regard him as his father. This is puzzling for the boy, because all he feels towards the Nibelung is a mixture of loathing and contempt.

By profession, the dwarf is a master metallurgist and blacksmith. Act I opens to reveal him attempting to forge a sword from the fragments of Notung, and complaining in a soliloquy that Siegfried has broken across his knee every sword which he has so far produced from the pieces. He is sure that with Notung Siegfried would be able to slay the dragon. (Siegfried is also sure that with a strong sword by his side he could leave Mime and fend for himself in the world.) Curious to learn about his true origins, he violently forces Mime to tell him the story of his mother and father and all he knows about Notung. Reluctantly, Mime agrees. Siegfried experiences a confusion of emotions, yet is relieved to discover that Mime is not his blood relation. He then goes off into the woods, threatening that if Mime has not reconstructed Notung before his return, he will beat him black and blue.

Wotan*, disguised as a Wanderer, now enters, but Mime has no trouble in recognizing him (the two met in *Das Rheingold*). The Wanderer hints that he may be able, with his store of wisdom, to help Mime, but Mime misses the point and simply tries to get rid of him. The Wanderer does not leave, but proposes a guessing game. He bets Mime that he can answer any three questions Mime cares to put to him. If he fails to answer correctly, then Mime may remove his head.

The Wanderer's purpose is clear: he wants Notung to be reforged and he wants Fafner killed, but he cannot arrange these matters directly. Therefore he will drop some obvious clues for Mime to pick up and give to Siegfried. Mime asks frivolous questions; the Wanderer gives correct replies. Then the Wanderer, in turn, asks Mime three questions, the final one of which defeats the dwarf. It is: 'Who can reforge Notung anew?' The wily Mime cannot answer. Wotan tells him that Notung 'will be reforged by the one who has never felt fear', which is virtually a code-phrase for Siegfried, as Mime quickly realizes. Wotan departs, telling Mime that he can keep his head for now: 'I leave it forfeit to him who has never learned to fear!' – another reference to Siegfried.

In the third scene, the music achieves an even closer harmony with the poetic text. Mime tells Siegfried that he cannot mend Notung; in that case, Siegfried says, 'I will have to teach you.' The orchestra then vividly describes Siegfried's labour in recasting and retempering his father's sword. Mime, meanwhile, is mixing a drugged drink. He realizes that Siegfried will soon be off to tackle an heroic project in the outside world – killing the dragon Fafner, Mime hopes. When Siegfried is tired after this battle, Mime plans to sedate him with the drug and kill him. His musings are interrupted by Siegfried's triumphant shout that the sword is ready. Holding Notung aloft, he brings down the curtain on Act I by slicing Mime's anvil in two with his magnificent, glittering sword.

Act II, set in a thick forest, opens with a testy encounter between Alberich* and the Wanderer. Alberich wants to make sure that Wotan is no longer meddling in the affairs of destiny. The Wanderer replies that there may be a new hero abroad called Siegfried, and he may indeed slay Fafner and seize the Ring, but he, Wotan, the Wanderer, has not persuaded him to do this. The Wanderer and Alberich rouse the dragon Fafner, who lies sleeping in his cave, to ask if he would like to hand over the magic Ring? Fafner says he intends to keep what he has. The Wanderer now leaves, while Alberich remains, although hidden.

Mime enters, leading Siegfried to Fafner's lair. To test Siegfried before his ordeal, Mime tries to explain to him what fear is, but the poor blond boy cannot grasp the idea. All well and good, thinks Mime, because that guarantees Siegfried victory in the fight with Fafner. An even better outcome, thinks Mime, would be if Siegfried and Fafner could actually slay each other.

While Siegfried waits for Fafner to awaken, there follows a delightful nature interlude, during which we hear the mur-

muring music of the woods and the wood birds. The song of one bird in particular catches Siegfried's attention. He tries to copy it on a reed pipe, but fails comically. Then he blows the same melody on his hunting horn (a gift from Mime), and the woods fill with the raucous blast of sound. Fafner is awakened by the noise. Siegfried, fearless and forthright, fights Fafner and stabs him to the heart. The dragon is as much surprised as wounded, saying that he has never heard of his conqueror. Revealing no momentous secrets, Fafner expires. By chance, a drop of the dragon's burning blood has spilled onto Siegfried's hand. He puts it to his lips, and now finds that he can interpret the Wood-bird's* song. It tells him to take the Ring and the Tarnhelm from Fafner's cave. While he does so, Mime and Alberich encounter each other. There is no love lost between the brothers and neither will agree to form an alliance to win the Ring for the Nibelung race. Each is out for himself alone.

We then witness a highly amusing scene between Siegfried and Mime. Not only can Siegfried understand the song of the Wood-bird; he can also understand that when Mime flatters him, he is actually threatening to kill him. Mime sings a beautiful, wheedling song, the burden of which is that 'I only intend to chop off your head!'. Siegfried saves him the trouble by felling him with a single blow from Notung, to the great delight of Alberich, who is watching from the safety of nearby cover. Rendering Siegfried a final service, the Wood-bird closes Act II by leading him to 'claim a glorious bride', who lies waiting for him, wrapped in enchanted sleep on a nearby mountain top. Siegfried hurries away to do so.

The final Act of *Siegfried* leads up to the fateful and loving meeting between Siegfried and his intended wife, Brünnhilde.* But first, Wotan (still disguised as the Wanderer) beseeches Erda,* the Mother of Earth, to tell him whether or not it is true that the 'swift-turning wheel of fortune' can be stopped. She replies that since her love affair with him her vision has been clouded. She only desires to sleep. The Wanderer therefore informs her that he is now resigned to the passing of his own power, if Siegfried and Brünnhilde – the race of the Wälsings* – can inherit his realm.

The Wanderer, leaving Erda, hurries forth to bar Siegfried's way to Brünnhilde. Only if Siegfried destroys Wotan's spear* can he successfully make his way to Brünnhilde, for so Wotan ordained it. It is a supremely difficult scene for Wotan to play because he is compelled to remain disguised, unrecognized and unacknowledged, and finally to let himself be thoroughly humbled by the rising power of his grandson. Notung shatters the sacred spear, and Wotan finally leaves, to prepare himself for death.

Heedless of such historical niceties, Siegfried races through the flames to find Brünnhilde. When he arrives, he is puzzled. Brünnhilde is not a man. This is the first time in his life that Siegfried has ever seen a woman. (For that matter, Brünnhilde is also his aunt.) He feels fear for the first time as well. Nevertheless, he kisses and awakens her.

Brünnhilde at first welcomes her future husband, but, when she remembers her former glory becomes sadly depressed. She thanks Siegfried for rescuing her, but now asks him to go on his way. He refuses. He feels the full force of love in his heart and will not be denied. Brünnhilde catches his mood and responds. In a joyful duet they rhapsodize on passion. And for the first time in a Wagner opera since *Das Liebesverbot*, we have a pair of lovers who, instead of falling dead, at the finale determine to celebrate love completely: 'eyes together, mouth to mouth . . . virginal light flaring into frenzy'. The opera truly closes on a pinnacle of ecstasy – although we are well aware that the composer has not yet finished with his convoluted drama, and that this happy ending is itself only an interlude before the final twilight of the Gods, the *Götterdämmerung*.

Siegfried (W, S, G)

Siegfried is the clarion-voiced *heldentenor*, dwelling in harmony with nature, brave and fearless, ignorant and free, simple and trusting. He is the child of brother and sister (Siegmund* and Sieglinde* – see *Die Walküre*); thus even the incestuous circumstances of his birth proclaim freedom from inhibition. His grandfather was Wotan,* the Lord of the Gods, who founded the house of Wälse,* to which Siegfried belongs. Siegfried's symbolic purpose in the *Ring* is to introduce liberty into the affairs of men, in the hope that the ills of the Gods can be put right.

IN *Siegfried*

A hero by his very nature tends to be a self-justifying entity. He does nothing except be brave. He faces dangers which other people fear to face precisely because he lacks the capacity to be afraid. There is something automatic about the heroic response to the complexities of the world. The hero is always energetic; he is always healthy; he is nearly always cheerful, taking life as it comes. More than one commentator has acknowledged that, in his unvarying consistency, Siegfried has the prime characteristics of a crashing bore. Others have remarked that by his callous treatment of Mime* he could have qualified for early entry into the *Hitlerjugend*. It is true that his behaviour towards Mime is oafishly cruel, but Siegfried displays freedom's virtues as well as its vices.

For example, he is capable of a great deal of personal learning, even though he is not a born intellectual. He is curious to know what it must feel like to have natural parents. The only human being he has ever known in his life is his warped-minded foster-father, Mime. When he discovers that his mother died giving him birth, he learns (just like Parsifal*) what it is to feel guilty grief. When he hears the Wood-bird's* song, he is keen to try and understand what it means. When Mime describes something called fear, he would very much like to know what it is. When he has slain the dragon, Fafner,* he would like his victim to shed some light on his own origins, but, to his regret, Fafner is both incurious and uninformed. And when he finally arrives on the summit of Brünnhilde's* cliff, and learns indeed what fear feels like, he presses on regardless, falls in love and learns that love is also fear's antidote.

IN *Götterdämmerung*

Despite these noble attributes, it is perhaps both foolish and selfish of Siegfried to seek fame in the world, leaving Brünnhilde at home: was there any reason to leave her behind? Siegfried is undeniably powerless to resist the effects of Gutrune's* amnesiac drug, but his death is ultimately caused as much by pride as by forgetfulness. When he has the opportunity to return the Ring* to the Rhinemaidens,* he is only restrained by a childish wilfulness. The Rhinemaidens *command* Siegfried to restore the Ring, but no hero-tenor submits to *commands*, from whatever quarter issued. And thus he dies. Finally, Siegfried is seen as an instrument whose death is necessary to permit Brünnhilde to understand in the light of her grief that the Ring must be given back to the Rhine: love is a mightier inspiration on earth than even Siegfriedian heroics.

Wieland Wagner* offers another interpretation of the plot. For him, the death of Siegfried was the essential ending of the drama, while the closing scene with Brünnhilde and the motive of redemption should somehow be understood as superfluous. In this analysis, Siegfried's death is as tragic and pessimistic as Wieland's reading of the rest of the cycle: a story of inevitable, entropic decay. Thomas Mann* tended to agree with him, although Wagner himself regarded Siegfried as an untragic, because guiltless, character.

Siegfried's Funeral March

The richly poignant, yet stirring march in Act III of *Götterdämmerung*, linking scenes 2 and 3, which accompanies Siegfried's funeral procession. It is sometimes staged separately as a theatrical spectacle. Wieland Wagner* insisted that the death of Siegfried, not Brünnhilde's* subsequent scene of redemption and death, marked the true ending of the *Ring* cycle.

Siegfried's Rhine Journey

The glorious orchestral passage in Act I of *Götterdämmerung*, linking Scenes 1 and 2, which describes Siegfried's journey along the Rhine towards the land of Gunther,* Hagen* and the Gibichungs.*

Siegfrieds Tod (*Siegfried's Death*)

Operatic poem written in November 1848, which was gradually expanded over the years into the mighty drama of the *Ring*. *Siegfrieds Tod* corresponds to what we now hear in *Götterdämmerung*.

Sieglinde (W) (Mentioned in S)

Hunding's* wife, Wotan's* daughter, mistress to Siegmund* (her brother), by whom she becomes Siegfried's* mother – Sieglinde (soprano) is saddled with a very confused set of personal relationships.

Her greatest quality is the capacity for heroic love, regardless of convention, which she doubtless inherited from Wotan. She is not deterred by the incestuous implications of her feelings for Siegmund, but rather embraces her fate joyously.

This spirit temporarily falters during the flight from Hunding, and she is rendered positively suicidal by Siegmund's demise. But as soon as Brünnhilde* tells her she is to become the mother of a hero, her courage returns and she disappears into the woods, alone and unprotected, to prepare for her labour.

Sieglinde dies giving birth to Siegfried,

according to Mime's* account in the third opera of the *Ring*, which is named after her child. Yet Sieglinde has preserved the fragments of Siegmund's magic sword, Notung,* so that Siegfried shall be able to confront Fafner* when the time is ripe. In *Siegfried*, Brünnhilde eventually tells Siegfried his mother's name, although Mime, his foster-father, had declined to reveal it to him. See also 'Incest'.

Siegmund (W)

The noblest loving *Heldentenor* in the whole of the *Ring* (Siegfried* notwithstanding), if you can forgive his incest* with Sieglinde* and the adulterous abuse of Hunding's* hospitality. Siegmund, Wotan's* son, has been trained in a hard school. His wolf-like father, under the name of Wälse, raised him to be self-reliant and god-defying. Wotan did this in the hope that Siegmund would one day develop into an independent hero and slay Fafner,* the giant, seize the magic Ring, restore it to its guardians in the Rhine and thus free him from fear of Alberich.*

At first, all goes according to Wotan's plan. Siegmund falls in love with Sieglinde. She is his sister, but they have been separated since early childhood. Both have suffered great unhappiness in life. Now the goddess of Spring, Freia, brings them together, helps them to recognize and love each other, and, by so doing, reveals Wotan's purposes to us in the audience. He wishes Siegmund to be armed with a magic sword, Notung,* which has been waiting for him, stuck in a tree at Hunding's house, for many years, and with this sword to work deeds of heroism, one of which might be the slaying of the giant, Fafner.* Wotan also intends that the union of brother and sister should serve to breed a race of heroes for the further protection of the gods. Siegmund duly extracts the sword, swears devotion to Sieglinde and rapturously carries her off to bed.

In the morning, armed with Notung,

Siegmund and Sieglinde flee Hunding's house. There is a pursuit. Wotan is ready to allow Siegmund to kill Hunding, but his wife, Fricka,* goddess of matrimony, has other ideas. She cleverly proves that Siegmund will not do for the purpose Wotan has in mind. The Lord of the Gods has erred by smoothing Siegmund's path for him. This is contrary to Wotan's treaty with Fafner and Fasolt.* Wotan is compelled by Fricka's arguments to withdraw his protection from Siegmund, and Siegmund falls to Hunding. Wotan must now cast around for a new hero to solve his logistical problem, one whom he will not personally train for this end.

It is in some ways a pity that Siegmund does not fit the bill, since he is a far more likeable character than his headstrong son, Siegfried, by whom he is eventually replaced in Wotan's master plan. When Brünnhilde* offers him immortal life in Valhalla,* Siegmund tells her he would rather go to hell with Sieglinde than enjoy eternity in paradise without her. So passionate is his eloquence, that even the stern Valkyrie is moved. She changes her father's plan, risking her own life, and promises Siegmund he can live with Sieglinde. But Wotan overrules her decision and Siegmund dies.

Siegrune (W): *see* Valkyries

Sintolt the Hegeling (W)

Name of a hero captured on the field of battle by the Valkyrie Helmwige. We are told he is the mortal foe of Wittig the Irming.*

Slezak, Leo (1873–1946)

Austro-Czech tenor who was notable as Tannhäuser,* Lohengrin* and Walther von Stolzing*, especially at the Metropolitan Opera, New York (1909–12), where he often performed under Toscanini* and Mahler.* Although he was a serious and dedicated artist, he had a wonderful sense of humour. His swan in *Lohengrin* once started to pull away prior to cue, and Slezak was heard to whisper loudly, 'When does the next swan leave?'

Solti, Sir Georg (b. 1912)

British conductor, born in Hungary, who has devoted his gifts and energy to the performance and recording of Wagner's greatest operas. Originally a pianist, Solti studied under Bartók* and Kodály. However he quickly developed into an able conductor and this work began to absorb his talents. An important landmark in his career were his two seasons as assistant to Toscanini* at the Salzburg Festival, 1936–7. His career as a conductor was interrupted by the war, after which he became musical director of the Munich Opera (1946–52). In 1959, he made his debut at Covent Garden, which was so successful that he was invited to become their musical director (1961–71). Thanks to his direction of Wagner in London the operas won even wider popularity in Britain. He has since conducted in almost every great musical capital and his recordings have brought him many honours, including six awards of the French *Grand Prix du Disque*. He was knighted for his services to music. He conducted the Bayreuth 1983 *Ring*.

Spear of the Grail (P)

Reputed to be the actual spear that the Roman centurion, Longinus,* used to pierce the side of the crucified Christ and thus the second most holy relic in Christendom after the Grail* itself. In Wagner's opera, the spear has been given into the keeping of the Grail servants under Titurel.* When he resigns the leadership in favour of his son, Amfortas,* the spear is lost to the wicked magician, Klingsor.* Klingsor uses it to wound Amfortas in the same anatomical spot that Longinus pierced Christ. The wound refuses to heal because only the spear that made it can also make it well again, and no ordinary mortal can recover the spear from Klingsor's magic grasp. The Grail prophecy is that a 'pure fool' will one day come and restore the spear to its rightful keepers, after he has shattered the power of Klingsor. This comes to pass in the course of *Parsifal*.

According to legend, Joseph of Arimathea conveyed the spear to a band of original Grail knights from whom it was subsequently reclaimed by Heaven. A contrary tradition maintains, however, that Longinus' spear was dug up at Antioch during the First Crusade.

Spear, Hagen's (G)

The spear on which Siegfried* swears he has been true to Brünnhilde* and on which Brünnhilde swears he has been false. Later it is the spear with which Hagen* stabs Siegfried in the back.

Spear, Wotan's (R, W, S)

Wotan's* spear was plucked from the Tree of Life (see 'Yggdrasil') and is engraved with the treaties and compacts by which he rules the world. It symbolizes his power, based on the authority of law. His spear is both a weapon and a totem of honour. It is used to kill Hunding,* for example, in *Die Walküre* and yet it prevents Wotan from killing the giants in *Das Rheingold* when they come to claim Freia.* His hands are bound by his bargain to pay them an acceptable wage for their work in building Valhalla.* Similarly, his spear cannot be used to destroy Alberich* directly, since Wotan, who craves power, may not seize it by force. Finally, the spear is shattered by the 'free' power represented by Siegfried, whom Wotan himself has created in the hope that Siegfried one day will set the world to rights, even at the price of Wotan's overthrow.

Spohr, Louis (1784–1859)

German romantic composer. He was an unreserved supporter of Wagner's mature style, which he anticipates in his use of chromaticism and the leitmotiv*, and in his abandonment of set 'numbers', in three of his own operas: *Faust* (1816), *Zemire und Azore* (1818–19) and *Jessanda* (1822).

Spontini, Gaspare Luigi Pacifico (1774–1851)

Italian composer, whose French opera *Fernand Cortez* (second version, 1817) strongly influenced the young Wagner.

Spring Song (W)

The glorious passage of music, indicating the long spring night during which Siegmund* and Sieglinde* first identify their feelings of love for each other, towards the end of the first act of *Die Walküre*.

Squires, Four (P)

A body of sopranos and tenors, attendant on the Grail knights, who effectively assist in the dramatic development of the opening act of *Parsifal* by asking Gurnemanz* questions about Kundry,* whom they do not like, and by replying to his inquiries about the latest state of Amfortas'* health. They suffer from certain youthfully hidebound preconceptions until Gurnemanz broadens their horizons.

Stabreim

The unrhymed alliterative verse which Wagner set much store by and used for his text of the *Ring*. His own appreciation of poetry was narrowly technical. Generally, he thought poems were created by turning prose drafts into rhyming couplets. The *stabreim* effect was intended to reinforce the notion of the *Gesamtkunstwerk** by creating a unity in multiplicity, designed to make a cumulative impact on the mind of the listener.

Stanislavsky, Konstantin Sereyevich (Konstantin Sergeyevich Alekseyev), 1863–1938)

Russian theatre and opera director, the father of 'method' acting who once testified, 'Wagner's feeling for staging and his dream of the festival in Bayreuth are the most grandiose creations of the entire nineteenth century in the field of theatre.'

Steersman (H)

Tenor leader of the sailors' chorus on Daland's ship, who falls asleep on watch in Act I and thus fails to notice the ghostly arrival of the Flying Dutchman. His singing provides many of the sea motifs later developed in contributions by more important characters.

Steersman (T I)

Minor baritone role, the helmsman of the ship on which Isolde* flees to Brittany to join the ailing Tristan.* He tells the company that King Marke's* ship is in close pursuit and that, if it comes to a fight, there will be no possible escape.

Stein, Heinrich Freiherr von (1857–1887)

German scholar and writer who was appointed Siegfried Wagner's* tutor in 1879. His principal works were *Heroes and the World* and *Origins of the New Aesthetics*. Wagner had a considerable influence over his theories.

Stern, Daniel

Pen-name of Cosima Wagner's* mother, Marie Catherine Sophie de Flavigny, Countess d'Agoult.*

Stewart, Thomas (b. 1926)
American baritone, who sang Donner,*
Gunther* and Amfortas* in 1960 at
Bayreuth, where he appeared regularly
until 1975, including the Flying Dutch-
man*, Wotan* and Wolfram von Eschen-
bach* in his repertoire. He has also sung
Hans Sachs* (at Nuremberg) and
Kurwenal* (in New York).

Stolzing, Walther von (M)
Heroic but impatient young Franconian
knight who wishes to marry Eva,* daughter of one of the Mastersingers, Veit
Pogner.* Walther is a symbol of poetic
and passionate youth. His senses immediately respond to the impact of hot
blood and natural beauty, whether of the
land or of the flesh. But he also has grit. A
strict song-contest has been set up as a
means of choosing the right suitor for Eva,
and Walther enters, but he is no orthodox
competitor.

Not everyone would brave a band of
pettifogging old songsters in their cham-
bers and sing to them of joys forgotten in
the pursuit of finicky metrical precision.
Walther stands firm in the belief that
poetry begins with a vision, not with a
calculator. He has no time for all these
'stanza-rhyming packs of poetasters! –
everywhere judges, markers with
grudges!' It is no surprise to us that his
song is rejected, nor that Walther thinks
he must resort to elopement to secure his
love.

The wise old shoemaker and Mastersinger Hans Sachs* persuades him otherwise
and teaches him a great deal of wisdom
about poetry. In many respects, says
Sachs, inspiration comes too easily to
youth. For the most part, young men lack
the experience to fashion a sublime work
of art. The true test comes in mature
years, when – perhaps at some distance
from the original source of his inspiration
– a man can recall his dreams and by his
learning and artistic discipline give those
old dreams new life. He shows Walther

how, and Walther is able to write a song
that will sweep all Nuremberg off its feet,
not to mention Eva Pogner.

Walther duly wins the song contest,
besting Beckmesser.* But he refuses to
join the Masters' guild until Sachs has
completed his education for him, insisting
that no poet is an island: he is part of a
mainland of tradition and owes a great
debt to those who ploughed there before
him.

Strassburg, Gottfried von (fl. 1210)
Author of one of the major mediaeval
versions of the story of *Tristan und Isolde*,
to whom Wagner is heavily indebted for
his libretto. Gottfried's limpid, mel-
lifluous verse translates the twelfth-
century tale of the Anglo-Norman poet
Thomas from thunderous passion into
something of a lyric idyll. It should be
noted that Thomas, like Wagner, played
down the power of the drug philtre in
order to heighten the independent human
passions, but Gottfried restored it to its
full, compelling potency.

Strauss, Richard (1864–1949)
The last of the great Romantic composers,
Richard Strauss excelled in his tone poems
and operas, including *Der Rosenkavalier*
(1911). His early enthusiasm for the operas of Wagner led to his being hailed as
'Richard the Second'. In 1889 and 1891,
he worked as musical assistant at the
Bayreuth Festival and Cosima tried to get
him to marry into the family, but he
resisted. His article on the staging of
Tannhäuser, published in the *Bayreuther
Blätter* (1892), is still of interest to students today.

Strauss had a close and questionable
relationship with the Nazis during the
Second World War, although he was
cleared of complicity with them. Of all the
post-Wagnerian composers of opera,
Strauss has been by far the most successful, absorbing the master's influence, but
nearly always in a relatively conservative
fashion.

Stravinsky, Igor (1882–1971)

Russian-born composer, notably of ballets and other orchestral music, including the famous *The Rite of Spring* (1913). He visited Bayreuth in 1912. Recalling his experiences nearly a quarter of a century afterwards (1936), he writes,

The performance which I saw there would not tempt me today even if I were offered a room gratis [he had had trouble finding accommodation]. The very atmosphere of the theatre, its design and its setting, seemed lugubrious. It was like a crematorium, and a very old-fashioned one at that, and one expected to see the gentleman in black who had been entrusted with the task of singing the praises of the departed. The order to devote oneself to contemplation was given by a blast of trumpets. I sat humble and motionless, but at the end of a quarter of an hour I could not bear any more. Crack! Now I had done it! My chair had creaked making a noise which drew on me the furious scowls of a hundred pairs of eyes. . . . I do not want to discuss the music of *Parsifal* nor the music of Wagner in general. . . . What I find revolting in the whole affair is the underlying conception which dictated it – the principle of putting a work of art on the same level as the sacred and symbolic ritual which constitutes a religious service. . . .

Sucher, Rosa (1849–1927)

German soprano who was Sieglinde* in the first complete cycle of the *Ring* at Leipzig in 1878. After making her London début as Elsa* in 1882, she gave Senta,* Elisabeth,* Eva* and Isolde* later in the season, singing the two last-named roles in the first London productions of *Die Meistersinger* and *Tristan*. At Bayreuth (1886–99) she sang Isolde, Kundry,* Eva, Venus* and Sieglinde*. She was especially notable for the intensity and warmth of her Elsa, Sieglinde and Isolde.

Sulzer, Dr Johann Jakob (1821–97)

Swiss government official with whom Wagner grew friendly in the late 1840s and who helped Wagner financially.

Swan, The (L)

The form which Ortrud* compels Prince Godfrey* of Brabant to assume after cursing him with a spell. In this guise, Godfrey provides river transport for Lohengrin.* Lohengrin hopes to release Godfrey through the power of the Grail,* but Elsa's* failure to refrain from asking Lohengrin to reveal his name prevents this. Only by an extempore prayer does Lohengrin move the Grail to disenchant Godfrey.

Wagner got the germ of the idea of the swan from Wolfram von Eschenbach,* but mythical swans abound in both classical and mediaeval legends – from Leda to the Walloon-French epic *Le Chevalier au Cygne* – and it was not difficult for Wagner to appreciate the symbolic value of this creature. Parsifal* makes his appearance as a swan-shooter in Wagner's final opera.

Talvela, Martti Olavi (b. 1935)

Finnish bass who gave a good account of Titurel at Bayreuth in 1962 and has since sung all the main bass Wagnerian roles there.

Tannhäuser

Opera in three acts; text by the composer, based on a miscellany of popular and romantic mediaeval sources. It was first performed at Dresden on 19 October 1845, but did not win the immediate success Wagner and his creditors desired. A new version opened in Paris in 1861 but was destroyed by the claque and members of the Jockey Club, who maintained a barrage of boos against which no opera could survive. It was withdrawn after three performances.

Wagner wrote most of *Tannhäuser* 'in a state of burning exaltation that held my blood and every nerve in fevered throbbing', between the summer of 1843 and the spring of 1845, having been distracted in the meantime by two choral compositions: the choral paean of welcome for the King of Saxony and his funeral oration and chorus for the burial of Weber* at Dresden. He was, as ever, in dire need of money. Most of the income from *Rienzi* was being absorbed by old debts, and this opera, together with *Der Fliegende Holländer*, had not been given quite as widely as Wagner optimistically hoped. As usual, he was also living generously beyond his current means.

Wagner turned to German mediaeval literature for his financial and artistic salvation. The historical Tannhäuser* (*c.* 1200–*c.* 1270) was a German lyric poet who became transformed into an international legend. He was probably a crusader; he travelled widely, lived well as a professional minstrel singer and left a number of lyric lays, dance songs and gnomic poems. His legend is written in the popular ballad, *Danhauser* (1515), which tells the story of a wandering minstrel enticed to the court of Venus. He later repents of his sensual sins, but is denied absolution by the Pope and so returns to Venus for eternity, although a miracle has by now induced the Pope to relent. An ironical twist in the story is that the Pope is damned for failing in his office as dispenser of Christian forgiveness, whereas the minstrel can frolic in the arms of Venus until Judgement Day before receiving his penalty. Other sources include Jacob and Wilhelm Grimm's *German Sagas* (1816–18), E. T. A. Hoffman's* collection of stories, *The Serapion Brethren*, Ludwig Bechstein's *Legends of Thuringia* (1835) and Tieck's *The Faithful Eckart and Tannhäuser*.

By general consent, *Tannhäuser* is a more original, more subtle conception than *Der Fliegende Holländer*. The latter 'still held to the design of conventional opera,' according to Robert Jacobs, 'it being divided into "numbers", some of which even had cadenzas'. The joining of the situations in the earlier work, Wagner himself admitted, 'was imperfect'. In *Tannhäuser*, he would try to do away with 'operatic diffuseness'. He would present his hero with greater freedom, torn not by external forces, but by inward, psychological conflict – conflict Jacobs defines as 'the conflict between the desire of the flesh for pleasure and of the spirit for redemption'.

Tannhäuser shows an advance in technique over *The Flying Dutchman*; Wagner replaces set-piece songs with 'thematic signatures', but does not yet modulate these leitmotivs to express several moods or conflicts in one character simultaneously – as happens, for example, in the *Ring*. Baudelaire noticed something of this in his 1861 essay on 'Richard Wagner and Tannhäuser in Paris', where he discerns a new 'totality of effect'. Wagner now begins to transcend the conscious mind for the first time, and to discover the musical symbols for conventionally repressed desires – lust, power, revolt, self-assertion – and their full opposite in self-denial. Instead of arias, which are civilization's renderings of acceptable thoughts, Wagner found an equivalent in sound for the more devious and less acceptable wanderings of the mind – for a mind roaming the inner sea (like the Flying Dutchman's*) or a mind excluded from the inner pleasures of the Venusberg* (like Tannhäuser's). In both cases, the music manages to convey the depressed state of the victim very precisely – just as we feel elsewhere a jubilant hero's triumph of will (over Senta,* over Elisabeth*).

The first performance of *Tannhäuser* was disappointing. The hearty tenor Tichatschek* could not quite grasp the depths of the complex character he was meant to portray and Schröder-Devrient* was embarrassed by her role as the Queen of Lust. The notorious 1861 Paris production, even though it incorporated the many improvements to the score which Wagner inserted after the Dresden run, was simply destroyed by the Parisian philistines: the management wanted the opening ballet to be deferred till Act II, since this was when the members of the Jockey Club arrived at the opera, and these bloods naturally wished to see their mistresses perform in the *corps de ballet*. Wagner refused; the gentlemen-jockeyists booed. The work only slowly recovered from this assault in succeeding years.

To produce the *Tannhäuser* that we know today, Wagner merged two distinct tales. The first is the seduction of a Wanderer by Venus*. The second is the minstrel contest at the Wartburg*. This allowed him an opportunity for writing big operatic 'numbers' and for evoking Venus's sensual attractions; during the contest at the Wartburg, Tannhäuser cannot help but recall the idyllic days of delight he has passed beside Venus. This, in fact, produces one of the opera's electrifying high points, only to be compared with Venus's later appearance in Act III, when Tannhäuser returns from Rome.

The story begins at the Court of Venus, deep inside the Venusberg* (or Hörselberg) Mountain, near Eisenach. We see a vast, Ludwigian grotto, a blue lake, naïads, sirens, dancing nymphs, bacchantes and all the other paraphernalia that led D. H. Lawrence on several occasions to pronounce *Tannhäuser* 'pornographic'. Tannhäuser has his head in Venus' lap and 'in the arms of love fiercely glowing seems to bask in the charms of Pleasure o'erflowing'. Mist descends. Tannhäuser and Venus are alone.

The occasionally incongruous, martial overture has given way to subtle and erotic ballet music, which is in turn replaced by the ambivalent themes of Tannhäuser's longing: both to stay where he is, enchanted, and to leave the Venusberg for ever.Like Arindal* before him and Siegfried* afterwards, Tannhäuser feels the need to be up and doing things in the world: 'Not lust alone the heart desireth!' This is a repudiation of Wagner's message in *Das Liebesverbot*, and we must sadly conclude that piety makes better art; or else it was not just piety, and the composer genuinely believed that people would prefer a holy love unto death rather than

eternity in the arms of Venus. Eventually, Tannhäuser's spirited song of freedom drowns Venus's angry curses: 'If thou never to me returnest Accursed the human race shall be,' she storms, but it is in vain.

Tannhäuser is released from her spells and finds himself in a valley by the castle of the Wartburg, beside a rural shrine to the Virgin. He praises God for his release and acknowledges that he has sinned and needs salvation. It is important to stress that Venus is meant to be a devil in this work, otherwise it is hard to understand the nature of Tannhäuser's offence. For the modern sensibility, particularly, the element in the opera which condemns sensuality has to be reinterpreted at more than its face value. It is quite clear that Tannhäuser yearns for the physical in woman – both in Venus and in Elisabeth. As Robert Jacobs stresses;

In the Pilgrim's Chorus, in the Hymn to Chaste Love, in 'O Star of Eve', in Elisabeth's Prayer, he seems to be drawing not away from but *towards* the Venusberg. This music exhales a delicious melancholy, a sense of denial, a longing. . . . When at the end Tannhäuser, about to reenter the Venusberg, is redeemed by the sight of Elisabeth's corpse, the chorus sings a banal hymn and then [we hear] the yearning melody of the Pilgrims' Chorus *upon every crochet of whose accompaniment the strings make a fascinatingly irreligious slur* [my italics].

In a literal sense, Wagner condemned Tannhäuser's 'going to the devil', but musically he longed to give him the tangible delights of love.

By an operatic coincidence, Tannhäuser's former comrades (*Minnesinger* Knights) now meet with him. We hear from Henry the Writer* that Tannhäuser used to be inordinately proud, and from Wolfram von Eschenbach* that it is plain to see he is 'proud no longer'. In fact, our hero is very low indeed and in no mood for jovial company, until Wolfram mentions the Landgrave's niece Elisabeth – 'that magic name'. Tannhäuser hears that she has been quite bewitched by his magic voice ever since the last song contest at the Wartburg and agrees to accompany the party back to see her. 'To thee, to thee,' cries the minstrel-knight, uplifted and charged by the restoration of loving memories.

In Act II the scene moves to the minstrel hall at the Wartburg. Elisabeth is equally overjoyed by her man's return – 'I am more foolish than a child' – but cannot seem to get a sensible answer out of him as to where he has been. When she puts the question directly, the reply is an ironic evasion: 'The God of Love brought me back to you.' Wolfram, we notice, is not so pleased by the favourite's return. 'For me no joys are waiting,' he tells us, 'And every hope doth flee!' Reintroductions completed, we move on to the new song feast. The Landgrave provides a little national map-reference ('We are the champions who fight for German right and might'), before choosing a new theme for his *Minnesinger* to extemporise on. The winner is to be the one who can most movingly persuade the company to accept his interpretation. With no hint of prescience, Hermann the Landgrave* bids them, 'Say – what is Love?'

This has an immediately troublesome effect upon Tannhäuser, who begins to day-dream, no longer concentrating on the proceedings. When Wolfram defines love as 'pure and tender', Tannhäuser looks puzzled: surely there is more to the matter than this? When Walther emphasizes love's moral qualities, Tannhäuser involuntarily mutters that this sounds too cold: 'He can never have felt soft caresses and rapturous joys.' Biterolf* (another Knight and *Minnesinger*) calls Tannhäuser a blasphemer, insisting that love is a martial rather than an erotic inspiration, 'a defender of the faith, an arm to shield the good', and shows that he is ready to fight for this narrow, repressive nostrum. But Tannhäuser quite accurately retorts that he is a prater: 'Tis certain thou hast never gained the joys that I have often drained!'

Since no man likes to be accused of being so undesirable that women refuse his caresses, Biterolf makes as if he would like to love Tannhäuser to death on the spot, but a fight is averted. The songs continue. When Wolfram begs that his serenade shall be declared the winning song, Tannhäuser angrily rises to laud the stronger joys of dalliance with a mistress of the erotic arts, his voice painting an increasingly plain portrait of decadence, until only the obtuse can fail to realize who his mistress must be: 'He hath with Venus dwelt.' Horror, outrage and repulsion seize the assembled throng (and their troubled minds): like all staunch puritans, they would prefer to kill him than forgive him.

It is the saintly Elisabeth who restrains them. She says that Tannhäuser's horrid revelations have already killed her (is this only a metaphor?), but counsels them to think not of revenge but of God. Their Christian duty is to try to achieve Tannhäuser's salvation: 'I plead for him, the Saviour died for him too!' The Landgrave is still troubled: 'This curse-beladen son of sin – how shall I punish him?' Eventually, it is agreed that Tannhäuser's path to salvation lies towards Rome. He must join the weary Pilgrim's march to St Peter's and seek the Pope's blessing.

Act III takes us back to the wayside shrine and the spot where Tannhaüser 'landed' after his ejection from the Venusberg. Elisabeth is scanning the faces of passing pilgrims, hoping for news of the return of her errant knight. When all seems lost, she prays to the Virgin for 'renewed purity' and begs God to 'take me from this earth away', if the blood sacrifice of her own life will appease him and grant Tannhäuser grace.

Tannhäuser does return, but chances to meet Wolfram instead of Elisabeth. Wolfram wants to know if he managed to obtain grace; Tannhäuser sullenly answers that he only wants to know the way back to Venus. 'Speak not of Rome!' he snarls, then relents enough to tell

Wolfram that his journey has been fruitless. Yes, he did make the trip. Yes, he did obtain his audience with the Pope (probably Urban IV). But all the answer he got from the Holy Father was 'Didst thou in Venus' mount delay, So art thou damned for aye and aye, Salvation *never* can be thine.' And as a further gloss on this uncompromising example of Papal charity, Tannhäuser was told that he would find salvation 'only when the Pope's staff shall shoot forth green leaves' – in fact, one assumes, never.

Thus, denied Elisabeth, Tannhäuser has decided that he must have Venus, and it is to her that he now calls. All Wolfram's horror does not prevent the mist of love from rolling on stage and Venus from shimmering forth out of the gloom. There is a struggle of wills between the moral Wolfram (aided off-stage by the spirit of holy Elisabeth) and Tannhäuser, hellbent on his desires (aided on stage by the glorious Siren of Love). Wolfram and Elisabeth win only when the former utters the name of the latter; this is a more powerful token than any rival aphrodisiac, especially since Wolfram claims that Elisabeth has just died to save Tannhäuser's soul. Her spirit is 'fluttering over them', and her funeral bell can be heard ringing in the distance. Wolfram then tells Tannhäuser that he is redeemed; Venus tells herself that she has lost him; and Tannhäuser falls dead in Wolfram's arms. The Pope's staff is now carried on stage covered with sprouting buds and green leaves. 'Great is the Lord and grand are his ways,' we are told, for 'see this miraculous mark of heavenly salvation!'

The ending of the opera is too good to be true. Feasible alternatives were available to Wagner, but he rejected them. Would it have been a violation of any essential dramatic principle if Tannhäuser had *not* died of salvation? Would this variant have diminished in any way Elisabeth's grand and tragic gesture of self-sacrifice? Does not Tannhäuser's hasty exit in a sense

diminish our belief in its value anyway? Of course she ostensibly yearns to save by her death his spiritual, not earthly, self. All the same, one may conjecture that, if Wagner had let Tannhäuser live, he could have made his hero honour Elisabeth's sacrifice by choosing to survive chastely in memory of her, without Venus. Would it not also have been pleasant to see the Pope punished (as he was in the original saga of *Danhauser*) for his patent error in denying the central tenet of Christianity: that anyone who truly repents may gain absolution? The modern audience, more able to condone sensual love and less able to condone uncharitable prudery, is likely to think so.

The same audience, however, stunned by the music, is likely to regret that Wagner succumbed to the forces of conventional operatic and social morality at a point when his narrative imagination might have stretched a little further outside orthodoxy in the direction of the Venusberg, where the devil, after all, has by far the better tunes.

Tannhäuser (T)

Based on the thirteenth-century German lyric poet of the same name (*c.* 1200– *c.* 1270), Tannhäuser in Wagner's hands is not a pleasure-loving mediaeval adventure-seeker, but a troubled, nineteenth-century *Angst*-finder. Behind the characterization one cannot help but detect the philosophic preoccupations of the new industrial age; discipline, duty, dignity and dedication. At a deep level, Tannhäuser clearly represents some of Wagner's own guilty insecurities. Had not the composer himself wallowed in the Venusberg* more than once, and would he not do so again whenever temptation proved too strong? More generally, he is there to reveal the huge power of sex over men's souls and to suggest that spiritual love alone can provide an antidote.

Most of Tannhäuser's action in the opera is internal and psychological. We meet him first when he is clearly under a spell and therefore not responsible for what is happening. He manages to tear himself away from the charms of Venus – 'For freedom still I yearn!' – only to lapse into a debilitating depression. He temporarily revives when he encounters Elisabeth* again, but his mind is still captive to Venus, as it has been for most of the opera. He is incapable of concealing this during the song contest: when his companions realize he has loved Venus, a devil, he is driven to Rome, to seek absolution. The Pope rejects his plea for grace, and poor Tannhäuser can only succumb once more; Elisabeth's sacrificial intervention alone prevents him from going back into the Venusberg. And so he dies.

This is hardly the tenor hero – as Tichatschek* discovered in the first production in 1845. One's only regret with regard to Tannhäuser is that he protests his (after all very great) measure of innocence all too little – especially in the light of the fact that Wagner the composer makes the attractions of Venus the lover sound so infinitely superior to those of Elisabeth the saviour.

Tantris (T I)

The whimsical name Tristan* calls himself when he seeks Isolde's* medical aid for the festering wound he received while slaying her fiancé, Morold.*

Tarnhelm (R, but present throughout the *Ring*)

A magic helmet, or 'wish-helmet', which Alberich,* through the power of the Ring,* commands Mime* to forge for him. It is operated by secret rhymes which Alberich devises. The wearer who learns the passwords can transform himself into any shape he pleases, become invisible, or instantly transport himself to any place of his choice. In general, the power of the Tarnhelm seems to be unlimited and arbitrary, although, when in danger, its wear-

ers rarely manage to wish themselves to safety.

But, just like the Ring, the Tarnhelm seems cursed. It is the cause of Alberich's downfall, since Wotan* catches him while he is hopping about under the Tarnhelm, disguised as a toad. When Fafner* acquires the gold, he uses the Tarnhelm to change himself into a giant dragon, both to guard his treasure and to ward off attack. But Siegfried* comes to kill him precisely because he *is* a dragon, for that is the creature heroes are meant to slay. Again, it is largely the accursed Tarnhelm which allows Siegfried and Brünnhilde* to be deceived by Hagen's* plot in *Götterdämmerung*. Without the helm, Brünnhilde would never have mistaken Siegfried for Gunther* (see *Götterdämmerung*), and there would not have been a subsequent problem of mismarriage and jealousy.

The Tarnhelm motive itself is a truly bewitching piece of musical magic. It perfectly symbolizes the power which the helmet bestows: that of preventing the left hand from knowing what the right hand is doing. The Tarnhelm is really a metaphorical mask of *self*-deception, a mask which Wagner in real life wore on many occasions.

Tausig, Carl (1841–71)

Polish pianist of exceptional virtuosity and composer, who, in his last years, was associated with Wagner. At fourteen, Tausig met Liszt,* who took him on his concert tours. Tausig became the most celebrated of the first generation of the pupils of Liszt, some of whose faults, according to detractors, he picked up. Certainly, up to the 1860s, Tausig was regarded as something of a ranter at the keyboard, but later he became a really fine performer. Tausig made a piano transcription of *Die Meistersinger* which is still in use today, and shortly before his death worked hard to help Wagner found the Bayreuth theatre.

Tchaikovsky, Pyotr Ilyich (1840–93)

Russian composer, who, it seems, had to put up some resistance to the overwhelming energies of Wagner's music in order to preserve his own style. It is, therefore, not surprising that on his only visit to Bayreuth (1876) he should have reviewed the *Ring* (for the Russian paper *Russky Viedomosty*) somewhat crabbily:

I have dwelt on this matter at some length with the design of calling the attention of my readers to this prominent feature of the Bayreuth megalomania. As a matter of fact, throughout the whole duration of the festival, food forms the chief interest of the public; the artistic representations take a secondary place. Cutlets, baked potatoes, omelettes – all are discussed more eagerly than Wagner's music.

Tchaikovsky goes on to note that the greatest musical spirits of the day, himself apart, were significantly absent from the proceedings: 'Verdi, Gounod, Thomas, Brahms,* Rubinstein,* Raff, Joachim and von Bülow'* had not come to Bayreuth. He asks the question, 'If I, as a professional musician, had the feeling of total mental and physical exhaustion after the performances of each of the parts of the *Ring* – how great must be the fatigue of the amateurs!' But finally he responds to Wagner's spell: 'If the *Ring* bores one in places, if much is incomprehensible . . . if the harmonies are open to objection . . . even if the immense work should fall into oblivion . . . yet the *Nibelungenring* is an event of the greatest importance to the world, an epoch-making work of art.'

In a private letter to his brother Modest, he writes, 'Musically, it is inconceivable nonsense . . . after the last notes of the *Ring* I felt as though I had been let out of prison.' Even so, the Russian master felt it necessary to acquaint himself with Wagner's other operas. He called *Lohengrin* 'the crown of Wagner's work' and felt that *Parsifal* had been written by a 'great master, a genius, even if he has gone somewhat astray. . . .' On the other hand, *Tristan* he dismissed as 'an endless void, without movement, without life'.

Telramund, Frederick, Count von (L)

A noble courtier seduced from the path of virtue by the witch-like Ortrud.* His political ambition allows him to listen to Ortrud's lies about Elsa's* character and thus embolden himself to claim the throne of Brabant for his own. Ortrud also spurs him on to seek vengeance after his battlefield humiliation by Lohengrin,* telling him it was a magic spell that alone defeated him. This is a subtle half-truth, since, although Lohengrin is protected by enchantments, these derive not from the black arts but directly from God. Telramund finally loses his life because he persists in believing Ortrud's original cruel untruth: that Elsa murdered her brother Godfrey.*

Ternina, Milka (1863–1941)

Croatian soprano, who was the 1898 Covent Garden Isolde* and the 1899 Bayreuth Kundry.* She made her American début at Boston (1896) in Brünnhilde* and Isolde, and first appeared at the Metropolitan Opera in 1900 as Elisabeth.* According to the *New York Times* she had 'an overwhelming plenitude of warm mellow tone'. She also sang Ortrud* and Sieglinde.*

Thomas (Anglo-Norman poet): *see under* Strassburg, Gottfried von

Thomas, Jess Floyd (b. 1927)

American tenor, the 1961 Bayreuth Parifal*, who has since sung Siegfried,* Tannhäuser,* Lohengrin*, Walter von Stolzing* and Tristan.*

Thorborg, Kerstin (1896–1970)

Swedish mezzo-soprano, who sang Wagner in London 1936–9. She was one of Ernest Newman's* favourite interpreters of Wagnerian opera. He singled out her acting for special praise; writing of her

Kundry,* 'she walks like a goddess, sits like a statue, and not a gesture is wasted throughout the whole evening. All in all, I would rank her as the greatest Wagnerian actress of the present day.'

Thuringia
Historic region of Germany, now in the south-western part of the German Democratic Republic, chosen by Wagner for the setting of his opera *Tannhäuser*.

Tichatschek, Joseph Aloys (1807–86)
The silver-voiced Bohemian tenor who created Rienzi* and Tannhäuser.* He was the prototype *Heldentenor*, but such was his beauty of voice that he also sang *Spieltenor* in purely lyrical works. Wagner's friend, Peter Cornelius,* rated his Lohengrin* very highly, although King Ludwig* disagreed. Berlioz* described him as irresistible in *Rienzi* whereas Wagner thought 'Tichatschek has a brisk and lively nature, a glorious voice and great musical talent' but that this was not enough to stop him from being a 'childish clown'. Wagner may have been right: at the première of *Tannhäuser* (1845) the impassioned Tichatschek delivered his entire outburst in praise of Venus* directly to her rival, Elisabeth!* Wagner's temper was not improved when Tichatschek fell hoarse for a week after the first night.

Titurel (P)
For his own dramatic convenience, Wagner turns the legendary Titurel of Wolfram von Eschenbach's fragmentary poem into Parsifal's* father, but, by tradition, Titurel was father to Frimutel and Trevrizent and only Parsifal's great-grandfather.

In the opera, Titurel, the founder of the Grail knight* brotherhood, is now world-weary. He has abdicated in favour of his son Amfortas* (in the legend, his grandson) and only the periodical unveiling of the Grail* keeps him alive on earth. Why

this should be so is not made clear. If the Grail guarantees perpetual youth to its ministers, what has damaged Titurel? His subsequent death is one of the prices exacted by the Creator as punishment for Amfortas' sins, since the Grail can no longer be unveiled while Amfortas is in such extreme pain.

In keeping with his sepulchral position, we do not see Titurel on stage, but simply hear his impressive bass voice from behind a curtain.

Titurel's high-handed rejection of Klingsor's* original application to join the brotherhood is responsible for much of the misery brought upon the Grail prior to the opening of the opera.

Tolstoy, Count Leo Nikolaevich (1828–1910)
Russian novelist and political theorist, whose opinion of Wagner's compositions was virtually unprintable. For example, he believed that *Siegfried* was the supreme example of 'counterfeit art – mere hypnosis and maniacal ravings'. Bayreuth, he suggested, was a place of intolerable fetishism: 'To sit in the dark for four days in the company of people who are not quite normal, and through the auditory nerve subject your brain to the strongest action of sounds best adapted to excite it, is a guaranteed method of reducing yourself to a peculiar condition in which you will be enchanted by absurdities.'

Toscanini, Arturo (1867–1957)
One of the greatest virtuoso conductors of all time. After studying the cello, piano and composition in Italy, he became a professional cellist. At the age of nineteen, while on tour with an Italian opera company in Brazil, he was called upon to replace another conductor who was taken ill, and promptly directed *Aida* entirely from memory. For the next ten years he conducted in Italian theatres, where, above all, he was the champion of Wag-

ner, whom he called 'the greatest composer of the century' but who was still little known in Italy. Appointed artistic director of La Scala in 1898 (at the age of thirty-one) he made his début with *Die Meistersinger*. From 1908 until 1915 he was principal conductor of the Metropolitan Opera, and he subsequently conducted other great orchestras all over the world. He declined to conduct under the Nazis, however, so that the German people were deprived in the 1930s of the passionate interpretations of Wagner at which he excelled. His attention to detail of phrasing could cause delays: under his direction, *Parsifal* at Bayreuth took more than an hour longer than in modern renderings.

Traubel, Helen (1899–1972)
American soprano, who enjoyed great success in New York in the late nineteen thirties. She succeeded Flagstad* in 1941 as the leading interpreter in the United States of Brünnhilde* and reigned supreme in the role until Flagstad made her come-back after the war.

Triebschen
A villa standing just outside Lucerne, on a wooded tongue of land projecting into the nearby lake, which became Wagner's home in the spring of 1866. King Ludwig* paid the bills. Wagner had been compelled to leave Bavaria because of his scandalous liaison with Cosima [Wagner],* the wife of Hans von Bülow.*

Tristan und Isolde
Opera in three acts; text by the composer, based on German mediaeval legends and on the poem of the same name by Gottfried von Strassburg.* The opera was written 1857–9, and the first performance took place, under Hans von Bülow,* on 10 June 1865 at Munich.

This quite overwhelming opera, in some ways Wagner's most intensely passionate work, is for once a more magnificent achievement than even he, the sublime egotist, suggested. In a note to Liszt he wrote, 'Since I have never enjoyed in life the true happiness of love, I shall erect a monument to this most beautiful of all dreams, in which from beginning to end this love shall for once be completely fulfilled: I have sketched in my mind a *Tristan und Isolde*, the most simple but full-blooded musical conception.' If this is taken literally, Wagner craved a love so intense that only death could satisfy its fury, for the work itself defines love as a spiritual absolute of self-negation. Fulfilment comes from death. But if we listen to the music of *Tristan*, what do we hear? The most life-affirming rhapsodies ever written on a stave. It is probably safer to trust the ear than the composer's outpouring of musical theory.

In April 1857 Wagner moved into a lovely house, appropriately called 'Das Asyl*' ('The Sanctuary') on the estate of a wealthy patron, Otto Wesendonck.* Shortly afterwards, he was in the full throes of a passionate love affair with Wesendonck's wife, Mathilde [Wesendonck].* This emotional turn of events (Wagner was still married to a very jealous Minna [Wagner]*) led him to interrupt the writing of the *Ring* and turn to *Tristan und Isolde*.

In July, Mathilde, with her husband's reluctant consent, moved into a mansion next door to 'Das Asyl'. By September, Wagner was presenting her with the finished poem of *Tristan und Isolde*: 'On this day, at this hour, I was born again,' he wrote. '. . . A lovely woman . . . threw herself into the sea of pains and troubles so that she might create for me this glorious moment, might say: "I love you.". . . At last the spell of my yearning was broken.' The next ten months were probably the sweetest of Wagner's entire life.

And so personal relationships drifted into operatic forms. Wagner loved a woman who was plighted to his friend, just as Tristan* loved Isolde.* But Tristan and Isolde, unlike Wagner and Mathilde, could not live for ten months on King Marke's* private estate in connubial joy. They had a single night, followed by a long death. Wagner eventually plumbed something of their feelings when he, too, was forced to realize that his relationship with Mathilde could not be continued. She was a wife and mother, she was not contemplating sharing in a suicide pact, and the middle-class world was beginning to gossip. Wagner fled to Venice, then Lucerne (where he completed the score of this new choral-symphonic hymn to the dream of love) finally Paris. He accepted that his future could not lie in the inspiring arms of Mathilde Wesendonck. Love was renounced in life and its renunciation was preserved in art.

We cannot credit the new work entirely to his personal love affairs. The score of *Siegfried* had in any case been giving him increasing trouble, until Wagner interrupted it to make a fresh start with *Tristan*. Much of the difficulty was philosophical. Wagner was tired of characters who were in violent disaccord with his own modish beliefs (he was reading Schopenhauer*). Wotan,* Alberich,* Siegmund* and now Siegfried* were all riddled with 'corrupt desires'. By contrast, Tristan offered Wagner mental balm, since the hero's consummation lies in renouncing the world and seeking death as the only fit apotheosis of love.

The other good reason pressing Wagner to interrupt his lengthy labours on the *Ring* was nothing new. He needed cash. Breitkopf & Härtel* had finally refused to publish the text of the *Ring*. The Grand Duke of Weimar had not yet procured him an amnesty from exile and was jibing at the costliness and difficulty of mounting the *Ring* in production. Wagner decided to write a new, lucrative work – a work on the scale of *Tannhäuser*, which was bringing in large royalties from Berlin and Vienna, although not enough to satisfy either his outgoings or his creditors. Wag-

ner therefore rushed enthusiastically into composing *Tristan*. The finest irony is that *Tristan* turned out to be a complex, revolutionary opera that bewildered singers and conductors alike. It was anything but practicable to stage, was not performed until 1865 (five bitter years after its completion) and, even, then, did not prove instantly lucrative.

Although the sources of both *Lohengrin* and *Tristan* yielded wonderful operas, *Tristan* is a greater love story than the tale of Elsa* and Lohengrin.* Wagner took the Tristan legend from the mediaeval German poet, Gottfried von Strassburg, and gave it modern flesh. In Gottfried's poem, written early in the thirteenth century, the lovers owe their feelings entirely to a drugged drink. Wagner, however, had the insight to begin his first act at a point when Tristan and Isolde had already come to care for each other, but dare not admit it to the world, or even to themselves; their love potion simply removes a few impediments to a preexisting passion.

The opera opens on board ship. Isolde, daughter of the King of Ireland, is being ferried to Cornwall by Tristan, to be married to his uncle King Marke. Tristan (an orphan, brought up at King Marke's court) has killed Isolde's former lover, Morold.* Morold inflicted a wound on Tristan that refused to heal, and Tristan, very ill, sought help from Isolde, who possessed fabled powers of healing (her mother seems to have been a sorceress apothecary). When Isolde saw that the dying Tristan's sword had a sliver missing which exactly matched the splinter which she had removed from Morold's dead head, she attempted to kill him too, but the apocalyptic power of his gaze prevented her. She is passionately disturbed by Tristan. We can detect that she loves him, but she is not entirely sure. When Tristan went on to woo her, she believed that he must care for her, but then he announced that he had only done that on his monarch's behalf and that she must accompany him back to Cornwall, there to be married to Marke.

And so her feelings are frenzied. She first wishes the 'defiant ship to be dashed to pieces', then vents her fury on Tristan. Turning to her maid, Brangäne,* she asks, 'what think you of this menial?' The servant cannot believe she means Tristan: 'what – the marvel of every kingdom, the man esteemed of all, the hero beyond compare, fame's protector and shield?' – how can such a man be termed a 'menial', such as she is herself?

But Isolde instructs Brangäne to 'command' Tristan, who has avoided her, to come and attend her immediately. There Tristan stands at the front of the ship in the company of his faithful retainer Kurwenal,* scorning, or so it seems to Isolde, to look in her direction. Brangäne delivers the message. Tristan evades the issue by suggesting that it is not seemly for a knight bachelor to talk to a king's fiancé on shipboard; but his servant is more explicit: 'Tell Dame Isolde,' says Kurwenal, 'that he who is giving Cornwall's crown to an Irish maid . . . cannot himself belong to the maid!' Kurwenal regards Isolde as a captive princess and has no real idea of the tentacles of love already encircling both master and this 'Irish maid'.

Isolde is made more furious by Tristan's refusal. She laments, 'How shall I, unloved, endure the peerless man ever near me?' Her feminine confidence begins to be shaken. Notwithstanding Brangäne's reassurance ('Why – where is the man who could look on you without loving you?'), Isolde calls for the casket of potions packed by her crafty mother to see if it contains an elixir to solve her problems. Brangäne brings the box and selects the love potion; Isolde, mortified and vengeful, rejects that in favour of some old-fashioned poison. If Tristan will not talk to her, he shall talk to no one! For the second time in her life, Isolde decides to murder Tristan.

Kurwenal announces the approach of land, and Isolde tells him to bid his master

to come to her and drink a toast of atonement for the wrongs he has done her. Tristan does come, asking to know how he has offended. Isolde repeats the story of the death of Morold. Tristan catches Isolde's hysterical mood and, baring his breast like Richard III with the Lady Anne, tells her to plunge his sword deep inside if a revengeful thought still lives in her heart. Isolde shrewdly suggests that it might be hard to explain that to the Cornish on her arrival.

Instead, she begs him to drink a cup of forgiveness with her, and waves Brangäne forward with the supposedly deadly draught. Tristan understands what is happening, and begins to sing in gnomic riddles: 'The mistress of silence would have me silent. I grasp what she conceals and conceal what she does not grasp.' With heady madness, proving he really does love Isolde, Tristan swallows what he believes to be poison. In a gesture of solidarity (and a foretaste of what is to occur in the finale), Isolde seizes the cup and drains the dregs. Both stand on stage, expecting to convulse and die.

But Brangäne has exchanged the philtres, so that both the would-be suicides have supped the love potion instead. The silent pause continues until it becomes clear to all that life, for the time being, is going to go on. The love potion serves to remove their wordly inhibitions, and waxing ever more lyrical and ecstatic, Isolde claims her Tristan and Tristan hugs his Isolde. The union is perfect, the external world dissolves for them, they live for this moment only in and through each other. The impending close of the act disturbs them mightily, for the ship has docked and King Marke is at hand, waiting to claim his lovely new bride, brought forth from Ireland by his favoured heir and nephew, Tristan the Honourable.

Act II opens in Isolde's Cornish garden at night. Brangäne now repents of having switched the potions, since Isolde seems bent on foolish nocturnal trysts with Tristan, which can only lead to grief. Isolde, clearly in raptures, begs her not to blaspheme, since the goddess of love herself must have forced her to administer such an elixir of delight. Isolde moves to make a prearranged signal to Tristan, telling him the coast is clear, but Brangäne warns her that the courtier Melot,* Tristan's alleged friend, may be plotting against them. Isolde dismisses this; Melot arranged the nocturnal hunt that even now will draw the King away from home, freeing Tristan to join her. The worldly-wise Brangäne tells her that this must be a ruse of Melot's; but Isolde signals to Tristan, just the same.

Tristan joins Isolde for an extended love-duet in which they contrast the vice of 'Day', which keeps them separated, with the virtue of 'Night', which permits them secret embraces. Jarring notes are occasionally struck by Brangäne ('Have a care'), but these are unheeded, until Kurwenal* rushes in headlong to warn them of the King's imminent arrival.

Marke and Melot and the rest of the court appear. Melot is triumphant that the lovers have fallen into his trap. Marke, more in sorrow than in anger, asks Tristan why he has destroyed not just his own honour but *all* honour, since Tristan was the source of honour? Tristan cannot answer, since the King would not understand that these questions of chivalry are no longer of any consequence, compared to his own discovery of absolute and eternal love. Instead he provokes a fight with Melot and allows himself to be fatally wounded in the ensuing sword-play. The curtain falls on Act II.

Act III is entirely concerned with what happens to love beyond the grave. We see Tristan, dying from his wounds, asleep in the grounds of his own castle on the high cliff near Kareol* in Brittany, whither he has been spirited by the devoted Kurwenal. Kurwenal tells him he has sent for Isolde, which rouses Tristan to a fever pitch of expectation – 'Can you see the ship? Can you see the ship?' he beseeches, his agitation doing nothing to

aid his recovery. Kurwenal says no several times, until, yes, a ship can be seen – ah, there it seems to be heading for the reef; no, it is safe again, and Isolde is here. While Kurwenal goes to guide Isolde to Tristan, in the hope that her skill can heal his body, Tristan, left alone, rises unsteadily to his feet, tears off his bandages and attempts to totter towards his arriving lover, but weakness and unconsciousness prevent him. As Isolde dashes forward, Tristan falls and then expires, with one last gasp breathing her name. Isolde tries to revive him, but gradually perceives that this is not possible – and perhaps not appropriate.

Meanwhile, a second ship, bearing King Marke, arrives at Kareol. Melot and Kurwenal engage in combat which proves fatal for both before Marke can explain that Brangäne has confessed to him her part in chemically inducing the lovers to break the chivalric code of honour. Now he is here to resign Isolde most willingly to Tristan. In fact, all is forgiven, but it is all too late. (Marke has not grasped the fact that Tristan and Isolde were in love *before* the potion was concocted.)

All this is ignored by Isolde, since she, too, is passing from this earth. She sees a vision of Tristan resurrected and transformed and is surprised that no one else can see it. She beholds Tristan in his glory – 'high in the air, with heavenly harmony pouring out of him, enveloping her round and penetrating her through and through'. Perfume seems to fill her being and seize her soul. Shall she dive forward – 'let herself be engulfed and sink, unconscious, into highest bliss?' she asks.

On this effulgent note the opera closes, with our knowledge that Isolde has been filled with a joy so grandiloquent that she will immediately die of sheer ecstasy. Whether or not she is deceived by her vision of an afterlife, her act asserts the rule of love over all, particularly death.

Symbolic opera on such a scale is patently not meant to be taken as a literal model for our own behaviour. Wagner was, in fact, carrying out his project of erecting a monument to love. The opera is infinitely more human than *Lohengrin*, since it does tell the story of the eternal triangle and the deaths seem partly justified by conventional wrongdoing. But this is not the whole point either. The work is a talismanic affirmation of *living love* and *loving life*. It is not a crude exemplar, but, through the moody mists of Schopenhauer's* philosophy we can perceive that the ideal is being offered. We are enjoined to feel passion more keenly. We are encouraged to yearn for some small fragment of the ecstasy the lovers generate on stage. When the audience is robbed of Tristan and Isolde's love by its disappearance in death and a final curtain, the reaction is simple – our spirits rebel. We want to suggest that such extreme love *can*, in fact, survive in our world. To put it crudely, we want more, we want our share, we want to put the clock back, we want to hear the opera again. In that special sense, this opera always affirms the supremacy of love, because we, the audience, will always affirm the value of that of which we are deprived.

In this, we are aided in every bar by the music; theme and variation are subtly interwoven in an extended symphonic poem. At last we have something of a 'music drama'. The new opera is about universal feelings – love, grief, despair, redemption – but the new virtuoso is the orchestra, which almost seems to become more human and alive than the singers. The orchestra can 'tell' us long before the actor singers what has happened and how they should be feeling. For example, when Tristan and Isolde swallow the love potion, we already know from the music that they have a repressed longing for each other, and so no new dramatic emphasis is necessary. Contrast this with Siegfried* drinking Gutrune's* potion in *Götterdämmerung*, where the music mimics all the effects of swallowing and circulation. Again, when King Marke discovers the

lovers embracing at night, there is no sudden exclamation from the brass. We know how he feels, since his despair has already been communicated to us.

Wagner frequently explained to those who were confused by *Tristan und Isolde* that 'what was not clear in the words was made so in the music'. Through the sophisticated use of leitmotivs*, representing sorrow, anger, desire, magic, fate, death, yearning, heroism, day, night, the love potion, impatience and love's bliss, we can, if we listen carefully, keep our bearings at any point in the developing drama. The use of these short rhythmical themes attached to persons, places and passions is far more subtle in *Tristan* than in the *Ring*.

Tristan (T I)
A Cornish knight, nephew to King Marke,* this legendary lover is by far the most complicated character in what is possibly Wagner's greatest opera. Like Siegfried* (the composer had just been working on *Siegfried*), he is at the height of his youthful powers and tested in battle, but, unlike Siegfried, he has been educated and given social polish. He is of royal blood, with a fine awareness of the virtues required of kingly aristocrats. In effect, his entire dilemma is one of honour versus love. It is out of absolute reverence for King Marke's* commands that he avoids Isolde's* company during the sea voyage home to Cornwall, despite knowing that he loves her. It is out of loyalty to his oath to Marke that his love is fresh and strong, for Tristan has wooed Isolde by royal command on King Marke's behalf. Thus, when Isolde offers him a death potion, he can at once perceive what it is and why it is given and why he willingly wishes to swallow it. Anything, even death, would be better than this tortured tension between his duty to man (the king) and his duty to woman (Isolde).

Then, as soon as the potion is swallowed, Tristan's love for Isolde becomes his ruling passion. Obviously, as King

Marke later emphasizes, he is now under a spell. But we must also assume that the potion only serves to reveal to lovers what is already in their hearts – or if not that, that it perhaps removes consciousness of any external loyalties.

Tristan, however, is not blinded to the human world and its concerns. He does understand that his love for Isolde is really a forbidden desire not least because it is too intense to survive its frail human context. His passion would empty oceans and blast mountains. When King Marke confronts him with his 'petty human offence', he cannot begin to explain what has happened, since the scale is disproportionate. How can he tell his old liege lord that the grief of kings does not weigh one jot in the balance when compared to his love for Isolde? Of course, his original decision (to die on shipboard) was instinctively correct. Thus he lets Melot* exact revenge and commits a form of suicide, rather than unhinge the world any further.

The only question remaining is how far Tristan is really aware that Isolde will come to the same conclusion, spiritually and physically? Will she join him in love beyond death, and will she perceive that there may be emotion that transcends annihilation? And even if she does, will the audience be seduced by her glorious *Liebestod** into a similar conviction?

Twain, Mark (Samuel Langhorne Clemens, 1835–1910)

American author of lively popular tales such as *Tom Sawyer* (1876) and *Huckleberry Finn* (1884). He was also a substantial travel writer and overseas correspondent. He sent back some very funny despatches from Bayreuth in 1891, although he also held Wagner's work in considerable admiration, *Tannhäuser* in particular.

But this is what he says about *Parsifal*:

In this opera there is a hermit named Gurnemanz* who stands on the stage in one spot and practises [singing] by the hour, while first one

and then another character of the cast endures what he can of it and then retires to die. . . . When we reached home we had been gone for more than seven hours. Seven hours at five dollars a ticket is almost too much for the money.

Uhlig, Theodor (1822–53)

German violinist, composer and critic. A violinist in the Dresden opera orchestra from 1841, he was an early, and highly articulate, champion of Wagner, whose radical political outlook he shared. The two men carried on an extensive correspondence after Wagner went into exile (1849–52).

Unger, Georg (1837–87)

German tenor: the first Siegfried.* His vocal technique was improved by Julius Hey (a Munich singing teacher, engaged by Wagner) especially for the première of the *Ring*, and Wagner also coached him personally. It was suggested by Hey that Wagner even tried to 'influence Unger's temperament'. The master was troubled by what he decided was Unger's 'black outlook on life. You must become more gay and sunny,' he said.

Urlus, Jacques (1867–1935)

Dutch tenor, who, after singing Tristan* in London in 1910, gave the 1911 and 1912 Bayreuth Siegmund.* From 1912 until 1917 he was the principal Wagnerian tenor at the Metropolitan Opera House.

Valhalla (R, but present throughout the *Ring*)

Wotan's* gleaming palace, built by the giants Fasolt* and Fafner* in return for the promised possession of Freia,* goddess of Spring. When that payment is resisted, the giants accept, in lieu of Freia, the Rhinemaidens'* stolen gold, including the magic Ring* and the Tarnhelm.*

Wotan's difficulties all stem from his original desire to own a glorious palace. He has created Valhalla for two ignoble reasons: he wishes to exalt his own ego, and to possess a fortress-sanctuary to protect him from the dark forces of Alberich* and his dwarfs, of whom he is afraid. Valhalla, as in legend, is filled with heroes, removed from the battlefield at or near their deaths and carried heavenward, to be revived for a second life in service to their new lord, Wotan. By this means, the Lord of the Gods plans to amass an immortal army to save him from his foes.

Wotan's wife, Fricka,* wants Valhalla built because she hopes it will encourage her husband to stay at home, rather than travel abroad having affairs with other women.

Yet, at the end, neither Wotan nor Fricka is satisfied. Valhalla is overthrown by the consequences of Wotan's original sin in paying for its construction with stolen loot. In the last act of *Götterdämmerung*, the gleaming palace and all its inhabitants are burned to ashes.

Valkyries (Walküren, Die) (W)

Sisters to Brünnhilde,* the Valkyries are named Gerhilde, Helmwige, Ortlinde (sopranos), Grimgerde, Rossweisse, Schwertleite, Siegrune and Waltraute* (mezzo-sopranos). Waltraute makes a reappearance in *Götterdämmerung*. The nine sisters are daughters of Erda,* the Mother of Earth, and were born as a result of her love affair with Wotan,* Lord of the Gods. Wotan employs them as 'bold Valkyries, who would avert the doom that the Wala [Erda] made Wotan fear – the shameful defeat of the gods'. The Valkyries have the task of assembling an army of human heroes to defend Wotan's palace, Valhalla,* from enemy attack. Their methods of doing this are frequently cruel. First, they help to provoke war in the world in order to see which men are the bravest warriors. Those heroes who fall in battle are swiftly resurrected and carried off to bear arms in Valhalla. But even those champions who survive the field, should they be earmarked as fine fighters, may also find themselves 'persuaded' to ride to Valhalla against their will.

Once these heroes have been lured, or metaphorically knocked on the head, a life of slavery awaits them. Brünnhilde apart, the Valkyries live in fear and trembling of Wotan's wrath, being little more than the slaves they make of the mortals. Wotan claims that he fashioned them to be 'hard-hearted, stern and strong', but when they ask him to show mercy to Brünnhilde, one bark from him is enough to cower them all. See also 'Brünnhilde', 'Waltraute'.

Van Dyck, Ernest Marie Hubert (1861–1923)

Belgian tenor who sang at the French première of Lohengrin* at Paris in 1887 and Parsifal* at Bayreuth in 1888–1912, with great success. Eventually he gave other major Wagnerian roles in a voice that was full and generous.

Varnay, Astrid (b. 1918)

American soprano, born in Sweden, who made her Wagnerian début at the Metropolitan Opera House as Sieglinde* in 1941. She also gave Elsa* and Elisabeth.* She was the 1948 Brünnhilde* at Covent Garden and sang Brünnhilde, Isolde,* Ortrud, Kundry* and Senta* at Bayreuth 1951–67. Varnay's acting was of a high quality, but her voice was even finer. Between the eras of Flagstad* and Nilsson,* Astrid Varnay was the finest Wagnerian soprano.

Vaterlandsverein (Fatherland Society)

A radical group in Dresden, which Wagner joined just prior to the Revolutions of 1848–9.

Veasey, Josephine (b. 1930)

English mezzo-soprano, who sang Waltraute* (1963) and Fricka* (1964) at Covent Garden. She has since given Brangäne* and Venus* there and Kundry* in Paris.

Veccio, Cecco del, Roman Citizen (Ri)
Henchman of Baroncelli,* representative of the fickle Roman people who first support, then destroy, their Tribune, Cola Rienzi.*

Venus (T)
In German legends the goddess Aphrodite was identified first with Holda, goddess of Spring, who is benign, and then with Venus, a pagan love-witch and daughter of the devil. In Wagner's hands, Venus (soprano) is officially wicked, attempting to keep Tannhäuser* to herself through constant acts of unlawful seduction, but the music belies her status. Not for the first time, the devil seems to get the best tunes, and it is clear that Wagner was strongly attracted to venereal enchantments, whatever is said in the libretto. By Act III Venus loses Tannhäuser for good, thanks to Elisabeth's* heroic act of self-sacrifice. Not all her soft suggestions that he should 'Drink from my lips the draught of love divine' can win Tannhäuser's hand – or even save his life.
The 'goddess of love' is called 'Frau Minne'* in *Tristan und Isolde*.

Venusberg, The
A mountain near Eisenach* in the depths of which Venus (or, in some legends, Holda, the goddess of Spring) is said to hold her court. It is here that she detained Tannhäuser for many months of amorous enchantment. Wagner's original title for *Tannhäuser* was to have been *Der Venusberg*. The mountain is known by the alternative name of the Hörselberg, after the nearby River Hörsel.

Verlaine, Paul (1844–96)
French poet, associated with the Symbolists, who wrote the 'Parsifal' sonnet, containing the line 'Et, ô ces voix d'enfants chantant dans la coupole . . .', which T. S. Eliot later quoted in *The Waste Land*.

Vianesi, Auguste Charles Leonard François (1837–1908)
Like other Italians of the day, the conductor Vianesi was found wanting as an exponent of German operas. He conducted at Covent Garden for ten years after 1870, directing the first performance in London of *Lohengrin* (1875) and *Tannhäuser* (1896), but without showing, according to some critics, the least understanding of the spirit of the scores.

Vickers, Jon (Jonathan Stewart) (b. 1926)
Canadian tenor, who sang Siegmund* at Bayreuth in 1958 and has since sung Parsifal* and Tristan* at Covent Garden since 1957.

Victoria, Queen of England (1819–1901)
Queen Victoria met Wagner during his London visit of 1855, after the *Tannhäuser* overture had been repeated at a concert by royal command.

Villiers de Lisle-Adam, Jean-Marie-Mathias-Philippe-Auguste Count de (1838–89)
Aristocratic French poet, who was obsessed with Wagner and Wagnerism. He visited the composer in 1869 and again in 1870. His prose-poem 'Azrael' is dedicated to Wagner.

Vinay, Ramón (b. 1912)
Chilean baritone, later tenor, who then resumed his career as a baritone. At Bayreuth, from 1952 until 1957 he sang Tristan,* Parsifal,* Tannhäuser* and Siegmund;* then (as baritone) Telramund* in 1962.

Vogelgesang, Kunz (M)
One of the Mastersingers, a furrier by trade (tenor), who adds an occasional commentary during the more formal

scenes of *Die Meistersinger*. He seems to
be less hidebound by tradition than his
colleagues, since he is one of the few,
apart from Sachs,* to speak up on behalf
of Walther von Stolzing's* wild but
beautiful song in Act I.

Völker, Franz (1899–1965).
German tenor who sang Siegmund* at
Covent Garden (1934, 1937) and was also
a fine Lohengrin.*

Völsunga Saga, The
Icelandic heroic saga (c. 1270); one of
Wagner's primary sources for the *Ring*
cycle.

Wächter, Eberhard (b. 1929)
Austrian baritone who gave fine accounts
of Wolfram* and Amfortas* at Bayreuth
(1958), and has also sung Kurwenal.*

Wagner, Adolf (1774–1835)
Wagner's uncle, who worked as a writer
and translator.

Wagner, Adrian
Richard Wagner's great-great-grandson,
a contemporary rock-musician and the
composer of a mainly electronic symphony in nine movements called *The Last
Inca*.

Wagner, Albert (1799–1874)
Wagner's brother, a singer and stage
director.

**Wagner, Carl Friedrich Wilhelm
(1770–1813)**
Wagner's father. Carl Wagner was an
actuary at the town court in Leipzig.
Wilhelm Richard was his ninth, and last,
accredited child. In November, 1813, six

months after the birth, Carl Friedrich died
during the epidemic of typhus that followed in the wake of the Battle of Leipzig.
His widow, Johanna, now found herself in
difficult financial circumstances, from
which she was rescued by a second marriage to Ludwig Geyer* (a portrait painter, poet and actor), which took place in
August 1814. It has been suggested
(although never proved) that Geyer was
Wagner's natural parent, as he was of
Wagner's beloved step-sister, Cäcilie,
who was born a significant six months after
the Geyer nuptials. But there is a strong
physical resemblance between Richard
Wagner and his eldest brother Albert to
be set against this.

Wagner, Cosima, *née* Liszt (1837–1930)
Richard Wagner's second wife, Cosima,
was the illegitimate daughter of the composer Franz Liszt* and the writer Countess Marie d'Agoult.* By the time of her
birth, the passion between her parents was
cooling. When she was two, they agreed to
separate for all but the three summer
months, and when she was seven, they
parted for ever. She was brought up in
Paris by the governors of Liszt's new
mistress, the Princess Wittgenstein,* who
actively discouraged any reference to
Cosima's own mother. Her father toured
the concert platforms of Europe making
infrequent visits home. When he settled
down, it was to be with the Princess in
Weimar, not in Paris with his daughter,
and Cosima came to regard herself as an
orphan exile. She did not forgive Liszt
easily, even when he lay helpless on his
deathbed. The child of intellectuals who
disregarded family ties, she had no
alternative but to become another intellectual – but one who harboured clear
domestic ambitions, born of a sense of
grievance.

Her first attempt to satisfy these was
disastrous. At the age of nineteen she
married the gifted but solitary aristocratic
musician, Hans von Bülow.* Within a

matter of months, she knew she had made a mistake. He had no desire to share his artistic concerns with a woman, whereas Cosima's greatest yearning was to create a home which was a salon, to get herself included in the important work of a great man. As soon as she met Richard Wagner (briefly in 1853, and again in 1857) she realized his potential to fulfil this dream. He was a genius who craved to be looked after by everyone.

When Cosima finally abandoned von Bülow in 1869, she already had four daughters and a fifth child was expected. Two of the children (Daniela and Blandine) were von Bülow's; the other two (and the unborn child) were Wagner's. She knew that von Bülow had never really wished to marry her. He had done so as a favour to Liszt, his musical mentor. When Cosima gave birth to Eva in 1857, von Bülow sat at her bedside and said, 'I forgive you,' to which Cosima replied, 'I need no forgiveness, I need understanding!'

Now, she flung herself body, heart and soul into serving the life of Richard Wagner. Between 1864 and 1869, she had turned herself into an indispensable extension of the master's will, giving him children (Isolde,* Eva* and eventually Siegfried* [Wagner]), giving him support and constant encouragement, giving him an unswerving *alter ego* in the attractive form of a woman twenty-four years his junior.

In 1879, Cosima defined her duties thus, '. . . my happiness rests in the fulfilment of my office . . . to make it possible that the Master – despite unpleasantness of all sorts – can put his work aside and end the day happily in the evening. So is my day's work accomplished.'

There was a price to pay. As a result of this irregular union, Liszt was estranged from Wagner until 1872. King Ludwig* was compelled to ask Wagner to leave Munich because of the scandal over Cosima, whom he refused ever to set eyes on again. And Cosima herself was compelled to follow her father's example of bringing bastard children into the world. Fortunately for her, the death of Minna Wagner* in 1866 permitted marriage to Wagner, although this did not occur until 1871.

Eventually, Wagner was unfaithful to Cosima; Cosima averted her gaze, concentrating on her mission. Her chief duties were to transcribe Wagner's autobiography and to write a detailed daily diary of his doings.

Cosima was prostrated by Wagner's death and was determined to worship his memory. At all costs, the festival at Bayreuth must survive. It was this task to which she committed herself for almost the next quarter-century, producing, directing and casting performances of the operas. She was not the finest judge of the work, but by no means the worst. When she retired in 1906, after a severe illness, the theatre was at least financially flourishing. She lived on to a great age, dying on April Fool's Day 1930 at 92. Four months later, her only son Siegfried, Richard Wagner's most treasured creation, followed her into the grave.

Cosima subordinated her life and will to that of one man. But this very act of continuous submission only proved that she was mistress of a will equally strong, as all those who came into contact with her in later life have amply testified. The only person to whom she bowed in acknowledgement was her husband, Richard. And to her, he was nothing less than a god.

The Diaries (1869–83)
Brilliantly edited by Martin Gregor-Dellin and Dietrich Mack, the diaries of Cosima offer the clearest picture we shall ever obtain of the sad, manic, intolerably gifted man to whom she was eventually married. They were written as a panegyric to Richard Wagner, but also to expiate her own guilt for abandoning her first husband Hans von Bülow, and two of her children. In the words of the editors, the diaries contain 'the fervent jottings of a wife

totally absorbed in her husband's mission and who has no wish to bequeath to posterity anything other than this great passion of her life'.

She began the diary on 1 January 1869 and ended it on 12 February 1881, the night before Wagner died. The volumes were dedicated to Siegfried Wagner, who never bothered to read them, then fell into the hands of Eva Wagner* [Chamberlain]. She left them to the town of Bayreuth, on condition that they were not published until thirty years after her own death (in 1942), and then they remained in a bank vault until a mass of litigation obtained their release in 1974.

Cosima was conventional at heart, although both illegitimate and an adulteress. She wished Siegfried and her daughters to 'understand' why it was necessary for her to make an alliance with Wagner. His 'great work' was to be an excuse for many sins, both his and now hers. Her life henceforth would be justified by a higher morality: that of fostering his genius. She was, therefore, no feminist, and her view of women included advice to her daughters 'to be for husbands that firm, sacred, inviolate plot of earth in which they may lay their thoughts and feelings, secure from any of life's storms'.

Elsewhere, the volumes faithfully record the painstaking composition of *Parsifal*, as well as Wagner's painful insomnia. We read of the Wagners' occasional opposition to Bismarck's imperialism and their hopes for a renewed liberty arising in America. We see Wagner as a father, given to mad horseplay; we also see genius descending to bad temper when Liszt beats him at whist.

Musically, Cosima shows how Wagner in old age harked back to the composers of his youth, doing justice to the baroque. He described Beethoven's* Hammerklavier Sonata as 'like being taken into the workshop of the Will'. But, unsurprisingly, no justice whatsoever is done in these diaries to those women who essentially

inspired much of his greatest writing – to Judith Gautier,* for instance. Nor, according to the *Sunday Times* (1 November 1981) to Carrie Pringle,* an English singer who appeared as a Flower Maiden* in the 1882 Bayreuth *Parsifal*.

Wagner, Eva (1867–1942)

Wagner's censorious daughter (also known as 'Evchen'), who heavily edited her parents' letters and diary manuscripts to try to preserve the family reputation. She was past forty when she married Houston Stewart Chamberlain.* Their union proved childless. She was alienated from the family in 1930 because control of the Bayreuth Festival passed to the English-born Winifred Wagner,* Siegfried Wagner's* widow. Eva then left Bayreuth to live with her step-sister Daniela at Triebschen. See also Wagner, Cosima: *The Diaries*.

Wagner, Franziska (1829–95)

Wagner's niece, daughter of his brother Albert [Wagner]* and husband of Alexander Ritter, a composer and brother of Karl Ritter (see 'Ritter family'), with whom Wagner was associated in the early 1850s.

Wagner, Isolde (1865–1919)

Also known as 'Loldi' or 'Loldchen'.

Wagner's daughter (not von Bülöw's,* as is made clear by Wagner's poem to Isolde on the occasion of her fifteenth birthday). In later life she married Franz Beidler, a musician. Siegfried Wagner* fell out with Beidler, and a family estrangement followed. In 1913, the rift worsened when Isolde, in the interests of her son (b. 1901), tried to get herself legally proclaimed Wagner's child. She was unsuccessful, however, in the courts.

Wagner, Johanna (1826–94)

The adopted daughter of Richard Wagner's eldest brother, Albert.* She pursued a successful career as an operatic soprano, creating the role of Elisabeth* in the unhappy *Tannhäuser* production of 1845 and giving a good account of Ortrud* in the first Berlin *Lohengrin* (1859).

In the early 1860s, her singing voice vanished, and so she resorted to the spoken drama, making a second successful career. After ten years, her voice returned as suddenly as it had disappeared, so that she could sing Schwertleite* and First Norn* in the Bayreuth première of the *Ring* in 1876.

She was by all accounts a marvellous actress, and, at its best, her singing voice was full and bright.

Wagner, Johanna Rosine (*nèe* Pätz, 1774–1848)

Wagner's mother, to whom he was extremely attached. The daughter of a mill-owner, she had been widowed twice by her late forties, but managed to bring up a large family (nine children in all, of whom two died in infancy), despite the practical difficulties. Wagner inherited both her small build and her superabundant energy. There is still debate about her legitimacy (was she the daughter of Prince Constantin of Weimar, who arranged for her education?) as well as that of her famous son (did Wagner suffer all his life from a sense of bastard inferiority?). We shall probably never know the truth.

Johanna's education had been interrupted at the age of fourteen by marriage to her first husband, Wagner's father (Carl Friedrich Wagner*), who was critical of her literary ignorance. When he wanted to name his children after the heroines in works by Goethe* and Schiller (Ottilie, Klara, Luise, Rosalie), she had to confess she knew nothing of their books.

Wagner was particularly impressed by his mother's strength of character. She always warned him against the temptations of going on the stage because her second husband, Ludwig Geyer,* was an actor and she did not think much of the prospects of that career. Instead, she encouraged Wagner to think of a future in the nobler arts of poetry, music or painting, and Wagner paid dutiful attention to her wishes.

Wagner, Julius (1804–1862)

Wagner's elder brother, who was a goldsmith by trade.

Wagner, Klara (1807–75)

One of Wagner's sisters, Klara Wagner became an opera singer, but the early loss of her voice ended her career. She married Heinrich Wolfram (1800–74), also a singer.

Wagner, Luise (1805–72)

One of Wagner's sisters. Initially an actress, she retired on her marriage to Friedrich Brockhaus,* the publisher.

Wagner, Minna (*née* Planer; 1809–66)

Wagner's first wife. At the age of sixteen, Minna Planer was seduced by an unscrupulous army officer and gave birth to an illegitimate daughter called Nathalie, whom she always passed off as her sister. Later, Minna found employment as an actress. In 1834, the young Wagner became musical director of a theatre company at Landstädt, to which Minna Planer was attached. He fell head over heels in love with this pretty woman, three-and-a-half years his senior. She was the belle of the town. He thought it a feather in his cap to make her his mistress, as indeed did several other gentlemen. Eventually, she returned his love in full. Two years after their first meeting, they were married in haste (on no cash) in Königsberg.

In the first year together, Minna left home twice in pursuit of a merchant whom she fancied. Wagner forgave her; but the newly-wed couple remained at odds. His huge artistic ego needed a great deal of servicing. Her insecure personality also required constant and trivial attention.

Wagner respected Minna a great deal for sharing his Paris privations in the years 1839–42, and also for obtaining in 1862 an amnesty for his role in the Dresden rising of 1849. But theirs was always a marriage in search of an iceberg on which to crash. This eventually materialized in the formidable person of Cosima von Bülow, *née* Liszt (see 'Wagner, Cosima'). There had been an assortment of preliminary ice-floes for Minna to negotiate: Jessie Laussot,* Mathilde Wesendonck,* Mathilde Maier* and Friederike Meyer, to mention a few. But Cosima was too much for her, and the marriage sank. Cosima and Wagner decided to live together, whether anyone protested or not, and after 1864 Minna found herself alone.

The marriage had been really off course from 1849. All Minna had ever wanted was a 'normal family life', with a steady income and a respectable position in the community. It was a sadness to her that the union was childless. Yet she had made the best of the difficult years in Paris and looked forward to the comfortable companionship of her husband in middle age. Instead, in 1848–9, he had joined a revolution, lost his job and been sentenced to exile from the homeland which was also hers. She was shattered. His head was filling fast with a fantastic project to stage an ambitious opera (about a ring) for which she did not care two pins, and when he was not scribbling libretti he was chasing petticoats. She began to despair. Finally, she let him have his fancy women and his operas, retiring sorrowfully to Dresden, where she died in bitterness.

Wagner, Ottilie (1811–83)

One of Wagner's sisters, Ottilie married Hermann Brockhaus, a philologist, brother of the publisher Friedrich Brockhaus,* who married Luise Wagner.*

Wagner, Rosalie (1803–37)

One of Wagner's sisters, an actress, married to a professor at Leipzig University, Oswald Marbach (1810–90). She died in childbirth.

Wagner, Siegfried Helferich Richard (1869–1930)

Also known as 'Fidi', 'Fidichen', 'Fidel' or 'Friedel', Siegfried, Wagner's much-prized son, survived the hazards of celebrated parentage to become a composer and conductor in his own right.

At his birth, the doting Wagner began to compose the lovely *Siegfried Idyll*. As a youth, he allowed Siegfried to study under his friend Humperdinck.* By 1892, Siegfried was assisting at Bayreuth and in 1906 he produced *Der Fliegende Holländer*. From then until 1930, Siegfried remained the General Director of the Bayreuth Festival, but often in the shadow of his mother, Cosima Wagner*, who was Artistic Director until 1906 and a constant psychological presence for the remainder of his days. Four months after she died, Siegfried also expired, as if his will had been broken with hers.

Siegfried's own musical tendencies as a composer were towards fairy opera of an experimental variety. He wrote twelve operas, the favourite among which was *Der kobold*, first performed in Hamburg in 1904. (A kobold is a sort of gnome which is inhabited by the soul of a prematurely deceased child awaiting redemption by deliberate sacrifice on the part of its host.) Siegfried's writing is more adventurous rhythmically than harmonically, but chiefly appeals owing to its attractive use of melody, for which he had real flair.

Wagner, Wieland Adolf Gottfried (1917–66)

Richly imaginative producer and stage designer, the son of Siegfried Wagner* and brother of the present Bayreuth Festival Director, Wolfgang Wagner.* His premature death was widely mourned.

Wieland specialized in stark symbolic sets ruled by electric light. He believed that the Electrical Director of an opera house was as important as the conductor of the orchestra. His inclinations suited the post-war modernism of the revived festival of 1951. Wieland banished solid rainbow bridges and shattered swords. In their place he created ample well-lit space for the imagination.

He produced *Parsifal* as early as 1937 and *Die Meistersinger* in 1943 and in the course of his career designed all Wagner's major operas, from *Rienzi* to the *Ring*. After Cosima's policy of rigid adherence to the Romantic conventions of 1876 (or what she *said* were the conventions of 1876), Wieland provided welcome novelty. His 1954 *Tannhäuser* set was a chessboard. At the climax of Elisabeth's* intercession for Tannhäuser,* the move was shown by the White Queen breaking the rules of the game and rushing forward to protect the threatened Black Knight.

Wieland produced the first tilted sets for the *Ring*, now so widely copied in opera houses around the world, but his Bayreuth productions were gradually phased out after his death, the last to go being *Parsifal* in 1973.

As a youth, Wieland was one of Hitler's favourites. On his seventeenth birthday he received a large Mercedes motor car, with the Führer's compliments. On a subsequent occasion, he was given the even more valuable present of exemption from German military service. Hitler was known affectionately as 'Uncle Wolf' by both Wieland and Wolfgang Wagner.

Wagner, Wilhelm Richard (1813–83)

I cannot live like a dog. I cannot bed in straw or satisfy my soul with gin. Mine is a highly susceptible, intense, voracious yet uncommonly sensitive and fastidious sensuality, which must somehow or other be flattered if my mind is to accomplish the agonizing labour of calling a non-existent world into being.

Wagner to Liszt.

The least contradiction provoked him to incredible anger. Then he would leap like a stag, roar like a tiger. He paced the room like a caged lion, his voice became hoarse and the words came out like screams: his speech splashed about at random.

Edouard Schuré, who knew Wagner in Paris in the 1860s.

When the conversation turns upon his fame [then] twenty times a day he falls upon my neck, and rolls on the floor, caressing his dog Peps and talking perpetual nonsense to him – while all the time he curses the Jews. . . .

Liszt on Wagner

The grudge is as necessary to my nature as gall is to blood . . . and so I let fly.

Wagner to Liszt

Wagner is thirty-seven to thirty-eight years of age, of medium stature, has brown hair, an open forehead; eyebrows brown; eyes greyish blue; nose and mouth proportioned; chin, round . . . Special characteristics: rapid in movements and speech. . . .

Warrant for Wagner's arrest, 1849.

Richard Wagner was a man with an inordinate number of needs, some real and some imaginary. It is a complication of his life that he usually confused imagination with reality, and so felt all his desires with equal force. In no particular order, these basic necessities may be said to include luxury, love, praise, music, money, poetry, sex, soft clothing, vegetarian food, horseplay, world fame, power, bad jokes, disciples, an 'ideal' house and a tranquil domestic routine. When these needs were satisfied, his personality was able to produce more original creative work than almost any other human being who has ever lived, but the service price was high. Wagner the man was often rude, manic, churlish, paranoid, depressed, suicidal, racist and prostrated both physically and mentally. He was almost always in debt. He was almost always paying court to the wives of his friends. If the wives responded, the friends were distressed and some demon in him was satisfied. If the wives did not respond, he very often fell out with his friends anyway for trivial reasons. He was almost always a tyrant in his personal dealings. His artistic ego was by far the noisiest of the nineteenth century.

This could be dignified as the necessary corollary of supreme artistic ambition, but, if so, we are still left with the puzzle as to why Wagner became such a manically ambitious man in the first place. Some sort of explanation can be found in the circumstances of his childhood and early manhood.

Firstly, Wagner early suspected that his paternity was open to question. His mother was a reassuring woman, but her domestic life had undeniably gone through a number of upheavals. Here then is a prime motive for Wagner's later desire for the security and certain identity which fame seems to offer. The talent he had inherited gave him grounds for hope. Born with manic energy as well, Wagner then grew up in an environment where his family and teachers encouraged him to see the sky as the limit. His self-selected 'peer group' were the immortals: he compared himself to Homer and Shakespeare, rather than to mundane school friends. However, his intimate domestic circle was not exactly ordinary. At home he was waited and doted on in an artistic ambience where many of his close relatives were painters and singers. A bright child like Richard was therefore expected and encouraged to achieve the highest renown. 'What struck me [about my mother] was the strange enthusiasm and almost pathetic manner in which she spoke of the great and beautiful in art,' said Wagner. Desperate to gratify these expectations, he had no idea at all how cold the outside world could be. Wagner was one of the most spoilt young men in Germany when he first left home.

Never afraid of hard work, he was yet unable to accept that the world did not owe him respect. The contrast between the total acceptance he had found in the warm home nest and the realm of employment which saw no reason to accept him on any but its own terms was traumatic. His greatest crisis, therefore, lay in establishing a true external identity, in finding financial and critical recognition of his worth, a level of worldly success on which he could operate. He knew he might not be his father's child; he knew deep inside that he had to be more than the *Wunderkind* his mother uncritically extolled; on the other hand he was convinced that he had unique, original talent of his own to develop. His solution of the problem was unorthodox.

With no very settled idea of how to behave towards his fellow-men and women, Wagner simply proceeded to follow his inclinations until stopped in his tracks. There were certainly enough early brakes and reverses to contend with: his first operas were not a success, his capacity to get into debt was phenomenal, Paris in the 1840s was an unforgettable disaster. But his energies (some of them bitter) seemed to grow in proportion to these setbacks. It took a great deal of power to stop Wagner, especially a Wagner (the name means 'Waggoner') that had gathered speed. Because of his gifts, many people forgave in him actions that they would have damned in lesser men; in short, he got away with being absolutely outrageous – with friends, lovers, family, creditors, admirers, fellow-composers – for most of his seventy years.

We may conjecture that it is because in his formative years no one quite realized and satisfied Wagner's need to find a firm identity that he left us with such a monumental body of artistic work, all blatantly craving for our recognition and attention. This work is not a crude cry for help, but it *is* a plea for communication so powerful as to exceed the aesthetic dimension. Wagner's art flows, like all art, from joyous and miserable experience, but some of the heights and depths also derived more especially from a sense of cosmic isolation and self-ignorance. His achievements might have been equally profound had his life been happier. But the chances are that his music would have been less in quantity and reduced in tragic intensity.

It is possible that much of the finished grandeur of Wagner's music depends precisely on the less amiable sides of his nature: on his *Angst*, his sense of self-loathing and his fear of loneliness, which he sublimated partly by projection onto 'enemy' targets, such as the Jews.

Wagner could rarely enjoy a mature relationship with man, woman or child (how fond he was of dogs!), because he could not accommodate himself to the possibility of rejection. That is why in real life he could never credit others with actual existence. They are forms and shadows, idolaters or detractors, people who played two-dimensional roles in the often fictional dramas of his private and professional life, but they are never whole people who can be allowed an independent existence of their own.

Thus, alone in the world, protected from ultimate human contact by his wilful solipsism, Wagner nevertheless asked through his operas for confirmation of the existence of sympathetic, kindred spirits.

Wagner, Winifred Marjorie, *née* Williams (1897–1980)

Born in Hastings, England, she was brought up in the house of the pianist and conductor, Carl Klindworth, who was an acquaintance of Wagner's. At the age of eighteen, she became engaged to and married to Wagner's only son, Siegfried.*

She was just thirty-three when her husband died in 1930, but by then Winifred had absorbed all things German, and it was no surprise that, by the terms of Siegfried's will, she was entrusted with the direction of the Bayreuth Festival. Lacking any qualifications for such a post, Winifred appointed the director of the Berlin State Opera, Heinz Tietjen, as artistic director at Bayreuth.

Winifred offered help and support to Hitler* at an early stage in the rise of the Nazis. She is reputed to have become the dictator's mistress; whether this was true or·not, there was certainly a close relationship between Winifred the Wagnerian Germanophile and Hitler the Wagnerian Anglophile, who always admired the British for managing to acquire an empire. Winifred also kept the family in line with German foreign policy. She threatened her daughter Friedelind (b. 1918) with 'extermination' if she should broadcast anti-German propaganda on the American radio, which at one stage seemed likely.

After the war, Winifred's position was uncomfortable. She was put on trial for complicity with the fascist regime, found guilty and fined, although remaining unrepentant. It was partly through her energetic efforts that the festivals were recommenced in 1951 under the direction of her two sons, Wieland* and Wolfgang,* who were lessees. In 1973, she helped create the Richard Wagner foundation. In 1975, she announced to an embarrassed world that she would be quite happy to see Hitler back again, but perhaps this can be attributed to traditional English eccentricity as well as to her overt and dedicated fascism. After her outburst, which was broadcast on West German television, Wolfgang Wagner forbade her to set foot in the Bayreuth Festspielhaus, even though she was still the legal owner.

Wagner, Wolfgang Manfred Martin (b. 1919)

Son of Siegfried and grandson of Richard, Wolfgang Wagner has been sole director of the Bayreuth Festival since the death of his brother, Wieland,* in 1966. His reign has been stormy. First, there was the replacement of Wieland's celebrated stark productions by more Romantic interpretations. Wolfgang's production of the

Ring in 1970 was almost unanimously praised. The tilted circular set, a symbolic ring, was broken up during *Das Rheingold*, to be restored again only towards the end of *Götterdämmerung*, when the wrongs of Alberich* and Wotan* had been set to rights. Then came the controversial *Ring* of 1976, the year of Bayreuth's centenary, which outraged traditional Wagnerians. Pierre Boulez* conducted, and Patrice Chéreau designed the sets. The result was an analytic interpretation of both music and text. Wotan* appeared in a frock-coat, Fricka* in a tea-gown, Erda* was a writhing Beckettian shape in the final stages of labour and the *Götterdämmerrung* Rhinemaidens* appeared to be prostitutes soliciting for business on the parapet of a hydroelectric power station. There was an outcry as a result, with the older Wagnerian Germans denouncing the French as traitors to the sacred memory of Teutonic culture. Some who saw it threatened to murder those responsible, including the festival director: 'A curse and destruction to you and the French *Ring* team. What you have done to Richard Wagner's legacy is a crime. One ought to put all those concerned in front of a firing squad!', was a representative, but anonymous, comment. An equally anonymous 'Honest German' added, 'Since the *Ring* of 1976, I have again learned to *hate* the French nation and the French from the bottom of my heart.' Perhaps the 'again' was revealing. That centenary year, fist fights broke out in the Bayreuth auditorium and every curtain call was punctuated by boos from one section of the audience. In fact, what Wolfgang, Chéreau and Boulez had really done was to render the gods more intelligible in terms of the nineteenth-century values of Wagner's own contemporaries.

Wagner Societies of Patrons
These societies were widely established to help fund the Bayreuth Festival. Emil Heckel started the first in Mannheim in 1871; the London Wagner Society was founded the next year. Today there are Wagner Societies throughout the world. In Germany, there is an organization of West German Wagner Societies, the *Richard Wagner Verband*, which can be contacted via the Festival Theatre: 8580 Bayreuth 2, Postfach 2320, West Germany.

Wagner Tuba (Bass Tuba in F)
An instrument specially developed by Wagner for the *Ring*, to bridge the gap between the horns and trombones. Wagner wrote for a set of four Wagner tubas: two tenor tubas in B flat; two bass tubas in F. Wagner's idea seems to have been inspired by instruments which he saw in Adolphe Saxe's workshop in Paris in 1853, but it is not known which firm produced the tubas which Wagner had made for the Bayreuth Festival.

'Wahnfried'
Wagner's villa in Bayreuth, which today houses the Richard Wagner Museum. It was basically designed by the artist himself and, after building delays, he lived there from 1874 until his death nine years later. In 1945, an Allied bomb destroyed one-third of the residence, but the building was restored and the Wagner family continued to occupy it until 1973.

For many months, Wagner schemed and planned his vision of an ideal dwelling. He told King Ludwig* that he had 'survived like a fugitive' for too many years and now needed somewhere which would provide a 'proper sphere for my work'. The building of 'Wahnfried' lasted two long years, Wagner becoming increasingly intolerant of any further delay. Finally, the dream abode was ready. All that remained was to set three plaques in the front wall. They read, in translation: 'Here where my delusions found peace, let this house be called by me, "Peace from Delusion".' However, in private letters and jokes to friends, Wagner called the place 'Ärgersheim' ('House of Annoyance'), because of the struggle to get it ready in time.

The museum today houses a huge collection of Wagner memorabilia, including Franz Liszt's* Steinway grand piano.

Wala (W)

Alternative name for Erda,* the Earth Mother.

Walker, Edyth (?1867–1950)

American soprano who sang Ortrud,* Fricka,* Erda* and Waltraute* at Covent Garden in 1900. At the Metropolitan Opera (1903–6) she added Brünnhilde* to her repertoire. In 1908 she sang Ortrud* and Kundry* at Bayreuth, and her Isolde* at Covent Garden in the same year was acclaimed.

Walküre, Die (The Valkyrie)

Music drama in three acts, being the second work in Wagner's tetralogy of the Ring and the first in his poetic trilogy the Ring of the Nibelungs. Text and music by Richard Wagner, based on a variety of thirteenth century Icelandic, Nordic and German poems and legends. Die Walküre was first given in Munich on 26 June 1870. The first performance of the opera as part of a complete Ring cycle took place in 1876 in Bayreuth. The writing of Die Walküre was completed between 1854 and 1856, when Wagner was in his early forties.

In Die Walküre, Wagner picks up the themes established so successfully in Das Rheingold, but now on a grander scale. The work is much longer. This music drama needs to be divided into formal acts. The orchestral score grows in sophistication. Whereas, in Das Rheingold, some thirty of the ninety motives to be heard in the Ring were quoted in rapid succession, but none was developed to a musical conclusion, now, in Die Walküre,

with its stormy opening and six-four rhythm, we are going to hear music sometimes tested to destruction. If Das Rheingold is easy listening for the novice, the first Act of Die Walküre is very advanced musical writing indeed. This opera, nevertheless, is so passionate that the music (especially, perhaps, in Act I) will carry the audience through any difficulties.

As Siegmund* bursts into Hunding's* hut, wounded and exhausted, seeking shelter from the storm, he rushes headlong into one of the most enigmatic love scenes in all opera. He is met and tended by Sieglinde,* wife of Hunding. Siegmund is captivated by something familiar about her face. He cannot help but stare. She feels similarly moved. Their stares, lightly accompanied by thoughtful music, grow almost exaggeratedly long.

When questioned, Siegmund is coy about revealing his identity, only giving his name as 'Wehwalt', the 'sorrowful one'. He relates how ill-luck has dogged him all his life. Sieglinde responds with understanding, indicating that she, too, is no stranger to sadness. Again, they stare at one another. They are still staring when Hunding enters, instantly suspicious. He demands to know who the interloper is and abuses his wife for providing him with hospitality. Siegmund retorts by defending Sieglinde's generosity and ignoring Hunding's question. Hunding is troubled by the emotional force behind Siegmund's observations and disturbed to see how strong a physical resemblance there is between the stranger and his own wife.

Eventually, Siegmund breaks silence and tells a version of his life history. He says he is the child of 'Wolfe'*, but his mother was killed and sister carried off by a marauding tribe when he was still young. Later, his father also disappeared after a subsequent raid. Since then, known as Wehwalt, he has wandered like a nomad. But he has always found it difficult to establish friendships: 'I do not see the world as others do. . . . What I thought was right, others thought was wrong.'

167

Hunding merely interjects sarcastically, 'So few greet you with joy when you turn up as a guest!'

We then hear Siegmund's most recent news. He was asked for assistance by a woman oppressed by her kinsmen. They wished to compel her to marry a man she feared. Siegmund agreed to help and there was a fight. The woman's brothers were slain. More kinsmen arrived to avenge these deaths. The woman was killed and Siegmund chased off after defending himself so valiantly that his weapons were hacked to pieces in his hands. This explains the presence of 'Siegmund the Wehwalt' in Hunding's hut. He is on the run.

Alas, this is no sanctuary, since Hunding is one of the very men he has so recently been fighting. In great anger, Hunding warns him to prepare for a battle to the death the next morning; 'but this night, the laws of hospitality protect you'. Siegmund and Sieglinde cast eyes at each other yet again as Hunding retires to bed. Sieglinde follows Hunding out to prepare his evening drink.

Left to his own devices, Siegmund laments that he has never found the sword his father once promised him 'in his hour of need'. Surely that hour has come? Alone, wounded, weaponless, trapped in his enemy's house, how will he survive without further assistance? A light gleams briefly in the ash-tree around which the hut is built. There is something metallic hidden in the tree-trunk.

Sieglinde returns and reveals that she has taken the daring step of drugging her husband's drink. She tells Siegmund that there is a sword with which he can defend himself, buried up to the hilt in the wood of the tree. A mysterious shaft of light indicates the spot. The sword was put there by a peculiar one-eyed old man (Wotan*). He proclaimed that the sword should belong to the one who could draw it from the tree. All those who have tried have hitherto failed. Now, Sieglinde feels convinced that the sword is intended for Siegmund. She proposes directly and frankly that Siegmund should also become her lover if he can pull the sword from the tree.

The door blows open. Bright moonlight shines in. The couple see the glorious illumination of the magical spring night fill the surrounding countryside. Sieglinde compares Siegmund's arrival to the arrival of spring in her own heart. Love and spring, she exults, are again united. They again discuss their affinities. Both seem to recognize each other's features, as if from a past life. Sieglinde believes she can almost identify her companion's very voice and when he finally tells her that his father's true name was 'Wälse'* (Wotan's alias at the time), she jumps up, calls him 'Siegmund' by name and claims him as her long-lost brother. Siegmund hails her as 'Sister and Bride', because he firmly intends to become her husband, despite the fact that their relationship is too close in terms of blood. Sieglinde readily agrees. There is no flicker of protest when Siegmund grasps the sword (Notung*), pulls it easily from the ash-tree and closes Act I by taking Sieglinde off to bed in her own husband's house, with the words 'Holiest Love' rising from his jubilant lips.

In Act II, we are privy to a powerful domestic row between Wotan, the Lord of the Gods, and his wife Fricka,* concerning the events of the previous scene. Wotan is looking forward to the fight between Siegmund and Hunding because he is sure Siegmund will triumph, aided by the magic sword, Notung. Then perhaps Wotan can induce Siegmund to kill Fafner* and retrieve the Ring,* the one thing Wotan cannot do for himself, since a treaty binds Wotan to do Fafner no violence.

Fricka, goddess of matrimony, however, has altogether different ideas. She simply wants Siegmund slain. First, he has offended against the laws of marriage by committing adultery with Sieglinde. Second, he has offended against the laws of nature by committing incest with the same party. And third, she is irked by his very existence, since he is Wotan's bastard son. Wotan resists her arguments, until she shrewdly points out that, by giving Siegmund a magic sword and permitting Brünnhilde to assist him in battle, Wotan is actually breaking his treaties. For if Siegmund triumphs over Hunding and then destroys Fafner, Wotan will be to blame. Such logic is inescapable. Sadly and reluctantly, Wotan gives Fricka his oath not to protect Siegmund in the forthcoming fight.

Brünnhilde enters, surprised and alarmed to find her father so melancholy. He explains what has happened, commanding her expressly not to offer Siegmund any further aid, comfort or protection. Brünnhilde at first refuses, whereupon Wotan flies into a furious musical rage. Matters calm down, but Wotan confides that he is truly broken-hearted about abandoning Siegmund, his own child, to a bloody death. He is equally perplexed as to how he can ever create a hero to act consistently on behalf of his own interests, who yet retains free will.

With Wotan's dilemma unresolved, we return, in the third scene of Act II, to the story of Siegmund and Sieglinde, now fleeing from Hunding and his clan, who are tracking them down with dogs. The forbidden lovers arrive at a rocky pass. Sieglinde swoons with guilty distress. Siegmund offers heroic comfort, and says he will destroy any shame attaching to her name by slaying her accuser, Hunding, in battle.

A little reassured, Sieglinde falls into an uneasy sleep. The sleep produces a nightmare. Most of this troubled dream concerns the fear that Siegmund will abandon her. It is therefore a mercy that she cannot see the arrival of Brünnhilde, who announces in funereal tones that Siegmund has been called to his death in Valhalla.* Brünnhilde attempts to persuade Siegmund to welcome the journey with the promise that he and his real father, Wotan (the 'Wälse'), will be

reunited. Siegmund says he would prefer to go to hell or slaughter Sieglinde on the spot than abandon her to the wilderness of Hunding's wrath. So moved is the Valkyrie by this evidence of Siegmund's passion that, solely on her own initiative, and contrary to Wotan's command, she assures him that he shall love Sieglinde and live, even promising him total victory over Hunding in the coming fight.

We thus witness a contest of heavenly wills, Fricka versus Wotan and Wotan versus Brünnhilde (which practically amounts to Wotan against himself, since he would dearly love to save Siegmund). However, rule must prevail, and in the fight, when Brünnhilde shelters Siegmund with her shield, a ferocious Wotan materializes himself, shatters Notung with his spear* and allows Siegmund to be killed by the sword of the exultant Hunding. Brünnhilde quickly gathers up the distraught Sieglinde, together with the broken fragments of Notung, and flees from the scene of her disobedience. Wotan kills the ignoble Hunding with one baleful glare, then angrily turns to pursue his all too wilful child, Brünnhilde.

The final act of *Die Walküre* is full of splendid dramatic and musical contrasts. It opens with some of the most popular and graphic music ever written: 'Ride' of the hard-hearted and grim-visaged Valkyries.* It ends with Wotan's poignant and passionate forgiveness of his wayward daughter, once he has succeeded in mastering his own internal thunderstorm.

First, we meet the Valkyries bent on their grisly task of persuading dead heroes to join Wotan's conscript army of Valhalla. The incentives are the traditional ones: fine scenery, female company and a share in godly glory. Then Brünnhilde turns up, bearing Sieglinde across the saddle of her steed, Grane,* instead of the customary male. She tells her sisters what has occurred, and asks them to lend her a horse, so that she can bear Sieglinde to safety, away from Wotan's avenging wrath. They are horrified and refuse. Sieglinde begs for the release of death, until Brünnhilde informs her that she is pregnant with Siegmund's son, whom she must bear and call Siegfried.* Sieglinde pauses to absorb the news, then rallies, since that much comfort shall remain for her.

Her recovery is interrupted by the thunderous arrival of Wotan. He commands the cowering Valkyries to hand Brünnhilde over. He is more angry than they have ever seen him before. He decrees that Brünnhilde will be staked out on a mountain-top, chained in an enchanted sleep and cursed to fall in love with the first mortal man who wakes her. At one and the same moment, she will lose her immortality, liberty and virginity. Brünnhilde proudly pleads for death rather than suffer any such degradation. In mournful motives of the highest beauty and pathos, she gradually wins her father's forgiveness, but not without a typical display of family cunning. She gives Wotan the news that Sieglinde is pregnant with Siegfried and also possesses the shattered fragments of Notung. Perhaps this child, when grown up, will turn out to be a hero mighty enough to kill Fafner, seize the Ring and deliver Wotan from his terrible fear of Alberich,* without compromising Wotan's bargain with the giants?

Wotan is finally persuaded, pressing his daughter to his bosom. He now understands that, in her disobedience to his commands, she was only obeying his 'higher' will, for his desires really are divided and he desperately longs for the arrival of a hero champion to solve his problem. Accordingly, Wotan modifies Brünnhilde's sentence. She shall still be placed in enchanted sleep on the mountain-top, but the man who awakens and claims her as bride will have to be a veritable Hercules, who can not only brave a circle of protecting fire (Loge*), but also has the power to shatter Wotan's spear with his sword. The only hero who could qualify for this task is Siegfried, as we come to see in the next opera of the cycle, bearing his name.

Wälse and Wälsing (W)

Siegmund's* true familial name. Derived by Wagner from the *Völsunga Saga*, it is an obvious alias for Wotan,* Siegmund's actual father.

Walther von der Vogelweide (T)

Minnesinger (tenor) colleague of Tannhäuser* at the court of Hermann,* Landgrave of Thuringia, who is as outraged as the rest of the company by news of Tannhäuser's illegal and immoral sojourn in the arms of Venus.* Walther's song in the Wartburg Contest (tenor) takes a conventionally moral view of love.

The character is closely based on the historical poet of the same name (*c.* 1170–*c.* 1230), who was celebrated as the greatest German lyric poet of the Middle Ages. His poetry emphasizes the virtues of a balanced life, regardless of personal considerations. In politics and religion, he stresses faithfulness, sincerity, charity and self-discipline – virtues that had not been especially prominent in his own life (which was marked by political intrigue). One should take his contribution to the song contest as being quite in keeping with the real Walther's career – beautiful, but tinged with hypocrisy.

In *Die Meistersinger*, the young knight Walther von Stolzing* claims that he was taught to sing by Walther von der Vogelweide.

Waltraute (W, G)

The second noblest Valkyrie (mezzo-soprano) after Brünnhilde.* She shows no exceptional qualities during the course of events as told in *Die Walküre*. However, in *Götterdämmerung* she dares to undertake an independent mission in defiance of her father Wotan,* who has forbidden any of his minions to leave Valhalla.* Her purpose is to ask Brünnhilde to save the gods by returning the magic Ring* to its rightful owners, the Rhinemaidens.* She says that Wotan is resigned to death, except for one tiny part of his will, which still hopes for salvation, provided by Brünnhilde. Waltraute makes it clear to her sister that 'The world's future all depends on the Ring. Cast it from you, down in the waters; Valhalla's grief shall be ended when you fling it back in the Rhine.'

Unfortunately, at this point the Ring holds far more significance for Brünnhilde as Siegfried's* token of love than it does as a symbol of mere world salvation. She refuses. Waltraute accuses her of disloyalty and rushes home to Wotan, full of woe.

Wanderer: *see* Wotan

Wartburg
A hill overlooking the ancient German city of Eisenach,* on which is built the castle of the Landgraves of Thuringia. It is famous in German legend as the seat of a lively court frequented by vagrant poets and musicians, such as Walther von der Vogelweide* and Wolfram von Eschenbach,* as well as featuring centrally in Wagner's opera *Tannhäuser*.

Weber, Carl Maria Friedrich Ernst von (1786–1826)
German composer, primarily responsible for the transition from Classical to Romantic in opera. He worked as musical director at Prague and later at Dresden. His principal operatic contribution is the delightful *Der Freischütz* ('The Freeshooter'),· first performed in Berlin in 1821. Weber was sometimes a guest at the home of Wagner's parents. In his autobiography Wagner writes, 'I received my first impressions of music from this master. . . . Nothing pleased me so much as *Der Freischütz*. . . . That inspired me with enthusiasm for music. I often saw Weber go past our house. I always regarded him with reverent respect.'

As a child, Wagner could play the overture to *Der Freischütz* by ear. Wagner was also influenced by Weber's two later Romantic operas, *Euryanthe* (1823) and *Oberon* (1826).

In 1844, Wagner, who had succeeded Weber as conductor at Dresden, personally arranged for the shipment of Weber's ashes from London to Dresden, where they were finally interred.

Weber, Ludwig (1899–1974)
Austrian bass. Weber joined the Bavarian State Opera in 1933, and in 1936 sang Pogner,* Gurnemanz,* Hunding* and Hagen* in London, where he later gave Daland* and King Marke.* He joined the Vienna State Opera in 1945. From 1951–60 he sang regularly at Bayreuth. Weber was as happy in the dark role of Hagen as in the portrayal of the humane King Marke.

Wehwalt (W)
The sad pseudonym, meaning 'woeful', adopted by Siegmund* on first encountering Sieglinde* in the hut of her husband, Hunding.*

Weigl, Joseph: *see Schweizerfamilie, Die.*

Weingartner, Felix (1863–1942)
Austrian conductor who was much influenced by his personal contacts with both Wagner and Liszt,* as can be seen from his memoirs. Surprisingly, his own conducting was along strictly classical, non-Wagnerian lines.

Weinlig, Christian Theodor (1780–1842)
German organist and composer, who from 1823 held Bach's old position of cantor of the Thomasschule in Leipzig, where he taught Wagner musical theory for a short but, for Wagner, fruitful period.

Weissheimer, Wendelin (1838–1910)
German conductor and composer whom Wagner met in the late 1850s. Weissheimer later published an account of Wagner's dramatic turn of fortune when King Ludwig II* offered to clear Wagner's debts (*Experiences of Richard Wagner, Franz Liszt, etc*, 1898). Wagner fell out with Weissheimer, partly because his wife, Cosima [Wagner],* did not like him.

Wellgunde (R, G)
One of the Rhinemaidens (soprano).

IN *Rheingold*
Wellgunde helps her sisters to tease Alberich* for being ugly. It is alleged that the maidens only victimize strangers to drive them away from the vicinity of the Rhine gold. If so, it is somewhat ironic that the Rhinemaidens should also give Alberich the key to the gold by explaining how it may be stolen. Wellgunde is as culpable as Woglinde,* because it is she who tells Alberich how to fashion the Ring from the Rhinegold.

IN *Götterdämmerung*
Wellgunde sings with her sisters to Siegfried* of the fate that lies in store for him, unless he throws the Ring* back into the waters of the Rhine; but Siegfried is deterred from complying by their presumptious manner. Wellgunde helps Woglinde to drown Hagen* in the grand finale of the cycle, Act III.

Wesendonck, Mathilde (1828–1902)
Artistically inclined wife of a Rhineland businessman, Otto Wesendonck*. It is no surprise to find that Wagner's wooing should have taken a musical form. His 1853 piano sonata is dedicated to Mathilde, who at the time of its composition was twenty-five years old. The next year, the couple grew closer, and from the fruits of their relationship Wagner conceived his idea for an opera based on the legend of Tristan and Isolde, with Mathilde firmly cast in the role of Isolde to his Tristan. We not only owe Frau Wesendonck our musical thanks for this, but also for being the inspiration behind some of Wagner's loveliest melodic writing: for the *Wesendonck Lieder*, for Sieglinde,* and for the nature themes in *Siegfried* as well as in *Parsifal*.

In 1857, Wagner and Mathilde shared their lives, living in houses side-by-side on the estate of Mathilde's sad but complaisant husband, Otto. The affair came to an end when Minna Wagner arrived at their idyllic love-sanctuary ('Das Asyl'*) and insulted Mathilde to her face. In August 1858, Wagner and Mathilde parted and all their future meetings had to be conducted on a conventional basis.

Of Mathilde, Wagner once wrote, 'I laid the whole festival [of my music] at the feet of one beautiful woman. . . . She was the wish-child [Brünnhilde?] who divined my most secret thoughts.'

Wesendonck, Otto (1816–96)
A rich businessman from the Rhineland who settled in Zurich in 1851, where he and his wife Mathilde* met Wagner. He built a large villa for himself and his family on land just outside the city, but then made the generous mistake of offering Wagner the use of a summer house, called 'Das Asyl',* situated in the estate grounds. His wife, Mathilde, fell violently in love with the composer and Otto found himself forced to take the role of *mari complaisant* for the sake of his children.

However, many commentators have suggested that Otto carried his forgiveness to extremes by continuing to lend Wagner money even after the affair had finished. Wagner himself seemed to think so, since he began to disparage Wesendock both behind his back and in his published autobiography, *My Life*:*

'. . . it became really intolerable to me to give up whole evenings to conversations and entertainment in which my good friend Otto Wesendonck thought himself bound to take part at least as much as myself and others. His anxiety lest, as he imagined, everything in his house would soon go my way rather than his gave him, moreover, that peculiar burdensomeness with which a man who thinks himself slighted throws himself into every conversation in his presence, something like an extinguisher on a candle.

Whitehill, Clarence Eugene (1871–1932)

American baritone and bass-baritone, who studied with Cosima Wagner* from 1904 at Bayreuth, where he sang Wolfram von Eschenbach (1904),* Amfortas (1908, 1909)* and Gunther (1909).* He sang Wotan* in a complete *Ring* under Richter* at Covent Garden in 1905, and sang again there in English-language Ring cycles in 1908 and 1909 (under Richter) and in 1922 (under Albert Coates)..

Wibelungen, Die

A semi-historical essay which Wagner wrote in 1848, just before starting *The Nibelung Myth.as a Sketch for a Drama.*

Wieland der Schmied (Wayland the Smith)

The title of a projected opera about the lame blacksmith which Wagner never managed to write. It was sketched as a drama at the beginning of 1849 and worked out more elaborately in 1850 in Paris. Adolf Hitler* toyed with the idea of completing the project on Wagner's behalf.

Wilde, Oscar Fingal O'Flahertie Wills (1856–1900)

Gifted Irish playwright and wit, most famous for *The Importance of Being Earnest* (1895) and for his trial and conviction for homosexuality in the same year. He championed the Wagnerian cause in late Victorian England, despite the untruthful malice of his much-quoted remark: 'I like Wagner's music better than anybody's. It is so loud that one can talk the whole time

without other people hearing what one says.'

Wille, Eliza (née Sloman; 1809–93)

Novelist and supporter of Wagner in his Swiss years.

Windgassen, Wolfgang (1914–74)

German tenor, son of a tenor, born into an intensely musical family. Windgassen's singing was famed for its lyrical grace and beauty. He gave the 1951 Parsifal* at Bayreuth and sang there almost every year until 1970. His roles, besides Parsifal, included Siegfried,* Lohengrin,* Tristan,* Walther von Stolzing,* Erik,* Loge,* Tannhäuser* and Rienzi.* He also sang regularly in the Wagner seasons at Covent Garden 1955–66. His voice was a lightish *Heldentenor*, especially charming and delightful in the *Siegfried* woodland passages, and his Tristan was also notable.

Winkelmann, Hermann (1849–1912)

German tenor, one of the finest of the first generation of Wagner singers, Winkelmann was coached by the composer himself. In London with the Hamburg company in 1882, he sang Lohengrin,* Tannhäuser,* and Tristan,* and in the same year, on Richter's recommendation, sang Parsifal* at its Bayreuth première. Wagner greatly admired his fluid vocal phrasing.

Wittgenstein, Princess [Carolyne] (1819–87)

Unhappily married to a Russian aristocrat, Princess Wittgenstein later met and fell in love with Liszt,* with whom she lived until 1860. At first, she was a supporter of Wagner, but relations became strained when she was estranged from Liszt. Cosima [Wagner]* blamed her for much of the difficulty in her own childhood.

Wittich, Marie (1868–1931)
German soprano, who gave Sieglinde,*
Isolde* and Kundry* at Bayreuth 1901–9.
Her performances at Covent Garden
(1905–6) as Elsa,* Elisabeth,* Isolde,*
Sieglinde* and Brünnhilde,* however,
were disappointing on account of her poor
health.

Wittig the Irming (W)
Name of a hero captured on the field of
battle by the Valkyrie* Schwertleite. He is
described as the mortal foe of Sintolt the
Hegeling.*

Woglinde (R, G)
One of the Rhinemaidens (soprano).

IN *Rheingold*
After teasing Alberich* in a most unpleasant fashion, it is Woglinde who im-
prudently reveals to him that, in order to
steal the sacred Rhine gold, he will have to
pronounce a curse on love for ever, which
he immediately does.

IN *Götterdämmerung*
Woglinde joins her sisters in begging
Siegfried* to return the Ring to its home in
the Rhine, but this plea is couched in a
threatening form calculated not to appeal
to the brash and fearless hero. Later,
Woglinde joins her sister Wellgunde* in
drowning Hagen* in the waters of the
Rhine.

Wolf, Hugo (1860–1903)
Austrian composer, one of the supreme
masters of the German *Lied*, who died in a
mental asylum.

Wagner had a strong influence on the
younger man, although there were few
contacts between them. The fifteen-year-
old Wolf queued for four hours for a
standing place to hear the first Vienna
Tannhäuser in November, 1875. At the
final curtain, he clapped until his hands

were bruised, huzzaing so lustily that
people turned to look at him rather than at
the famous composer, who was present.

In December, Wolf tried to get Wagner
to appraise his early compositions, but the
great man brushed him aside with shatter-
ing condescension, saying that nothing
could be divined from an artist's juvenilia.
'Look at my *Rienzi*,' he said. 'There are
poor things in that!'

When he first heard *Parsifal*, Wolf sent
a postcard to his friend Henrietta Lank,
'Parsifal is without doubt by far the most
beautiful and sublime work in the whole
field of Art. My whole being reels in the
perfect world of this wonderful work, as if
in some blissful ecstasy, becoming ever
more enraptured and blessed – I could die
even now, a thought that has not occurred
to me for a long time.'

Wolfe (W)
The name by which Siegmund* says he
knew his father. It is obvious that this
'Wolfe' is, in fact, Wotan. (It is interesting
to note that Wieland* and Wolfgang*
Wagner used to refer to Hitler* as 'Uncle
Wolf'.)

Wolff, Fritz (1894–1957)
German tenor who sang Loge* in 1925 at
Bayreuth, where he reappeared regularly
as Loge, Parsifal* and Walther von Stolzing* in the years up to 1941. He also sang
at Covent Garden 1929–33 and 1937–8,
giving Lohengrin,* Walther, Loge, Erik,*
and Parsifal. In the last-named role he was
especially admired by Ernest Newman.*

Wölfing (W)
The name (meaning 'little wolf') by which
Siegmund* claims he has often been
known, since his father before him was
called 'Wolfe'.

Wolfram von Eschenbach (T)
A minnesinger in love with Elisabeth* of
Thuringia, who overlooks this silent wor-
shipper in favour of his close friend,
Tannhäuser.* Wolfram is the upright
Christian baritone who strives throughout
the opera to save Tannhäuser from the
devil. His paean of praise to love in the
famous Wartburg song contest scene
stresses spiritual purity and tenderness –
the kind of unspoken love he offers the
saintly Elisabeth. He has the satisfaction
in the end of knowing that both Tannhäuser and Elisabeth die in a signal state of
grace and that the sacrifice of his own
feelings has been worthwhile (like that of
Sachs in *Die Meistersinger*).

The character is based on the famous
impoverished Bavarian knight, Wolfram
von Eschenbach (*c.* 1200–*c.* 1220), who
wrote the epic poems *Parzifal*, *Titurel* and
Willehalm, as well as the lyric octet *Tage-
lieder*. Of these the most important is
Parzifal, a wondrous and complex creation running to 25,000 lines in sixteen
books.

Wagner took the poem as holiday reading to Marianske Lazne in 1845. It seems
to have exercised no great initial effect,
but he read it again in April 1857 and this
time his mind was overwhelmed by Wolfram's epic idealism and instantly filled
with a network of ideas which were eventually to emerge as his own *Parsifal*.
However, by 1859, Wagner had finished
with the poem, having got what he wanted
from it. In a letter of that year to Mathilde
Wesendonck* he offers some of the least
accurate literary criticism: 'Just look how
easy Master Wolfram made things for
himself!' In the opera *Parsifal*, Wagner is
preoccupied with his hero's conquest of
sensuality; in the poem *Parzifal*, Wolfram
is more comprehensively preoccupied
with his hero's conquest of self, and yet
Wagner commented that he was 'disgusted by Wolfram's superficiality'! The
epic *Parzifal* and the fragment *Titurel* are
prime sources for Wagner's *Lohengrin*.

**Wolzogen, Hans Paul Freiherr von
(1848–1938)**
German writer on music and librettist,
editor of the *Bayreuther Blätter* and author of numerous studies of the master.
He lived in Bayreuth from 1877 onwards,
where he remained an influential figure.
His father, Karl August Alfred von Wolzogen (1823–83), had been director of the
court theatre of Schwerin.

Wood-bird, Voice of the (S)
An off-stage soprano impersonating a
song-bird whose words become intelligible to Siegfried* after his lips have been
dashed with a drop of Fafner's* magic
dragon's blood.

Her message is to tell Siegfried to avoid
Mime's* murderous plots, to take the
Ring* and the Tarnhelm* from Fafner's
cave for himself and to claim a glorious
bride, Brünnhilde,* who lies chained in
enchanted sleep on a mountain-top ringed
by fire. The bird then guides him to the
location of Brünnhilde's rock.

Previously, Siegfried had tried to copy
the Wood-bird's motive, first on a clumsy
reed pipe, and then on his fine hunting
horn.

World Ash-Tree: *See* 'Yggdrasil'

**Wotan (L, R, W; but present throughout
the *Ring*, in *Siegfried*, as the Wanderer)**
(See also Ravens of Wotan, Spear of
Wotan; Wälse; Wolfe; and Yggdrasil)
Wotan is the Lord of the Germanic Gods
whom Ortrud* in *Lohengrin*, for example, invokes as the god of power, who
might help her win the throne of Brabant.
In Scandinavian legend, he is known
variously as Odin and Woden, from which
of course the word Wednesday is derived.

Wotan is one of the leading protagonists
in the *Ring* and the main purpose of this
cycle of four operas is to present the
reasons for his rise, decline and fall. We

see him in *Rheingold* as the leader who has brought law to an anarchic planet; indeed, he rules the world by virtue of his compacts and bargains struck with the other inhabitants: with Loge,* the giants (Fafner* and Fasolt*) and Erda.* These treaties (see 'Yggdrasil'*) are engraved in runes upon his spear* of authority, hewn from the Tree of Life, Yggdrasil.* But by the final act of *Siegfried*, Wotan has transformed himself into a rootless 'Wanderer', a law-breaker deprived of authority, fallen from grace in the pursuit of power and glory. All that remains for him is hope; he himself is outlawed from power. Wagner's moral purpose could not have been more clearly stated.

This downfall is due to three major frailties in Wotan's character: imperialism, hubris and lack of nerve. First, he revels in ruling. Many commentators, including Wotan himself, have noticed how little difference there is between his personality and that of his black foe Alberich.* They both crave world dominion, and, if Wotan were not restrained by his runic treaties, he would be indistinguishable from Alberich, except in his ability to enjoy somewhat exploitative love affairs with a number of women (whereas Alberich has to patronize prostitutes). Wotan and Alberich are alteregos: the light and dark shades of a single passion. Wagner's message is again unmistakably clear: beware power-crazed men, even when they come in their legal and civilized disguises.

Wotan's second weakness is his love of grandeur. This commits him to a speculative building project (the palace of Valhalla*) for which he cannot pay. The only moral escape from his dilemma would be to forego Valhalla and resign the power game to Alberich.

Yet resignation would only intensify Wotan's already incapacitating fear of Alberich, an uncontrollable displacement anxiety, which is his third weakness. Wotan is determined to purchase Valhalla partly because it will serve as a fortress, a wolf's lair, where his enemy will be unable to get at him. It is to be the ultimate bunker. Wotan will fill this fortified palace with selected heroes from the world's great battlefields. Some of these men, we learn, will be 'shamefully tricked and deceived' into signing up. Although these martial spirits will enjoy the privileges of an afterlife, Wotan's basic motive is the opposite of heroic. He is hoping by this means to amass such an army of knights that Alberich will never dare to take him on in combat.

IN *Rheingold*
We see Wotan wriggling on the horns of his dilemma. He is eager to keep the palace of Valhalla,* but reluctant to pay the price agreed with the giants. He cannot bilk his way out of the deal because his word is his bond. Loge* suggests stealing Alberich's gold. They could return the Ring to the Rhinemaidens and keep the balance to pay off the giants. Wotan assents, but is corrupted by the Ring as soon as it sits on his finger. It seems to divine his desire for glittering riches and world-conquest. By the opera's end, Wotan is irrevocably compromised and, as Erda indicates, effectively doomed. He has permitted the Ring to pass to the giants, paying for Valhalla in stolen gold, hoping that something else will 'turn up' to save him from his fate.

Wotan's character possesses excessive grandeur, balanced by intelligence and a curiosity which leads him into many love affairs. Yet his relations with women are as much instrumental as loving: a means of acquiring information or children that can be of use to him. Wotan could never have uttered a curse on love, as Alberich does, since part of his personality always remains open to the generosity of love. But these two power-seekers are not so very different in their relationships with others. When Wotan drops his guard, he can inspire love, as we shall see in the case of Brünnhilde,* but this happens all too rarely.

IN *Die Walküre*

It has to be admitted that Wotan – like Alberich – does not tamely surrender to fate. His new plan is to use a human hero, Siegmund,* his own son by a mortal woman, to try to gain the Ring from Fafner the giant. This plan aborts because Wotan's jealous wife, Fricka, points out that since Siegmund would be little more than Wotan's creature, he, by this scheme, he would still be breaking his contract with Fafner. What is wanted is a truly free spirit and only when, at the end of *Walküre*, Brünnhilde* tells him the news of Siegfried's impending birth does he see the possibility of re-seizing the initiative. Where Siegmund failed, surely Siegfried will succeed?

During this political plotting, we see Wotan's character develop in complexity. As his options narrow, his will seems to turn against itself. On the one hand, his desire for power wants Siegmund to live and flourish. On the other, his legalistic will wants him to die. Brünnhilde is very much a victim of the situation; when she disobeys Wotan's legal command to let Siegmund die, she is really only carrying out Wotan's simultaneous but contradictory wish that Siegmund should survive. This conflict takes on external, symbolic form in a titanic thunderstorm. Yet again, Wagner is showing that extreme emotional distress and depression will follow whenever any human being pursues ends in contradiction with his fundamental nature. Wotan is first and foremost a lawgiver.

And yet, Wotan is a revolutionary. He strongly desires to change the conservative customs by which the world lives. He tells Fricka to 'learn that a thing may happen, although it has not happened before'. He excuses incest* on the grounds that the authentic desires aroused by the goddess of Spring (Fricka's sister, after all), quite naturally proved stronger than Fricka's own notion of 'marital law'. Thus Wotan has progressive visions: he is an attractive innovator although still far too slippery for his own good.

We are naturally tempted to share Wotan's self-pity and grief in Acts II and III of *Die Walküre* when he complains of being 'the least free of all living' and also 'the saddest of creatures'. And yet he continues to harden our hearts against him by his autocratic and mean-spirited pomposity. We learn that he is a cheat (deceiving heroes into Valhalla) and a tyrant (he cannot brook any form of opposition from any of the Valkyries including Brünnhilde). In fact, the most terrible admission that Wotan can bring himself to make is that he is 'weak'. Wotan's pride is still one of his three destructive demons.

IN *Siegfried*

Now calling himself the 'Wanderer', Wotan begins to recognize that he cannot save himself. Much of his effort in this opera will be devoted to handing over his inheritance to the fearless hero, Siegfried – who is, of course, his grandson. He still wants to 'cheat' by interfering with destiny. For example, Siegfried only acquires Notung,* the magical sword, because Wotan 'prompts' Mime* to tell Siegfried how he can forge it. Yet for himself and the gods he begins to accept that the end is in sight. Hubris still compels him to boast to Erda that he has 'willed' this end, although even Wotan ultimately recognizes the force of the inevitable. But Wotan has done all he can to save his race; he resigns himself to death with a becoming nobility, reaping in the world of Wagner the just reward for imperious folly.

IN *Götterdämmerung*

We learn from the Norns* and Waltraute* that Wotan has locked himself up in Valhalla with all his family and men. He has chopped down the Tree of Life and its branches lie stacked around his palace. He is waiting for the end of the gods in Loge's flames.

However, Waltraute tells us that some old ambition still flickers deep in his heart. Although in *Siegfried* he said to Erda that he was resigned to death, he whispers within earshot of Waltraute that 'all could still be saved if only Brünnhilde would return the Ring to the Rhinemaidens'. Wotan's old habits die hard.

Yggdrasil

The mythological 'World Ash Tree' or 'Tree of Life' beneath which rises the sacred fountain of wisdom. The legend runs that Wotan* sacrificed one of his eyes to the giant Mimir in return for a drink from the fountain. Then he plucked a rune-covered branch from the tree and fashioned himself a spear. In order to decipher the runes and thus obtain world-knowledge, Wotan wounded himself with the spear and hung in torment on Yggdrasil for the space of nine days and nights. He was not freed until this self-inflicted punishment had engendered wisdom.

Although he is possessed of deep wisdom, Wotan's vision has been restricted by the loss of his eye, so that he only imperfectly understands the forces of nature. He needs to consult the earth-goddess, Erda,* at moments of crisis (for example, in *Rheingold*). He is unaware that by mutilating the World Ash Tree he has caused it to wither and the flow from the spring of knowledge to dwindle. In *Götterdämmerung*, we learn from the Norns* just how much trouble Wotan's Faustian clamour for knowledge has caused. The rope of destiny they have been spinning no longer hangs from its proper perch on Yggdrasil but has been moved to a common fir-tree and when Siegfried* shatters Wotan's spear,* the Lord of the Gods even has to order the felling of Yggdrasil to provide firewood for the burning of Valhalla* in the final conflagration.

Young Siegfried

Wagner's poem of 1851 which he subsequently turned into the text of the opera *Siegfried*.

Zemina (F)

A fairy or fate and partner to Farzana.* She opposes the liaison between her queen, Ada,* and the mortal Arindal,* disparaging it as an 'unworthy match'. But her wicked tricks come to nothing, since the opera is played out to a happy ending for the lovers.

Zimmermann, Erich (1892–1968)

German tenor, the most famous buffo and character tenor of his day, especially valued for his David* (in which he made his Bayreuth début in 1925) and Mime.*

Zorn, Balthazar (M)

A tenor Mastersinger of Nuremberg, and pewterer by trade, who contributes to the song contest scenes.

Zumpe, Hermann (1850–1903)

German conductor who, from 1872, helped Wagner to complete the score of the *Ring*. Zumpe gave a famous series of Wagner performances in Munich in 1900. In his own lifetime he was compared to Richter,* Mottl,* and Levi,* especially as an exponent of Wagner.

Zweter, Reinmar von (T)

Minnesinger bass at the court of Hermann,* Landgrave of Thuringia, who helps swell the choral quintet (sometimes quartet) which colours the solos of Tannhäuser* and Wolfram von Eschenbach.*

Non-operatic Music

Wagner said, 'I would never have been able to compose in the manner in which I have done so up to now had Beethoven not existed.' The special truth of this remark can be demonstrated by listening, for example, to some of his earlier orchestral works, in particular the Symphony in C Major, first performed in Prague in 1832. In this work, Wagner parades his ample command of traditional technique and also that 'classical' ability to develop musical themes which many of his detractors openly questioned when confronted by the mature operas.

Wagner's major surviving non-operatic works are as follows (dates are of first performances unless it is stated otherwise):

Orchestral

Overture in B flat (1830)
Overture in C (1830)
Overture in D (1831)
Overture to *König Enzio* (1832)
Symphony in C (1832)
Overture to *Columbus* (1835)
Overture, *Polonia* (1836)
Overture, *Rule Britannia* (1837)
Incidental music for the play *Die Letzte Heidenverschwörung in Preussen*, by J. Singer (fragment; 1837)
Overture to *Faust* (1840)
Trauermusik, for reburial of Weber's remains, for band (1844)
Huldingungsmarsch, for military band (1864)
Siegfried Idyll, for small orchestra (1870)
Kaisermarsch, with unison male voices (1871)
Grosser Festmarsch (*Centennial March*, for the centenary of the Declaration of Independence of the USA; 1876)

Choral

Neujahrs-Kantate, for mixed voices and orchestra (1834)
Nicolai Volshymne, for mixed voices and orchestra (1837)
La Descente de la Courtille, for mixed voices and orchestra (1840)
Gesang zur Enthüllung des Denkmals Sr. Maj. des hochseligen Königs Friedrich August des Gerechten, for male voices and brass (1843)

Das Liebesmahl der Apostel (for the unveiling of the memorial for King
Friedrich August I of Saxony), for male voices and orchestra (1843)
Gruss seiner Treuen an Friedrich August den Geliebten, for unaccompanied
male voices (1844)
Hebt an den Sorg (An Webers Grabe), for unaccompanied male voices
(1844)

Piano

Fantasia in F Sharp (1831)
Polonaise in D, for four hands (?written 1832)
Sonata in A (written 1832)
Albumblatt in E (*Lied ohne Wörte*; written 1840)
Eine Sonate für das Album von Frau M[athilde] Wesendonck, in A flat
(written 1853)
Albumblatt in C (*In das Album der Fürstin M[etternich]* (written 1861)
Ankunft bei den Schwarzen Schwänen (Albumblatt), in A flat (written
1861)
Albumblatt für Frau Betty Schott, in E flat (1876)

Songs for voice and piano

Sieben Kompositionen zu Goethes Faust (written 1831, revised 1832): 'Lied
der Soldaten'; 'Bauer unter der Linde'; 'Branders Lied'; 'Lied des
Mephistopheles' (I); 'Lied des Mephistopheles' (2); 'Gretchen am
Spinnrade'; 'Melodram Gretchens'; 'Der Tannenbaum' (text by G.
Scheurlin; 1839)
'Adieux de Marie Stuart' (text by J. P. de Béranger; written 1840)
'Les Deux Grenadiers' (text by H. Heine, trans. F. A. Loeve Veimar; 1840)
Fünf Gedichte für eine Frauenstimme (*Wesendonck Lieder*; texts by M.
Wesendonck; written 1857–8): 'Der Engel'; 'Stehe Still'; 'Im Treibhaus';
'Schmerzen'; 'Traüme'

Arrangements

G. Donizetti, *La Favorite* (vocal score; published ? 1840)
G. Donizetti, *L'elisir d'Amore* (vocal score; published ? 1840)
F. Halévy, *La reine de Chypre* (vocal score; published ? 1841)
F. Halévy, *La guitarrero* (vocal score; published ? 1841)
C. W. Gluck, *Iphigénie en Aulide* (performing version, 1847; vocal score
published 1858)
G. P. da Palestrina, *Stabat Mater* (performing version, 1848)

Of all these works, the two which are probably the most frequently
performed today are the exquisite *Siegfried Idyll* (a serenade,
written as a birthday present for Cosima Wagner* in 1870 in
gratitude for the birth of their son Siegfried [Wagner])* and the
Wesendonck Lieder (now usually performed with orchestral accompaniment). Of the other works, the early Overture to *Faust* is often
played. Of Wagner's arrangements, the performing version of

Gluck's *Iphigénie en Aulide* is of especial interest for the light it throws on Wagner's thoroughly professional understanding, and disinterested love, of other composers' music; in particular, the overture is always performed today in his arrangement.

Wagner's Literary Works

The more important of Wagner's voluminous writings are listed below. Two useful published collections are Albert Goldman and Evert Springchorn, trans. H. Ashton Ellis, *Wagner on Music and Drama* (London, 1970) and Robert L. Jacobs and Geoffrey Skelton, *Wagner Writes from Paris* (London, 1973).

Theoretical Works

The German Opera (1834)
Pasticcio (1834)
On German Music (1840)
A Pilgrimage to Beethoven (1840)
On the Overture (1840)
The Wibelungs (1848)
Art and Revolution (1849)
The Art-work of the Future (1849)
Art and Climate (1850)
Judaism in Music (1850; revised 1869)
Opera and Drama (1851; revised 1868)
The Music of the Future (1860)
State and Religion (1864)
What is German? (1865–78)
German Art and German Policy (1867)
Beethoven (1870)
On the Destiny of Opera (1871)
Actors and Singers (1872)
Modern (1878)
Public and Popularity (1878)
The Public in Time and Space (1878)
Shall we hope? (1879)
Open Letter to Herr Ernst von Weber (concerning vivisection; 1879)
Religion and Art (1880)
What boots this Knowledge? (1880)
Hero-dom and Christianity (1881)
On the Human Womanly (1883)

Technical Works

The Virtuoso and the Artist (1840)
Concerning the Royal Orchestra (1846)
A Project for the Organization of a German National Theatre for the Kingdom of Saxony (1849)
A Theatre at Zürich (1851)
On the Performing of 'Tannhäuser' (1852)
Remarks on performing 'The Flying Dutchman' (1852)
Gluck's Overture to 'Iphigenia in Aulis' (1854)
On Franz Liszt's Symphonic Poems (1857)
The Vienna Court Opera House (1863)
Report to His Majesty King Ludwig II of Bavaria upon a German Music School to be founded in Munich (1865)
On Conducting (1869)
The Rendering of Beethoven's Ninth Symphony (1873)
On Poetry and Composition (1879)
On Operatic Poetry and Composition (1879)
On the Application of Music to the Drama (1879)

Autobiographical Works

An End in Paris; The Artist and the Public (1841)
Autobiographical Sketch (1842)
A Communication to my Friends (1851)
My Life (published privately, 1870–81; 1st ed. for the public 1911)
The Work and Mission of my Life (1879)

Recollections

Recollections of Spontini (1851)
Recollections of Ludwig Schnorr von Carolsfeld (1868)
A Recollection of Rossini (1868)
Recollections of Auber (1871)

Richard Wagner.